# POLITICAL AND SOCIAL HISTORY
# OF THE UNITED STATES

## 1492–1828

POLITICAL AND SOCIAL HISTORY
OF THE UNITED STATES

VOLUME I (1492–1828)

BY HOMER C. HOCKETT
PROFESSOR OF AMERICAN HISTORY
OHIO STATE UNIVERSITY

VOLUME II (1829–1925)

BY ARTHUR MEIER SCHLESINGER
PROFESSOR OF HISTORY
HARVARD UNIVERSITY

UNIVERSITY COLLEGE,
NOTTINGHAM.

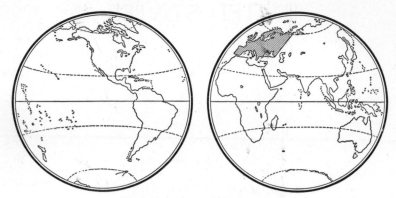

EUROPE IN THE XV CENTURY

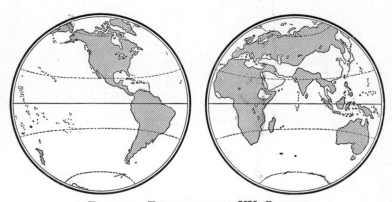

EXPANDED EUROPE OF THE XX CENTURY

# POLITICAL AND SOCIAL HISTORY

OF THE

# UNITED STATES

1492–1828

BY

## HOMER C. HOCKETT

PROFESSOR OF AMERICAN HISTORY
THE OHIO STATE UNIVERSITY

New York

THE MACMILLAN COMPANY

1926

COPYRIGHT, 1925,

By THE MACMILLAN COMPANY.

Set up and electrotyped. Published June, 1925. Reprinted
October, 1925; May, 1926.

Norwood Press
J. S. Cushing Co. — Berwick & Smith Co.
Norwood, Mass., U.S.A.

TO

THE MEMORY OF THE

## TWO FRIENDS

WHOSE UNFAILING FAITH WAS

MORE THAN RICHES

# PREFACE

W<small>HOSOEVER</small> by literary art can lend new charm to a twicetold tale has no need of other excuse for telling it. He who essays the oft-repeated story of our country must needs use art to win the praise of those who already know it well. But the writer of a text-book, whose primary purpose is didactic, may be pardoned for dismissing the initiated reader from his thought and centering it upon the student who looks to the text as a book of facts and interpretation rather than as a source of literary entertainment. An accurate, impartial, and clearly-stated summary of the findings of scholars must be his aim. If these be set forth with skill enough to entice the student into more intimate acquaintance with his country's story, it is well.

Even this is no slight undertaking, as any one who has attempted it will readily testify. The story of a nation is no longer a simple tale. No longer may the historian be content with a mere tracing of the evolution of government. While political development still properly forms the central theme of history, the operation of the deep-seated social and economic forces which give it much of its significance must be made plain. Moreover, the story must be given its proper setting in the larger whole of world history. The writer must correct old errors, avoid old prejudices, present new views, offer suggestive interpretations. Even if he contributes little that is not already known, the task of sifting out from the voluminous and daily increasing literature of history that which is both true and significant demands no small measure of critical judgment as well as scholarship. These things being equal, the story is "his at last who says it best," and I can only "try my fortune with the rest."

In the present volume, the notes appended to each chapter are neither comprehensive bibliographies nor mere collateral reading lists. They are designed to introduce students, and teachers if necessary, to a rather severely restricted list of secondary works and to give some clue to the value of each. As a rule, each work is first mentioned where its connection with the text is most obvious, and frequent citations of it thereafter are avoided. A few particularly important articles in periodicals and annuals are cited, but this valuable field of literature is hardly touched, for once invaded, it would prove difficult to impose reasonable limits upon the number of citations. Bibliographical details, such as names of publishers and dates of publication, will be found at the end of the volume, in the List of Books, which may thus serve as a guide in purchasing for college libraries.

The writer is happy to acknowledge his indebtedness to his colleagues in The Ohio State University, Professors Arthur C. Cole, Carl Wittke, and Edgar H. McNeal, who read the manuscript in whole or in part and gave helpful suggestions and criticisms. He is likewise indebted to Professor Clarence E. Carter, of Miami University, and Dr. Richard H. Shryock, of Duke University. His special thanks are due to the author of the companion volume, Professor Arthur M. Schlesinger, of Harvard University, who gave every page careful scrutiny. Many imperfections were corrected by the aid of these friends; those which remain are to be charged only to the author.

HOMER C. HOCKETT.

THE OHIO STATE UNIVERSITY,
    May, 1925.

# CONTENTS

# CONTENTS

# LIST OF MAPS

Vera Cruz

Mexico City

Porto Bello

Cartagena

Lima

DEMARCATION LINE

SPAIN'S EMPIRE IN AMERICA AT CLOSE OF XVI CENTURY.

# POLITICAL AND SOCIAL HISTORY OF THE UNITED STATES

## 1492—1828

### CHAPTER I

### EUROPEAN BEGINNINGS IN AMERICA

#### SPAIN'S COLONIAL EMPIRE

If a visitor had come to the earth from another world five hundred years ago, he would not have found its largest cities and greatest wealth in North America, nor would he have found mature and highly cultured states in Europe. A sparse population of copper-skinned savages roamed the American wilderness, while European nations were in the making, slowly taking form out of the older universal state, and just beginning to recover the literature and art of classical civilization which had been submerged a thousand years before when the Roman empire was overrun by barbarians. Passing by the ruins in Egypt and the Tigris-Euphrates Valley of other dead empires, the visitor would have come at last, in India and China, to the cities, the wealth, the luxury of hoary civilizations where philosophy and letters flourished when the peoples of Europe were skin-clad nomads.

The visitor might readily have predicted the spread of culture from these oriental centers to the more backward regions of the earth. But the future was not in the hands of the eastern peoples. They had ceased to be impelled to change by internal forces. Asia and the whole world were to become the sphere of activity for the restless new nations of Europe. Between the fifteenth and nineteenth centuries these gained the mastery of the earth.

The history of the last five centuries is largely the story of this expansion of Europe and the development of the white man's civilization. Culture has undergone more change during this

1

period than in all the previous ages. The advance of scientific knowledge and the vast enlargement of life on the material side are the distinguishing characteristics of the modern era. No less real, it may be hoped, is the gain in the freedom of the spirit through the progress of religious and political liberty and the increase of educational opportunity. These changes have come with, and in part because of, the expansion of Europe, from the impulses gained in far-flung enterprise and in the building of society in the earth's waste spaces.

The widening of the geographical possessions of the European stock has involved also rivalries and wars among the European states, the overthrow of ancient empires, the extermination of weak peoples, and has brought each nation of today face to face with problems affecting the entire human family.

The history of America is a part of this larger story. The discovery of the western continents was a first fruit of the awakening of Europe, and their occupation was an early stage of its expansion. For two centuries or more its rival nations contended for the mastery of the New World. Then colonies ripened into independent states, with their own institutions and ideals bearing the impress of the American environment, ready to make their contribution to the world order.

Down to the fifteenth century European life centered about the Mediterranean Sea. Even in the best days of Rome, Europeans had little or no contact with Asia beyond a line reaching from the Caspian Sea to Calcutta, although they drew their gems, fine fabrics, and spices from China, India, and islands still more remote which their traders did not themselves visit. During the rude ages which followed the disintegration of Roman power commerce languished and geographical knowledge contracted. Then the Crusades brought the men of Europe once more into western Asia, revived the intercontinental trade, and begot new interest in the lands of the East. Across central Asia and around the eastern and southern coasts to the Persian Gulf and Red Sea and thence by land, goods were now carried to the cities of the Black and Mediterranean seas, where they were received by the merchants of Italian towns who distributed them in Europe or passed them on to other merchants from the countries of the North.

It was about the middle of the thirteenth century that European began to penetrate into eastern Asia. Most famous of these travelers was Marco Polo, a merchant of Venice, who just at the close of the century (1298) wrote an account of his wanderings. For two hundred years more the interest in geographical inquiry increased with accelerating pace until the fifteenth century ushered in a veritable golden age of discovery.

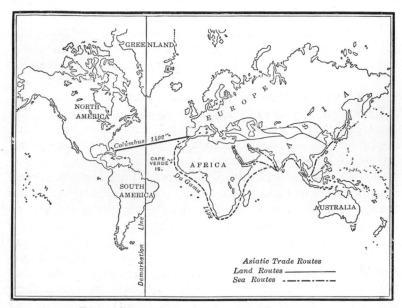

TRADE ROUTES AND VOYAGES OF DISCOVERY.

In this memorable epoch the art of printing began to disseminate knowledge while the compass and astrolabe transformed navigation. Timid, land-hugging seamen gave way to bold mariners who, urged by curiosity, love of adventure, missionary zeal, or desire to expand commerce, explored all seas.

Portugal was the pioneer in the new enterprise. She had attained national unity while the other countries of Europe were slowly emerging from feudalism; her location also favored her leadership as the center of action shifted from the Mediterranean Basin to the Atlantic. Her navigators gradually disclosed the contour of the African coast and dispelled the old belief in sea monsters and boiling oceans, and before the end of the century (1498) found an all-water route to India around the Dark Continent.[1]

Out of the crowd of seamen in Portuguese employ who took part in these explorations emerges one of the few men whose names will live forever.   This man was the Italian known to the English-speaking world as Christopher Columbus.   Obscurity veils his early life, denying us knowledge of the year of his birth and even of the origin of his great adventure.   He is known to have been a diligent student of the scientific writings of his time, and to have shared the concept of the earth as a sphere, which was held by the enlightened men of the fifteenth century.   What he sought by sailing westward, however, is not certain.   It is possible that he knew of voyages to lands in the Atlantic the record of which has been lost, and that these were the object of his quest.

The story of the struggles and triumph of the great discoverer need not be retold.   Winning at length the support of Isabella of Castile, late in the summer of 1492 he fared forth upon the untried waters, the first of the pioneers whose dauntless faith and courage were to conquer the New World.

Thus was inaugurated the era of expansion in two hemispheres. After the return of Columbus from his first voyage, to prevent conflict between Spain and Portugal the Pope issued the Demarkation Bull of 1493, granting to Spain the lands which she should discover in the West.   Soon afterwards the two nations agreed by treaty that the boundary between their claims should be the meridian three hundred and seventy leagues west of the Cape Verde Islands.

These adjustments laid the foundation for Spain's claim to nearly the whole of America.   It was soon strengthened by exploration.   When the successors of Columbus began to suspect that a continent lay between them and the lands of silk and spice, they made prolonged efforts to find a waterway to the "South Sea."   Knowledge of the geography of the Atlantic

[1] It was long believed that the conquests of the Turks cut off the old lines of communication between Asia and Europe through the eastern Mediterranean, ruining the Italian commercial cities and providing Portugal with the incentive for seeking a new route to India. It is now held that the rise of the Turkish power had little if anything to do with the voyages of the Portuguese.

coast from Chesapeake Bay to Cape Horn was a by-product of this quest.

Interest in a waterway to Asia did not lead the Spanish to despise the new-found land. On the contrary their imagination invested it with impossible delights and riches. The fountain of youth, the seven golden cities — what wonders might it not hide? Men were freed from belief in such fables only by learning the truth. Discovery was a great experiment in reality. Nevertheless, reality was so marvelous that it made the era of Spanish exploration an age of romance and adventure, a chapter in history which reads like the tales of Greek heroes. Native empires welcoming the white conqueror as the Fair God whose coming had been foretold by their prophets, captive princes paying as ransom the price of a kingdom in gold — these and other stories are almost as incredible as would have been the finding of the fountain of youth. And back of all the glamour in the tales of the *conquistadores* is the vision of native peoples melting away under the cruel hardship of unwonted toil as slaves in the mines, of multitudes crushed by the Juggernaut of "civilization."

Santo Domingo was chosen as the site of the first Spanish colony, and exploration and settlement proceeded from this center in ever-widening circles. Cuba was soon won, and in 1519 Hernando Cortez began the conquest of Mexico. The Aztec Indians of this land had made considerable progress. They cultivated the soil, dwelt in populous towns, and in their religious and governmental institutions had attained a much higher organization than the tribes farther north. However, in conflict with the invaders, who had firearms and horses, the very civilization of the natives proved to be a weakness, for Cortez, in a short campaign, by seizing the most fertile districts, compelled them to submit.

Francisco Pizarro, in a similar way, conquered Peru (1532–1538); and within a half-century after the first voyage of Columbus the Spanish power was established throughout Central and South America, save in Brazil, the coast of which was east of the demarcation line.

Within what is now the United States the Spanish were less successful. Attempts to imitate the exploits of Cortez and

Pizarro failed.  The most notable of such efforts were those of Ferdinando de Soto and Francisco Coronado, about 1540.  De Soto, who had been with Pizarro in Peru, landed on the northeast coast of the Gulf of Mexico and penetrated to northern Georgia, thence making his way to the Mississippi, crossing it not far from where Memphis now stands, and reaching the neighborhood of Hot Springs, Arkansas.  His hope of conquest was baffled by the primitive character of the Indian culture.  The tribes, still partly in the hunting stage, suffered only inconvenience from the destruction of their huts and crops, and avoiding the slow-moving Spaniards, harassed them continually without exposing themselves.  Nor was there among the natives north of the Gulf any accumulated wealth to satisfy the desire for plunder as had the gold and silver of the Incas (Peruvians) and Aztecs.  Disappointed and broken by hardships, De Soto died in the wilderness, and his followers made their way to the Spanish settlements in Mexico.

Coronado's expedition was due to rumors which had reached Mexico of rich native cities to the northward.  Hoping that they would prove to be the fabled cities of Cibola, he penetrated into what is now New Mexico, where he found the adobe structures of the Pueblo Indians.  In the hope of success farther on he divided his party, one section reaching the Colorado River at the Grand Canyon, the other crossing the Great Plains and reaching the neighborhood of the Missouri River in eastern Kansas.

On the far Pacific coast the successors of Cortez attained the shores of San Francisco Bay.  But aside from St. Augustine in Florida and Santa Fé in New Mexico, Spanish colonization made no progress north of the present Mexican boundary until the eighteenth century.  South of the Rio Grande, however, Spain established a great empire.  The age of romance and adventure passed, but the lands, mines, and commerce of the New World continued to lure the Castilian.  The Crown encouraged emigration by land grants and advances of supplies.  Before either France or England possessed a single settlement in America, Mexico City had a population of fifteen thousand whites and ten times as many natives.  Lima, the capital of Peru, contained two thousand Spanish families.  There were schools, hospitals, and other public institutions in each of these cities, and each

boasted a university with scholars whose reputations extended
to Europe.

After the first half-century the government adopted regulations laying upon the white landholders the responsibility for
the welfare of their native dependents and forbidding their
enslavement.   The government labored in conjunction with the
Church to convert the Indians to Christianity, and in the missions

FARTHEST EXTENT OF SPANISH EXPLORATIONS IN NORTH AMERICA IN
XVI CENTURY.

instruction in industrial arts was given as well as in religion.
The Spanish policy was one of assimilation, while the English
treated the weaker race as an obstacle to be pushed from their
path.

Spain intended that the wealth produced in the colonies should
enrich herself only; hence foreigners were entirely excluded,
and even Spanish trade was strictly regulated.   Twice a year
government fleets sailed from Cadiz or Seville for Vera Cruz,
Cartagena, and Porto Bello, and the trade of the merchants was

limited to these semiannual voyages.  All colonial exports had to be brought to the ports named, where fairs were held for the exchange of goods.  Few commodities except the precious metals could bear the cost of transportation for long distances, and remote settlements like those in New Mexico and the Argentine were condemned to stagnation or illicit traffic, which was punishable with death.  Despite slight concessions to England after the War of the Spanish Succession (see page 106), this policy remained substantially unchanged to the end of the colonial period.

Despotic in rule at home, it was not to be expected that Spain would grant political liberty to her American subjects.  The government of her possessions pertained to the Crown, which acted through the "Council of the Indies."  The colonies were divided into viceroyalties, with subdivisions for local administration.  In 1600, the viceroyalty of New Spain comprised Mexico, Central America, and Venezuela ; that of Peru the South American settlements below Venezuela.  Colonial officers were appointed by the Crown and were almost invariably Spaniards.  American-born subjects were excluded from all important offices, and self-government in the English sense, by officers acting under laws made by representative assemblies, was nowhere to be found in the Spanish dominions.

On the whole, the Spanish colonization of the New World was a notable achievement, to which English-speaking historians have done scant justice.  "The Spanish colonial empire," writes Professor Bourne, "lasted three centuries, a period nearly as long as the sway of imperial Rome over western Europe.  During these ten generations the language, the religion, the culture, and the political institutions of Castile were transplanted over an area twenty times as large as that of the parent state.  What Rome did for Spain, Spain in turn did for Spanish America."

Spain became in the course of the sixteenth century the richest and most powerful state of western Europe.  From the mines of Mexico and Peru such a quantity of the precious metals flowed into her coffers as Europe had not received from any source since Roman times.  Not unnaturally her success obscured her errors, so that her policy influenced other nations when they came to establish colonies.

### First Efforts of France and England

While the Spanish rulers were showing Europe the pathway to empire, the kings of France were busy with schemes of expansion nearer home or distracted by civil wars. Nevertheless their banner was carried to the St. Lawrence. In three voyages between 1534 and 1541 Jacques Cartier examined the great northern river, attempted a settlement at Quebec, and reached the bold height which still bears the name he gave it, "Mont Real." Cartier sowed the seed of a New France in the woods of North America, but the harvest was long delayed.

England's rulers, like their neighbors across the Channel, for a long time showed little interest in lands beyond the sea. Although the first European who explored the coast above Chesapeake Bay sailed under the English flag, he was an Italian (John Cabot, 1497) whom the penurious Henry VII allowed to embark at his own expense. Upon his return the King gave him a trifling present for finding "the new isle," a discovery on which his successors based their claim to half a continent.

England under Henry VII was still one of the lesser states of Europe, and had been exhausted by a long series of wars. Not until the middle of the sixteenth century did interest in colonization awake. Then the English began to reflect that ship-building materials from Baltic lands, wines from the Mediterranean states and Rhine Valley, oriental goods by way of Portugal, and gold and silver through the channels of trade were evidences of an odious and dangerous dependence. Colonies in America would doubtless supply all of these necessities and give the kingdom an economic self-sufficiency which might be a matter of life or death in time of war. Besides, they were convinced that their country was overcrowded. Many landlords had given up grain-raising for wool-growing, in order to meet the increasing demand of the looms of the Netherlands. This change had both reduced the food supply and thrown laborers out of employment. The care of the poor was rendered more difficult by the dissolution of the monasteries (1536) which had been the great dispensers of charity. Colonies would give employment to the poor, it was urged, and prevent idleness from breeding vice and crime.

When Henry VIII divorced his Spanish queen (1533) and

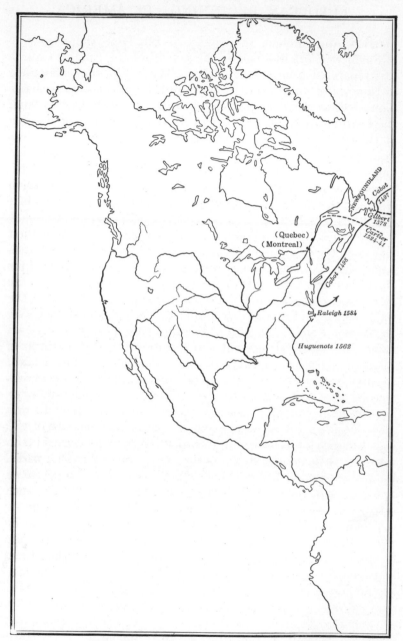

FIRST EFFORTS OF FRANCE AND ENGLAND.

married Anne Boleyn in defiance of the Pope, the friendship of Spain was forfeited and at the same time the English Church was separated from that of Rome.   When Elizabeth, daughter of Henry and Anne, came to the throne in 1558, Spain, as champion of Catholicism, supported the claim of Mary of Scotland, the legitimate heir in the eyes of those who denied the legality of Henry's divorce.   Elizabeth, convinced that her throne was insecure while Mary lived, at last consented to her execution and Spain prepared for war.   The defeat in 1588 of the "Invincible Armada" with which Philip II attempted the invasion of England, left her free to pursue colonial projects without fear of Spain's power.

In the years just preceding the war Englishmen made their first serious attempts at colonization.   As lord of vacant lands under the feudal law, Queen Elizabeth in 1578 gave a patent for an American fief to Sir Humphrey Gilbert.   Gilbert lost his life in a storm at sea and his plans came to nought; but within the six years allowed him for establishing a settlement, his relative, Sir Walter Raleigh, secured a renewal of the patent in his own name.   In 1584 Raleigh sent an expedition to select a site for a colony on Chesapeake Bay, but his agents chose Roanoke Island, in Albemarle Sound.   Several times during the next few years recruits were sent to Roanoke, but in each case, on one pretext or another, they abandoned the settlement.   The last attempt was made in 1587.   After landing his passengers the master of the vessel returned to England for supplies, arriving just at the moment when the country was threatened by Philip's Armada. He was detained by the war crisis, and when the colony was visited again, in 1591, the whites had disappeared.   The best conjecture is that they had found homes among some friendly native tribe.

In spite of these reverses Englishmen did not lose interest in the colonization of America.   They continued to discuss the benefits of "western planting," but for a time they limited their activities to an occasional trading voyage.

## The Planting of Virginia

One of the early acts of James I (son of the unfortunate Mary Queen of Scots) who succeeded Elizabeth in 1603 was to make

peace with Spain.   The peace was favorable to further attempts
at colonization, for although Spain refused to acknowledge that
the British had rights in America and watched the development
of their plans with a jealous eye, there was no great danger that
she would renew hostilities.   Raleigh had exhausted his resources
in his efforts at Roanoke and had fallen from grace at court.
It was some of his friends, however, who decided to make a new
trial.   Taught by experience that great losses must be expected
before profits could be realized, they abandoned the feudal grant
and adopted a form of business organization which was proving
a great success in the case of the British East India Company.
This was the "joint-stock plan," under which the total capital
was divided into shares, each of small amount, to be sold to many
persons.   The device brought together a larger sum than one
person could command, and discouragement was much less
likely to defeat an undertaking in which profits might be slow
in coming.

Upon application of the promoters the King granted them
(1606) a charter which created two joint-stock companies known
as the "London Company" and the "Plymouth Company."
To each was given a tract of land with exclusive rights of colonization and trade.   The companies aimed at profit, but also hoped
to benefit England and carry Christianity to the Indians.   They
therefore urged the public to buy stock not merely as an investment but as a patriotic and Christian duty.

It was an ill-equipped and ignorant Europe that essayed the
mastery of North America.   More than a century had passed
since the tiny caravels of Columbus had plowed the first paths
to the new "Indies," and still practically nothing was known of
the geography or resources of the region to which three small
ships bore the first settlers of the London Company in the spring
of 1607.   It was well for the English that the Atlantic margin
of the continent was hospitable.   A stern shore line like that of
the Pacific coast, where mountains almost meet sea and harbors
are few, would have repulsed them.   Instead, the indentations
of the shore led like open doors to a wide and fruitful plain which
welcomed them with the fair promise of a genial climate and
abundance.

Even so the contest with nature taxed them to the utmost.

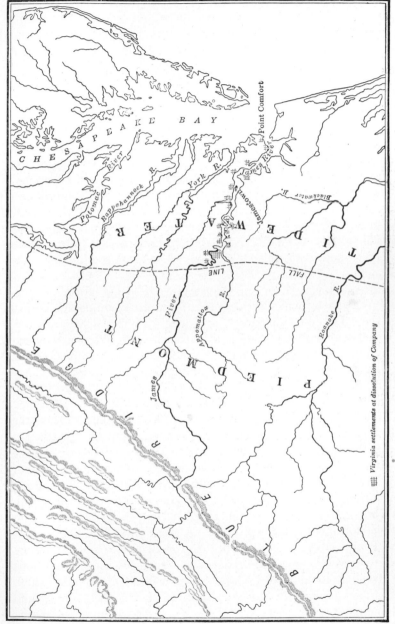

PHYSICAL FEATURES OF EARLY VIRGINIA.

▦ Virginia settlements at dissolution of Company

Although, unlike the Spanish, they did not believe in fables, the Virginia colonists cherished illusions woven of the vain fabric of their dreams, hopes of producing wine, silk, and spices and of finding mines of gold and silver, hopes which diverted effort into fruitless channels when the real problem was to become acquainted with the environment and adapt themselves to it.

They began by examining the James River. Like other streams which flow into the Chesapeake from the west, the James is a broad though short river, navigable by small vessels as far as the tides ascend. The lowland, or tidewater, area of Virginia is bounded by the fall line, the edge of a more elevated plain known as the "Piedmont," which stretches away to the Blue Ridge of the Appalachians, and is cut into a number of strips or "necks" by the rivers which flow across it. Of these the chief besides the James are the York and Rappahannock, and, at the northern limit, the Potomac.

After a few days' survey of the James the settlers fixed upon the spot still called Jamestown. Nature was in her most engaging mood in this spring of the long ago, as if to welcome these suitors for the favors of the New World. The woods had again put on their luxuriant garments of green and adorned themselves with garlands of many-hued wild flowers. Through fair meadows and forests of tall and goodly trees the waters of limpid streams flowed in virgin purity. Under the verdant carpeting of the earth showed here and there the red of the luscious strawberry. At first sight the sea-worn travelers fell in love with the beauteous land. But as the summer came on supplies ran low and they did not know how to cultivate the native food crops. Bad water and insufficient food, and the malarial surroundings, brought on fevers and dysentery, from which nearly all suffered and many died. When cooler weather came, the survivors regained their strength, but they were able to procure food for the winter only by trading with the Indians for their surplus corn. With the second summer came again sickness and inability to till the soil. For several seasons this cycle of hardships recurred, and more than once it seemed the colony must be abandoned.

A few score half-starved men, weakened by illness, beset by savage foes, and quarreling among themselves, illy sheltered by miserable huts on a river-edge in the far-off wilderness, three thousand miles across seas from their native land — such phrases seem more fitting to describe castaways than builders of empire. Yet in such feeble efforts began the overseas dominions of modern England. Little by little conditions improved. Although the death rate among newcomers was startling, the survivors of one sickly season generally were immune thereafter, and the number of dependable workers gradually increased.

Visits to the natives for maize and search for gold and a waterway to the Pacific led to active exploration of the tidewater section. In this work Captain John Smith took the leading part. By these journeys a substantial knowledge was gained of nearly the whole of that part of Virginia which was to be the seat of settlement during the seventeenth century.

Knowledge of the real character of the country aided in the adjustment of life to actual conditions. Success required that the colony should not only sustain itself but produce something which could not be grown or made in England and for which there was a considerable demand. Such a staple was found in the native tobacco plant. Its cultivation began about 1614 and within a few years it became the chief product, affording Virginia its permanent economic basis.

But the Company did not prosper. The stockholders were of two classes: those who bought shares and remained in England were known as "adventurers," while those who emigrated were called "planters." Many of the planters were men of little or no means, for the Company was glad to give a share of stock to an able-bodied man who would "adventure his person." This practice was in harmony with the patriotic purpose of relieving England of its overpopulation. The Company undertook to maintain the planters at the common expense for a period of years, but during that term all products were to be sold for the benefit of the adventurers. At the end of the period the lands in the "plantation" were to be divided among the stockholders of both classes.

This plan did not furnish the incentive needed to draw forth the best efforts of the planters, and harsh measures were required to keep them at work. The severe discipline and the unwholesome climate caused much discontent, and with the high death rate made it difficult to obtain immigrants. A great step was

taken when the joint-stock period ended in 1616.  Although the
adventurers had received no profits, a "land dividend" of one
hundred acres was awarded to each planter.  Soon after this a
grant was promised for each immigrant — to be given to him
if he paid the cost of his passage across the Atlantic, otherwise
to the person who did so.  This practice, with the size of the
grant fixed at fifty acres and known as the "head right," became
the basis of the Virginia land system.

About the same time the Company began to offer large tracts
to "societies" which would purchase shares of stock.  These
societies were expected to find their own immigrants to supply
the labor needed on their "particular plantations," as they
were called.

Under the stimulus of these new plans Virginia began to grow
rapidly.  Plantations appeared along the banks of the James,
both above and below Jamestown.  They were usually far apart,
for tobacco growers desired plenty of room to expand operations.
Another class of inhabitants also appeared.  These were the
"indented" servants, who were bound to work for a time for the
person who defrayed the cost of their passage.  The owners of
particular plantations imported many such servants, some of
whom were promised lands of their own upon the expiration of
their terms.

These changes in the economic system were accompanied by
changes of equal importance in the government.  The arrangements for government were at first quite incidental, but the Company's enterprise was carried on so far from home that some
provision was necessary for preserving order.  Under the charter
of 1606 the King retained the right to govern the settlers through
a council in London which appointed members of the Company
in the colony as a subordinate council, to rule according to
instructions sent out from time to time.  While as agents of
government this council received orders from the King, as business managers for the Company they were subject to the
instructions of the adventurers.

The plan was too clumsy to work well, and under a new charter
of 1612 the Company was made a self-governing corporation, with
the privilege not only of managing its business affairs but of
governing the people in the plantation.  It was authorized to

hold a meeting in London four times each year, known as the "General Court," at which a majority of the stockholders present could elect officers and make "such Laws and Ordinances for the Good and Welfare of the said Plantation" as they thought "requisite and meet," so long as they were not contrary to the laws of England.  For the transaction of routine business there was a smaller body including the officers chosen by the General Court.  From this time the London Company was commonly known as the "Virginia Company." [1]

For six years after the granting of the new charter the planters were ruled by governors and councilors chosen by the General Court and sent out to Virginia.  This policy seemed arbitrary and unwise to the liberal members of the Company, led by Sir Edwyn Sandys and the Earl of Southampton, who believed that unless the planters were content the Company could not prosper. The personal rights of the people in Virginia had been repeatedly violated by the code of discipline which it had been thought necessary to adopt.  Moreover, as stockholders the planters were probably entitled to vote in the General Court if it had been possible for them to attend.  Along with the new land policy, therefore, the liberal faction persuaded the Company to establish a Virginia branch of the General Court.  Sandys's enemies charged that he said it was his purpose "to make a free and popular state . . . in which the people should have noe government putt upon them but by their owne consents."  The governor and council were still to be chosen by the General Court, but Governor George Yeardley's instructions of 1619 directed him to call upon the free inhabitants of each plantation to choose representatives to join with him and the council, at Jamestown, in passing ordinances for the welfare of the colony.

The settlements were grouped for this purpose into eleven "boroughs," and the representatives were called "burgesses." The ordinances passed by the assembly were subject to the approval of the General Court, while those of the General Court were equally subject to the approval of the assembly.  The

---

[1] A second charter of 1609 is passed by as a mere step in the transition from the first to the third.  Its most notable feature was the new definition of the bounds of the Company's grant — along the coast two hundred miles each way from Point Comfort, and " up into the land throughout from sea to sea, west and northwest."

Virginia assembly of 1619 is memorable because it marks the extension to America of the British principle of representative government.

A few years after this notable event the Virginia Company's career was brought to a close. An Indian massacre in 1622 gave the King an excuse for action against the charter. The Sandys-Southampton faction belonged to the party in Parliament which was seeking to restrict the royal prerogative, and the King became fearful that the discussions in the General Court were making it a "seminary for a seditious parliament." Having created the Company by his own act, even the arbitrary James felt bound as by a contract which he could not revoke without appearing to show cause before a court of law. Under a charge of mismanagement, therefore, he obtained from a subservient court in 1624 a decision by which the Company lost its charter.

The change did not involve much alteration of the government of Virginia so far as the settlers were concerned. After a short interval they were allowed to continue to elect representatives to an assembly, but the King instead of the Company appointed the governor and councilors. The governor became the agent of the Crown, acting under the terms of the royal commission and such instructions as were issued from time to time.

The earnest entreaties of the colonists had much to do with the King's decision to continue the assembly. In America as at home Englishmen were attached to representative government, and already they were particularly jealous of the principle of taxation by legislators of their own choosing, as is shown by an act of the assembly of 1624 declaring "That the Governor shall lay no taxes . . . upon the Colony, its lands or goods, other way than by the authority of the General Assembly."

The assembly lost the right of assenting to measures decided upon in England relating to Virginia, and its acts became subject to veto by the governor. Gradually the government in the colony conformed to the pattern of that of the mother country. After many years (in 1676) the burgesses and councilors separated into two houses; the one suggests the British House of Commons, the other the Lords. It was but natural that in the new country Englishmen should follow in general the forms which long usage had made habitual.

Under the Company Virginia was a proprietary colony; with the Company's dissolution it became the first of the royal colonies and the model for all the later ones.   Although as a business venture the Company was an utter failure, it won enduring fame as the founder of a new dominion.   At the time the charter was revoked the colonists numbered twelve or thirteen hundred, scattered in nineteen settlements, all situated on the banks of the James River.   Many persons believed that the colony could not survive unless the King continued the support which the Company had given; but his neglect compelled the Virginians to rely upon themselves and proved that they no longer needed the fostering care of a guardian.

## SELECT BIBLIOGRAPHY FOR CHAPTER I

(A full list of books and articles cited in this volume, with names of publishers and places and dates of publication, will be found on page 400.)

**Spain's Colonial Empire.**   The events in Europe which bear upon the discovery and early colonization of America are well reviewed by Cheyney, *European Background of American History*.   Abbott, *Expansion of Europe*, also deals with the European background.

Cheyney's volume is one of the twenty-eight composing *The American Nation: A History*, edited by A. B. Hart.   Each is the work of a recognized authority on the period covered by it, and while the merits of the volumes vary, the series is perhaps the most useful single work covering the whole of American history.   A valuable feature is the chapter on the authorities used, which appears at the close of each volume.

Winsor, *The Narrative and Critical History of America*, is a coöperative work of great learning, each chapter of which was prepared by a specialist. The eighth volume reaches into the nineteenth century, but the great bulk of the work is on the colonial period.   Volumes I and II deal with the early voyages, the aborigines, and the Spanish conquest.

Another work of modern scholarship which supplements *The American Nation* at many points, is Channing, *History of the United States*.   It is still in progress.   It begins with the Europe of Columbus; the fifth volume, issued in 1921, brings the narrative to 1848.

Fiske, *The Discovery of America*, tells the story of the early explorations and settlements, particularly of the Spanish, in a fascinating way.   This writer's books are noteworthy for literary excellence rather than historical scholarship, in which respect they leave somewhat to be desired.

Of the older general histories, Bancroft, *History of the United States*, is written in a tone of extravagant patriotism, and, at times, with inattention to the sources.   It ends with the adoption of the Constitution.   Hildreth,

*History of the United States to 1820,* is more soberly and accurately done, but is rather dull reading.

Most of the good lives of Columbus are voluminous. That by Markham combines brevity, accuracy, clearness, and readability.

One of the best of the older works on Spanish America is Helps, *The Spanish Conquest in America.* In addition to the story of the conquest it treats the problem of the Indian and negro.

Moses, *The Establishment of Spanish Rule in America,* gives a good account of the system of government.

Bourne, *Spain in America,* contains an excellent summary of the whole subject indicated by the title.

Richman, *The Spanish Conquerors,* is a briefer summary. It is one of the fifty volumes of *The Chronicles of America,* edited by Allen Johnson. This series, like *The American Nation,* is the product of a group of scholars. Each volume gives a complete treatment of a topic. While the style is rather popular, the series as a whole maintains a high level of accuracy and trustworthiness.

**First Efforts of France and England.** Bourne, Channing, Fiske, and Winsor, in the works cited above, deal with the French and English efforts of the sixteenth century. The standard history of the activities of the French for the period is Parkman, *Pioneers of New France.* See also Winsor, *Cartier to Frontenac;* Wood, *Elizabethan Sea-Dogs;* and Munro, *Crusaders of New France.*

Beer, *The Origins of the British Colonial System, 1578–1660,* analyzes the economic background of the English attempts at colonization, and marks out the lines within which most recent studies of British expansion and colonial administration have been carried on. An older study of value is Seeley, *The Growth of English Policy.*

**The Planting of Virginia.** In addition to Channing and Winsor, the following general accounts of the English colonies become important with the beginnings of Virginia:

Doyle, *The English in America,* is the standard English treatise on the subject. Volume I deals with Virginia, Maryland, and the Carolinas;

Tyler, *England in America,* brings the narrative to 1652;

Osgood, *The American Colonies in the Seventeenth Century,* is a most careful and critical account of institutional history;

Fiske, *Old Virginia and Her Neighbors,* tells the story of the southern colonies with the writer's characteristic charm; Johnston, *Pioneers of the Old South,* covers similar ground.

A recent scholarly political history of seventeenth-century Virginia is Wertenbaker, *Virginia under the Stuarts.* Three books of great merit, dealing with particular phases of the history of that colony, all by Bruce, are: *The Economic History of Virginia in the Seventeenth Century; The Institutional History of Virginia in the Seventeenth Century;* and *Social Life of Virginia in the Seventeenth Century.*

# CHAPTER II

## PURITAN COLONIZATION

### THE PILGRIMS AND PLYMOUTH

The love of adventure, the hope of gain, and the desire for political and religious liberty have been the mainsprings of emigration from the Old World to the New. While the Virginia Company was vainly seeking profits on the banks of the James River, other Englishmen, self-exiled for conscience' sake, were making homes on the shores of Cape Cod Bay.

Back of the beginnings of New England is the religious history of the mother land. The Anglican Church, which had separated from the Roman under Henry VIII, took definite form under Elizabeth (1558–1603). As then established it was a compromise and included both Catholic and Protestant elements. Extremists on both sides were therefore dissatisfied; Catholics were offended by the departure from the old faith, while Protestants were displeased by the retention of what they termed the vestiges of Romanism.

The discontented Protestants, called "Puritans," did not agree among themselves. The Nonconformists believed in one national church, and were content to remain within the establishment, departing from its practices, so far as they dared, in the direction of "purer" forms of worship. They desired more preaching and simpler ceremonies. Some of them (the Presbyterians) wished to substitute Calvin's plan of church government for the episcopal system. There were other Puritans whose dissent was so decided that they withdrew from the Anglican communion. Desiring the separation of church and state and congregational control in religious matters, they were called "Independents," or "Separatists."

Under Elizabeth the Catholics were persecuted, for the plots on behalf of Mary of Scotland brought all English Catholics

under suspicion of disloyalty.  James I, on the contrary, as the
son of a Catholic, was leniently disposed towards them, but disliked the Nonconformists extremely.  He feared that their
agitation for changes in the Church would end in the curtail-
ment of his prerogative.  He therefore formed a close alliance
with the Anglican party, and put his view in the epigrammatic
form, "no bishop, no king."  The King had good reason to fear
the Puritans, for in truth they were the heart of the political
group which stood for the rights of Parliament.

The Separatists were objects of the King's particular displeasure.  One congregation of them, to escape his persecution,
left their home at Scrooby in Nottinghamshire and fled to Holland.  For several years they dwelt in Leyden, where they
enjoyed religious liberty; but as their livelihood could be won
only by labor as wage-earners, and their surroundings were non-
English, they became discontented.  They desired a new home
where they might maintain an English community and become
independent in worldly estate.

When they heard of the particular plantations in Virginia,
they planned to settle in that colony, and their application for
lands was promptly granted when Sandys and his liberal friends
gained control of the Virginia Company.  Sandys's father, the
broadminded Archbishop of York, owned the house in which the
Scrooby congregation had held its meetings before removing
to Holland, and Elder Brewster, one of the representatives of the
Pilgrims in their negotiations, had been the steward of a manor
belonging to the Sandys family.

On the voyage the vessel, the famous "Mayflower," ran out of
her course, and near the end of the year 1620 landed her passengers
on the shores of Cape Cod Bay.  Winter being at hand, the
company decided to remain.  After some days spent in seeking
a proper site, a point on the west side of the bay, already known
as Plymouth, was chosen.  This region was beyond the bounds
of the Virginia Company, and by planting their settlement on
lands for which they had no grant the Pilgrims became "squatters."  They proceeded by an act of "squatter sovereignty" to
set up a government.  Before landing the men drew up the "Mayflower Compact," forming a "civil body politic," each member of
which pledged himself to submit to the will of the majority.

The Mayflower Compact was not an assertion of independence, but arose from necessity, since for the time being there was no other means of preserving order.  Nor can the Compact properly be called a constitution, as it did not provide a plan of government.  This was left to evolve as needed.  At first public business was carried on by a "general meeting" of the men.  This assembly determined what was for the good of the colony and dealt with offenders, exercising both legislative and judicial functions.  For executive duties it chose a governor and one or more "assistants."

It was not long before the general meeting became impracticable, as settlement scattered more and more widely.  Then it was decided that each community should send delegates to the "General Court," which took the place of the original general meeting, and hold its own "town meeting" for local business. Each "town" also had its church, the members of each congregation choosing their own pastor and transacting all business. relating to ecclesiastical affairs.

Plymouth colony thus became a little republic.  For that age it was remarkably democratic in spirit.  The Pilgrims were plain people of the yeoman class.  A few were superior to the rest in social rank, according to the standards of the time, and a few others were non-members of the congregations who in one way or other had strayed into the company of the Pilgrims. Some of these formed a disturbing element.  Two were finally banished and one was hung for murder, but until charged with their offenses they were allowed a voice in the general meeting. The democracy of Congregationalism tended distinctly towards democracy in government.  Not until 1660 did the colony adopt a property qualification for voting; still later it added the requirement of church membership.

The Leyden congregation was so poor that the money for the removal to America had to be borrowed from capitalists in London.  To meet this debt the men of the colony established fishing stations and posts for trading with the Indians on the coast of Massachusetts and Maine and in the valley of the Connecticut River.  For sustenance they relied upon the produce of their fields and fisheries.

Conditions of life were hard in the Plymouth colony.  In

spite of an unusually mild winter half of the original group died
the first season. The soil was unproductive; wealth and
numbers increased but slowly. The first settlers numbered
about one hundred, and others came from Leyden a little later;
but that source of immigration was soon drained. Thereafter
Plymouth grew chiefly by an overflow from Massachusetts Bay.
In effect Massachusetts gradually absorbed the smaller colony.
Although a land patent was obtained from the New England
Council (the successor of the Plymouth Company of 1606),
all efforts to secure a royal charter failed, and Plymouth was
finally (1691) incorporated with its neighbor. While short-
lived as a distinct commonwealth, it made a memorable contribution to American life. For practice of the Christian virtues
and for devotion to the principles of political liberty history
offers few parallels to the peasants who founded the "Pilgrim
Republic."

### MASSACHUSETTS BAY

The Massachusetts Bay colony, which became by far the
most populous and powerful of the New England communities,
was not founded until Plymouth was nearly a decade old. It
owed its origin to the discord between the Puritan party and the
King. James I held an exalted notion of the royal powers. In
the quaint phrase of an American historian of the eighteenth
century (Stith), "he had been bred up under . . . one of the
brightest geniuses and most accomplished scholars of that age,
who had given him Greek and Latin in great waste and profusion,
but it was not in his power to give him good sense." In his own
opinion he was responsible to God alone for his conduct as ruler.
Parliament, he thought, should provide funds without meddling
with the way in which the government was carried on. He could
not avoid applying to Parliament for funds, however, and the
House of Commons, the stronghold of Puritanism, would not
grant money unless the King would enforce the laws against
Catholics and treat Nonconformists leniently. Because of the
friction which came with every effort to deal with Parliament,
James summoned it as seldom as possible; in the twenty-two
years of his reign there were but eight sessions.

Under Charles I, who came to the throne in 1625, the situation grew still worse. When Parliament refused taxes for an unwise war, Charles levied forced loans. Parliament then drew up the Petition of Right, which the reluctant King signed in 1628 in order to obtain a money grant. In the growth of the British constitution the Petition of Right ranks in importance with the Great Charter wrested from King John in 1215. It made illegal the collection of money without authority of an act of Parliament.

Almost immediately another dispute arose. The House of Commons tried to punish some of the Anglican clergymen who leaned towards Catholicism. The King forbade the proceedings and decided to be rid of the troublesome Puritans. He therefore dissolved Parliament in 1629 and did not summon another session until 1640. In France and elsewhere rulers were setting up autocratic monarchies and Charles hoped to do the same. He and Archbishop Laud began to enforce conformity with a strong hand, while the disheartened Puritans turned their hopes towards New England as a land of promise.

The way was already prepared for a Puritan migration. The Plymouth Company of 1606 had done little more than license trading and fishing vessels to visit the New England coast. Among a number of stations which its licensees had established was one at Cape Ann. In 1628 some of the owners of this station purchased lands from the reorganized Plymouth Company, and in the next year they obtained a royal charter. This charter was much like the third one of the Virginia Company. It created a trading corporation, which was made proprietor of any colonies which it might set up within its grant, and given the right to govern them in accordance with English law. As in the case of the Virginia Company, the stockholders, called "freemen of the Company," met in General Court to manage affairs and elect officers consisting of a governor, deputy governor, and eighteen "assistants."

Upon the abrogation of the Virginia Company's charter, the King had declared his intention of retaining the government of future colonies in his own hands. If Charles I had foreseen the results of creating "The Governor and Company of Massachusetts Bay," he would doubtless have adhered to this resolution of his father, for during the summer following the dissolution of Parliament in 1629 the Puritan leaders set on foot a plan to utilize the new trading corporation in founding in the New World "a bulwark against the Kingdom of Anti-Christ." To bring this about it was arranged, by an agreement signed at Cambridge, that all stockholders who did not wish to emigrate to America should transfer their rights under the charter to the members of the Company who would go. John Winthrop, who had been prominent in the contest between Parliament and King, was chosen governor, and by March, 1630, he and many others were ready to sail. During that year seventeen vessels carried some two thousand persons to Massachusetts Bay. Thus began the "Puritan Exodus," or "Great Migration," which peopled Massachusetts in the course of a decade with sixteen thousand souls.

The lands around Boston Bay filled up rapidly. Salem, Boston, Charlestown, Watertown, and Newtown (Cambridge) were founded within a year or two. The coast plain was narrow, and the higher levels back of the plain were strewn with glacial boulders which made cultivation of the soil difficult. The early towns were generally located on level terraces only slightly above the reach of high tide. In the cultivation of these lands and in the neighboring fisheries, along with the Indian trade, the early inhabitants found their occupations. Settlement spread inland less rapidly than along the coast for want of navigable streams such as made tidewater Virginia a "sylvan Venice." The soil did not lend itself to the production of a single staple like tobacco, but was tilled for food. The dispersing influence of the plantation was lacking, and the congregational system in the church made for compact settlement.

In none of the early colonies did the English know how to deal with the wilderness. They were decidedly what the frontiersmen of a later day would have called "tenderfoots." Occasionally a man showed exceptional capacity to adapt himself to the primitive environment. John Smith of Virginia, Edward Winslow and Captain Miles Standish of Plymouth, were quick to learn woodcraft and the art of dealing with the natives. In many ways, such for example as the cultivation of maize, the natives became the white men's teachers. It took time to evolve the bold and adventurous type of pioneer who loved the wilds and feared no danger or privation; but Smith and Standish were forerunners of the true type. Most of the early-comers were merely transplanted English villagers who were pitifully unprepared to face the hardships of an untamed land.

The Bay Colony paid its full toll in human life and suffering before the day of security and comfort was attained. Although free from the fevers which plagued the Virginia lowlands, New England endured far greater extremes of heat and cold than either Virginia or the British Isles. Deaths from exposure in winter were not uncommon. During the first few years the influx of population overtaxed the capacity to produce food, and semifamine prevailed. Upon women and children the severities of life fell like a blight. In Plymouth the first May found only four women alive of the eighteen who landed in January, and many indeed of those who came to Massachusetts Bay merely passed through "on the way to Heaven."

The leaders were disappointed but not discouraged by the unexpected privations. Winthrop abandoned hope of improving his temporal fortune with the words "we may not look for great things here." Thomas Dudley, his associate, found conditions "short of our expectations." But the chief purpose of these men was not material gain; according to Winthrop they sought to build "a City of God on earth," and New England they called the "New Canaan."

In contrast, the motives of many of the inhabitants were purely worldly. Within the tract granted to the Company there were seven little settlements in 1630, remnants of the fishing and trading ventures licensed during the twenties. The total population of these was small, but the Puritan chiefs added to the "ungodly" element by bringing in many indented servants. Winthrop alone had twenty such servants in his household. While many persons of this class may have been honest and capable, they came as a rule from the least promising portion of the English nation. When, then, we read the judgment of the old Puritan divine — "God hath sifted a nation, that he might send choice grain into this wilderness " — we do well to remember that he was not speaking of the common run, whom he would have regarded as chaff.

The great body of the Puritan immigrants belonged to the middle class of small farmers, tradesmen, and craftsmen who felt the continual pressure of poverty and were accustomed to follow the lead of the minister and squire. With these, religious and economic motives were doubtless mingled in varying degrees. As to the numbers of the rank and file, it is rather startling to learn that of the two thousand who came in 1630 only about twelve were "freemen of the Company" and signers of the Cambridge agreement.

Social distinctions, almost wanting in Plymouth, were marked in Massachusetts Bay. Slaves were never numerous, but Indians and negroes of this status were at the bottom of the scale. Indented servants came next. The third class included those who did not own land or pursue a trade as independent workmen but labored for hire. The farmers and skilled craftsmen composed yet another group, the body of the Puritan population probably, and inferior socially only to the small class of leaders. The last were the gentry, and alone enjoyed the then significant title of "Master," since transformed into our universally used "Mister."

The gentry belonged to the social rank which in England composed the majority in the House of Commons and as country squires or magistrates held the county offices. Many of them, especially the clergymen, were trained in the universities. They were aristocrats by tradition and profession. They were brave and honorable idealists, but they belonged to a narrow and bigoted age. Social distinctions were to them real indexes of worth. They could suffer from the pinch of rising prices without perceiving why smiths and carpenters should raise their scale of charges. Women's activities were restricted to the home, and when they appeared in public, as at "meeting," they were expected to maintain a modest silence.

Hardly less than the Stuart kings the Puritan rulers believed themselves chosen of God to govern. John Cotton, the pastor at Boston, and for a long time the most influential of the ministers, declared that he did not conceive that God "did ever ordain [democracy] as a fit government for either church or commonwealth. If the people be governors," he asked, "who shall be governed?" In similar vein Winthrop held that "the best part is always the least, and of that best part the wiser part is always the lesser." Democracy has "no warrant in Scripture."

"Among nations it has always been accounted the meanest and worst of all forms of government."

These opinions were not universal, for Thomas Hooker, pastor at Newtown, held that the choice of magistrates belonged to the people, who also had the right to set the bounds of their authority. But Hooker came of yeoman stock, and owed his education at Cambridge University to "free" food and tuition provided for poor students who rendered menial services!

The aristocratic and popular elements in the colony began to clash almost at the beginning. The Cambridge agreement placed all of the privileges granted by the charter in the hands of the dozen aristocrats who composed at the time the entire body of stockholders. They were thus the General Court; and by election all of them were also assistants.

This handful of men had the legal right to govern all of the other emigrants to Massachusetts, but some of the others, dissatisfied with this monopoly of power and privilege, soon demanded admission to the Company as "freemen." As with their families they represented a considerable fraction of the population the assistants hesitated. They feared that if they refused the demand, there would be an exodus to Plymouth or some attractive unsettled spot. On the other hand, to grant it and admit the new freemen to the General Court might cost the old group its control.

To retain their power the assistants violated the charter. They decided to admit the new freemen, but allowed them only the privilege of voting for assistants "when these are to be chosen," reserving to themselves the legislative power and the choice of governor. At about the same time they "ordered that for time to come no man shall be admitted to the freedom of this body politicke but such as are members of some of the churches within the lymitts of the same."

Although the people were ignorant of this breach of the charter, discontent soon showed itself again. Watertown protested against a tax laid by the Court of Assistants. "It was not safe to pay moneys after that sort," said the townsmen, for the act seemed to be a case of taxation without representation. Governor Winthrop's explanation that the Court was "in the nature of a parliament" was given in such a tone of rebuke that the men of Watertown not only receded from the ground they had taken, but apologized for their "error."

All might now have gone smoothly had not the laws passed by the assistants favored the upper classes by limiting the wages of artisans and laying penalties upon the poor man whose stock wandered from the woodland to the unfenced fields of his betters.  Perhaps some rumor of the true nature of the charter raised doubts of the competence of the Court of Assistants to pass such laws.  In any case, in 1634 a group of freemen from several of the towns asked Winthrop to show them the charter. He produced it, but frankly told the delegation that the freemen did not have men among them who were qualified to share in legislation; he intimated that the assistants would lend an ear to the suggestions of a committee chosen by the freemen.  From this time on the towns sent deputies to act with the assistants at each meeting of the General Court, and the "suggestions" of the deputies speedily became in practice a share in legislation.

By these changes the freemen obtained their charter rights, but the leaven of democracy worked very slowly.  The people were too thoroughly imbued with belief in the superiority of the gentry to choose farmers or artisans as officials.  The influence of the aristocracy, lay and clerical, continued to be enormous. The aims of the magistrates and clergy were so identified and their coöperation so close that the government is sometimes described as a "theocracy."  The popular element in the law-making body only slightly offset the influence of the assistants, but incessant conflict resulted from their different viewpoints, and after an unusually warm dispute in 1644 they decided to sit as two houses.

In the events narrated we can trace the evolution, step by step, of a constitution from the charter of a commercial corporation.  A colony which, like Massachusetts, enjoyed self-government is called a "corporate" colony, to distinguish it from the proprietary and royal types, in both of which a large degree of control was exercised from without.

The Massachusetts Puritans professed allegiance to the English Church but put into practice the purified service which they had advocated in England.  In effect they really separated from the English Church and gravitated towards the congregational system of Plymouth. Yet the union of church and state was preserved and a Puritan establishment resulted. As Winthrop put it, he and his associates had come "to seek out a place of cohabitation under a due form of government both civil and ecclesiastical." In addition to the denial of the franchise to all non-members of the church, no churches were allowed except of the approved type, and the clergy assembled in synods were habitually consulted on political questions.

Closely connected with the church-state system was the scheme of public education. The Puritan ideal required an intelligent and well-trained ministry and a body of believers sufficiently educated to hearken with understanding. Out of such religious impulses sprang Harvard College (1636) and schools sustained at public expense (see page 68).

It must not be supposed that events in New England passed wholly unnoticed by the King. Malcontents from the colony complained that the Puritans were setting up an independent church and state, and as early as 1634 a royal commission ordered Massachusetts to submit its charter for scrutiny. The colonial authorities delayed their reply and sent an agent to persuade the English officials to forego their inquest. Meantime fortifications were erected and other preparations made for defense. The Crown took steps to enforce the surrender of the charter, but decisive action was prevented by the disturbances in England which led to the Civil War of the forties.

The designs of the King were a part of his plan for enforcing conformity throughout the British dominions. New England escaped chiefly because of distance. In Scotland the Presbyterian "Covenanters'" resistance caused the failure of the King's experiment at rule without Parliament. By various devices, including the exaction of "ship-money," Charles succeeded for a decade in raising funds, but when his ecclesiastical policy provoked armed resistance in Scotland, an army became necessary, and the only way to obtain sufficient money for the payment of the soldiers was to call Parliament and ask for a grant. Parliament demanded reforms before it would vote taxes, and the quarrel which followed culminated in war between its supporters and those of the King. Broadly speaking, the King's camp contained the Anglicans, while the Puritans of all varieties

upheld the cause of Parliament. Beginning in 1642, the Civil
War ended seven years later in the triumph of the parliamentary
party and the trial and execution of Charles I.

These events directly influenced the progress of colonization.
The Puritan emigration coincides with the period of Charles's
personal government. With the meeting of Parliament in 1640
the movement was checked. In fact, many Puritans returned
to England, and the triumph of their party there gave the impulse for a considerable migration of Royalists to Virginia, where
the English Church was established by the laws.

## EXPANSION AND UNION IN NEW ENGLAND

In Massachusetts the occupied area was extended, not as in
Virginia, by granting land to individuals (see page 39), but by
the incorporation of new towns by groups.[1] The first step was
an application to the General Court. If the Court approved
the petition, the group was recognized as incorporators of the
town and a tract of land was assigned to the corporate body.
The incorporators then laid out the lands and assigned plots to
their own members and other persons at their will.

The town soon became one of the most significant of the institutions of New England. It early gained the right, as we have
seen, of sending representatives to the General Court. It also
became the unit of local self-government. The town meeting
was the body through which the inhabitants acted. It passed
by-laws relating to local interests, it elected officers to administer
these laws, it chose the deputies to the General Court. In
different towns the privileges of the inhabitants varied somewhat.
Only freemen of the Company could vote for deputies in any of
them, but in other respects some of the towns gave non-freemen
equal rights. Some of them, in short, were little democracies.
Although, taking the population as a whole, only a small percentage of the adult men were fully enfranchised, so many were
in constant contact with public business that Thomas Jefferson
was led, many years later, to call the town meeting "the best
school of political liberty the world ever saw."

[1] Note that the word "town" in the New England sense means "township" rather
than "village." It is also used to denote the corporate body.

Massachusetts soon became the mother of other colonies. A fur-trader named John Oldham found a trail leading to the Connecticut River and brought back such a glowing report of the lands in the river valley that a new migration was begun in that direction. Lacking good land, and somewhat dissatisfied in other ways, some of the Newtown people and others from neighboring towns, under Pastor Hooker's lead, started the movement in 1635. Within two years Windsor, Hartford, and Wethersfield had been founded, and the total population was about eight hundred. In 1639 a plan of government was adopted, known as the "Fundamental Orders of Connecticut."

Like Plymouth, Connecticut was a squatter colony, for the followers of Hooker had no legal title to the lands taken, and the Fundamental Orders, like the Mayflower Compact, rested on the assent of the people. But being more specific than the earlier compact as to the details of the government, they mark another step in the evolution of the idea of a written constitution.

The Connecticut government and church were very much like those of Massachusetts, but the Fundamental Orders, instead of requiring the voter to be a church member, left his qualifications to be determined by the town. In 1659, however, a property qualification was adopted by the General Court which stood with slight change until the nineteenth century. After nearly a generation Connecticut obtained a royal charter (1662) which gave a legal sanction for the institutions which had been set up without permission.

While the settlements on Connecticut River were taking form, another appeared farther west at New Haven, on Long Island Sound. The New Haven people differed but little from the Puritans of Massachusetts and Connecticut, but most of them came directly from England. The story of New Haven repeats the tale of government-making which we have noted in the case of Connecticut, but this colony was united with Connecticut when it was given a charter.

About the time that Connecticut received its first white inhabitants other groups from Massachusetts began the settlement of Rhode Island. These emigrants did not leave voluntarily, like the pioneers of Connecticut, but were expelled on account of their religious views. Winthrop and Cotton and their

like were not advocates of toleration.  Having left England in
quest of a land where they might establish the kind of society
which seemed good to them, they were prompt to cast out all
who differed in opinion.  Hence it was that Roger Williams and
Anne Hutchinson and their disciples were banished for holding
and disseminating doctrines which the Puritan leaders held to
be false.

Williams with five others came in 1636 to the head of Narragansett Bay, where they founded Providence.  A little later a
party of Mrs. Hutchinson's followers founded Portsmouth on
the island in the bay.  Still later a third town was begun at
Newport.  These and other settlements were at first uncon-
nected.  Each had its government resting upon the voluntary
agreement of the inhabitants.  In spite of rivalries there was a
strong tendency to unite under a general government, and after
several half-successful experiments a permanent union was
formed under a charter granted by Charles II in 1663.

There was no favored church in Rhode Island.  Owing partly
to the influence of Williams who preached toleration — a rare
doctrine in that age — and partly to the fact that the colony
was the common refuge of several sects, it was from the first the
home of religious freedom.  There were many contentions
among the sects, and Rhode Island was regarded by her neighbors as a hot-bed of disorder; but she clung to freedom of
speech and worship even while they drove out heretics and
hanged Quakers.  America offered a unique opportunity for
experiments in new types of society for which Europe had no
room.  Rhode Island was the first experiment in "full liberties
in religious concernments."

New Hampshire and Maine were the scenes of early efforts
at colonization by proprietors, but both of them owe more to
Massachusetts than to any proprietor.  Some of her religious
exiles went to these northern districts, and the expansion of her
shipping and trade interests sent others.  Her charter could be
construed to include portions of both New Hampshire and
Maine, and she gradually extended her control over them.  In
the case of Maine the union lasted until the nineteenth century,
but in 1679 New Hampshire was detached and made a royal
province.

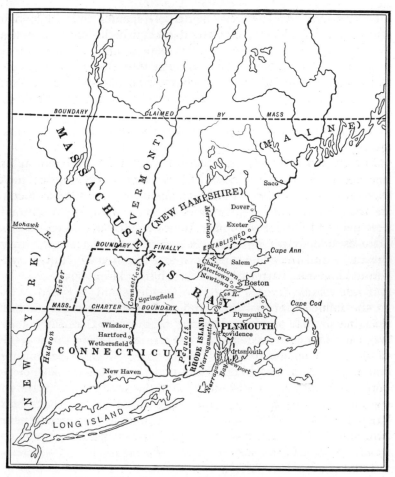

CHIEF NEW ENGLAND SETTLEMENTS BY 1640.

All along the New England coast the native tribes had been almost destroyed by a plague shortly before the coming of the Pilgrims. In consequence there was little trouble between the settlers and the Indians for several years. The English recognized the moral obligation to pay the Indians for their lands, but the red men regarded their sales only as admitting the whites to a share in the use of them. The migration into the Connecticut Valley caused the first war, by crowding the Pequot tribe into a narrow space between the white settlements and the hostile tribes of the Narragansett Confederacy, which dwelt upon the west shore of the bay of the same name. In 1637 the hard-pressed natives murdered and plundered John Oldham, the trader, and committed other acts of violence. To punish them a joint force was raised by Massachusetts, Plymouth, and Connecticut, which surprised the Pequots and almost exterminated them. Their lands were thus opened for occupation by the conquering race.

The Pequot War revealed the advantages of coöperation in meeting a common danger. Massachusetts, Plymouth, Connecticut, and New Haven were so similar in their institutional life that before 1640 synods representing the clergy of all four were held to promote a common policy in church affairs. Some disputes had arisen by this time over boundaries and other questions, and the people began to feel the need of an organization able to deal with questions involving the interests of more than one colony.

Out of this situation came the New England Confederation of 1643. A Board of Commissioners was created, consisting of two men from each colony. At the annual meeting the vote of six was to determine action on any business within their powers, which included the making of war and peace, the promotion of justice between the confederates, and the rendition of fugitive servants and criminals. The Confederation worked none too well. Massachusetts exceeded in population the other three members combined, and on more than one occasion refused to be bound by the decision of their commissioners. The incorporation of New Haven with Connecticut against her will almost destroyed the Confederation. It is important historically because it shows the tendency of the colonies to unite as they became conscious of common interests. In this way, and also in the powers given to the commissioners, the Confederation foreshadowed the union under the Constitution. In 1643 New England and the Chesapeake Bay colonies were, of course, too far apart to dream of union. Even Rhode Island, because she was not orthodox, was repeatedly denied membership in the Confederation.

## SELECT BIBLIOGRAPHY FOR CHAPTER II

**The Pilgrims and Plymouth.** The best history of Plymouth is Goodwin, *The Pilgrim Republic.* Channing, Doyle, Osgood, and Tyler all have chapters on Plymouth. Consult also the works on New England cited in the next section.

**Massachusetts Bay.** The standard account of the northeastern group of colonies is Palfrey, *History of New England.* Although rather old it is painstaking, accurate, and still valuable.

Fiske's book on this group is *Beginnings of New England.* In *The Chronicles* series is Andrews, *Fathers of New England.* An excellent recent study is Adams, *Founding of New England.*

A good non-political account is Weeden, *Economic and Social History of New England.*

**Expansion and Union in New England.** The authorities cited above provide an adequate treatment of this section for the general student. Osgood's discussions of the land system, the evolution of the colonial governments, and the New England Confederation are especially good.

# CHAPTER III

## FILLING IN THE COAST PLAIN

### MARYLAND

A little while before Pastor Hooker led his flock to the fine bottom lands of Connecticut the beginnings of a new colony were made near the mouth of the Potomac (at St. Mary's, 1634). This was Maryland, which Charles I had granted to Cecil Calvert, second Lord Baltimore.

Maryland arrests attention chiefly because it was the first successful proprietary colony. Baltimore's patent gave him the right to make laws "with the advice, assent, and approbation of the freemen." He construed this provision to mean that the colonists might approve or reject bills which he drew, but the representatives of the settlers insisted that theirs was the right to enact laws subject to his veto; and he was compelled to accept their view. In course of time the bicameral system evolved in Maryland, as in Massachusetts and Virginia, but the members of the upper house, or council, were selected by the proprietor instead of by the people or the King. The governor, also, was the appointee and agent of the proprietor. Maryland, in short, was governed much like Virginia, with the proprietor taking the King's place. It will serve as the type of the proprietary colony.

Baltimore offered a thousand acres to any man who would import five others to settle upon the land, and over them the grantee was given the rights of an English "lord of a manor." Few manors were ever created. As in Virginia many immigrants came as indented servants. For them the inducement was held out of a grant of fifty acres when their terms of service expired. For many years the poor servant's opportunity to rise in the social scale was better in Maryland than in Virginia, until the latter adopted a similar practice.

In other features of its institutional life Maryland was not so different from Virginia as to call for particular study. To this statement there is one exception. Baltimore was a Catholic, and many of his coreligionists were among the early immigrants. Within a few years they were outnumbered by the Protestants, who were inclined to reënact the harsh anti-Catholic laws of England. To protect the Catholics Baltimore procured the passage in 1649 of a Toleration Act which insured religious liberty for all Christians.

## THE DEVELOPMENT OF VIRGINIA

By the time Maryland was founded Virginia had fully recovered from the set-back given by the Indian massacre of 1622, and was again growing rapidly. A census taken in 1635 showed a population of five thousand. Plantations had taken up the lower valley of the James and its tributaries and were spreading to the northward beyond the York. When the Civil War ended with the execution of the King, Virginia proved to be a congenial refuge for the discomfited supporters of the alliance between the Crown and the Episcopacy. Far from changing the trend of development in the colony, the coming of the "Cavaliers" gave added impetus to the growth of the plantation system, since many of them were men of wealth who soon acquired large estates in land.

It was easy for men of means to get both land and labor for the large-scale production of tobacco. Head-right certificates and the right to the labor of indented servants were purchased and sold, and land grants were made to holders of head rights on easy conditions, including "seating" within a certain time, — by which was meant the clearing and cultivating of a small acreage and the erection of a cabin, — and the payment of an annual quitrent to the King. The requirements were quite commonly evaded.

Although negro slaves were first brought to Virginia in 1619, the number of servants of this class was small for many years as compared with the number of white servants; but in time the planters found the labor of the blacks, who were permanent bondsmen, more advantageous than the temporary servitude of persons of their own race. By the close of the seventeenth century negro slavery was well established as the chief labor system of the plantation.

Besides the planters and servile whites there were many small landholders who came at their own expense and received fifty acres for each member of their families, including sometimes a servant or two. Some of the more energetic indented servants also became landowners when freed. From these two sources there arose a sturdy yeomanry. The more shiftless of the servants, many of whom had been transported in punishment for petty crimes, upon attaining their freedom formed the class known as the "poor whites."

The planters sought the bottom lands along the navigable streams. The most productive soils were found there, and they wished to load their tobacco upon ocean-going vessels at their own wharves. From England they received in payment not cash but whatever goods they needed. There was little place for the retail merchant or the free handicraftsman. The lack of these classes and the dispersion of the population delayed the growth of towns until late in the eighteenth century.

In the development of Virginia there was no such activity of groups of men as has been described in New England. Grants of land were made directly to individuals. The diffuse population required a large territorial unit for purposes of local government, and nothing like the New England town was possible. In 1634 the assembly divided the colony into eight counties, modeled after the shires of England. These replaced the earlier boroughs. New counties were created from time to time as settlement spread. In each the free adult white males annually voted for two burgesses to represent them in the assembly. With this act the average man's participation in government began and ended. There was no county meeting with functions like those of the town meeting in the North. The duties of local administration were performed by officials appointed by the governor and council. The chief of these were the sheriff, the lieutenant (commander of the militia), and the justices of the court. Usually, if not always, the elected burgesses as well as the appointed officers were wealthy planters.

It has often been said that Virginia was aristocratic and that Massachusetts was democratic. But the statement is hardly

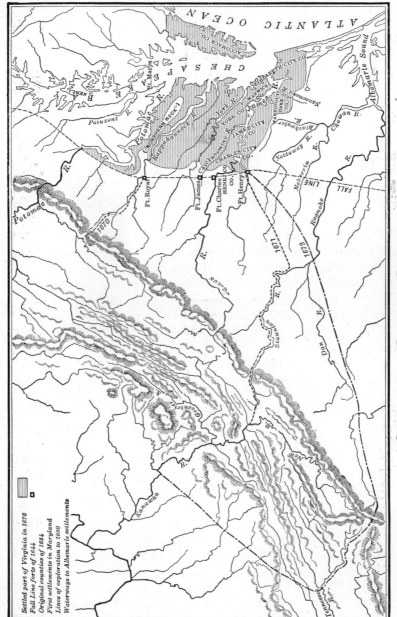

Settlements in Chesapeake Region by 1676.

true. The range of the voter's activity was narrower in the southern colony, but for a long time the franchise was less restricted. The Virginia system developed a keen sense of responsibility on the part of the governing class, and trained men for leadership as few other plans have ever done. It was no accident that so many statesmen of the first rank in the early days of independence hailed from the Old Dominion.

## Expansion, 1650–1676

Tidewater Virginia is almost as large as England, and afforded ample room for expansion during the seventeenth century. By the middle of the century immigrants were crossing the Potomac from the Maryland side and taking lands in the "northern neck." Among them were the ancestors of George Washington, John Marshall, and other great men of later times. The new-comers from the North, reaching the banks of the Rappahannock, met other pioneers coming from the old settlements on the James and York.

The plantations continued to hug the river banks, and the quest for good lands pushed the frontier to the fall line along the streams while great spaces between them remained almost unbroken wilderness, traversed only by bridle paths. During Indian disturbances in the forties, military posts were erected at the falls of the chief streams, and by 1650 interest was awaking in the more remote interior. Within the next generation exploring expeditions to the West and Southwest reached the Carolina Piedmont and the upper waters of the Tennessee and Great Kanawha rivers beyond the Appalachian watershed — the first visits of Englishmen to the "western waters."

These expeditions opened the fur trade with distant tribes, and tempted some of the planters at the fall line to divide their attention between tobacco-growing and the Indian trade. To and from these westmost plantations the traders came and went, and their ways of life began to show the characteristics of the typical American frontier.

The agricultural advance towards the West halted at the fall line until a decade or two of the eighteenth century had passed. However, ascending some of the streams which fall into the James from the south, the whites found themselves in touch with other streams which led them to the Roanoke, and soon after the middle of the century they began settlements on Albemarle Sound in North Carolina.

Few great planters were to be found on the frontier. It was the small landowners, as a rule, who were pushed by social and economic forces towards the outer rim of settlement. Rich planters who had acquired large tracts of the best lands in the river valleys had little reason to seek new homes, while indented servants who had served their time, or yeomen immigrants, could hardly get land at all except in the newer parts of the colony.

As time passed jealousies and suspicions arose between the planters and the small landowners. The planters became fearful that the poorer element might gain control of the assembly, and to preserve their power Governor William Berkeley withheld writs for the election of burgesses during the whole period from 1660 to 1676. In 1670 the assembly thus irregularly prolonged imposed a property qualification upon the voters.

While the common people were still angry over this reactionary law the Indians of the Piedmont began to give trouble. The governor was so slow in taking steps for the defense of the frontier that the people in the danger zone believed he was trying to avoid hostilities in order to save his profits in the fur trade. Exasperated at last beyond endurance by a man who "bought and sold their blood," the frontiersmen took matters in their own hands, and chose one of the fall-line planters, Nathaniel Bacon, Jr., to lead them against the savages. The governor, enraged in his turn, refused to give Bacon a commission, and his followers turned their arms against the administration. Gaining the upper hand for a time, the insurgents called an assembly which restored manhood suffrage; but Bacon died during the turmoil, his discouraged followers submitted, and their work was undone. "Bacon's Rebellion" (1676), so called, shows how decidedly the frontier tended to foster an independent and democratic spirit.

New England's expanding population spread along the valley of the Connecticut River, which contained the only considerable body of good land, but its course led settlement northward instead of westward. The earliest river town in Massachusetts was Springfield, which was founded soon after Hartford and its neighbors of the Connecticut colony. By 1676 the valley was occupied as far as Deerfield, although the strip of settled land along the coast was as yet hardly thirty miles wide.

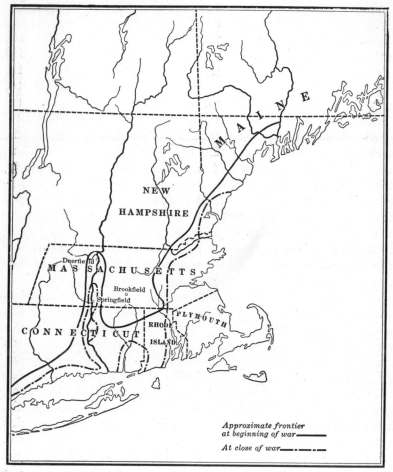

EFFECT OF KING PHILIP'S WAR.

Just when the Indian war broke out in Virginia, the expansion of New England was checked by King Philip's War, in which the tribes made a united effort to resist the white advance. Using their favorite tactics of surprise, the natives fell upon the exposed towns with savage fury. Beginning in the summer of 1675 the conflict raged desperately for two years. Of ninety towns forty were attacked and twelve destroyed. The frontier was driven back and the whites lost a thousand men. In the crisis the New England Confederation was revived and the united strength of the colonies was brought to bear in the struggle. The Indians were finally crushed, and when next New Englanders suffered the horrors of Indian war, their enemies were remoter tribes in alliance with the French of the St. Lawrence basin.

## RIVALRY WITH THE DUTCH

The confusion in England during and following the Civil War was not conducive to the planting of new colonies. The execution of Charles I was followed by an Interregnum when Oliver Cromwell ruled with a strong hand supported by the army; but after his death came reaction and the "Restoration" in 1660 of the Stuart line in the person of Charles II. Then the country, weary of strife over religious and political dogmas, turned again to worldly matters. The new King had spent the years of the Interregnum in exile, and an easy-going, pleasure-loving disposition led him to avoid repeating the offenses of his father and grandfather, lest he be compelled "to go again upon his travels." Desiring to please, he lent himself readily to the schemes of men who began to push plans of commercial and territorial expansion with great vigor.

One of the aims of these "mercantilists" was to destroy the Dutch maritime power. The Dutch states had recently won their independence from Spain and had conquered the East Indian possessions of Portugal. With an enthusiasm born of freedom and success they had then begun to look around for other opportunities.

About the time of the coming of the Pilgrims to Plymouth the Dutch West India Company was formed with an ambitious program embracing projects as widely separated as the slave traffic on the African coast, rivalry with the Portuguese in Brazil, and trade with the North American Indians. Until they were driven from the Connecticut Valley by the men of Plymouth, the activities of the Dutch in the Indian trade extended from the Connecticut to the Delaware, which they called "South River."

On the site of New York City they built the village of New Amsterdam; but Fort Orange on the Hudson, near the modern
Albany, was the key-point for the fur trade.

Excursions from this post first made known the geography
of the New York lake region, and the course of the Delaware
from source to mouth.   Central New York was the home of the
most powerful native confederacy of North America, the League
of the Iroquois.   The five (later six) tribes composing this
alliance were the terror of the other natives, from New England
to the Mississippi, and from Canada to Carolina.   With them,
owing to the mutual benefits of trade, the Dutch had the happy
fortune to establish friendly relations which were never seriously
disturbed.

The West India Company, like the Virginia Company, tried
to shift the burden of bringing in settlers to private shoulders.
The "patroonship," like the particular plantation in Virginia,
was a grant of land to an individual or group of men on condition of importing immigrants.   The Dutch went beyond the
English, however, in giving to the patroon the political as well
as the economic rights of a feudal lord over his tenants.

Several patroonships were attempted, but the only successful
one was Rensselaerswyck, established by Kiliaen van Rensselaer.   It embraced the present counties of Albany and Rensselaer and completely surrounded Fort Orange.   The ill success
of the patroonships led to other devices to induce immigration.
Lands were offered on liberal terms to persons of small means,
and sometimes free passage was provided.   Peasants from
Holland, indented servants who had served their time in Virginia,
and New Englanders in great numbers were attracted to New
Netherland.   They settled on Long Island, on the mainland
near the mouth of the Hudson, or at Fort Orange, for most of
the Hudson Valley, as one contemporary put it, was "little
fitted to be peopled," having only "here and there a little corn
land, which the Indians had prepared by removing the stones."

The government of New Netherland lacked the liberal features
found in the English colonies.   There was no representative
assembly, and the people had only a small share in local government.   In this respect New Netherland resembled the Spanish
colonies much more than it did the English.   The lack of

political privileges caused much discontent among the English element, and they would doubtless have obtained the right of representation if Dutch control had lasted a little longer.

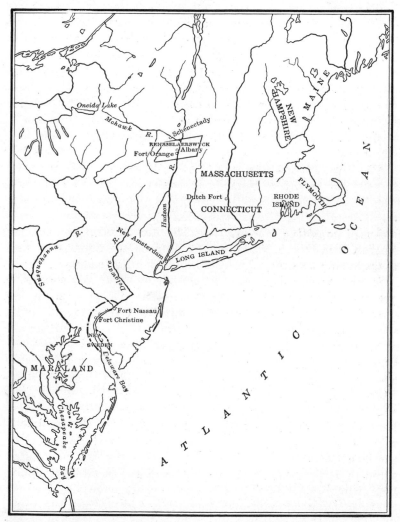

REGION OF DUTCH AND SWEDISH ACTIVITY, 1609–1664.

The Dutch had slight success in the Delaware Valley. They tried to maintain a trading post in what is now New Jersey, almost opposite the site of Philadelphia, and patroons and others attempted to settle on Delaware Bay. Their failure was due in large part to the hostility of the Indians. The Swedes fared better. They built Fort Christina on the site of the future Wilmington, in the late thirties, and it was soon the center of a group of small hamlets. The Dutch regarded the Swedes as intruders, but being allies in the Thirty Years War then raging in Europe, they contented themselves for the time with a protest by the governor at New Amsterdam. With the end of the war, however, came the bloodless conquest of New Sweden (1655) by a force from New Netherland.

The elimination of New Sweden was the prelude to the conquest of New Netherland by the English, who claimed the whole coast from Nova Scotia to Florida. Having no active interest in the middle region in the early decades of the century, they had not interfered with the Dutch except in the Connecticut Valley, although Delaware Bay was clearly within the grant to Lord Baltimore. By the middle of the century, however, the growing naval power of the Dutch had aroused the English, who were then as now jealous of their supremacy on the seas. A large share of the carrying trade of the English colonies had fallen into the hands of their enterprising competitors. To regain the monopoly of this trade and to encourage English shipping, Parliament began to pass restrictive laws known as "Navigation Acts." One of these, dating from 1651, forbade the importation into England, or any English possession, of goods from Asia, Africa, or America, except in vessels owned by Englishmen or English colonists, and manned chiefly by English sailors. Imports from European countries might be brought into the English possessions only by English ships or ships of the producing country.

This act was aimed directly at the Dutch, and with other causes led to war, during which an attack was planned (1655) against New Netherland. The forces of New England were to be employed; but Massachusetts held out against the other members of the New England Confederation, and the war ended without hostilities in America.

Similar causes brought on a second war in 1664. The English now thought the time ripe for ejecting the Dutch. An expedition against New Netherland was carefully planned and was actually on the way across the sea before war was declared. Reenforced by some Connecticut volunteers it appeared before New Amsterdam and received its surrender.

## NEW NETHERLAND BECOMES NEW YORK

The region of which the Dutch were dispossessed, from the Connecticut to the Delaware, was given to the King's brother, the Duke of York.[1] The Duke in turn transferred the portion between the lower Hudson and the Delaware to Lord John Berkeley and Sir George Carteret, retaining the Hudson Valley and Long Island for himself, under the name of New York.

The Dutch inhabitants accepted the change of masters quite readily. Their property rights were respected, holders of petty offices were allowed to serve out their terms, and the Dutch local government was replaced so gradually as to cause no annoyance. Complete religious liberty was allowed, and those who wished to leave the province were permitted to do so. Few availed themselves of this privilege, and the descendants of the Dutch stock form to this day an important element in the New York population.

The English inhabitants were sorely disappointed because the conquest did not bring representative government. Perhaps because the people had no representation during the Dutch period, the Duke's patent, unlike Baltimore's, did not require their assent in legislation. Instead it gave him "full and absolute power . . . to . . . govern and rule," so long as his laws were not contrary to the laws of England.

At the outset Governor Richard Nicolls told the English that they might "assure themselves of equal if not greater freedoms and immunities than any of his Majesty's colonies in New England." In fulfillment of this promise he proclaimed the "Duke's Laws," based upon the New England codes and including some features of the system of town government. They permitted the freeholders (landowners) of each town to elect local officials,

---

[1] An agreement with Connecticut fixed the boundary between that colony and New York, but the Vermont region was in dispute between New York and New Hampshire until after the Revolution.

but the town meeting, with its right to pass local laws and to choose delegates to the legislature, was wanting. The law-making body consisted of the governor and his council aided by a judicial tribunal known as the "Court of Assizes."

To the English inhabitants Nicolls's promise meant the right of the freeholders to elect deputies to act with the governor and council in law-making. The history of New York for a generation after the conquest turns on the struggle for this right. In 1683 the Duke seemed to be on the point of yielding; he allowed Governor Thomas Dongan to permit the election of an assembly, but upon his accession to the throne in 1685 as James II, he changed his mind. Three years later he was overthrown by the Revolution of 1688, and in the general reorganization which followed New York gained at last the coveted privilege (see page 86).

## The Carolinas

The conquest of New Netherland filled in the gap between the English possessions in New England and on the Chesapeake. At the same time new colonizing efforts were made in the territory claimed by Spain. Lords Berkeley and Carteret were members of a group of courtiers who were eager to undertake colonial ventures. Lord Berkeley's brother William, governor of Virginia, was also of this group. To them and others, eight in all, the King gave a patent in 1663 for lands south of Virginia, under the name of Carolina. As later defined the tract extended from the southern limits of Virginia (36° 30') to the thirty-first parallel, and to the Pacific on the West.

Within this grant were already the settlers on Albemarle Sound, who had come in from Virginia. They formed a nucleus which slowly expanded, while far to the southward, on the coast, a second settlement was begun in 1670 and named Charleston. Attempts in the intermediate region, near Cape Fear, failed. The wide interval between these occupied centers necessitated separate governments and led at length to the division of Carolina. In each the ordinary type of proprietary government came about in time.

Owing partly to their later origin and partly to broad belts of "pine barrens" which paralleled the coast a few miles inland,

BEGINNINGS OF CAROLINA AND GEORGIA.

there were no settlements in the interior of the Carolinas before
the eighteenth century. Although almost from the beginning
fur-traders ascended the rivers and trafficked with the natives
in the Piedmont, this back country did not receive its in-

habitants much before 1750, when they came in mostly from the North.

In economic life these southern settlements developed much like Virginia. Religious toleration prevailed, but the Anglican Church was favored by the laws.

## THE JERSEYS AND PENNSYLVANIA

The land granted to Berkeley and Carteret was named New Jersey. Immigrants from New England, especially, came to add to the sparse Dutch and Swedish population which already fringed the banks of the Hudson and Delaware. Through successive purchases New Jersey gradually passed under the control of Quakers, and many persons of this faith came from England to escape the persecutions to which dissenters were still subjected in the British Isles. For a time the province was divided into two parts, known as "East Jersey" and "West Jersey," with separate governments.

Among the Quaker proprietors of the province was William Penn, son of a British admiral, whose family connections gave him much influence at court in spite of the adoption of the faith of a despised sect. While a student in college Penn became interested in political philosophy, and under the influence of Friends' doctrines his views on government took a decidedly liberal turn. The desire to provide an asylum for those who were oppressed for conscience' sake, and to try out his theories of government, as much as the hope of gain, led him to obtain from Charles II, in 1681, a patent for a vast tract west of the Delaware River, which was named Pennsylvania in honor of Admiral Penn. The next year he acquired from the Duke of York a somewhat doubtful title to Delaware. The latter claim brought him into dispute with Lord Baltimore, but with the aid of the powerful Duke the Quaker courtier gained the territory.[1]

Penn's charter contained some restrictions upon his powers as proprietor which were not found in the earlier grants of this

[1] A further dispute over the boundary between Pennsylvania and Maryland was not settled until 1760. In accordance with the agreement then reached between the heirs of Penn and Baltimore, the present boundary was surveyed by Mason and Dixon, in 1767. The arrangement gave Pennsylvania a strip many miles wide within the original Maryland grant.

type. Acts of the assembly were to be sent to England for approval; appeals were to be allowed from the courts of the

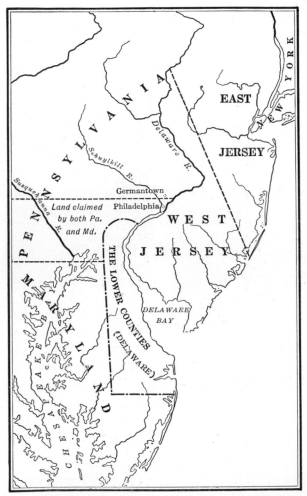

BEGINNINGS OF NEW JERSEY, PENNSYLVANIA, AND DELAWARE.

province; and the obligation to enforce the navigation acts was imposed. Taxes were to be laid only with the consent of the assembly "or by Act of Parliament."

The later colonies, Pennsylvania in particular, escaped the

hardships endured by the early inhabitants of Virginia and New England, for the conditions of success were better understood. Pennsylvania grew rapidly from the start. Penn advertised widely and even visited the Low Countries on the continent, selling lands outright subject to a modest quitrent. Indented servants were promised fifty acres when they attained freedom. Religious liberty was promised to all who believed in the existence of God, although only Christians were to be allowed to take part in government.

Penn's first immigrants settled along the Delaware. Philadelphia was laid out upon its banks in 1682. The next year Germantown was founded near by, by people from the lower Rhine Valley, who sought escape from religious persecution and the poverty caused by almost continual war. Population then spread northward along the river and up the tributary Schuylkill.

The plan of government which Penn devised was artificial and clumsy but unusually liberal, for the voters were allowed to elect the council as well as the lower house. The proprietor depended upon the governor, whom he appointed, to protect his interests. A few years showed that his rights were not sufficiently guarded by this arrangement, and in order to regain the usual right of a proprietor to appoint the members of the council, he agreed that it should relinquish its share in legislation. As a result, Pennsylvania, unlike the other colonies, had a legislature of only one house.

The settlements on the lower Delaware, known as the "lower counties," were for awhile under the same government as those around Philadelphia, and sent their representatives to sit in the assembly; but Delaware was given a separate assembly in 1703.

## GEORGIA

A half-century passed after the founding of Pennsylvania before the English filled in the last gap along the coast plain. James Oglethorpe, founder of Georgia, was, like Penn, a philanthropist, who sought to open a new door of opportunity for the prisoners for debt in English jails. The British government had other reasons for encouraging his plan, as it wished to forestall the Spanish in occupying the vacant territory, still claimed by both nations, lying between Florida and South Carolina. Parliament therefore, for the first time in the history of British colonization, granted financial aid. A secondary object with Oglethorpe was to provide an asylum for the persecuted Protestants of Catholic countries, and soon after he began his settlement at the mouth of the Savannah River, in 1733, Germans from the Salzburg came to the upper river. Scotch Highlanders, too, came and took the risk of locating not far from the Spanish settlements in Florida.

The character of the settlers and the purpose of the undertaking seemed to forbid the usual type of government. The colonists were given no part in it, and control was vested in a board of trustees for a period of twenty-one years, after which Georgia was to become a royal province. Slavery was prohibited, as well as the importation of intoxicants, and the amount of land which might be held by one person was limited in order that settlement might be compact and easily defended. These restrictions so hampered the growth of the province that one by one they were given up. Progress was more rapid after the change to a royal province in 1752, and at that time a representative assembly was established.

## SELECT BIBLIOGRAPHY FOR CHAPTER III

**Maryland ; Development of Virginia.** See citations under **The Planting of Virginia**, in Bibliography for Chapter I.

**Expansion.** The story of the explorations which opened the fur trade to the West and Southwest from the fall line in Virginia is told, with documents, in Alvord and Bidgood, *First Exploration of the Trans-Alleghany*. The studies of Bruce (see page 20) become invaluable for this period of Virginia history. Books previously cited cover the political history.

The spread of the New England population is the theme of Mathews, *Expansion of New England*.

**Rivalry with the Dutch.** Dutch and Swedish colonization is covered by Fiske, *Dutch and Quaker Colonies*, and by Goodwin, *Dutch and English on the Hudson*. A standard work of the old type is Brodhead, *History of the State of New York*. Volume I treats of the Dutch period.

**New Netherland Becomes New York : The Carolinas, Jerseys, Pennsylvania, Georgia.** The conquest of New Netherland and the founding of the later colonies are covered by Andrews, *Colonial Self-Government;*

by Channing, *United States*, II, and Winsor, *America*, III.  Osgood, *American Colonies*, II, discusses the institutional development.

New York under the English is dealt with by Brodhead, II; and Fiske, *Dutch and Quaker Colonies*.

Ashe, *History of North Carolina*, is the best for that province.  McCrady, *History of South Carolina*, is a good modern work.

The Jerseys and Pennsylvania compose the subject matter of Fisher, *The Quaker Colonies*.  Sharpless, *A Quaker Experiment in Government*, is commendable.  Of various lives of Penn the one by Fisher, *The True William Penn*, may be mentioned.

For the founding of Georgia see Greene, *Provincial America*.

# CHAPTER IV

## PROVINCIAL AMERICA

### The Westward Movement

At the close of the seventeenth century the inhabited districts in the English colonies still formed a mere fringe along the seacoast, broken by patches of swamp and forest, and nowhere extending far inland save along the courses of the navigable rivers. By the middle of the eighteenth century, however, the widening fringe had reached the mountain barrier which separates the Atlantic slope from the Ohio Valley.

To the northward, in New England, population had reached the Massachusetts-Vermont line. In New York expansion had been slow in getting under way. Just when New Netherland was coming under its English masters a few Dutch families had settled at Schenectady, the Mohawk-River gateway to the land of the Iroquois. For more than half a century Schenectady remained a lonely outpost on the exposed frontier. In 1698 over fifteen thousand of the eighteen thousand inhabitants of New York were still on Long Island or near the mouth of the Hudson.

The lack of representative government long caused immigrants to avoid the province. The narrowness of the Hudson Valley and its stony soil were additional deterrents. The land system was uninviting. Oftentimes as the result of fraud on the part of the recipients of land grants, large holdings prevailed and formed the basis of a provincial aristocracy which controlled political and social life. On some of the great estates a system of tenantry existed which was quite out of keeping with the prevalent freehold tenure in America. Small landowners were crowded out, and young men sometimes left New York for other provinces where lands could be obtained more easily and held more securely.

The expansion of New York really began in the eighteenth century when the frontier was thrust up the Mohawk by German

SPREAD OF POPULATION, 1700–1760.

immigrants. Driven from their homes in the valley of the Rhine by persecution and hard times, like their kinsmen who had founded Germantown, they came to New York by thousands during the first quarter of the century, and their settlements on the Mohawk marked the farthest advance of the frontier in that province before the Revolution.

In Pennsylvania the opening of the century found population on the banks of the Delaware and its navigable tributaries, with a few outposts on the Susquehanna. Through the mountain wall which barred the advance of the farmer the Susquehanna and Delaware led northward to the Indian country of the "finger lakes," inviting the adventurous trader to compete with New Yorkers in the commerce with the redskins. Although by the royal patent of 1664 the western boundary of New York was a line drawn due north from the source of the Delaware, the prosperity of that province rested so largely upon the fur trade of the lake country that vigorous efforts were made to forestall the Pennsylvanians. The assertion of a protectorate over the Iroquois was the means of compelling the southern traders to turn their attention elsewhere.

Threading the passes of the mountains traced by the western branches of the Susquehanna, the Pennsylvanians now came upon the upper waters of the Alleghany and began to traffic with the tribes of the Ohio Valley. It is not unlikely that they crossed the mountains as early as 1725; before the middle of the century their posts were to be found at several points in the Ohio country, between the river and Lake Erie.

Prominent in this trade were the so-called "Scotch-Irish." They were Protestants of Ulster, in northern Ireland, who came to Pennsylvania in great numbers, and to the other colonies to a less extent, in the early eighteenth century, because of British laws which discriminated against the people of the smaller island in favor of English commerce and of the Anglican Church.[1]

Germans, who had shared in the making of Pennsylvania from the beginning, continued to come in great streams. Some of those who had gone to New York came later to Pennsylvania by way of the Susquehanna. Others came directly from the Fatherland. Many of them were from the Rhine Palatinate, and possessed so little of this world's goods that they were compelled to defray the expense of their transportation by pledg-

---

[1] The "Scotch-Irish" were people from the Scottish lowlands who had been colonized in Ireland by James I as a means of holding the native Irish in check.

ing their labor for a term of years, much like the indented servants of early Virginia.

Greatly to the annoyance of the government officials, the immigrants were disposed to help themselves to lands when they could not pay for them. The Scotch-Irish declared that "it was against the laws of God and nature that so much land should lie idle while so many Christians wanted it to work on and raise their bread." While both stocks produced many a fur-trader and pioneer, the Germans especially as a class became thrifty farmers. The coming of these foreigners filled up the lower valley of the Susquehanna, giving rise to Lancaster and neighboring towns, and bringing the settled area up to the mountains.

Virginia was the only province in which there had been any considerable westward advance during the seventeenth century. By 1675, as we have seen, her people had reached the fall line. Just at the turn of the century French Huguenots formed a settlement on the James above the falls, the first in the Piedmont. Fourteen years later Governor Spotswood brought a number of German redemptioners to the upper Rappahannock to work local iron ores. To his zeal was due the organization a little later of two counties in the Piedmont. The pioneers moved in only tardily, however, and before it was filled up Germans and Scotch-Irish moving southward from Pennsylvania crossed the Potomac and took lands west of the Blue Ridge (1730–1750).

In North Carolina the Albemarle settlements did not expand beyond the mouth of the Chowan until after a war with the Tuscarora Indians in 1712.[1] In fact the occupation of the Piedmont of both Carolinas was due largely to the continuation of the movement of Germans and Scotch-Irish from Pennsylvania. Where Staunton Gap breaks through the Blue Ridge the convenient pass formed an exit for the pioneers to the headwaters of the Roanoke and other southern rivers.

## THE FRONTIER

In one sense, the first English colonists in America were frontiersmen. The primeval woods formed the somber back-

---

[1] After their defeat this tribe was removed to New York and became the sixth nation of the Iroquois League.

ground of their rude cabins, and the howl of the wolf was the nightly accompaniment of their slumbers. However, they suffered but a temporary deprivation of their accustomed ways of life, and speedily transformed their surroundings. It was in the "back settlements" of the mid-eighteenth century, stretching from the Mohawk to the Savannah, that the typical frontier society first formed.[1] From this frontier onward, the real pioneer kept in the van of the movement westward and formed the "cutting edge" of civilization in its attack upon the wilderness. His type was permanent. His isolated cabin of rough logs, often without floor or windows, stood in the midst of a tiny clearing where a few trees had been felled or perhaps only deadened to make room for a little patch of corn. His few hogs ranged the neighboring woods, fattening on acorns and beechnuts until needed for the table. But he "loved the gun and scorned the plow." His long muzzle-loading flint-lock was his most intimate friend, and hunting was at once recreation and business, the source of food, raiment, and income. Venison supplied the larder and deerskin took the place of cloth in the making of garments. Peltries he bartered for the few commodities which he could not provide for his family through his own efforts. Of these the chief were salt, ammunition, and hardware, brought by the trader or obtained by occasional visits to a post or distant town.

Accident and disease were met with rough readiness; barring wounds, if alive, the frontiersman was usually well. Life was a prolonged adventure with danger ever near. Any night might bring the savages to burn, scalp, and torture. Wild almost as the Indian, certainly as bold and freedom-loving, the frontiersman endured hardship as his daily lot and despised the soft life of the old communities, while his Amazon-like companion

---

[1] A vivid picture of the mid-eighteenth century frontier is given by Schnell, a missionary representing one of the German sects in Pennsylvania, who in 1743–44 made a journey on foot along the entire frontier from Pennsylvania to Georgia. Unarmed, except with a hatchet with which to cut a path through the forest, he ascended the Shenandoah Valley, penetrated the Blue Ridge to the Virginia Piedmont, and passed southeastwardly through North Carolina to the sands of the beach which he followed to Charleston. Six years later, on another journey through the Shenandoah Valley, he found a sleeping place each night in a settler's hut, and swimming James River, came to an Irish settlement near the site of Fincastle. Here the people " lived like savages," having no clothing but deer skins, and no food except deer and bear meat and Johnny-cakes. For thirty miles after leaving this settlement he saw no house.

dauntlessly reared a numerous brood and skillfully wielded ax
and gun, sometimes even against the Indian.

## Urban Life

Europe could show nothing so primitively simple as the life
of these pioneers, but America was by no means all frontier at the
close of the colonial period.  While the towns on the coast still
lacked many of the pleasing features of the maturer culture of
the Old World, they had far more in common with eighteenth-
century Europe than with the United States of our own day.
Boston, for a long time the largest of the provincial towns, may
be taken as a mirror of urban America.  It stood upon a rocky
peninsula, and from the sea appeared to lie in crescent form with
the country rising gently behind it to sunny fields and green
woods.  A long wharf jutting far into deep water afforded dock-
ing facilities for the largest vessels of the time.  Along the north
side of this wharf was a row of warehouses for storing articles of sea-borne commerce.  Creaking windlasses, hand-turned,
slowly swung heavy casks and bales to and from the wooden
sailing vessels, a hundred of which would hardly have shipped the
cargo of one modern ocean freighter.

By the waterside massive two-wheeled carts rumbled to and fro,
drawn by lean horses.  At intervals along the harbor and bay
were a dozen or more yards where sailing craft were built.  From
the foot of the wharf a principal thoroughfare ran straight to the
Town House, a quarter of a mile away.  It was broad and well
paved, but to right and left ran narrow lanes, typical of the place.
Typical also was the lack of regularity in the lay-out of the
streets.

In the closely-built districts near the waterfront were the shops
of retail merchants and craftsmen, whose families occupied the
upper stories of the houses.  Farther off were the homes of the
wealthier people, built of wood or brick,[1] two or three stories
high, but with little beauty of design.  They were set in wide,
deep lots which gave ample space for outbuildings, gardens of
vegetables and flowers, and even orchards.

In this quaint little city of the olden days the ears were never

---

[1] King's Chapel, built 1749–1754, was probably the first stone edifice in Boston.

greeted by the whir of machinery. No tall chimneys belched forth smoke to dull the brilliance of the sunlight and impart an unnatural murkiness to the day. No shriek of whistle disturbed the perpetual calm. Locomotive and factory were deep in the womb of the future. Void were the avenues of street-cars and automobiles, of telephone poles and lamp posts. Water-driven grist-mills (there was one on Mill Creek within the town) and saw-mills of primitive type marked the limit of man's success in harnessing nature's forces.

In the houses of wealthy merchants were fine imported furnishings, but conveniences were unknown. Heating arrangements were most primitive and there was an utter absence of sanitary plumbing. Open fire-places provided the only opportunity for cooking and the only source of artificial warmth. In winter they consumed enormous quantities of wood at an alarming cost, yet did not redeem the houses from almost arctic cold. In such a domicile many of the habits now deemed essential to decency were quite impossible. Each morning a negro servant kindled the fire and assisted the master to dress, but a scanty washing of hands and face was the nearest approach to a bath.

Breakfast done, the substantial citizen was ready for his counting-house. A two-wheeled, one-horse chaise was the favorite conveyance, but in fine weather walking might be preferred, since from house to office could hardly be more than a fifteen-minute jaunt. Mayhap this morning walk led by the quarter where farmers from the countryside and other marketmen exposed for sale the necessities for the evening dinner. In this case a black attendant carried home the well-filled basket. Fish, meats, vegetables, and fruits in great variety were sold in season, at prices which would make a modern housewife gape with astonishment. A twelve-pound codfish for two pence sterling, a turkey for two shillings, "butchers' meat" (beef, mutton, and pork) for as little as one penny per pound, illustrate the values of the times.

Somewhere near the wharf the merchant had his counting-room, a bare, dingy, dimly-lighted office where, along with middle-class clerks who worked for wages, young men of the higher ranks learned to "cast" accounts and mastered the details of "big business." All work moved at the pace set by hands, horses, and sails. Did the merchant wish to send a message, no telephone at his elbow emancipated him from bondage to the ubiquitous servant. Amanuenses with goose-quill pens laboriously wrote letters in triplicate, one for the office records, the others to guard against the mishaps attendant upon transmission to distant correspondents. These letters, if bound to England, would be delivered in eight or ten weeks at a cost of a shilling each, but if the destination were a neighboring province, a week or less might suffice for carriage.

Like the nag that drew his chaise the merchant jogged through the day at a leisurely pace. At one o'clock he met his friends for an hour at the "Exchange," and with that he reckoned the day's work done. The afternoon and evening belonged to family and friends. But amusements were few. Neither music nor drama afforded diversion. Plays were forbidden, and music either in the home or outside was seldom to be heard. A "consort of music" was given at the court room in 1732, but a dozen years passed before there was another. Rare animals were exhibited now and then. Within one six-year period Boston enjoyed opportunities to view a sea lion, a lion, and a polar bear. Sleight-of-hand performers, rope-walkers, and puppet shows came more often, but were probably the delight of the populace rather than of the gentry. Gentlemen preferred to stroll with their ladies on the Common, or to drive to a country inn for dinner. Some of the richer families had country seats where they gave great house parties. The men loved fishing and shooting, too, and paid many a visit to the woods and streams. For more extended outings there were cruises along the coast of Maine.

Dances were the chief social events, and the great annual ball given by the governor was the climax of the season. Both men and women appeared on these occasions in resplendent attire. Silk, satin, velvet, and broadcloth, of many hues, and ornamented with buckles, buttons, and lace of silver and gold, found a fitting setting in parlors walled with elaborately carved or painted panels. Even in the dim light of tallow or bayberry candles such a gathering was a brilliant spectacle.

Puritanical Massachusetts forbade the sale as well as the use of playing cards, but the law was disregarded by the fashionable set, and merchants of high standing sometimes impaired their fortunes by gambling. The use of strong drink was universal and as a class the aristocracy vied in bibulous habits with their poorer neighbors who indulged their convivial propensities in the public houses or taverns. Yet a drunken man in the streets was a rare sight, and excessive drinking was condemned, although usually on economic rather than moral grounds. No organized temperance movement arose until many years after the close of the colonial era, although John Adams must have uttered the thought of many when he remarked that "if the Ancients drank wine as our people drink rum and cider it is no wonder we hear of so many possessed with devils."

The tone of Boston society was probably caught quite accurately by the English visitor who wrote: "Both the ladies and gentlemen dress and appear as gay . . . as courtiers in England on a coronation . . . and the ladies here visit, drink tea, and indulge every little piece of gentility, to the height of the mode; and neglect the affairs of their families with as good a grace as the finest ladies in London."

Not all persons enjoyed the ample leisure of the merchant and his family. The slow processes of production meant long and toilsome hours for those who worked with their hands. Wage-earners in the modern sense were relatively few, and organizations of workers as distinguished from employers quite unknown. In the ship-building industry, for example, the yard owner might be himself a shipwright, and wield hammer and saw elbow to elbow with the little group of journeymen and apprentices who formed his working force. Of these the journeymen worked for wages, but the apprentices, who were young men learning the craft, worked for their "keep" as members of the master's household. The intimacy of master and man made the members of the group sympathetic, and prevented the antagonisms which in later times have divided "capital" and "labor." That the lot of the Boston workmen was happy as compared with that of the same class in England is indicated by the immigration of ship carpenters.

The ordinary clothing of workmen was of coarse imported woolen stuff made up at home. It was better economy for the townsman to buy imported cloth than to divert labor to its manufacture. Ready-made imported clothing could also be had.

On the "Lord's Day" a carefully preserved best suit was brought out, while a second-best was donned for the non-working hours of week-days.

Black slaves and white servants rendered menial service in prosperous homes of the middle class as in the houses of the rich. Ships sometimes brought "transports" (persons condemned to service in the colonies for petty crimes, or sometimes young persons who had been kidnapped) from the British Isles, whose service might be purchased for a term. When a ship arrived with such passengers, heads of families visited the wharf to choose likely boys from among those who ran up and down to display their condition. Poor families who found the support of children beyond their ability often "bound" them out to work for more fortunate persons, who in turn engaged to teach the boys a trade and the girls "housewifery."

There was little extreme poverty in New England as yet, but Boston was beginning to face the problem of pauperism. "Gentle folk" in reduced circumstances were aided privately by relatives or friends, but "rates" were laid for the maintenance of an alms-house where paupers of the "meaner sort" were cared for "in decent manner, suitably to their" station. Never in town or country did one meet a "strolling beggar."

The alliance of church and state which had made early Massachusetts an intolerant theocracy no longer existed. Toleration of Anglicanism had come in the last quarter of the seventeenth century under pressure by the Crown, and general freedom of worship had followed as Puritanism lost its original harsh and uncompromising character.

Love of display, social gayety, and the desire to get on in the world suggest that eighteenth-century Boston was losing the piety of earlier days. If so, she made outward atonement by the strict observance of the Sabbath. This vestige of seventeenth-century Puritanism still survived in full vigor. At sundown on the seventh day of the week every counting-house, shop, and tavern closed and remained shut for the space of twenty-four hours. During that interval neither man nor beast left the town, or walked by the waterside or on the common.

Boston churches and meeting-houses numbered about one for each thousand of the inhabitants. Congregationalism still led in numbers, and two thirds of the houses of worship were of that faith. Anglicanism came next, and several minor denominations were represented by one or two meeting-houses each. The era of handsome edifices had not yet dawned. Plain, rectangular, without tower or steeple, bare inside except for high, square pews, without organs,[1] unheated and unlighted by artificial means — in these temples on Sabbath mornings the congregations, seated strictly according to rank, witnessed the baptism of infants with icy water, and listened to the reading of sermons which were never finished before the sands of the hourglass ran out.

Congregationalism had not yet lost the somber character due to Calvinistic theology; the terrors of hell still seemed more real than God's grace and mercy. The hold which the sermon retained upon the minds of the people indicates, however, not only an interest in introspective religion, but a paucity of rival intellectual stimuli. There was Harvard College, to be sure, and the public library, but neither ministered as yet to a large percentage even of the leisure class, nor, indeed, to needs different from those met by the sermon. "At a town which is about six miles from Boston they have a University," wrote an English visitor, "where their clergy and other young gentlemen are sent to be educated." Founded to insure a trained ministry and magistracy, the college of John Harvard after more than a century was still true to the original purpose, and comparatively few "other young gentlemen," especially those who looked forward to a mercantile career, thought it worth their while to go there.

"They have a library there too," wrote the Englishman just quoted, "but they say they are in want of some modern books." As late as 1723 the Harvard library contained none of the writings of Addison, Bolingbroke, Swift, Steele, Dryden, Pope, or Locke. A generation later it is described as containing "above five thousand volumes" on theology, the classical languages and literatures, history, biology, mathematics, and philosophy.

The subjects studied in the four-year course leading to the degree of bachelor of arts may be inferred from the regulation governing the award: "Every scholar that on proof is found able

---

[1] An organ was bequeathed in 1713 to one of the Congregational churches, but proving unacceptable for use in worship, passed to King's Chapel, where it was used for many years.

to read the originals of the Old and New Testament [and translate] into the Latin tongue and to resolve them logically; withal being of godly life and conversation . . . is fit to be dignified with his first degree."

As for the public library, it had been started in 1673 and until destroyed by fire in 1747 was kept in a room of the Town House. Its great folios certainly did not circulate, but were doubtless consulted more or less at least by the clergy. Books were in demand, as the number of printers and booksellers shows. The Exchange was surrounded by the shops of book dealers, who displayed the works of Latin and Greek writers in profusion but found little need of carrying in stock "contemporary" literature (although Addison's *Spectator* seems to have been widely read), or even the classics of Milton and Shakespeare. Five printers supplied the retailers with reprints of English books and with the works of American writers. The latter were chiefly sermons. Even the efforts at poetry dealt mostly with theological themes. A "best-seller" in its day was Wigglesworth's *Day of Doom*, which has been called the "epic of fire and damnation." In this age of the beginnings of the English novel the colonies produced no fiction.

No newspaper appeared in the seventeenth century. The *Boston News Letter*, first issued in 1704, was the pioneer Anglo-American journal. For fifteen years it had no local rival, but by 1730 the Boston public was supplied with news of "the most remarkable occurrences, Foreign and Domestick," by three weekly papers. They afford even more evidence than the printed books that literary impulses were astir. They offered encouragement to writers of prose and verse, and printed some essays in the vein of the *Spectator* which showed promise.

Boston contained several primary schools "for people of all ranks," and its people were credited with being "as careful of the education of their children" as the English. Since 1647, the Massachusetts laws had required the maintenance of a school in every town of fifty families and a college preparatory school in each of the larger ones. These schools, although not free, were open to all and were the forerunners of the public education in which modern America takes so much pride. Instruction in the primary schools included reading, writing, arithmetic, spelling, and the catechism. In the Boston Latin School the boy who looked forward to a course at Harvard made a beginning in the classical languages, while the farmer's lad who wished to go to college got his start in Greek and Latin under the local minister.

At the close of the colonial period Boston had a population of twenty-five or thirty thousand. New York, older but less populous; Philadelphia, the junior of the New England metropolis by fifty years yet now outranking it in numbers; Charleston in South Carolina, almost contemporary with Philadelphia in origin — these were the other "great towns" of the Atlantic seaboard. Salem in Massachusetts, Newport in Rhode Island, Baltimore in Maryland, and Norfolk in Virginia, while much smaller, were also important places.

While in culture and in material civilization all of the towns were much alike, there were some noteworthy differences. New York, like Boston, had many narrow, crooked streets, while Philadelphia and Charleston were laid out with streets crossing at right angles. Philadelphia streets were well lighted as well as paved, and had sidewalks of flat stones. Charleston was unpaved, except for brick footways about six feet wide, separated from the drive by a line of posts. Its streets were foul and ill-smelling, and neglect of sewage made it unsanitary. It was subject to annual epidemics of smallpox, yet as the favorite residence of the South Carolina planters it was noted for its gay and lively society.

Many New York houses were built in the style introduced by the Dutch colonists, with gables on the street. Philadelphia and Charleston were cities of brick. Three-story structures of uniform design gave the former a monotonous appearance that drew unflattering comment from visitors. In Charleston only the better houses had glass in the windows. The Anglican churches of these two cities were stately edifices, in pleasing contrast with the homely meeting-houses of Boston. All had bells, and Christ Church, Philadelphia, had a set of chimes.

The Puritan strictness, which so carefully guarded Sabbath observance and banned dramatic performances, was not in evidence south of New England. The Philadelphia Quakers were quite as strict as the Puritans, but the community did not take its tone from them. Plays were a constant diversion of the upper class in the middle and southern colonies for twenty years before the Revolution. The first theater was built in Williamsburg, Virginia, in 1716, and New York had a "play house" by 1733. Taverns, court rooms, and warehouses were utilized before the erection of special buildings. The earliest theater buildings made little advance over these makeshift accommodations, but despite all handicaps patronage was sufficient after 1750 to support a small number of professional actors.

Musical instruments, such as spinnet, pianoforte, and violin, were quite common in the South, and Charleston had a St. Cecilia Society. Cards, dancing, gay parties, and hunting were in vogue everywhere, while horse-racing (not unknown in New England) and cock-fighting were followed with special devotion in Virginia and the Carolinas.

The proportion of blacks among servants increased steadily to the southward, until in the Carolinas practically no others were to be found. The labor group composed of master, journeymen, and apprentices, conspicuous in all of the northern towns, receded into the background or disappeared in the South, where slave labor quite overshadowed all other forms.

In New York and Philadelphia the schooling of children instead of being provided for by the public was regarded as the duty of the religious bodies. Schools were of the parochial or private type, and probably reached a smaller percentage of the boys and girls than the schools of Boston. In New York the Anglican Church, through the Society for the Propagation of the Gospel in Foreign Parts, established a number of elementary schools. In Philadelphia the Friends were especially active. Each of these towns had its college. King's, the forerunner of Columbia University, was founded by the Anglicans in 1754, while, in contrast, the Academy out of which grew the University of Pennsylvania (1755) was promoted by citizens of Philadelphia without regard to sect. Several of the smaller towns had institutions of higher education, the chief of which were William and Mary College, at Williamsburg (opened in 1696 and ranking next in age to Harvard), Yale at New Haven (1701), and the College of New Jersey at Princeton (1746). Charleston had neither college nor public schools. Wealthy families employed tutors, and others sent their children to "pay schools," but many young people grew up untouched by any instruction other than that which parents could give.

None of the colleges provided instruction in professional branches except theology, until the University of Pennsylvania opened a school of medicine in 1765. The boy who determined to become a lawyer or physician served a kind of apprenticeship, "reading law" in the office of an established practitioner until he could pass a mild examination for admission to the bar, or attending a physician and observing his methods until he absorbed such knowledge as his mentor possessed. A few fortunate young men attended English schools and universities, or studied law at the Inns of Court. Most of these came from the middle and southern colonies, and the superiority of the training obtained in the British Isles was a factor in the intellectual leadership of the statesmen of these provinces during the Revolution.

Free libraries supported by public funds were practically unknown. Only a few men of means accumulated private collections of as many as a thousand volumes. Philadelphia, Charleston, and some of the smaller places, among them Salem, organized library associations, the members of which raised funds by subscription for the purchase of books to be used on the circulating plan. Most famous of these was the Library Association of Philadelphia; founded (1731) as the result of Benjamin Franklin's efforts, it is still in existence.

By the end of the first quarter of the eighteenth century enterprising publishers in all of the important centers had followed the lead of Boston in establishing newspapers. For the most part they had only a local circulation, but they gained steadily in importance as disseminators of information and quickeners of thought.

In the intellectual and material equipment of provincial America nothing is more conspicuous to the modern student than the lack of knowledge of science and its applications. In this respect, however, the colonies were not far behind the rest of the world, for geology, botany, zoölogy, chemistry, anatomy, and physiology as we conceive them today were still blank pages in the book of human knowledge. All that was known on these subjects was briefly summed up under the term "natural philosophy." At the close of the colonial era only a generation had passed since Newton, the discoverer of the law of gravitation, had gone to his grave (1727).   Franklin was in the midst of the experiments which brought him international fame and honorary degrees from Yale and Harvard for "improvements in the electric branch of natural philosophy."   Not until the year of American Independence did the discovery of oxygen lay the foundation of chemistry, and another dozen years passed before Jenner announced the theory of vaccination.

Astrology, alchemy, and kindred superstitions still held sway over the minds of intelligent men, and medicine was on a par with these pseudo-sciences.   The medical books in common use dated from the previous century, and most of the remedies had less than no efficacy in the complaints for which they were given. There was much brewing of concoctions of herbs and barks, to which were sometimes added worms, wood lice, or vipers, making a broth quite worthy of Macbeth's witches.   Melancholia was thought to be due to worms in the brain, and fever was supposed to yield to the application of salt herrings on the soles of the feet.

None the less medicine was honored as one of the learned professions, and physicians deserved respect for their practical skill in the simpler forms of surgery and in the use of laxatives and purgatives.   Too often, however, their treatment was sadly overdone, as the case of Washington shows, even at the end of the century.   For a severe cold the doctors bled him profusely, scarified him with blisters and poultices, and dosed him with calomel and tartar emetic.   "Every medical assistance was offered," wrote a friend.   In this medical aid the modern practitioner sees the chief cause of Washington's untimely demise, for even his sound and vigorous constitution could not withstand such treatment.

### COUNTRY LIFE

The great majority of Americans cultivated the soil for a livelihood under conditions perhaps midway between those of the frontier and English rural life.   In general, land was so abundant and cheap that the cultivator found it easy to obtain possession of all that he could till, without the necessity of sharing the fruits of his labor with a landlord.   His toil was hard and incessant and his pleasures and comforts few; yet as compared with the peasant-tenant class of Europe from which he sprang he enjoyed independence and a rude plenty.

The stubborn soil of New England, even when with infinite toil it had been cleared of stones and timber, responded reluctantly to the efforts of the husbandman. The colonist who came to plant was driven to the sea. Many a farmer was also a sailor, at least in his youth, and on occasion made a hand on a fishing vessel. The farm belt hugged the coast, and in Massachusetts still extended hardly more than thirty or forty miles inland. The Connecticut Valley, the only exception, maintained its contact with the sea by way of the river rather than by overland connections with Boston Bay.

Although isolated farmsteads were not uncommon, the dwellings of the country people were frequently clustered in villages which the arable land surrounded. Such a community was the "town." The cultivator was a freeholder. His small, one-story house of logs or rough-hewn boards was unpainted, and unheated except by the fireplace in the room which served as kitchen, dining- and living-room, and in cold weather as bedroom. Strings of dried apples, pumpkin, and peppers hung in festoons from the ceilings. A large slab fitted with long pegs for legs did service as a table. Wooden trenchers, which were often merely square blocks hollowed out by hand, held food and served as plates from which two or more persons ate, sometimes with forks or wooden spoons, often with fingers. Homespun garments were the rule, made from wool grown by the farmer, spun and woven and made up into suits and skirts by the women of the household.

Toilsome as was the farmer's life, food at least was abundant. Soil, forest, and stream amply supplied the larder and yielded some surplus for the market. Fruits and vegetables, butter, cheese, barreled beef and pork, and wooden articles such as bowls, staves, ox-bows and ax-helves, whittled out by firelight in the winter evenings, were carried to town by ox-cart or sled, and brought a little ready money in the form of paper currency.

Rural life was even more monotonous than that of the town. Few homes contained any books except the Bible, psalm-book, and almanac. The last was magazine, cyclopædia, and speller, all in one.  It guided the farmer in sowing and reaping and in treating disease in man and beast; contained the record of expenses, crops, and the weather; and even vied with the Bible as the record of births and deaths.

The meeting-house was the center of intellectual and emotional stimulus and of solemn sociability.  The village tavern and schoolhouse were also important places for group gatherings.  At the tavern were posted notices of elections, sales, and other matters of public interest, and there men gathered to make trades, swap yarns, and discuss politics.

At meeting-house, schoolhouse, or tavern the men of each community assembled from time to time in town meeting, to pass by-laws and choose selectmen, constables, and other petty officers. Once a year each town meeting chose the deputies to the General Court.  In town meeting as elsewhere social rank counted. The voice of the gentleman was heard rather than that of clerk, mechanic, or farmer, and deputies were much more likely to be selected from the "best families" of each locality than from the plain people.

Immigration was infusing foreign blood into the Puritan stock, although the country felt this influence less than the towns.  Such names as Faneuil, Bowdoin, and Magee betray non-English origins.  The total mass of foreigners in New England was not great, but it showed quite diverse elements, including French, German, Dutch, Scotch, and Irish.  So many of the newcomers intermarried with Puritan families and were assimilated that the population retained its homogeneity.  It was becoming, however, a new "Yankee" race — a "new Nordic amalgam on an English Puritan base," differing from the English in character, dialect, and ideals.

The era of improved roads had not yet dawned even in Europe in 1760.  In America roads existed, of a kind, along the coast, and it was possible to go from Boston to New York in four days, with three days added if the journey was continued to Philadelphia.  For the most part, the streams were unbridged and crossing was possible only by ford, ferry, or canoe.  No hill was leveled, no valley filled, in road construction, and the surfaces were innocent of any harder finish than the native soil.  The best day's journey seldom exceeded forty miles, and twenty-five miles was a good average. Under favorable conditions travel by water was less arduous and as rapid, but with light winds two weeks might be consumed in such a voyage as that from New York to Albany.

The traveler journeying southward from New England found the character of country life gradually changing. In southeastern Pennsylvania he encountered the Germans on the most productive lands to be found anywhere in the colonies. Huge barns sheltered their stock and stored their grain, while smaller, simpler structures sufficed for the housing of the family. Negro servants were rare here, for the Germans despised the blacks and would not work beside them. Wife and daughters shared with husband and sons the labor of the fields, raising wheat for export and contenting themselves with Indian corn for their own sustenance. Dwelling in communities of their own kind and speaking a foreign tongue, the "Pennsylvania Dutch" formed an element which alarmed the English, as they seemed to be unassimilable.

Crossing the Potomac the traveler entered still another realm, where the roads became even more wretched, the inns more intolerable, and the population more diffuse. When Thomas Jefferson went to Williamsburg in 1760, at the age of seventeen, to enter William and Mary College, he had never seen a dozen houses grouped together. Williamsburg, the provincial capital, had about two hundred dwellings, and while Norfolk, the center of trade with the West Indies, was larger, Virginia — in fact, the South in general — was distinctly a region of country life. In most counties the courthouse and jail, although perhaps destined in later times to become the nucleus of a village, stood alone, unless flanked by a tavern or store.

In the absence of towns the country store, where almost everything could be bought, was becoming an important institution. Planters sometimes "kept store" in addition to their other activities, or set up their sons as storekeepers, as did Patrick Henry's father. But the plantation was the central feature of southern life. The house of the wealthy planter was of wood or brick, and, like the Washington home at Mt. Vernon, often stood upon elevated ground commanding a view of a river. The kitchen stood apart from the house, freeing it from odors and heat. Well-kept grounds surrounded the mansion, ornamented with flowers and trees. In the rear was the vegetable garden, and still farther removed were tobacco-barns, granaries, stables, the dairy and poultry houses, and the quarters for the negro slaves. These last consisted of cabins of logs or rough planks, and each was furnished with a bed, chairs, and a few cooking utensils.

The typical plantation consisted of four or five thousand acres, part of which was cultivated while part was woodland. The nearest neighbors were usually two or three miles distant. Many planters had much more land, and the population of their estates, mostly black, might run into the hundreds. A great planter, like a mediæval lord, sought to make his establishment as nearly independent as possible, and trained his slaves as carpenters, coopers, blacksmiths, tanners, shoemakers, spinners, and weavers, as well as house servants and field hands. Lumber, fuel, meat, grain, fruit, vegetables, wool, cotton, flax, rough furniture, shoes, flour, brandy, cloth, casks, all these were often produced on the estate. Articles for the "great house" and the personal use of its white occupants were generally brought from England, and the extravagance of the average planter (or his family) kept him in a chronic state of debt.

The planter who took his business seriously and was his own manager could not indulge in indolence. Yet a love of leisure was characteristic. There was much exchanging of hospitality, and entertainment was often on the grand scale. Idle hours were turned to good advantage by men of intellectual tastes. Some of the best private libraries in America were gathered in the homes of Virginia gentlemen. William Byrd II, who had been educated in England, possessed at his estate of "West-over," near Richmond, nearly three thousand volumes. He was a writer as well as a reader, and his *History of the Dividing Line* (the story of the survey of the boundary between Virginia and North Carolina) makes an effort, with some success, at literary grace.

The planter's children were taught by tutors who were in-mates of the house, or by the parish clergyman, or they attended a "neighborhood school" maintained by subscription. If the young men went to college, they attended William and Mary like Jefferson, or Princeton, like Madison; or sometimes went

abroad, like Byrd. A substantial part of the education of many
Virginians who attained prominence — Washington, Jefferson,
Madison, and others — was gained through careful reading in
their own homes.

The rural population was much given to games and sports.
Fox-hunting and horse-racing were favorite exercises of the
aristocrats, and public gatherings often gave occasion for boxing
and wrestling matches and other contests of skill and strength.
Elections and court sittings brought together at the Court House
men from all parts of the county to indulge in such sports, to
listen to speeches by prominent men, and to drink the liquor
which candidates for the assembly always provided in the
greatest abundance at such times.

## Economic Development

The eighteenth century was a time of rapid industrial development. New England, where the fisheries were from the beginning one of the chief occupations, enjoyed a great expansion
of this pursuit. Under the stimulus of an increasing market in
Europe the whale fisheries also developed from an intermittent
longshore business into a well-conducted enterprise which sent
Yankee vessels into every corner of the Atlantic. Ship-building
was on the increase. The forests supplied an abundance of
material, and Yankee shipwrights became so skillful that their
product was readily salable in Europe and the other colonies.
Ship-building was the chief New England manufacture in this
epoch. Rum, distilled from West Indian molasses, was the other
important manufacturing enterprise of this section.

Boston, Salem, and Newport were the centers of New England's
commerce. Hundreds of native-built ships cleared yearly from
these ports laden with lumber, the products of the fisheries, or
rum. The Catholic countries of southern Europe were the chief
buyers of fish, the poorer grades going to the West Indies to feed
slaves. Lumber was sold in the same markets, while most of
the rum was exchanged on the Guinea coast for gold, or negroes
to supply the slave market of the Spanish colonies. From the
West Indies came in this round of trade goods of European manufacture, sugar and molasses, and cash in the form of Spanish

silver coins.  Little of the export trade was with the mother country.  New England paid for English manufactures with the coin derived from the West Indian trade.

The middle colonies grew even faster than New England. By 1750 Pennsylvania, although founded so much later, took rank with Massachusetts and Virginia as one of the three most populous colonies.  The merchants of Philadelphia supplied much of the capital for the fur-trading ventures of the Scotch-Irish and bought for export the surplus produce of the German farmers.  From New York and Philadelphia the furs, grain, and flour of the middle colonies, like the fish and lumber of New England, went to the markets of southern Europe, the West Indies, and the Carolinas.  Manufacturing here took the form of flour-milling.  Among the non-English inhabitants were many mechanics who set up small manufacturing plants to supply their neighborhoods with a variety of articles, such as stoves and other iron products, glass, paper, and cloth.  Such small-scale manufactures were carried further in the middle colonies than anywhere else in North America.

In the South, North Carolina soon adopted the plantation of the Virginia type, with slave labor.  Tobacco was the chief crop, while in South Carolina indigo and rice, grown in the swamp lands along the coast, were the important staples.  Negro slavery was especially necessary on the plantations in the marsh region, which was unwholesome for whites.  The planters tended to congregate in Charleston, leaving their estates to be managed by overseers, and the result was a harsher type of slavery than that in Virginia, because it lacked the sympathy which sprang from frequent contact between owner and slave.  The growth of chattel slavery was stimulated by the slave traders.  In the Treaty of Utrecht (see page 106) England exacted from Spain the privilege of supplying her colonies with slaves (the Asiento contract).  To exploit this concession the British Royal African Company was organized, but independent traders, some of them New Englanders, claimed a share of the profits, and not content with the Spanish markets, developed that of the English colonies to the utmost.  By the middle of the century negroes composed nearly half of the inhabitants of Virginia, while in South Carolina they were far more numerous than the whites.

In contrast with the commerce of the northern and middle colonies, the chief trade of the southern provinces was with England. British or Yankee ships carried the plantation products to London, where some merchant acted as agent for the planter, selling his crop and purchasing the goods desired in return.

The people of the back settlements at first lived as self-sufficing family units, existing by hunting and the most primitive agriculture. Gradually the inland counties became farming communities, producing grain and stock, even in the Piedmont portions of the Carolinas and Virginia. A few men of wealth penetrated to the back settlements and took large tracts of land which they tried to cultivate with slave labor, but most of the settlers were poor men who disliked slavery and cultivated their small farms with their own hands. It was not until after the colonial period that the plantation reached the Piedmont and displaced the small-farm economy (see page 348). By the end of the colonial era the back settlements were producing an agricultural surplus which found a market in the tidewater for consumption or export. This productivity relieved Charleston and tidewater South Carolina, for example, of dependence upon Pennsylvania for foodstuffs, and created a demand for roads and other improved means of transportation to bring the output of the interior farms to the coast.

## RELATIONS OF FRONTIER AND COAST

The wealth and culture of provincial America were to be found in the coastal regions and were little in evidence among the fur-traders and farmers who were pushing westward. By the time the frontier had reached the mountains there was a sharp contrast between the society of the coast lands and that of the back country.

The settlement of the new regions was welcomed by the people of the coast as a protection against the Indians, but in every colony those in possession of political control took care to prevent it from passing out of their hands. Even when the population of the new districts exceeded that of the old, the system of government was such as to keep the interior communities in subordination to the minority on the seaboard.

In New England, where there was the nearest approach to
equality, few of the dwellers inland were eligible for seats in the
upper houses because of the high property qualifications.    In
the southern colonies the planters dared not share power with the
non-slaveholders of the Piedmont.    Everywhere the property-
owning class feared that popular government would lead to
taxation of those who possessed property for the benefit of the
poorer class.    In Pennsylvania the immigration of foreigners
aroused the apprehensions even of Franklin.    The ease with
which they acquired land made the ordinary property qualifications for voting and  officeholding an ineffectual barrier.[1]
New communities were therefore tardily organized as counties,
and then only allowed from one to four representatives each,
while the old counties where dwelt the "Quaker aristocracy"
enjoyed eight each — more than either their relative wealth
or numbers warranted.

Virginia allowed each of the new counties, like the old ones,
two representatives in the lower house, but made them so large
that their delegates represented many more inhabitants than
did those from the tidewater counties.    In South Carolina the
Piedmont had no separate representation before 1773.

The men of the back country did not meekly accept their
position of inferiority.    Many of them, including the Scotch-
Irish Presbyterians and some of the German sects, held the
Calvinistic theology with its democratic implications.    Under
the primitive conditions of the frontier these doctrines and the
actual equality of men inevitably begot the ideal of political
equality.    The backwoodsmen forgot those artificial distinctions
which had no meaning in the realities of their lives, and used
arguments which anticipated those of the Revolution, in their
demand for equal rights.

Although allowed so slight a share in the government of their
provinces, the frontiersmen actually regulated the affairs of their
everyday lives, and their actual liberty and self-reliance made
them all the more impatient with the restraints put upon them
by the governing class.    Before the Revolution a sharp contest

---

[1] At the close of the colonial era seven colonies imposed a freehold qualification upon the
franchise ; the other six accepted personal property as an alternative qualification.    For
officeholding the requirements were higher than for voting.

had begun between the people of the coast and those of the interior in most colonies. The unenfranchised workmen of the towns were potential allies of the men of the back districts in this contest, and in this division is to be found one of the bases of the political parties of later times.

## SELECT BIBLIOGRAPHY FOR CHAPTER IV

**The Westward Movement; The Frontier.** Ford, *Scotch-Irish in America*, Hanna, *The Scotch-Irish*, and Faust, *German Element in the United States*, are among the most important books dealing with the race elements which contributed most largely to the early pioneer stock. For the general significance of immigration see Schlesinger, "The Influence of Immigration on American History," in *New Viewpoints in American History*. Turner, *The Frontier in American History*, develops in a series of essays the significance of the westward movement. Turner is the pioneer scholar of the modern school to exploit this theme.

**Urban Life; Country Life.** Andrews, *Colonial Folkways*. Alice M. Earle has written several books on manners and customs in the colonial period. Among them are: *Child Life in Colonial Days; Colonial Dames and Goodwives; Colonial Days in Old New York; Customs and Fashions in Old New England; Home Life in Colonial Days; Stage Coach and Tavern Days.*

**Economic Development.** Weeden, *Economic and Social History of New England*; Andrews, "Colonial Commerce," in *American Historical Review;* Bell, "West India Trade," *ibid.*

**Relations of Frontier and Coast.** Turner, "The Old West," in *The Frontier in American History;* Hockett, *Western Influences on Political Parties to 1825*, 9–22.

# CHAPTER V

## ENGLAND AND THE COLONIES

While America was growing into vigorous adolescence, England was attempting to devise a policy for the suitable control of her lusty offspring. When the period of religious controversy passed, the Puritan party in Parliament was eclipsed by another group whose thoughts turned on economic interests. With this class the extension of trade had always been a chief consideration in colonization. At first they had operated, as in the case of Virginia, through private companies to which the King granted concessions. From the Restoration on the " mercantilists " gained more and more influence in the government, and in the eighteenth century practically became the government. Their rise is closely associated with the growth of the power of Parliament at the King's expense, and as their influence increased, British colonial policy more and more embodied their views.

British mercantilism, like that of the other states of western Europe in the same era, aimed at national self-sufficiency. Economic strength had a political purpose, the safety of the nation in its rivalries with other powers, especially when those rivalries led to wars. The intent was not merely to advance the prosperity of the commercial class, but to promote the welfare of the empire as a whole.

In the very year of the Restoration (1660) Parliament passed a navigation law which excluded all foreign vessels from colonial ports. It also required the colonists to send certain enumerated products only to England or another English colony. The main purpose of this provision was to bring the products of the West Indies to the mother country, but as tobacco was included in the list of enumerated goods Virginia and her neighbors were also affected. In 1663 a second act added the requirement that all articles bound for the colonies from European countries must first be brought to England and there reshipped for the colonial ports.

Charles II, working in harmony with the mercantilists, after some tentative plans, appointed a Committee of the Privy Council for Trade and Plantations (1675) to administer these laws and give general supervision to colonial matters. The purpose of the laws was to build up English shipping. A prosperous merchant marine was regarded as the foundation for the powerful navy which was essential for the protection of the colonies as well as England. Colonial industry was also to be made to supplement English industry, in order that it might help to free the Islands from dependence upon foreign countries.

By destroying Dutch competition these acts gave New England the lion's share of the carrying trade of the empire and greatly benefited her ship-building industry. The restrictions in the acts may have been meddlesome but they were not deliberately unjust, and valuable privileges were granted as offsets. Thus while tobacco could be shipped only to England, it enjoyed a monopoly of that market, for its importation from any other source than the English provinces was forbidden.

None the less the Crown had difficulty in enforcing the acts, for the colonists chafed under the restrictions and evaded them in all possible ways. Enumerated articles were shipped first to another colony and thence to Europe. New England shipmasters imported goods directly from European countries and distributed them throughout the colonies. The cost of such commodities was reduced somewhat, perhaps twenty per cent, below the prices quoted by British merchants.

The colonial governors were required to enforce the acts of 1660 and 1663, but they performed this duty so laxly that special collectors of customs had to be appointed with salaries paid by the English government. Their performance of duty sometimes led to violent resistance — to an insurrection in North Carolina and to the murder of a collector in Maryland. In Massachusetts the stand was taken that acts of Parliament were not in force unless reënacted by the colonial assembly. The collector for New England, Edward Randolph, found that colonial juries would not convict persons charged with violations of these laws; nine cases prosecuted by him resulted in eight acquittals. In the ninth the shipmaster was fined, the money going into the colonial treasury while the costs were assessed against the collector.  Taught by experience that Americans were likely to be guided by their interests rather than by their sense of loyalty, Randolph urged the government to set up admiralty courts to try such cases.  These courts would be free from local influence, because they dispensed with juries and left the decision on points both of fact and law to judges appointed by the Crown.

The self-willed conduct of Massachusetts in other matters irritated the King.  She had long been a thorn in the side of the Stuart rulers.  During the Civil War and ensuing disorders in England she had acted very much as if she were an independent state.  Soon after the Restoration, therefore, the King demanded that her people take an oath of allegiance; that the courts render justice in his name; that freedom of worship be granted to members of the Church of England; and that a freehold qualification for voting be substituted for the religious test.  When royal commissioners visited New England to see how these commands were obeyed, they found that only one — the issue of writs in the King's name — had really been complied with, and they departed in high dudgeon, declaring: "The king did not grant away his Sovereigntie over you when he made you a corporation.  When His Majestie gave you power to make wholesome laws and to administer Justice by them, he parted not with his right of judging whether those laws were wholesome, or whether justice was administered accordingly or no."

The obstinacy of Massachusetts at last led the Lords of Trade to advise the King that its government was conducted without the slightest regard for the authority or revenue of the Crown.  The outcome was a court process and judgment annulling the charter, in 1684.

By this time it was apparent that the charters of the corporate and proprietary colonies interfered with the plans of the government.  Down to 1679 Virginia was the only royal colony, but the design was now formed of changing all of the chartered colonies to the royal type and uniting them to simplify administration of the trade acts and other laws.  Following the Massachusetts case the Lords of Trade determined to proceed against the charters of Connecticut and Rhode Island and the patents for the Jerseys and Delaware, and to unite all of them with New

York and Massachusetts under one governor. Only the one charter was actually annulled, but Sir Edmund Andros was sent in 1686 as governor-general of the "Dominion of New England," with authority also over New York and the Jerseys, where he was represented by deputy governors.

James II probably carried the changes farther than the Lords of Trade intended. He ordered Andros to discontinue the representative assemblies. This done, Andros ruled New England with the aid of a council appointed by the King, although its members came from the colonies composing the Dominion. Landowners were required to secure new deeds, for which fees were exacted, and to pay an annual quitrent in recognition of the King as grantor of land. In spite of the abolition of the assemblies the towns were required to collect taxes, and when some of them refused, town meetings were forbidden save for the purpose of electing officers. The New Englanders, like the New Yorkers of the same period, protested vigorously against taxation without representation, again foreshadowing the stand taken eighty years later.

## THE REVOLUTION OF 1688

James, less cautious than his brother, asserted the royal prerogative in accord with his grandfather's theory of divine right, and revived the conflict which had made the seventeenth century a long struggle for supremacy between King and Parliament. He disregarded the charter rights of English municipal corporations as lightly as he did those of the corporate colonies, and, being himself a Catholic, he suspended the laws which excluded Catholics and dissenters from office. By this conduct he offended both the Anglicans who had supported divine right and the anti-Anglicans who held that the King was subject to the law.

The "bloodless revolution" drove James to seek refuge at the friendly court of Louis XIV of France. Parliament signalized its victory by giving the vacated throne to Mary, the Protestant daughter of the deposed monarch, and her husband, William of Orange, head of the Dutch state, and prescribing the terms on which the throne should be held thereafter.[1]

[1] By the Bill of Rights (1689) and the Act of Settlement (1701). The latter insured the Protestant succession by barring the Catholic descendants of James II.

To justify the turning of a hereditary ruler out of doors and choosing his successors, the parliamentary party appealed to the compact theory — that rulers derive their powers, not from divine right, but from the people, through an agreement to set up government for the protection of their lives, liberty, and property. The philosopher John Locke played the rôle of chief apologist. In language which found an echo in the Declaration of Independence in 1776, he wrote : "Whensoever the legislative shall . . . endeavor to grasp . . . an absolute power over the lives, liberties, and estates of the people, by this breach of trust they forfeit the power the people had put into their hands for [the preservation of their rights] and it devolves to the people, who have the right to resume their original liberty, and by the establishment of a new legislative (such as they shall think fit), provide for their own safety and security, which is the end for which they are in society. What I have said here concerning the legislative in general holds true also concerning the supreme executor [king], who having a double trust [as part of the legislature as well as executive] acts against both [trusts] when he goes about to set up his own arbitrary will as the law of the society."

With the overthrow of James II came the downfall of Andros and the end of the Dominion of New England. The denial of the right of representation was contrary to the spirit of the English revolution, and Connecticut and Rhode Island were allowed to resume their governments. The people of Massachusetts had high hopes of recovering their lost charter. A new charter was granted in 1691, but it did not restore all of the former privileges, for the governor was to be appointed by the Crown. The council, however, was to be chosen by the assembly subject to confirmation by the governor, and Plymouth and Maine were incorporated with Massachusetts. It was at this time that New York won the privilege of a representative assembly, but in that province this liberty rested not on a charter but upon the less secure basis of royal instructions. The Jerseys were restored to their proprietors, but they voluntarily surrendered their patent in 1702, and the two colonies were united as one royal province.

Although liberal principles underlay the revolution, it did not alter the direction which colonial policy had taken. The influence of the mercantile class, now acting with the landed aristocracy, become greater than ever. A new motive for desiring effective control over American resources in men and money arose with the beginning of the wars with France, the first of which broke out soon after the ejection of James II. They therefore continued to aim at the thorough administration of the navigation system, at the reduction of the colonies to the royal type, and at intercolonial union.

A new navigation act was passed in 1696, to correct defects in the earlier ones, and admiralty courts were established as advocated by Randolph. In the same year the Committee of the Privy Council for Trade and Plantations was superseded by the Board of Commissioners for Trade and Plantations (The "Board of Trade"). The membership of the new body was not confined to the ministry, but included other men who were experts in the work to be done. Its functions included the general supervision of colonial affairs.

## RISE OF PARLIAMENTARY GOVERNMENT

Logically, the Revolution of 1688 meant the supremacy of Parliament over King, but the subordination of the King actually came about so slowly as almost to escape observation at the time. The Frenchman Montesquieu, who wrote a great book (*L'Esprit des Lois*, 1748) praising the British government because it separated the legislative, executive, and judicial branches, misinterpreted the facts, for as the royal influence declined executive powers passed to ministers who were responsible to Parliament and a part of it. The outcome of this evolution was the cabinet system of our own times; it was already partially developed at the outbreak of the American Revolution.

One of the high points in the history of the passing of the King's power was the abandonment of the royal veto of acts of Parliament. It was used for the last time in 1707. In 1714 the accession of George I of the House of Hanover consigned the kingship almost to insignificance. George was a German prince, already advanced in years, only slightly acquainted with the English language, and not inclined to vex himself with British problems. He preferred to leave them to the ministers, and when the second George came to the throne in 1727 their position was already too firm to be shaken.

The ministry framed policies, but if these were not supported by the necessary legislation, its functions were at an end.  A new ministry possessing the confidence of the majority in the legislature, especially in the House of Commons, must then be formed, or an election held to determine whether the voters would uphold the ministry by returning a majority of members in sympathy with their program.

This development made the legislature the supreme power in the government.  The older writers on the English law had held that the power of Parliament was limited by "common right and reason," and implied that the courts might declare acts void if they violated fundamental principles of right.  It was Blackstone, in his *Commentaries on the Laws of England* (1765), who first expounded the doctrine of parliamentary supremacy.  "I know of no power," he wrote, "which can control the Parliament."

In the nineteenth century parliamentary government became responsible to the masses of the people, but in the eighteenth it rested on a basis which was far from popular.  The members of the upper house — the Lords Temporal and Spiritual — held their places as they still do by right of birth or position in the Church.  In the House of Commons members, although elected, were chosen under a very restricted franchise.  In the incorporated towns only those residents voted who belonged to the small group which held the corporate privileges.[1]  In the rural districts the usual test was the possession of land with a rental value of forty shillings or more per annum.

The apportionment of seats in Parliament had not been revised for something like two centuries, and some of the towns or "boroughs" represented had declined until they were almost or entirely without inhabitants.  Other towns had grown up, and some of them had become populous, yet members still sat in the House for the ancient boroughs while the new towns were without representation except as parts of the shire in which they were situated.

The owners of great estates were very influential in controlling the votes of the small landowners.  Perhaps, as a rule, the latter

[1] *Cf.* the freemen of the Massachusetts Bay Company.

voted as a matter of course for the candidate preferred by the local aristocrat. In the case of the "rotten boroughs," as they were called, the choice of members became practically a power of appointment by the owner of the land where the borough had stood. When it is added that corruption was rife, and that the buying and selling of votes and of seats in the House was a common practice, one can understand the charge (made in 1780) that the choice of a majority of the members was controlled by about one hundred and fifty men.

Instead of being representative of the nation Parliament was the representative of the merchants and landlords. The merchants were especially influential in the towns, and as wealth increased with the growth of commerce they came more and more closely into alliance with the landed aristocracy, partly through intermarriage, and partly through the purchase of estates for their own families.

For some decades after the Revolution of 1688 the Tory party sympathized with the exiled Stuarts while the Whigs supported the Act of Settlement. The son and grandson of James II, known as the Old Pretender and the Young Pretender, made some efforts to recover the throne, but the last of these, aided by the Scotch, was frustrated by the Battle of Cullodon, in 1745. The Tory party declined with the hopes of the Pretenders, and the distinction between the parties almost disappeared. Instead of two great opposing organizations a number of factions arose, each under the lead of a prominent politician.

To make up a majority in the Commons, a combination of two or more of these factions had to be arranged, and it was the game of the politicians to form these combinations. Each ministry, of course, must likewise be made up of representatives of the factions acting for the moment in alliance. These shifting alliances sought ends among which the spoils of office were not the least.

When George III came to the throne in 1760, he determined to regain the ground lost by his predecessors. Born and bred in England, he "gloried in the name of Briton." He indulged in no dreams of absolutism such as that of the monarchs of France and Prussia, but relied upon his control of patronage. By skillful distribution of offices he was able to gain control over the choice of a good many members of Parliament and thus built up a faction of his own known as the "King's Friends." These were able at times to defeat the ministry, and even, by coalition with other factions, to form a majority. Control of the Commons meant control of the ministry, in effect the personal rule of the King.

In all this George III carefully observed the forms of parliamentary government and ministerial responsibility; he simply played the game of the politicians and beat them at it. His success held some menace for parliamentary government by the aristocracy, for the King's Friends became a kind of revived Tory party with a royal "boss." Through his mastery of Parliament and the ministry George III became chiefly responsible for some of the measures which brought on the American Revolution. He was a well-meaning man of good character and high sense of honor, but he lacked statesmanship and was unusually headstrong. His influence reached its height in the ministry of Lord North (1770–1782). The failure to crush the American revolt discredited his leadership, and the current set again in the direction of parliamentary rule, but with a tendency towards liberalism which brought democracy at length through great reform acts in 1832, 1867, and 1884.

## British Mercantilism in the Eighteenth Century

The dominance of the mercantile and landed classes is a fundamental fact in explaining the relations between Britain and the colonies in the eighteenth century. They doubtless believed sincerely in the wisdom of their system of regulation, but there were occasions, then as now, where men yielded to the temptation to seek private gain at the general expense. Control over colonial industry was gradually extended. Some of the new regulations were in line with the provisions of the navigation acts. Such was the law of 1733 called the "Molasses Act." To force the continental colonies to buy their sugar and molasses from the British West Indies, and thus to build up the plantations there, the act laid prohibitory duties upon these articles when brought from the foreign sugar islands. This legislation is a good illustration of the union of policy and private interest; while in harmony with the idea of fostering colonial industries which supplemented those of Britain, it was enacted at the behest of a lobby of Englishmen who owned plantations in Barbadoes and Jamaica — and it is said that the agitation for the law originated with a resident of Boston who had a similar interest in the islands.

In keeping with the earlier policy also was the addition of naval stores, furs, and rice to the list of enumerated articles. Finding that the rice growers suffered from this restriction, a concession was made permitting that commodity to be sent directly to the countries of southern Europe, although it was still to go to the north of Europe by way of England.

A new departure was the regulation of manufactures. The prosperity of the rising factories of England must not be endangered by colonial competition. So thought the rulers. By successive enactments Americans were forbidden to make woolen cloth and hats for sale outside of the colony where made, and manufactures of iron were restricted to the making of bar- and pig-iron. Such laws were hardly needed, since there was as yet little incentive in the colonies to manufacture. Recognizing this, the great English economist, Adam Smith, whose book on *The Wealth of Nations* (1776) started a reaction against the whole theory of mercantilism and is regarded as the beginning of modern economics, called the restrictions "impertinent badges of slavery." [1]

Other laws sprang from the need of some general supervisory authority which could make uniform rules in matters affecting the interests of the colonies collectively, where separate action tended to confusion. Such were the acts creating a general postal service and regulating the currency. All of the colonies suffered from the lack of specie, and from time to time tried to make good the deficiency by issuing circulating paper. The whole matter of the currency was taken up by Parliament, as closely related to imperial commerce, and several acts were passed to regulate the value at which foreign coins should circulate throughout the provinces, or to prohibit paper money issues.

It is difficult to find any example of parliamentary legislation

[1] "Land is still so cheap, and, consequently, labour so dear among them, that they can import from the mother country, almost all the more refined or more advanced manufactures cheaper than they could make them for themselves. . . . In their present state . . . those prohibitions . . . are only impertinent badges of slavery imposed upon them, without sufficient reason, by the groundless jealousy of the merchants and manufacturers of the mother country." — *Wealth of Nations*, Book IV, Chap. VII, Part II.

for the colonies previous to 1763 which is not connected with the regulation of industry, and thus with the mercantile system. Many other kinds of legislation were proposed, including laws for raising a revenue by duties on imports, an excise, or a stamp tax. Especially during the wars with France there was strong temptation to levy troops and raise money by parliamentary action. But Parliament in the end always refrained from such legislation, and from regulations which would have touched the "internal police" of the colonies, such as the relations of individuals to one another. In matters affecting only its own inhabitants each colony was allowed to enjoy "home rule."

## The Crown and the Colonies

While except in industrial matters the colonies were hardly touched by Parliamentary acts, the Crown was a very real factor in their government. Colonial administration, in other words, was a function of the Crown rather than of Parliament. The governor in the royal colonies was the agent of the Crown in holding his province in line with the policies of the home government. He had a veto upon the acts of the legislature, and was under instructions to work for certain kinds of legislation and to withhold approval of other kinds. An example of the former class would be laws for raising troops or revenue for the French wars. His veto was to be given to all acts which tended to injure British commerce, such as those restricting the slave trade, or favoring American debtors at the expense of English creditors.

Strictly speaking, colonial laws were not in force even after receiving the governor's signature until approved by another crown agency, the Privy Council in England. Hundreds were actually disallowed because they were in conflict with the laws, interests, or policies of Britain. Moreover, the Privy Council, which in earlier centuries had possessed judicial powers and lost them so far as England was concerned, developed in the eighteenth century the function of a court of appeals for cases tried in the colonial courts.

The immunity of the chartered colonies, especially the corporate ones, from the control exercised in the royal provinces was a source of increasing dissatisfaction to the British politicians, and several proposals were made to set aside all of the charters by parliamentary act. The Whigs, however, always sensitive to property rights, looked upon charters as vested interests of the holders and defeated all such proposals. They sought the same end quite successfully by other means, such as purchase and forfeiture.

A number of chartered colonies had been converted into royal provinces during the last two decades of the seventeenth century. Thus New Hampshire had been detached from Massachusetts in 1679 and New York had become royal through the accession of the proprietor to the throne (1685). Misgovernment furnished the pretext for voiding the charter of Carolina and erecting two royal provinces (1728).[1] The Georgia charter provided for the reversion of government to the Crown after twenty-one years. Negotiations were carried on for many years with the Penn family for the purchase of their rights in Pennsylvania and Delaware, but without success, and these two provinces with Maryland remained proprietary until after independence was won, when the proprietors' rights were purchased by the states. At the close of the colonial period eight of the thirteen colonies were royal, and the influence of the Crown had increased correspondingly. Connecticut and Rhode Island remained corporate.

Even in the colonies which retained their charters the royal influence was considerably extended. The Crown had established the right (first set down in the charter to Penn) to confirm the appointment of governors for the proprietary colonies and to require them to give bond to execute the British laws relating to America. The right of appeal from the provincial courts to the Privy Council was also extended to the proprietary provinces. Even in the corporate colonies the right of appeal was asserted with increasing success. The collectors of customs and the admiralty courts are examples of imperial agencies which were everywhere independent of provincial control.

All of this administrative machinery was supervised in England by the Board of Trade. Besides drafting instructions for the governors and other crown officials, the Board gave colonial

[1] The King took over the government of South Carolina about 1719, owing to disturbances, and a few years later acquired the proprietary rights by purchase.

laws their first examination, and under the advice of the law officers, recommended their acceptance or rejection by the Privy Council.   The latter held the real authority, as it included the great ministers who acted nominally for the King but really for the aristocracy which dominated Parliament.

In part because the ministry desired to have at hand a source of information relative to American affairs, some of the larger colonies supported a representative in England known as the colonial agent.   These men were often skillful lobbyists and sometimes succeeded in preventing the passage of acts which would have been detrimental to the interests of their constituents.   The most famous of them was Benjamin Franklin, of Pennsylvania.   His success led other colonies to appoint him as their agent, and on the eve of the Revolution he was virtually an informal ambassador of the American people.

It must be remembered that the British control, whether by acts of Parliament or through the crown administrative agencies, was devoted mainly to securing the interests of the empire as a whole.   In spite of the elaborate machinery and of the royal governor's share in every act of legislation and administration, the Americans had large freedom of action.   In most matters with which each government dealt no one was concerned except the inhabitants, and the governor allowed them to have their own way as a matter of course.   Britishers when appointed to colonial offices were likely to remain at home, enjoying their income while their duties were performed by a deputy who was often a provincial bound to those whom he governed by intimate ties.

This situation helps to explain the lax enforcement even of the laws of which the British were most tenacious.   The Molasses Act, for example, was almost a dead letter.   By false papers, by covering the cargo from foreign ports with a layer of molasses-casks from the British West Indies, by slipping into some obscure inlet to make a landing — all these practices with the connivance of dilatory officials — Yankee skippers set the statute at naught. The duties collected were negligible.   To be sure, the act was not intended as a revenue measure, but the foreign molasses brought into Rhode Island alone, it is estimated, would have yielded something like £28,000 if the duties had been paid.

Even where the colonial will was in direct conflict with the governor's instructions the Americans frequently had their way. In such contests the weapon of the provincials was the control of the purse. Without acts for raising and appropriating money the governor's administration was paralyzed. For his salary also he was dependent upon the legislature in almost every colony. He was the servant of two masters, the Crown and the assembly, and not seldom compromised his instructions to save his income.

Especially during the French and Indian wars, when prompt action was needed in raising troops and funds, the necessity of dealing with so many provinces separately led bold minds to urge the short-cut of parliamentary action. The centralized power of the French government seemed much superior to the English system at times of crisis, and was regarded by many Englishmen as the model on which the British administration should be reconstructed. Sober judgment indicated that at least some plan should be devised by which the colonies would be brought into permanent coöperation, with a general legislative and executive body to deal with such a vital common interest as a war with the French. Several plans of union were suggested, some of them by Americans and some by British leaders.

The most notable of the proposals of union was the Albany Plan, which distinctly foreshadowed the Constitution of the United States. It was the work of a congress of delegates from seven colonies which met at Albany in 1754, at the instance of the British ministry, in the hope of bringing the colonies into joint action in the impending French and Indian War. The plan was drafted by Franklin. It provided for a council composed of delegates selected by the assembly of each colony, and a president-general appointed by the Crown. This body was to have power to carry on wars in which the colonies were involved, and to raise troops and collect taxes for this purpose. In addition it was to control all relations with the Indians, including trade and purchases of lands, to superintend the laying out of new colonies, and to govern them until the Crown erected them into distinct provinces.

These proposals were the fruit of actual experience and show a consciousness that the Americans could act to better advantage in union than separately. It was only advanced thinkers on either side of the Atlantic, however, who were able to appraise the plan at its true worth, and it was not put into operation. The British government thought that it savored too much of American autonomy, while the colonies, jealous of one another, needed another generation filled with sharp lessons to teach them the importance of union.

## The Conflict of British and American Opinion

Several generations of life in the New World, under conditions so different from those in England, had given the Americans views which were widely separated from those held by the British mercantilists. They regarded the provinces, not as establishments existing merely for the promotion of English commerce, but as commonwealths or states, comparable with England herself, inhabited by Englishmen associating together in all the manifold ways characteristic of political communities, and united with England only by having the same king. The train of events which had shifted authority from King to Parliament and made the merchants and landlords the masters of imperial policy meant comparatively little to them. They felt quite capable of managing their own affairs, and, indeed, were accustomed to doing so. Down to 1763 they were content with their lot under the colonial system as actually administered, although on many occasions they had shown irritation and a disposition to act according to their own judgment when the system pinched. Long enjoyment of immunity from parliamentary interference in matters of internal police had bred in them the belief that home rule was their right. The superiority of their charters to the enactments of their assemblies accustomed them to the concept of a superior law, and earlier English and European publicists supported the idea that even the unwritten British constitution fixed limits to the powers of Parliament.

Scholars are still disputing over the legality of the authority which Parliament sought to exercise in America after 1763, but apart from the question of law it was folly for Britain to attempt to rule Americans contrary to their wishes. At bottom this was the effective cause of the Revolution.

## SELECT BIBLIOGRAPHY FOR CHAPTER V

The period 1700–1750 has been called the "neglected half-century." It was studied less carefully than the seventeenth century by the older historians, and many of the fruits of recent researches are still in the monographic stage. There is now available, however, the posthumous work of Professor H. L. Osgood, *The American Colonies in the Eighteenth Century*, which covers these years exhaustively. Greene, *Provincial America*, and Channing, *United States*, give excellent general accounts.

**England and the Colonies.** The relations of the European nations which form the background of the British colonial system are treated in Abbott, *Expansion of Europe*, II. Beer, *Old Colonial System, 1660–1754*, continues the study presented in *Origins*. A standard but older treatise is Seeley, *Expansion of England*. Osgood, *American Colonies in the Seventeenth Century*, III, is also excellent on the early phases of the imperial system. Andrews, *Colonial Self-Government*, and Channing, *United States*, II, are brief but good.

**Rise of Parliament Government.** The changes in the British government after the Revolution of 1688 may be studied in Maitland, *Constitutional History of England*. Especially good on the ministerial system is Blauvelt, *The Development of Cabinet Government in England*.

**British Mercantilism.** Beer, *Old Colonial System, 1660–1754; British Colonial Policy, 1754–1765;* and *Commercial Policy of England towards the Colonies*, provide the most satisfactory survey of the subject. Egerton, *Short History of British Colonial Policy*, is also useful.

**The Crown and the Colonies.** Dickerson, *American Colonial Government*, is a good study of British administration of the colonies through the Board of Trade. Greene, *The Provincial Governor*, approaches the administrative system from another angle. Kellogg, *The Colonial Charter*, is essentially a study of the efforts to reduce the colonies to the royal type.

**The Conflict of British and American Opinion.** Tyler, *Literary History of the American Revolution*, I, contains many quotations which illustrate opinions of Americans on questions of relations with England. Merriam, *History of American Political Theories*, contains a fairly good summary of American views. McIlwain, *The American Revolution*, is a recent brilliant defense of the legal soundness of the American denial of the authority of Parliament. Van Tyne, *Causes of the War of Independence*, is a dispassionate product of present-day scholarship. It stresses the divergent development of the two parts of the English world as the fundamental reason for the separation. A discussion by a prominent English authority has just appeared — Egerton, *The Causes and Character of the American Revolution*.

# CHAPTER VI

## THE STRUGGLE FOR THE MISSISSIPPI VALLEY

### THE FRENCH IN NORTH AMERICA

"Heirs apparent of the Romans!" In exultant mood Horace Walpole thus described the English race as successive victories in the Seven Years' War foretold a triumphant end. The terms of the Peace of Paris in 1763 marked, indeed, a signal triumph for England over her rivals in the race for world-wide empire. For three quarters of a century, on sea and land, in every clime — on the battlefields of Europe, in the tropical jungles of India, in the dark forests of North America — the banner of St. George had contended against the *Fleur-de-lis* until France, defeated, exhausted, humiliated, accepted the victor's terms. With their defeat the French Bourbons made their exit from the North American mainland and the curtain fell upon the dramatic and colorful history of New France; the turbid waters of the Mississippi marked the eastward limits of the dominions of decadent Spain, and half a continent spread its invitation before the restless feet of the sturdy race whose multiplying paths ran westward from the margin of the Atlantic.

The French, like the English, failed to gain a permanent foothold in America during the sixteenth century. Shortly before the formation of the London and Plymouth Companies, however, a commercial concern began a settlement at Port Royal, near the present Annapolis, Nova Scotia (1605); and from this germ came the colony of rough fisher folk and trappers called "Acadia."

With the founding of Quebec on the St. Lawrence by Samuel de Champlain in 1608, a far more important chapter began in history of French effort. This settlement commanded a natural highway leading to the Great Lakes and the heart of the continent. The transition from the St. Lawrence to the Father of Waters is easy; at many points the low watershed between the

+Chief portages

FRENCH EXPLORATIONS AND SETTLEMENTS TO 1763.

99

two great drainage basins is crossed by portages.   On the Fox-Wisconsin route only a mile and a half of boggy plain separated the two river systems; indeed, during spring floods the waters of the two often mingled at the portage, permitting the passage from the Great Lakes to the Mississippi entirely by boat.

The English, seated upon the short rivers which fall from the Appalachians, found themselves cut off from the Mississippi Valley by the mountain barrier.   In contrast, the great river flowing by the cliff of Quebec from the mysterious woodland of the West lured the French into the vast interior.   Champlain's commercial company had little interest in the development of the agricultural possibilities of Canada.   Larger profits and quicker returns were to be had from the fur trade; and the pursuit of trade led the French to trace the intricate network of the streams, to find the portages, to reveal the geography of the Mississippi Basin.

Champlain himself was active in exploration.   In 1609 he examined the lake which bears his name.   Soon afterwards he accompanied a war party of Algonkins from the St. Lawrence against the Iroquois Confederacy.   Hostile from this time, the Iroquois made the shores of Lake Ontario so dangerous for the French that their first excursions to the westward followed the Ottawa River and Lake Huron.

Champlain visited Lake Huron in 1615, and when the Massachusetts English were first discussing the settlement of the Connecticut Valley, his agent Nicolet was penetrating the forests of far-off Wisconsin (1634).   Within three decades from this time Radisson and Groseilliers penetrated westward and northward of Lake Superior, possibly touching the upper waters of the Mississippi.

Frenchmen were not eager to leave the home land for the Canadian wilds.   The Huguenots, who might have gone in considerable numbers, were not allowed to emigrate.   At the end of fifty years the population of New France did not exceed three thousand, but this scanty number was scattered from the shores of the Atlantic to the banks of the Wisconsin, a distance of more than fifteen hundred miles.   Many times that number might have found sustenance within a few miles of Quebec.

This dispersion was due in part to restrictions on the fur trade which drove many to engage in it without license.   The wide wilderness offered a secure retreat for these adventurous spirits. Fear of arrest and punishment prevented them from frequenting the vicinity of Montreal or Quebec, and led them to seek a market among the Dutch or their English successors in New York, and their Indian allies of the Iroquois League. Many a "wood ranger" (*coureurs de bois*, the French called them) made his home in the wilds, taking a squaw for mate and rearing a dusky brood in a native village on the banks of the inland waters.

Close behind the explorer-trader went the missionary. The Jesuits in particular carried the cross to the remotest regions with a heroic devotion never surpassed in the annals of the Church. The priest and trader sometimes became companions in exploration, as when Father Jacques Marquette and Louis Joliet crossed to the Mississippi by the Fox-Wisconsin route and descended as far as the mouth of the Arkansas (1673).

Greatest among the seventeenth-century explorers was the Sieur de la Salle, the first white man to descend the Mississippi to its mouth. Coming to Canada in 1666, he spent several years in trading among the eastern tribes and in the Ohio country. Then he conceived the idea of developing the fur trade of the Mississippi Valley on a grand scale. Visiting France to promote his project, he obtained the grant of a monopoly of the fur trade of the valley. After misfortunes which would have discouraged a less resolute man, he began the descent of the river early in 1682, and reached its mouth in April. Two years later, having visited France again in the meantime, he came by sea in command of an expedition seeking the mouth of the Mississippi with the purpose of planting a colony there. Missing the goal, the party landed on the Texas coast, where after suffering great privation, La Salle's mutinous companions murdered him (1687). A few survivors succeeded in reaching the Illinois country.

The net result of La Salle's brilliant dream was the awakening of interest in the valley. It was a dozen years, however, before the project of a colony at the mouth of the river was revived. When the close of King William's War (see page 105) brought a favorable moment, a new expedition under the Sieur d'Iberville began a settlement at Biloxi (1699) in the present state of Mississippi. Within a few years the river was reëxplored in the hope of finding mines of copper, lead, and other metals.

In disregard of the protest of the Spanish, who claimed the coast of the Gulf both to the westward and eastward, the French gradually extended their settlements, founding New Orleans in 1718 and planting outposts on the Red and Arkansas rivers. Their occupation of the territory came in the nick of time, for an English expedition in quest of a site for a colony turned back in 1699 only because the French had preceded them by a few months. Traders from the Carolinas and Virginia had already reached the Mississippi. They relaxed their activity not a whit after the coming of the French, and the lower Mississippi Basin became the scene of keen rivalry.

The second quarter of the eighteenth century was a time of considerable French activity west of the Mississippi. Marquette and Joliet had abandoned their descent of the river when they became satisfied that it flowed into the Gulf of Mexico, and not into the Pacific, as they had imagined; but the hope remained that by ascending its branches a way might be found to the "Sea of the West." The trade of new regions served as a continual lure to exploration. The native tribes of the Great Plains were visited, and in 1739 two brothers, Pierre and Paul Mallet, are believed to have crossed the plains to the Spanish settlements in New Mexico.

About the same time Varenne de Vérendrye was planning the extension of the fur trade westward from Lake Superior. By a chain of forts he hoped not only to command the trade of the country around the Lake of the Woods and Lake Winnipeg, but also to extend French influence so far that "the discovery of the Western Sea may be accomplished." From one of these posts Vérendrye's son Pierre crossed the northern plains in 1742 and came in sight of the Big Horn range of the Rocky Mountains.

Monopolistic commercial companies played a large part in the early history of the French colonies, as in the English; but the paternalistic government maintained such close supervision that private initiative was almost stifled. In the eighteenth century both New France and Louisiana were under the Crown, and were governed much like provinces in France, the most highly centralized country of western Europe. A governor appointed by the King headed the military as well as the civil administration, checked by another official (*intendant*, or *commissaire-ordonna-*

*teur*) who controlled expenditures, had some judicial functions, and as agent of the King watched the governor's conduct. In Canada (New France) the bishop was also an official of no slight importance. From the body of the inhabitants, on the nomination of the governor and intendant, the Crown appointed a number of councilors, who with the officials possessed all executive, legislative, and judicial powers, subject only to appeal to the government at Paris. The council was dominated by the three great officials, as were the local officers, and the colonists in general were without any voice in government. On the other hand the village community of the mother country appeared, and through its assembly gave the people a large degree of control over their local church and industrial affairs.

A form of feudalism known as the "seignorial system" was introduced into Canada at an early date, and was the basis of the tenure of land so far as agriculture was pursued. It was also the basis of an order of nobility. Many of the names which one meets in the history of Canada bear the title "Sieur," the sign of the feudal lord. The tenants cultivated their lands in narrow strips, paid a portion of their produce to their lord, patronized his mill and oven, and labored for him a few days each year, like the peasants of France and Germany. In the remote settlements, as in the Illinois country, the feudal features of the land system were practically replaced by individual ownership.

Permanent settlements were begun in the Illinois country at about the same time that the beginnings were made near the mouth of the Mississippi. La Salle had established Fort St. Louis on the Illinois River in 1682. A mission was opened at Cahokia in 1699; a rival one was founded at Kaskaskia near by in 1700. Fort Chartres and Prairie du Rocher, in the same vicinity, date from 1720 and 1733. At Detroit the French appeared in 1701, for at last they could navigate the lower lakes in safety. Vincennes on the Wabash and other outlying posts marked the spread of the diffuse French population.

In origin the Illinois settlements were the result of expansion from the St. Lawrence Basin, but circumstances tended to associate them with Louisiana. The Fox Indians of Wisconsin were enemies of the French and interposed a barrier between Canada and the Mississippi. The river also afforded an easier

outlet for the produce of the villages on its banks than did the
old route through the Lakes.   Illinois was finally incorporated
with the southern province.   By the middle of the eighteenth
century the little cluster of villages, while maintaining some
activity in the fur trade, had become noted as the chief agricultural community in the French mainland possessions.   Quantities of produce were taken eastward to Detroit, but especially
southward to the settlements along the lower river and to the
French West Indies.

## RIVALRY OF THE FRENCH AND ENGLISH

From the outset the progress of French settlement was watched
with jealous eyes by the English.   Not long after the founding of
Acadia a band of half-piratical men from Virginia raided Port
Royal (1613).   A few years later (1622) the King granted the
region (called by the English Nova Scotia) to a proprietor who
tried to colonize it in spite of the presence of the French.
Every occasion of conflict between the two powers in Europe
was the signal for hostilities in America, and even in the intervals of peace the indefinite boundary between New England
and Acadia was the cause of constant friction.

During the second half of the seventeenth century the two
countries became rivals for the fur trade of the interior.   Radisson and Groseilliers, the discoverers of the Hudson Bay country,
offended by their treatment at the hands of the French authorities, turned to the English, and the Hudson Bay Company was
chartered (1670) as the result of their efforts.[1]   Its posts on the
shore of the bay were readily reached by ocean-going vessels
during the ice-free months, and ease of transportation gave its
traders a great advantage over the French of the lake country.

Englishmen also reached the upper Lakes and undersold the
French; or the friendly Fox Indians and French wood rangers
came down to the eastern shores of Lake Erie to meet the Iroquois
or New Yorkers.   This competition in the lake region was a
source of great distress to the Canadians, and in 1673 and 1678
the governor of Canada built forts at the site of Kingston (Fort

---

[1] The promoters belonged to that group which was so active in all sorts of schemes of
colonial expansion under the second Charles.

Frontenac) and at Niagara, to cut off the English from the north-west trade.

The Iroquois country was another field of rivalry. These tribes, dependent on the English at Albany for goods, were jealous of their position as middlemen between New York and the western Indians. In 1680, encouraged by the English, they began a war on the Illinois tribes to break up their traffic with the French. On the other hand, Jesuit missionaries won considerable influence over the Iroquois. The English considered the Jesuits as political agents of the French government, and tried to supplant them with English priests. In 1684 Governor Dongan obtained the acknowledgment by chiefs of the League of the dependence of the Iroquois upon the government of New York, and took them under its protection. Thereafter hostile encounters between the Canadians and Iroquois tended to embroil the English and French governments.

While Anglo-French relations from Hudson Bay to the Mississippi mouth were thus tending towards armed conflict, the spark which brought war was lighted in Europe. William of Orange, whom the Revolution of 1688 brought to the English throne, was already the chief enemy of the French King, Louis XIV, having led in the formation of an alliance to check his projects of expansion towards the Rhine. The pleadings of the exiled Stuarts added to the old enmity embroiled Louis with England in the first of a series of wars which ended only with the overthrow of Napoleon at the battle of Waterloo in 1815.

In 1689, when "King William's War," as it was called in America, began, wide stretches of wilderness separated the settlements in Canada from the English even in New York and New England where the frontiers were nearest. In America, therefore, the war was not fought by armies drawn up in battle array after the European manner, but on the French side consisted chiefly of a series of forays against the English settlements by parties of Indians led by a few whites. These raids fell first upon outlying towns in New Hampshire and Maine. Early in 1690 came an attack on Schenectady, in the Mohawk Valley. It was fortified, as was usual on the frontier, with a palisade of logs set upright, the lower ends planted in the ground. Taken by surprise, it was burned and most of the inhabitants slaughtered or captured.

On the other side, Connecticut and New York troops attacked Montreal, and a naval expedition from Massachusetts captured Port Royal. The war was ended, without permanent results for either participant, by the Peace of Ryswick, in 1697.

Only five years elapsed before hostilities began afresh. "Queen Anne's War," as the War of the Spanish Succession was called in America, like its predecessor, found its chief causes in Europe. It was waged to preserve the balance of power, England, Austria, and Holland joining to prevent the virtual union, as they feared, of France and Spain through the accession of a French prince to the Spanish throne.

In America the fighting was of much the same kind as in King William's War. In the end the Bourbon prince retained the throne of Spain, but at the price of great concessions in the Peace of Utrecht (1713–1714). Besides other changes in the political map of Europe, Gibraltar went to England. It was at this time that Spain consented to the Asiento contract (see page 78). France yielded Newfoundland, Nova Scotia (conquered by New England militia in 1710), and the Hudson Bay Territory, and recognized the British protectorate over the Iroquois.

Unfortunately the treaty did not define the boundary of Nova Scotia, and although peace prevailed between the two countries for more than thirty years after Utrecht, quarrels and hostile encounters continued along the disputed border.

After Queen Anne's War the rivalry of France and England became world wide and made new conflicts inevitable. Each had its chartered company seeking to control the commerce of the Far East. On the Guinea coast the rival traders competed for the commerce in gold and negroes, with the advantage on the side of the English because of the Asiento contract; while the dim forest glades of America witnessed many a dark encounter the story of which has never been told.

England avoided war because of the close relations between France and Spain. The ties of kinship between the rulers formed the basis of a defensive agreement known as the "family compact" (1733). This was but one of a complicated system of alliances which made it more and more difficult for any two European countries to go to war without involving others. In fact, the next armed conflict between France and England took place during the general War of the Austrian Succession, 1744–1748 ("King George's War" in America), which owed its inception to causes quite apart from their own enmities.

During the long peace after 1714 France built the strong fortress of Louisburg on Cape Breton Island, commanding the approaches to the St. Lawrence, guarding her interests in the fisheries, and encouraging the Acadians, now British subjects, to remember their former allegiance.   When war broke out in 1744 this stronghold became a shelter for privateers and a base for possible expeditions against the British colonies.   Its reduction therefore became a prime object in New England.   Governor William Shirley of Massachusetts took the lead in organizing an expedition which with some aid from the British navy succeeded in taking Louisburg in 1745.   Shirley would have followed up this success by an attempt at the conquest of Canada, but the British government gave him no encouragement, and the remainder of the war, so far as it concerned America, was a repetition of the old dismal story of Indian raids against the northern frontier.

To offset the success of the British, the French gained a position in the Low Countries so menacing to England that at the Peace of Aix-la-Chapelle (1748) she purchased the evacuation of the Netherlands by restoring Louisburg, to the great dissatisfaction of the Americans.

## The French and Indian War

The peace of Aix-la-Chapelle left unsettled the old dispute over the Acadian boundary and did nothing to remove the causes of rivalry in the Mississippi Valley.   Even while the peace commissioners were still disputing, the shadow of a new war fell across the upper waters of the Ohio.   English land speculators as well as fur traders were now becoming active west of the mountains, seeking control of choice locations in anticipation of the coming of the settlers.   In 1749 a group of Virginia gentlemen, in association with several prominent Englishmen, organized The Ohio Land Company, and sought for it a grant of a half million acres on the Ohio river, below the "forks."   The next year they sent Christopher Gist to "spy out the

land." These plans were the cause of special alarm to the
French. Hence the governor of Canada dispatched a party
under Céleron de Blainville (1749) from Lake Erie to the
Alleghany River and thence down the Ohio, to assert the French
claim. At the Miami River the expedition turned north, crossing
to the Maumee and returning to Canada by way of Detroit.
They found the Indians friendly to the British, with whom their

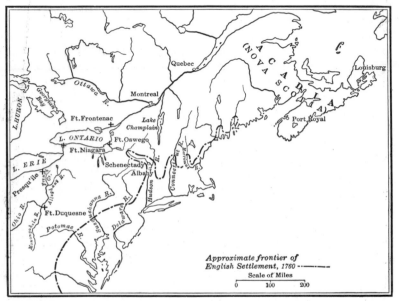

THE FRENCH AND INDIAN WARS, 1689–1763.

trade was large, and saw that vigorous action was needed to hold
the country against the English advance. Céleron's expedition
was therefore followed by an attack (1752) by Indians under
French control upon an Indian town on the Miami River (Pick-
awilliny) which was a center of British influence, and by the
building of forts at Presqu'île and on French Creek, as the first
of a chain intended to bar the English from the Ohio country.

The year 1753 found the people of two nations engaged in a
race for possession of the same territory, each determined to
repel the other's encroachments upon its "undoubted limits."
It was under these circumstances that Lieutenant-Governor

Robert Dinwiddie of Virginia decided to send George Washington with a formal message to the French commandant on French Creek demanding the withdrawal of the French as trespassers. Washington, then a young man of twenty-two, was already familiar with life in the wilderness through experience as a surveyor on the Virginia frontier.

The reply to the British demand was a polite refusal. It was followed by the building of Fort Duquesne at the forks of the Ohio, the key to the entire Ohio Valley. Meeting this challenge, the Virginia government sent Washington a second time with a force to drive out the intruders if they would not go peaceably. While still some distance from Fort Duquesne, Washington learned through scouts of the approach of an armed party with hostile intent, as he supposed. He surprised and defeated it, thus shedding the first blood in the new war; but a few days later, pressed by a superior force, he was compelled to surrender. The enemy was left in possession of the disputed country.

These events in the American backwoods involved Europe in another general conflict, the French and Indian War (in Europe called the Seven Years' War). England would gladly have confined the struggle to the western hemisphere; she withheld a declaration of war until France attacked her Mediterranean island of Minorca (1756), which enabled her to represent her enemy as the aggressor and thus to keep Spain neutral during the first years of strife.

In the campaign of 1755 the chief objective of the English was the recovery of the forks of the Ohio. General Edward Braddock was sent from England to command the combined force of regulars and colonial troops collected for this purpose. The two elements of the army did not harmonize. Colonial officers of the highest grade were ranked with British captains and jealousy destroyed the morale of the forces. American tactics, learned in the school of experience, in combat with savage foes in the woods, differed radically from those of the open battle-fields of Europe. The discord, combined with Braddock's tactless disregard of advice and inadaptability to his new surroundings, led to disaster. After a toilsome march across the mountains, as the army neared its destination, it fell into an ambush. From the shelter of the forest the unseen foe fired upon the regulars, who were unable to make effective reply.   The provincials, of whom Washington was one of the officers, fought frontier fashion, from behind trees, covering the retreat of the shattered army.

Against the western border, left exposed by this failure, the French now directed the savages, for most of the tribes quickly turned to the side which seemed to be winning.   "It is incredible," wrote a French captain, "what a quantity of scalps they bring us. . . .   These miserable English are in the extremity of distress, and repent too late of the unjust war they began against us."   To Washington, in command of a few hundred militia, fell the hard task of defending as best he could the harassed frontier.

The years 1756 and 1757 brought fresh disasters for the English.   The Canadian forces led by the able Marquis de Montcalm gained control of western New York and the Lake Champlain district.   In the crisis there came to the front one of the really great Englishmen of the century, William Pitt.   His statesmanship rose so far above the level of the place-seeking politicians of his day that he had not up to this time won a cabinet appointment.   Now as the dominating personality in a new ministry he became the organizer of victory.

When England declared war in 1756, a diplomatic revolution took place in Europe.   France, the ally of Prussia in the previous struggle, growing apprehensive of her rising power, joined with Austria and Russia, while England acted with Prussia.   Ambitious for the place of predominance among the states of Europe, France aspired also to rank as the greatest colonial and maritime power.   Grasping at both objects she dissipated her resources in the effort to put huge armies into the field while increasing her navy at the same time.

Pitt discerned the error of France and concentrated his effort upon the building up of British sea power, letting Prussia fight the battles of the alliance on the continent with the aid of money subsidies.   In consequence, British naval strength soon outdistanced that of France, and her sea power eventually won the war.   Moreover, Pitt put aside the incompetent army officers who owed their rank to seniority or favoritism and promoted young men to the positions of responsibility.   The later successes of Jeffrey Amherst and James Wolfe vindicated his wisdom.

Pitt also tactfully appealed to the loyalty of Americans, giving fairer recognition to colonial officers, and undertaking to pay for the operations of colonial troops outside of their own jurisdictions.

The population of the English colonies outnumbered that of the French about thirteen to one, but it was impossible to muster it in full force. The assemblies had to be appealed to separately in carrying forward war plans, for all schemes of intercolonial union came to nought.[1] While the English provinces were in little danger of actual conquest, the success of the French would have meant peace on terms which would have stopped British expansion. The task of the English, therefore, was to regain the offensive, and, if possible, to break down the French defense of the Ohio Valley and Canada.

This was Pitt's strategy. The superiority of the British navy began to tell in 1758, cutting off supplies and reënforcements for the Canadian armies, and coöperating with the land force under Amherst in a successful attack on Louisburg. The tide of war turned. Despite minor reverses in the Lake Champlain Valley, the year was one of victory. Fort Frontenac on Lake Ontario was taken, and an expedition under General John Forbes marched against Fort Duquesne. Defeating the enemy in a skirmish on the way, they found that the discouraged French had burned the fortifications and withdrawn. The new Fort Pitt erected at the forks of the Ohio was a monument to the British statesman.

Again, in the summer of 1759, a fleet in the St. Lawrence cut off succor for the French and enabled Wolfe to lay siege to Quebec, the chief stronghold of Canada. Nature was the ally of the defenders. Almost inaccessible cliffs guarded the approaches from the river side, and Montcalm hoped to avoid a combat until the early northern winter compelled his enemy to raise the siege. Wolfe, however, in mid-September, found a path which enabled him to scale the heights and force Montcalm to battle. The prize of victory was the possession of Quebec. The next year saw the fall of Montreal and the completion of the conquest of Canada.

Pitt aimed at victory so complete that England could dictate the terms of peace; but the final triumph was delayed by Spain's entry into the war in 1761. The Bourbon allies hoped that

[1] See page 95 for the efforts to form a union.

their united fleets might more than match the sea power of the English. The naval war of the final years only added, however, to the series of British successes, and involved Spain as well as France in the disasters of defeat.

During this final stage a shift in politics led to Pitt's resignation and the peace negotiations fell to his successors. By the treaties of Paris in 1763 France yielded to Great Britain Canada and all claims to territory east of the Mississippi, while Spain, in order to recover Cuba which Britain had taken, ceded Florida.[1] New Orleans went with Louisiana to Spain, but with this exception England now held the whole of North America east of the Mississippi. France retained only two little islands in the St. Lawrence, of importance to fishermen. In the Far East, also, the fruits of British generalship were garnered by the diplomats at Paris in the expulsion of France from India.

## THE PROBLEM OF THE WEST

The treaties of 1763 swept away all European opposition to English expansion to the Mississippi, but the management of this vast new estate was beset with difficulties. What policy should be followed with respect to the Indian occupants? Should white settlers be permitted to go beyond the Alleghanies, and if so, on what conditions? What additional provision was needed for the defense of the augmented empire? Finally, how should the great debt incurred in the war be met, and how should the vast sums be raised which were needed for this purpose and for administration?

These questions confronted the ministry in 1763. The Indian problem seemed most pressing of all. The time had come when Indian relations could no longer be left to the governments of the separate colonies. Sad confusion had resulted from the diversity of provincial laws, and the natives had suffered many things at the hands of unscrupulous whites.

The ministry resolved to take the responsibility for Indian affairs as an imperial matter. The Six Nations, while sympathetic with the British, had on the whole maintained a neutral

---

[1] This is equivalent to saying that Spain, like France, relinquished her claim to all territory east of the Mississippi. The boundary between the Spanish, English, and French claims in the Gulf region had been ill-defined.

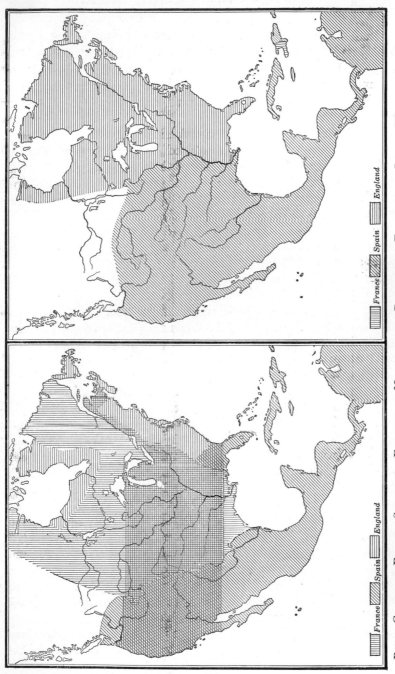

RIVAL CLAIMS OF FRANCE, SPAIN, AND ENGLAND IN NORTH
AMERICA, 1756.

France ▨ Spain ▨ England ▨

RESULTS OF FRENCH AND INDIAN WAR, 1756–1763.

France ▨ Spain ▨ England ▨

attitude during the war, but the more remote tribes in the Ohio
Valley and Northwest had sided with the French, chiefly through
fear that British success would mean the loss of their lands.    The
advance of the British farming frontier alarmed them, while
the French promised not to disturb their occupation and to
maintain profitable trade relations.

As the war drew to a close the restlessness of the Indians warned
the English of danger.    Unprincipled Frenchmen were playing
upon the fears of the natives to keep them at war even after the
white opponents had ceased to fight.    In 1763 the tribes of the
Northwest made a concerted effort against the English.    The
great chief Pontiac brought the natives far and wide into his
plan for striking a blow which would drive them back across the
Alleghanies.    At the same moment attacks were made on the
posts at Mackinac, Detroit, Presqu'île, and Fort Pitt.

Such attempts of the natives to defend their homes and hunting grounds have always ended in the same way.    However
severe the punishment suffered by the whites, the check has
been but temporary, and the flood has afterwards advanced more
irresistibly than before.    In 1764 two well-led expeditions to the
Ohio country reduced the tribes to submission.

The ministry, anticipating hostilities, had tried to avert
them by a Royal Proclamation relating to the regions acquired
by the war.    The Spanish and French settlements along the
Gulf of Mexico were designated as the Provinces of East and
West Florida, while for the French inhabitants of the St. Lawrence Basin the Province of Quebec was erected.    Between these
two lay the broad domain west of the mountains where dwelt the
natives.    This the Proclamation provided should remain in the
hands of the Indians, and all grants of land therein were forbidden "for the present."    The purpose of this prohibition was
perhaps primarily to assure the natives that their rights would
be respected and encroachments prevented until, by negotiations
from time to time with the proper officers, they might agree
to relinquish portions of their territory.    The ministry was also
desirous by this means to preserve the fur trade from the injury
which it would sustain from an inrush of settlers.

Following peace Indian affairs were placed in the hands of two
superintendents, Sir William Johnson for the "Northern Dis-

trict," and Captain John Stuart for the "Southern." The districts were subdivided, with subordinate officials in each

DISPOSITION MADE OF CONQUESTS IN FRENCH AND INDIAN WAR.

(Northern boundary of West Florida was fixed in 1767.)

division to enforce a uniform code for the protection of the Indians against traders and speculators. Purchases of lands were to be made only by the superintendents.

Within a few years most features of this plan were abandoned because of the cost, but the rule of land purchases by the superintendents was retained. Two great tracts were acquired in 1768 and 1770. The first, bought from the Six Nations by Johnson in the Treaty of Fort Stanwix, extinguished their claim to all lands east and south of a line running irregularly from the upper Mohawk to the Allegheny River and thence down the Ohio to the mouth of the Tennessee. The second purchase, by Stuart from the southern tribes, secured the lands east of a line drawn from the upper Tennessee River to the mouth of the Great Kanawha. These two treaties opened central and southwestern Pennsylvania and the West Virginia area.

By the time the French and Indian War ended many plans for new settlements were under discussion. The entire coast was parceled out in provinces, and if there were to be any new colonies, they would of necessity lie in the interior. A favorite project was to erect a new province between the Mississippi and the Wabash. That triangle of territory contained the old French settlements, which would be seed-plots for future growth. The scheme was favored by some of the army officers, who were concerned over the expense of transporting supplies from the coast for the garrisons which might be stationed in the old French posts, and thought that a portion of them might be raised by settlers. Others thought that interior colonies would yield new kinds of products which would make valuable additions to English commerce. Land speculators were more interested than any other class in the various schemes, but the distant Illinois country interested them less than the region just beyond the old settlements, which was more likely to be occupied promptly.

Out of the many plans which were discussed during the sixties one took very definite form, under the name of Vandalia. The promoters sought a grant from the Crown for a tract which coincided roughly with the cession obtained by Stuart, that is, West Virginia and eastern Kentucky. Franklin, in England, labored to secure favorable action, and Samuel Wharton, a Philadelphia Quaker, crossed the ocean for the purpose of lobbying with members of Parliament.

The question of new settlements brings out very well the

weakness of the ministries of that period as formers of policies. Frequent shifting of the political kaleidoscope made for vacillation and indecision, and prevented the pursuit of a consistent program. There were differences of opinion concerning the desirability of new colonies. While some of the ministers were favorably disposed, others believed that remote settlements would be of little value and hard to control. Lord Hillsborough, president of the Board of Trade, took this view, and held that the Proclamation of 1763 was intended to bar the whites from the transalleghany lands permanently. Lord Shelburne best represents the other position. He was a friend of Franklin, and of America, and decidedly liberal in his views.

Notwithstanding the fact, as Hillsborough urged, that the tract desired by the Vandalia Company lay within the charter bounds of Virginia, the ministry decided to make the grant, thus apparently setting Virginia's claim at nought, much as Charles I had done when he carved Maryland out of her unsettled domain and gave it to Lord Baltimore. The papers for the Colony of Vandalia were made out and were ready for delivery when the outbreak of the Revolution prevented.

While speculators were proposing and ministers debating schemes of settlement, the frontiersmen were paying scant heed to government plans or proclamations. In 1763 no settlements had yet been made west of the mountains, although some had reached westward-flowing waters in Virginia. The breaking down of the French barrier was the signal for overleaping the one interposed by nature. The densely wooded ridges of the Alleghanies lying in the path of the pioneers had hitherto diverted them southwestward along the valleys between the ranges, to the Shenandoah Valley of Virginia and the upland country of the Carolinas. Only the adventurous hunters and traders had followed the stream courses through the ranges, except here and there a squatter who had built a lonely cabin along the trails of the fur-seekers.

With peace came a rush through the passes. Southwestern Pennsylvania, western Maryland, the mountains of (West) Virginia, and northeastern Tennessee began to receive their inhabitants. By 1768 a cluster of "stations" dotted the branching waters of the upper Tennessee on both sides of the boundary between Virginia and North Carolina.   Hither in the early seventies came the Scotch-Irishman James Robertson from the Virginia frontier, and John Sevier, the Carolina Huguenot.

Opening out from the settled valleys of upper Tennessee into Kentucky was the great mountain gateway known as Cumberland Gap.   Kentucky, included within Virginia's charter grant, was a no-man's land, unoccupied by native tribes but used by many as a hunting ground.   Practically unknown to the English before the French and Indian War, it now became for them also a hunting ground.   Its well-watered blue grass lands of wonderful richness formed a natural pasturage which with the numerous salt licks had ages ago attracted the mastodon and other extinct mammals as they now drew the deer and bison.   Most famous of all the white hunters who visited this paradise in the sixties was Daniel Boone, whose Quaker parents had followed the stream of migration from Pennsylvania to the North Carolina Piedmont while Daniel was a youth.   Trained from boyhood to handle gun and knife, and inured to the life of the wilderness, his name became the symbol of all that is characteristic of the hardy pioneer stock which was about to sweep into the Ohio Valley.

## SELECT   BIBLIOGRAPHY   FOR   CHAPTER   VI

The works of Francis Parkman, under the general title of *France and England in North America*, give the classic account of French expansion in the New World, the rivalry with the English, and the final overthrow of French dominion.   For literary excellence as well as sound scholarship these volumes have not been surpassed in historical writing in America.   In *Montcalm and Wolfe*, which tells the story of the last French and Indian War, Parkman reaches his highest level.

Abbott, *Expansion of Europe*, II, gives the Old-World background of the Anglo-French rivalry in America.   Mahan, *Influence of Sea Power on History, 1660–1783*, discusses international relations with especial reference to the decisive part played by Britain's navy.

Thwaites, *France in America*, is a convenient one-volume summary of the whole topic stated in the title.   Fiske covers the subject in *New France and New England*.   Recent and brief is Wrong, *The Conquest of New France*.

Several volumes of the *Chronicles of Canada* are of interest on this topic.   Such are Colby, *Founders of New France*, and *The Fighting Governor;* and Munro, *Seigneurs of Old Canada*.

For Louisiana under the French, see Thwaites as above, Parkman, *La Salle and the Discovery of the Great West*, and Gayarré, *History of Louisiana*.

**The Problem of the West.** Parkman, *The Conspiracy of Pontiac*, tells the story of the Indian war of 1763. Carter, *Great Britain and The Illinois Country*, contains an excellent account of the projects of new colonies in the West after 1763. Alvord, *The Mississippi Valley in British Politics*, discusses the whole problem of the West from the point of view of the English government; he deals with the same theme more briefly in *The Illinois Country*. Roosevelt, *Winning of the West*, takes up the story of the actual movement of population after the Peace of Paris. Winsor, *The Westward Movement*, covers the same ground with less attention to the life and experiences of the pioneers and more to the formal political and diplomatic history. With these two writers may be compared Henderson, *The Conquest of the Old Southwest*, a more recent publication of popular character.

Boone's story is well told in Thwaites, *Daniel Boone*, and Bruce, *Daniel Boone and the Wilderness Road*.

# CHAPTER VII

## THE CONTEST OVER TAXATION BY PARLIAMENT

### THE POLICY OF GRENVILLE

In the face of a stupendous war debt the safety of the enlarged empire demanded increased expenditures for defense. The tardiness of the response of colonial assemblies to calls for troops, and the poor discipline of the militia and volunteers which America had contributed had called out bitter complaints by British officers during the late wars. Reliance upon such resources was perilous in a sudden crisis like Pontiac's War. A force of two thousand regulars under imperial control, judiciously distributed among the border posts, would provide adequate protection in case of Indian uprising or trouble from the French in the new Canadian possessions.

Indispensable as this program seemed, the expense involved was a serious problem. British taxpayers were already groaning under a burden which had been doubled by the war. Considerable economies might have been effected by purging the civil service of unnecessary offices created to reward the holders for political services, but the ministers lacked the courage to undertake drastic reforms. Besides, America was able to contribute something towards the cost of her protection, and it seemed only fair that she should be required to do so.

Two months after the signing of the Treaty of Paris there came to the head of the government as prime minister the man upon whom fell the chief burden of formulating the new defensive and financial program. This man was George Grenville. He was honest and conscientious and prized efficiency, but had little insight into the mind of Americans, and set about his task with slight anticipation of the reception in store for his plans.

It was clear to Grenville that the navigation system must be made a source of revenue in the colonies. He was amazed when his investigations revealed the extent of the evasion of the trade acts, and promptly tightened up the administration by appointing trustworthy collectors, sending vessels to patrol the American coast on the lookout for smugglers, and increasing the number of admiralty courts.   In April, 1764, the Sugar Act was passed.   It replaced the Molasses Act of 1733, and reduced the duty on foreign molasses from the prohibitory rate of sixpence per gallon to threepence, with the expectation that smuggling would cease and that the trade would yield a revenue. The new law laid duties upon a number of other imports, such as wines, silks, and coffee.

Grenville estimated that these imposts would yield about £45,000 per annum, while the cost of maintaining garrisons would amount to £360,000.   Of this he planned that one third should be raised in America, but he was at a loss for the best means of doing it.   Parliament passed a Billeting Act in 1765, which required the colonies wherein troops were stationed to provide them with quarters and certain supplies, and for the rest Grenville finally decided to recommend a tax requiring the use of stamps on a great variety of papers employed in everyday business transactions.   He announced the plan nearly a year in advance of asking Parliament to pass the bill, to give the colonial agents opportunity to suggest an alternative means of raising the sum desired from the colonies.   As they merely protested against any kind of direct tax, Parliament passed the Stamp Act in February, 1765, without debate.

The Sugar Act and the enforcement of the trade regulations aroused the merchants.   A duty of even threepence per gallon on molasses would kill the trade, they said, and injure British as well as colonial merchants, since it was the source of the specie for paying balances due England.   Imports from the mother country must cease if the Sugar Act were enforced.   To aggravate the situation a Currency Act of 1764 forbade the colonies to supply the deficiency of specie by issues of paper money.

The remonstrances of the merchants aroused little public attention.   In an attempt to awaken the fears of the people the Boston town meeting declared that if Parliament could tax trade, it could tax lands and houses.   But in form the Sugar Act was nothing new, and even the merchant class was more concerned with its practical effects than with the significance of the shift from a duty to regulate trade to one designed to raise a revenue. But indifference quickly disappeared with the passage of the Stamp Act. As almost everyone would have to use the stamps, the law brought home to every American the claim of a distant legislature to the right of taxing communities which sent no representatives to sit in it.

Even before the passage of the Stamp Act James Otis, of Massachusetts, published a memorable pamphlet against it, entitled *Rights of the British Colonies Asserted and Proved* (1764). In this he advanced the idea of a truly imperial parliament, composed of representatives from all parts of the empire, to regulate trade and lay taxes for imperial purposes. That the existing Parliament had such powers Otis denied, because of its unrepresentative character. Americans were not interested in gaining representation in Parliament; but in denying its right to tax unrepresented colonies Otis struck a responsive chord.

In Virginia Patrick Henry played a rôle somewhat like that of Otis in Massachusetts. He came forward in the House of Burgesses with resolutions declaring "That the General Assembly of this colony have the only and sole exclusive right and power to lay taxes and impositions upon the inhabitants of this colony." Supporting these resolutions, in a burst of that eloquence which made him famous as one of America's greatest orators, he cried, "Cæsar had his Brutus and Charles the First his Cromwell; and George III — ." Then as those about him exclaimed "Treason! Treason!" he concluded — "may profit by their example. If that be treason make the most of it!"

Otis and Henry had pointed out the constitutional argument with which parliamentary taxation could be combated. The stamps were not to go on sale until November 1, and there was ample time to organize resistance. Otis proposed a meeting of delegates from all of the colonial assemblies, and in October, 1765, twenty-seven, from nine of the colonies, met in New York.

This "Stamp Act Congress" is memorable as the first effort of Americans to act together in opposing the policy of England. The resolutions adopted are the most authoritative expression of colonial opinion up to that time. Owning their allegiance to the Crown, the colonists claimed also all of the rights and privi-

leges of subjects within the realm.   One of these rights was that
no taxes should be imposed upon them without their consent.
As their circumstances precluded representation in the House
of Commons, it followed, they held, that no taxes could be
consistently levied on them except by their respective colonial
assemblies.   It was the Stamp Act against which they directed
this argument.   As to the Sugar Act, professing "all due subordination" to Parliament, they protested against it as an unwise and oppressive restriction on trade.   Apparently they
regarded the duty as a trade regulation rather than a tax, and
the failure to denounce taxation in this form seemed to give
assent to its legality.

Meantime opposition had shown itself in other ways.   The
merchants, to give weight to their contention that enforcement of
the acts of trade would destroy their power to purchase British
goods, organized a boycott on imports from England, and their
appeals to the populace were in part responsible for several outbreaks of mob violence.   In one of these the mansion of Thomas
Hutchinson, chief justice of Massachusetts, was pillaged.   Under
the pressure of public opinion all of the stamp agents had resigned before November 1 arrived.   Business was temporarily
embarrassed for want of stamps, but soon went on as usual in
entire disregard of the law.

As for the Billeting Act, the Americans in their excited state
of mind could see in the presence of the troops only evidence of
a determination to intimidate them into submission.

When Parliament met and took up the American situation, a
change of ministry had taken place, and Grenville was no longer
in position to defend his policies from the vantage ground of the
premiership.   His friends insisted that the repeal of the Stamp
Act would be a surrender to rebellion.   With the support of Chief
Justice Mansfield, reputed to be the greatest lawyer of his time,
they maintained the doctrine of parliamentary supremacy and
ridiculed the idea that Parliament might lay an import duty,
as in the Sugar Act, but not an "internal" tax, such as the Stamp
Act provided.   They held that the colonies, like the new cities
of Manchester and Sheffield, were virtually represented in the
House of Commons.

The new ministry was in a quandary.   It must restore order

in America.   English merchants were feeling the effects of the boycott and were asking for the repeal of the Stamp Act.   But how could it be done without admitting defeat?   The House called Franklin before its bar and interrogated him.   He gave his opinion that the colonists would resist all internal taxes. Duties on commerce he thought they would accept unless may-hap the arguments in Parliament convinced them that they were wrong in making any distinction between internal taxation and taxation at the ports.   If troops were used to enforce the law, "they would not find a revolution, but they might make one."

Parliament was not indisposed to make concessions.   Some of the most influential members upheld the colonial view that parliamentary taxation was unjust and illegal.   Pitt was one of these, and Lord Camden was another.   Colonel Isaac Barré declared that he "rejoiced that the Americans had resisted," and referred to them as "Sons of Liberty."   It was finally deter- mined to repeal the Act, but to assert the theory of parliamentary supremacy in unmistakable terms.   In March, 1766, therefore, the repeal was voted, and at the same time a Declaratory Act was passed asserting that Parliament possessed authority to "bind the colonies and people of America, subjects of the crown of Great Britain, in all cases whatsoever."   Pitt would have added, "with the exception of taking money out of their pockets without their consent."   The rejection of his qualifying clause was ominous.

The repeal of the Stamp Act closed the first act of the dramatic contest which began in 1763.   The Americans celebrated the event with demonstrations of joy and loyalty.   If they noticed the Declaratory Act at all, they thought of it as mere words used to cover the retreat of the discomfited party, and not as a threat of further attempts at taxation.   That the other parts of Grenville's program remained in force also attracted little notice.[1]

None the less the issue remained unsettled, and the govern- ment still needed revenue.   The times called for a constructive statesman who could devise a means of harmonizing imperial

---

[1] At the same time that the Stamp Act was repealed the provisions of the Sugar Act were modified.   The duty on molasses was reduced from threepence to one penny per gallon and the impost on certain articles exported from England was to be collected on *exportation* instead of at the colonial port, lest the colonists object to "taxation at the ports." The changes made the Act more clearly than ever a revenue measure, yet Americans over- looked it as completely as they did the Declaratory Act.

necessities with colonial ideals of self-government. Few men on either side of the ocean saw the nature of the problem or gave it any thought. Franklin was one of the few. Otis was another. In England liberals like Pitt, Camden, and Shelburne might have found some workable plan if they had held power. Pitt was, indeed, called upon to form a new cabinet not long after the repeal of the Stamp Act, and Shelburne became one of his associates. Under a ministry so constituted there would have been no recurrence to the program of taxation. But Pitt was in ill health and another turn of the political wheel brought into office a man who was more clever than judicious. This was Charles Townshend, who now (1767) as Chancellor of the Exchequer became responsible for British finances. With him the contest over taxation entered its second phase.

## THE TOWNSHEND SYSTEM

Townshend's policy on the whole was a continuation of Grenville's. The elaborate machinery for managing Indian affairs was given up on account of the expense, but as to the keeping of troops in America, the enforcement of the trade acts, and the raising of a revenue, Townshend soon showed that he was in harmony with his predecessor. The New York Assembly had refused (1766) to comply with some provisions of the Billeting Act. Parliament therefore suspended the legislative functions of that body until it should yield (1767). New York was thus coerced into making an appropriation. Since her right to a legislature rested upon the grant of the King, its suspension by Parliament was a pronounced assertion of supremacy. If the rights of legislation and appropriation were not immune from invasion, it was difficult for Americans to see that they had any inviolable rights whatever.

The Chancellor next took steps to improve the method of enforcing the navigation acts. He procured the passage of a law creating a Board of Customs Commissioners to sit at Boston, and specifically authorizing the use of writs of assistance in the search for smuggled goods.[1] As to taxation, he boasted that he

---

[1] Writs of assistance were general search warrants. Otis had first come into prominence in 1761 as a defender of colonial rights by an argument against the use of such warrants.

knew a way to raise a revenue in America without arousing resistance. What he had in mind was new duties on imports which would take advantage of the implied admission of the legality of taxation at the ports, in the Resolutions of the Stamp Act Congress. The act passed at his suggestion laid duties on paint, paper, glass, and tea.

That this was a revenue measure could not be overlooked. The Sugar Act had declared that it was expedient to raise a revenue in America and had been little noticed; but three years of discussion had intervened since its passage, and the repetition of this phrase was not lightly passed by as before. Besides, the new act declared that the proceeds were to be used for the support of British officials in America, thus menacing the control over crown officers which the legislatures held through the power of the purse. Townshend was experimenting with colonial opinion, planning to add to the list of dutiable articles if the first attempt succeeded, until a considerable revenue was obtained.

As Franklin had hinted might be the case, the Americans now began to deny the right of Parliament to tax them in any way whatever. The lead in bringing them to the new point of view was taken by the Quaker, John Dickinson, in his "Letters of a Pennsylvania Farmer." "I have looked over every statute relating to these colonies from their first settlement to this time," he wrote. "Though many of them imposed duties on trade, yet those duties were always imposed with design to restrain the commerce of one part, that was injurious to another, and thus to promote the general welfare. The raising of a revenue thereby was never intended." "If Great Britain can order us to come to her for necessaries we want, and can order us to pay what taxes she pleases before we take them away, or when we land them here, we are as abject slaves as France and Poland can shew in wooden shoes, and with uncombed hair."

The merchants had been alarmed by the riotous outbreaks against the Stamp Act, fearing that lawlessness would divert the attention of the English government from the sound reasoning of the Americans. They were careful to exert their influence to preserve order during this new dispute. But they had less faith in petitions and remonstrances than in measures which would "touch the pocket nerve." Since the English seemed more sensitive to loss of profits than to arguments, non-importation agreements were again resorted to.  The merchants of Boston, followed by those of New York and Philadelphia, entered into covenants to discontinue importation until the Townshend Act was repealed.  In the southern colonies the planters took the lead in organizing the boycott, since many of the merchants were English and Scotch newcomers whose interests and sympathies were adverse to the program.  The boycott was enforced quite effectively in Philadelphia, fairly well in New York and Boston, and less successfully in the South.  The imports at Boston fell off almost fifty per cent; at Philadelphia they were reduced by more than two thirds.

The radicals aided in the enforcement of the agreements through local committees, and although threats were commonly used against offenders, the movement was for a time kept pretty well under control.

A new device was resorted to in 1768, as a kind of substitute for another intercolonial congress.  This was the Massachusetts Circular Letter.  It set forth the views of the assembly, and copies were transmitted to the assemblies of the other provinces inviting their replies and concurrence.

"The House have humbly represented to the ministry," so ran the letter, "their own sentiments, that his Majesty's high court of Parliament is the supreme legislative power over the whole empire; that in all free states the constitution is fixed, and as the supreme legislative derives its power and authority from the constitution, it cannot overleap the bounds of it, without destroying its own foundation; . . . that it is an essential, unalterable right, in nature, engrafted into the British constitution, as a fundamental law, . . . that what a man has honestly acquired is absolutely his own, which he may freely give, but cannot be taken from him without his consent; . . . that the acts made there [in Parliament], imposing duties on the people of this province, with the sole and express purpose of raising a revenue, are infringements of their natural and constitutional rights. . . ."  The obvious conclusion is, as the resolutions against the stamp tax had declared, that the people of each province could rightfully be taxed only by the provincial legislature in which they were represented.

Although couched in respectful terms, in England this letter was regarded as seditious, and Lord Hillsborough, now holding the newly-created office of Secretary of State for the Colonies, attempted to suppress discussion of it. Peremptory orders were sent to the royal governors to dissolve the assemblies of their provinces if they began to discuss the letter, while through the governor of Massachusetts a demand was made upon the assembly for its recall. When the assembly refused to rescind its action, the houses of Parliament joined in an address to the King proposing the arrest of colonial agitators for trial in England, under an ancient and almost forgotten law for punishing treasonable plots made outside of the realm. The only outcome of the proposal was further excitement of colonial resentment.

Notwithstanding the desire of the merchants to avoid violence, outbreaks occurred. In Boston an attempt was made to land the cargo of John Hancock's sloop "Liberty" in defiance of the revenue officers, who succeeded with difficulty in seizing the smuggled goods (June, 1768). Such deeds, and the defiant attitude of the legislature, brought down upon Boston two British regiments which were quartered in the town to overawe the inhabitants (October, 1768). The presence of the troops led to irritating incidents involving the soldiers and the less self-controlled elements of the population.

The climax came in the unfortunate affair known as the "Boston Massacre," in 1770. Beset by a mob of boys and young fellows who threw snowballs and clubs a squad of soldiers fired into the crowd and killed four persons. In the trial which followed John Adams defended the soldiers, and the commanding officer was acquitted because it could not be shown that he had given orders to fire. Two of the privates were convicted of manslaughter and given slight punishment. The affair had little real significance, except that it gave the radicals an opportunity to excite popular resentment against England. For several years, each anniversary of the "massacre" was made the occasion for a new appeal against "British tyranny."

Again the British government reconsidered its course. Townshend died. The new administration headed by Lord North was subservient to the King. The elements composing it were united in their belief as to England's rights over America, but the Townshend revenue law was costing too much in proportion to the sums it was bringing into the treasury. It was therefore determined to repeal the duties with the exception of a tax of threepence per pound upon tea. This was to be retained because, as the King said later, there must always be one tax to keep up the right. Thus, much as in the repeal of the Stamp Act, the government beat a "strategic retreat" but made no concession in principle.

As in the former case also colonial opposition relaxed. The non-importation agreement was abandoned except as to tea; but the merchants were growing weary of sacrificing profits and kept up the boycott on this article only half-heartedly. Although most of the tea used was smuggled in from Holland, little heed was given to the importation of small quantities which paid the tax. Even John Adams notes in his diary that he "dined at Mr. Hancock's . . . and drank green tea, *from Holland, I hope, but don't know!*"

## DIVISION OF OPINION IN AMERICA

Another reason for the lax observance of the tea boycott was that the merchant class, which led the opposition to Parliament at the beginning, was becoming fearful of the radical agitators whose conduct they could not control. They found that leadership was slipping from their hands. The arguments based on constitutional principles had kindled a back fire among the masses. With the British government on the one hand and the American radicals on the other, the upper classes were in a serious predicament. To press their complaints against England was to encourage the popular clamor, which might lead to worse things than British misrule. There was, indeed, an important group of Americans who were becoming convinced that the parliamentary party was right. An excellent example is found in Thomas Hutchinson. Although he disapproved of the Stamp Act, he was the chief sufferer from the violence which it stirred up — an experience which confirmed his dislike of radicalism. About the time of the repeal of the Townshend Act he was made governor of his province, and in this position he became an open champion of the British view-point.

The continuance of agitation after 1770, then, was due to radicals who aimed at reforms both in British and domestic relations. They determined not to allow the people to lose sight of the purpose of Britain in retaining the tax on tea. In Massachusetts their chief was Samuel Adams, upon whom had fallen the mantle of Otis.[1] It was he who drafted the Massachusetts Circular Letter of 1768, and who used the Boston Massacre to arouse the prejudices of the people. He was careful to let no occasion pass which might serve to keep alive the anti-British feeling. In 1772 it became known that the King planned to pay the Massachusetts judges, whose salaries had been appropriated by the General Court, from the customs receipts. Adams thereupon urged the appointment by the Boston town meeting of a committee of correspondence to keep in touch with other towns. The plan spread, and it proved to be an effective means of bringing the radicals together.

In Virginia, to mention only one other province, the social cleavage separated the great planters from the plainer people. The former chafed under the burden of their debts to British merchants, who were favored, as they believed, by the currency laws of Parliament. Then as later the planters were extremely individualistic and opposed to centralized government. Yet in Virginia as in the northern colonies, the zeal of the original leaders began to flag somewhat after the repeal of the Townshend Act, and this allowed the leadership to pass to a group of young men, most of whom were from the western counties.

Prominent among the young leaders were Thomas Jefferson, James Madison, and Patrick Henry. They thought that the older members of the Virginia assembly were not "up to the point of forwardness and zeal which the times required." Moreover, they were imbued with the democratic reforming spirit of the "West," and disliked the domination of the planting aristocracy only less than they did that of England. The three men named led the movement which eventually undermined the Church

---

[1] In 1769 Otis printed an article which drew upon him an assault by a British official. Insanity followed and he disappeared from public life. Both Samuel and John Adams were much influenced by Otis. The "brace of Adamses" were cousins. In contrast with the conduct of Samuel, John, as legal counsel for the officer who commanded the soldiers in the massacre, secured his acquittal of the murder charge. The state of public sentiment may be inferred from the fact that he did not forfeit prestige as a radical leader.

Establishment and the aristocratic system of land tenure, with its laws of primogeniture (inheritance of the entire landed estate by the eldest son) and entail (the prohibition of sale of a landed estate by the heir).

Following the adoption of the committees of correspondence by Massachusetts, Henry, Jefferson, and Richard Henry Lee secured the appointment of a committee of the House of Burgesses to correspond with similar bodies in the other provinces. The radicals elsewhere gradually secured similar action, thus creating an intercolonial organization.

While the radicals were thus busy the great majority of the people were unmindful of any probability of renewed contention. Indeed, all these preparations might have been to no purpose had not the British government blundered again. The ill feeling engendered by the controversies between 1763 and 1770 might gradually have declined if there had been no new occasion for friction. With the exception of more rigid trade regulations and the presence of troops, relations with England were on substantially the basis preceding 1763, and most provincials were content. In 1773, however, Parliament passed a new tea act which revived controversy without affording even the prospect of a contribution to the treasury.

The tea trade was a monopoly of the East India Company. The Company had a great quantity of tea stored in England, the market was glutted, and the Company was in financial straits. If the American market could be reopened, the Company would be relieved, especially if excused from paying duty in England on tea reshipped to the colonies. This duty was twelve pence per pound, which so much exceeded the cost of transportation across the Atlantic that, if remitted, tea would cost the consumer far less in America than in England. The new act not only granted this " drawback," but allowed the Company to appoint agents at the principal colonial ports to receive the shipments and sell the tea. The relaxation of the boycott, nominally maintained since 1770 because of the tax of three-pence, misled the ministry into supposing that larger quantities could be marketed if the price were lowered. Relief to the Company was only one object of the act. Although the duty in England was remitted, that payable at the colonial port remained unchanged, for, as Lord North admitted, "the king meant to try the case in America."

For the time being the new act brought the merchants and radicals once more into alliance.  The business of both legitimate tea importers and smugglers was threatened by the new methods of the East India Company, while the King's purpose was a direct test of colonial devotion to the principle of no taxation by Parliament.  Once landed and the duty paid by the agents, there was no doubt that the tea would find its way into the channels of trade and the whole American position against a duty for revenue would be subtly undermined.  The interest of the merchants no less than the principles at stake required that the tea must not be landed.

At Philadelphia, New York, and Charleston the Company's agents were persuaded to resign.  When the tea ships arrived at the first two ports, since there was no one to receive the cargoes and pay the duty, the shipmasters sailed back to England with their freight.  At Charleston the tea was placed in storage by the revenue officers for want of payment of the duty.[1]  At Boston, however, two sons of Governor Hutchinson held commissions as agents.  They would not resign, and the governor would not permit the issuance of clearance papers for the return of the ships.  With the issue thus drawn the radicals boarded the ships disguised as Indians (December 16, 1773), and "next morning tea lay strewn like sea weed along Dorchester beach."

## The Coercive Acts

With the "Boston Tea Party" the British plan of raising a revenue in America came to an abrupt termination.  Begun in good faith by Grenville, it had degenerated in the course of a decade into a policy of "shifts and devices," as Edmund Burke declared.  Provocative as had been the conduct of the King's government, moderate men like Franklin thought the Tea Party a blunder, for it was certain to force larger questions to the fore. Disregard of property rights put America in the wrong in the opinion of liberal Englishmen whose friendship was needed, and

[1] The Charleston consignment was sold at auction by the revolutionary government after hostilities began.

seemed to call for measures of coercion.  The early months of 1774 brought the enactment of five laws, two of which were the direct consequence of events in Massachusetts.

The first of these acts, the Boston Port Bill, forbade commerce with the guilty city until the inhabitants should compensate the East India Company for the destroyed tea.  The bill punished the innocent with the guilty, but the next law, the Massachusetts Government Act, by an extraordinary assertion of parliamentary authority, set at utter disregard the most precious rights of Americans.  It remodeled the government of that colony, converting it into a royal province of the standard type.  No longer were councilors to be elected, as provided by King William's charter of 1691.  Instead they were to be appointed by the Crown as in other royal provinces.  Judges and some other officers were also to be no longer chosen by the people.  Town meetings, hotbeds of sedition in the British view, were to be allowed only by permission of the governor, except for the performance of their routine functions.

Provincials regarded their charters as contracts which could be set aside only for cause duly proved before a court of competent jurisdiction.  Since they emanated not from Parliament but from the King, provincial opinion regarded them as quite outside the sphere of Parliament's authority.  The idea of converting the chartered colonies into royal provinces by act of Parliament had never before won favor even among the supporters of parliamentary supremacy.

A few liberals in Parliament vainly opposed the act.  The Bishop of St. Asaph declared, "The Americans have the same veneration for their Charters that we have for the magna charta."  The Duke of Grafton referred to the proposed changes as a "violation of the law of nature."  Whatever might be the correct theory of Parliament's relations to the colonies, statesmanship called for efforts at mutual understanding; but the majority was too much stirred to heed good counsel.

The next two statutes renewed the Quartering (Billeting) Act of 1765 and permitted the trial of royal officials in England on charges brought against them in the colonies.  In view of the fair trial given to the perpetrators of the Boston Massacre this Administration of Justice Act seemed insolent, and was in harsh contrast with the proposal to carry Americans to a less friendly locality for trial.

The fifth measure, the Quebec Act, was a consequence of the French and Indian War rather than of the friction with the colonies, but coming simultaneously with the other coercive acts and giving additional cause for discontent, the Americans classed it with them. The Treaty of Paris had promised that England would respect the religious liberty and legal customs of the French in Canada, and one purpose of the law was to carry out these pledges.

It also extended the boundaries of the Province of Quebec to include the Northwest. The Proclamation of 1763 had reserved this triangular area between the Ohio and Mississippi rivers as part of the Indian country. The few whites — French *habitants* and English traders — resident in the region had been left without government except such as might be exercised by the commander of the military forces. The union with Quebec now brought the region under the civil government of that province. The natural associations of the French residents, by race, religion, and trade, were with their kinsmen of the lower St. Lawrence.

However, the government of this Anglo-French province of Quebec was not representative, and its extension to the Mississippi and Ohio rivers tended to keep Englishmen from settling in the Northwest. The discouragement of English settlement in order to preserve the region for the fur trade was, in fact, an important purpose of the act. Scotch merchants of Montreal were rapidly gaining command over the trade and employed many of the French in the business.

The act disregarded the charter claims of Virginia, Massachusetts, and Connecticut to portions of the Northwest, and thwarted the plans of land speculators and promoters of projects of new colonies. These, it appeared, would have to be content with lands south of the Ohio, where the cordiality of the ministry towards the Vandalia project indicated that other grants might be made.

The religious prejudices of the Protestant inhabitants of the Atlantic colonies were aroused, moreover, by what could be interpreted as a plan to build up a strong Catholic province on their flank and in their rear.

If the Tea Party angered the British, the Coercive Acts —
"Intolerable Acts," the colonists called them — inflamed the
provincials even more. In Massachusetts Hutchinson was
replaced by General Thomas Gage, who as both civil and military
governor was to execute the new laws affecting that colony.
The radicals in their turn resolved to ignore the new government
and called for the election of a "provincial congress" to act as a
provisional government in planning resistance.

Whether this bold course would be supported by the other
colonies was the crucial question. Many of the moderates
thought that the quarrel should be ended by paying the East
India Company for the damage done to it, but the radicals would
not consent to this course, and they gained ground daily. The
popular movement brought the voteless workingmen of the
towns into union with the back-country people who clamored for
proportional representation in the assemblies, and led to the
meeting in several colonies of irregular bodies in which the common people were represented and began to influence the course
of events.

The radicals urged that the cause of Massachusetts was the
cause of all. The Boston Port Act was to go into effect June 1,
1774. The Virginia House of Burgesses set aside this day for
fasting and prayer. For this the governor dissolved the assembly. Some of the members then reassembled at the Raleigh
tavern and issued calls for a continental congress to consider the
"united interests of America," and for a convention in Virginia
to elect delegates. The choice of delegates to the First Continental Congress by every province but Georgia was the answer
to the question whether America would support Massachusetts.

The Congress assembled in Carpenters' Hall, Philadelphia, in
September, 1774. From only two or three colonies came delegates chosen by the assemblies; in others the choice was made
by "conventions" or irregular bodies composed with little attention to the legal right of the members to vote. The Congress
was fairly representative of colonial opinion, however, for it
included conservative as well as radical elements. Divergent
views had therefore to be reconciled if the body was to speak
with the "united voice of America."

The conservatives were led by Joseph Galloway, of Pennsyl-

vania. They hoped to formulate some plan of reconciliation
which would safeguard rights in future; and their program was
set out in the "Galloway Plan." It proposed a union of the
colonies quite like that contemplated by the Albany Plan of
twenty years before, with control over the common interests of
the colonies; but a new feature was the provision that no measure relating to such interests should become law without the
concurrence of Parliament and the general council of the colonies.
In essence this council was to be a third house of Parliament.

The Galloway Plan was a worthy effort in the direction of an
imperial constitution. Although cumbersome it might have
worked well enough to lead to something better; but it was
unacceptable to the radicals, who insisted that the British must
be forced to recognize the colonists' view of their rights. Consequently it was decided to draw up a Declaration of Rights and
Grievances as a kind of ultimatum.

The discussion of the contents of this Declaration showed the
divergence of view as to what American rights were. Some held
that Parliament was without legislative power over the colonies,
while others clung to the opinion that it had authority in matters
of general concern. Some ambiguity resulted from the attempt
to frame a statement which all could accept. In the end the
Declaration claimed all of the rights derived from "the immuta-
ble laws of nature, the principles of the English constitution, and
the several charters or compacts." Some Americans had long
maintained that even the navigation acts were not binding in
the colonies unless reënacted by their legislatures. This idea
seems to have been behind the provision of the Declaration which
denied the legislative supremacy of Parliament but promised
acquiescence in measures for the *bona-fide* regulation of trade.
External taxes were thus excluded, while the necessity was
recognized of some central body for controlling commerce.

In connection with the Declaration a demand was made for
the repeal of a number of laws which were held to contravene
colonial rights. A petition to the King was prepared looking
to the same end, and an appeal to British public opinion was
attempted through an Address to the People of England. No
petition was sent to Parliament, whose authority was now so
nearly repudiated. Canada was invited to make common cause

in an address to the inhabitants of Quebec.   Finally, in adjourning in October, the Congress resolved to reassemble in the following May in case the appeal for redress of grievances proved fruitless.

Another measure was intended to "put teeth" into the demand for justice.   This was the agreement known as the "Association." It revived and extended the non-importation agreements which had proved efficacious on former occasions, and threatened non-exportation to England and the West Indies after a year in case American demands were not heeded.   Members had great faith that commercial coercion would again win concessions.   A Maryland delegate believed that it would mean nothing less than bankruptcy for the English, while Richard Henry Lee declared that the same ship which carried the news of the Association to England would bring back redress.   To enforce the agreement a system of committees was to be organized throughout the colonies.

The efforts of the Congress seemed for a time likely to bring results.   Pitt, now Lord Chatham, commended the Declaration of Rights for "solidity of reason, force of sagacity, and wisdom of conclusion."   He hoped for some agreement, such as Galloway had outlined, which should define the powers of Parliament and the colonies respectively and prevent further controversy. Burke pleaded for a return to the old régime of the days before 1763.   Many merchants, alarmed at the prospect of a new interruption of trade, petitioned for such a modification of program as would avert that disaster.

The King, however, was determined not to yield, and an election showed that he had the support of the voters.   He refused to receive the petition of the Continental Congress.   A motion by Chatham for the withdrawal of the troops from Boston received only eighteen votes in the House of Lords.   Both houses by large majorities pledged their support to the King in putting down "rebellion," and in the course of the winter military and naval preparations were hurried forward.   Lord North, indeed, proposed to exempt from parliamentary taxation any province whose assembly would pledge itself to raise a stipulated sum for imperial purposes, but the offer, coming at the same time with the warlike preparations, was regarded by the provincials as an attempt to divide them.

Meantime, in America, party divisions crystallized, with the radicals, now called "Whigs," in the ascendant, especially in Massachusetts and Virginia. Conservatives began to fear that Whig plans must end in separation from England, and many who opposed the course of the British thought that such a cure would be worse than the disease. One part of these continued to act with the Whigs, still hoping for reconciliation. Another part believed that the Whig party was hopelessly under the influence of extremists, and sharing Hutchinson's opinions, became the party of the "Loyalists," or "Tories." It had a numerous following among the wealthy families in every colony who had social and political position and feared the rising power of the people. Many of the merchants in Massachusetts, New York, and Pennsylvania chose this side. The Quakers had strong Loyalist leanings, in part because peace was their creed. Even John Dickinson hesitated long enough to bring himself under suspicion of Toryism. The planters, on the contrary, were as a class moderate Whigs, and in Virginia worked well with the radical leaders from the western counties. Farther south Loyalism was strong in the back settlements. The old conflict between coast and interior caused the frontiersmen to lean to the side opposite to that taken by their antagonists.

Taking the colonies as a whole the Loyalists were numerous and of the most prominent class, but they agreed only in fearing that resistance to England might be carried too far. Lack of a positive program reduced their weight to the minimum. On the other hand the Whigs were active and well-knit. Their local committees suppressed the utterance of Loyalist opinions and rigidly enforced the Association by social ostracism, and if need be by physical violence.

The Whigs understood that the unyielding attitude of the King might lead to armed resistance as their own next step. The winter of 1774-1775 was therefore spent in collecting military supplies and drilling the patriot militia. They had no intention of starting hostilities, but by the spring of 1775 the situation was such that conflict was inevitable. Lord Dunmore, governor of Virginia, almost came to blows with the colonial militia, while Gage in Massachusetts found the authority of his government confined substantially to Boston.

In the gray light of early morn on April 19 a detachment of red-coated soldiers was in motion along one of the rude lanes serving as roads which led northwest from Boston. Word had come to Gage that the Whigs, led by Samuel Adams, were collecting arms and ammunition at Concord village. To prevent mischief, the governor had resolved to seize these stores, and, if possible, to arrest Adams. Hoping to accomplish his purpose by surprise, the troops had marched all night; but from rustics seized along the way they learned that the countryside was apprised of their approach. Now, as they entered Lexington through which their road led, they found upon the green about the meeting-house a company of provincial militia drawn up as if to dispute their passage.

LEXINGTON AND CONCORD.

Ordering his men not to fire unless the word was given, Major Pitcairn rode towards the Americans and commanded them to disperse. In view of the great disparity of numbers, Captain John Parker, commander of the militia, likewise gave the order to withdraw. The provincials were in the act of obeying when suddenly a single shot rang out. An American may have fired it, or in the confusion a red-coat may have mistaken Pitcairn's command. None the less, this shot, American or British, was the opening gun of the Revolution. Britain and her subjects had drifted into a war from which thirteen colonies were to emerge independent states.

After a brief engagement the troops proceeded to Concord where they overcame further resistance, but their return to Boston was converted into a rout by the Americans who lined the road and fired from the cover of the stone walls and trees.  Gage made light of these encounters in his report to the British War Department.  Not so the Americans.  The news of Lexington and Concord spread with amazing rapidity, and soon all of New England was represented in the force gathered at Cambridge for the siege of Boston.  Throughout the colonies the spirit of revolt was unleashed.  Patriots seized the reins of government and royal officials found that their power had vanished almost over night.  Instead of the redress of grievances hoped for, the Second Continental Congress found the country in tumult and war already begun.

## SELECT BIBLIOGRAPHY FOR CHAPTER VII

Channing, *United States*, III, covers the years 1761–1789.  Howard, *Preliminaries of the Revolution*, and Becker, *The Eve of the Revolution*, deal with the years preceding the resort to arms.  Van Tyne, McIlwain, and Egerton (see Bibliography for Chapter V) are indispensable for this chapter. Schlesinger, *The Colonial Merchants and the American Revolution*, is an excellent critical interpretation from the economic point of view.  A brief sketch by the same writer is *New Viewpoints*, chap. 7.

The most satisfactory history of the whole revolutionary era is Fisher, *The Struggle for American Independence*.  Fiske, *The American Revolution*, is rather popular and uncritical.  Excellent histories by Englishmen are those of Trevelyan, *The American Revolution*, and Lecky, *England in the Eighteenth Century*.  The chapters from the latter relating to the quarrel between England and the colonies have been published as *The American Revolution* (edited by J. A. Woodburn).

The *American Statesmen* series contains Tyler, *Patrick Henry*, Hosmer, *Samuel Adams*, and Morse, *John Adams*.  A standard life of Dickinson is Stillé, *Life and Times of John Dickinson*.  A new and adequate life of Otis is badly needed.

Lincoln, *The Revolutionary Movement in Pennsylvania*, gives some insight into the division of opinion in the colonies.

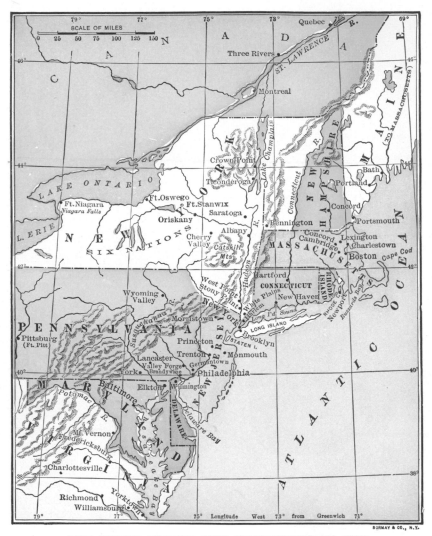

THE NORTH DURING THE REVOLUTIONARY WAR

# CHAPTER VIII

## THE WAR FOR INDEPENDENCE

The Congress assembled May 10, 1775. Few if any members desired independence as the goal of the struggle in which the country had become involved. Two months before, Franklin declared that he had never heard a word from any one in favor of independence. John Jay said later that the first talk of separation was heard in the autumn of 1775.

In explanation of resistance to a King to whom they professed loyalty the Congress issued a Declaration of the Causes and Necessity of Taking up Arms. This document placed all the blame upon the ministers. "We are reduced to the alternative of chusing an unconditional submission to the tyranny of irritated ministers, or resistance by force. . . . The latter is our choice. . . . We have counted the cost of this contest, and find nothing so dreadful as voluntary slavery. . . ." In the hope of retaining the moral support of English Whigs, who in Parliament had "nobly and strenuously asserted the justice of our cause," the Declaration assured them that "we mean not to dissolve that union which has so long and so happily subsisted between us," and concluded with a prayer that the Ruler of the Universe may "dispose our adversaries to reconciliation on reasonable terms." Had the British government at this time shown the conciliatory disposition which it did after Burgoyne's defeat (see page 154), it can hardly be doubted that separation would have been avoided.

Pending its response Congress did not shrink from military measures. It took control over the army at Cambridge, appointed officers, and called upon the provincial governments to raise arms and men. The conditions of American life had not developed tested military men among the Whigs, and Congress was compelled to rely upon civilians as officers. Henry Knox, who served with the artillery throughout the war, was a young

141

Boston bookseller.  Nathanael Greene, who won a reputation second only to that of Washington, was a Rhode Island blacksmith who was expelled from the Society of Friends because of his eagerness to fight his country's battles.  Washington, notwithstanding the fact that he had served with distinction in the French and Indian War, and that his military experience was quite as extensive as that of any of the Whig leaders, was himself essentially a civilian.  In choosing him as commander-in-

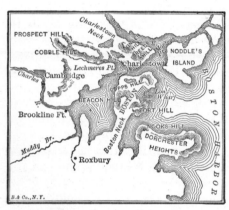

BUNKER HILL AND BOSTON.

chief Congress could not foresee that he was destined to win fame as one of the great commanders of modern times.  Indeed, his appointment was due in part to the fear that jealousy would prevent southern Whigs from serving wholeheartedly under a northern leader. Considerations of expediency, and faith in Washington's integrity and judgment, moved Congress quite as much as confidence in his military capacity.  As it proved, his moral qualities quite as much as his generalship made his name an anchor for the hopes of his countrymen in the dark days of the war.

Events now moved rapidly.  Before Washington could reach Cambridge the Battle of Bunker Hill had been fought.  In the middle of June the Americans tried to force Gage from Boston by planting batteries on high ground in Charleston.  The position was on a peninsula, separated from Boston by Charles River, and the Americans might have been forced to retire by the simple and safe expedient of threatening their single narrow path of retreat along the isthmus.  Gage preferred to show his belief in the superiority of the British regulars by sending Sir William Howe to take the position by assault.  This was accomplished, but only after two repulses, and then only because of the exhaustion of the ammunition of the Americans.  They lost less than half as many men as the British, and "all the advantages of victory were on their side."

Blundering generalship marked the British conduct of the war in its early stages. Gage, and Howe who soon succeeded him, rested inactive while Washington organized the patriot army, drilled the men, taught them the necessity of discipline, and made ready to occupy Dorchester Heights, south of Boston. When he took this position, early in March, 1776, Howe was at the mercy of his guns and agreed to evacuate the city.

Thus early in the war New England was rid of hostile troops. During the winter the Americans had directed a movement against Canada. The way for this expedition had been opened in May, 1775, by the pioneers of Vermont, who, under the lead of Ethan Allen and Benedict Arnold, attacked and captured the forts at Ticonderoga and Crown Point. These posts commanded the valley in which lay Lakes George and Champlain, the natural pathway to the St. Lawrence. If Montreal and Quebec could be taken, the patriots hoped that the Canadians would join in the war, and that Great Britian would soon be forced to concede satisfactory terms of peace.

Late in the year a force under Richard Montgomery followed the Lake Champlain route and succeeded in capturing Montreal (November, 1775). Another force under Arnold marched against Quebec by way of Maine, suffering great hardships in the wintry woods. Uniting before Quebec the two commands made an unsuccessful assault, in which Montgomery fell (December 31). In spite of reënforcements Quebec could not be taken, and Montreal, useless without it, was abandoned.

The Americans kept the foe on the defensive in the North during the first year. In the South the British made an attempt against the Carolinas, expecting help from the Loyalists of the interior. A body of North Carolina Tories set out for Wilmington, expecting to meet the British fleet there, but they were intercepted and defeated at Moore's Creek Bridge by a Whig force. In June came a futile attack on Charleston. Disdaining the tedious process of siege, the fleet tried to batter down the log fort on an island in the channel; but the solid shot buried themselves harmlessly in the soft palmetto logs, while the fire from the fort inflicted severe damage on the vessels.

## The Movement for Independence

The first year's fighting was inconclusive. Apart from the capture of Boston neither side had won a notable success. Yet the situation had altered greatly. The appeal of Congress for reconciliation had made far less impression upon the King than the news of the Battle of Bunker Hill. His answer to both was to proclaim that the Americans were rebels and to forbid commercial intercourse with them. Parliament followed with an act blockading the provincial ports. Many English Whigs opposed a warlike program. Even some of the army officers had no heart for the task of coercion which was assigned to them. For the time being, however, the King had his way, and ere long was hiring German soldiers to reduce his American subjects to obedience.

As the winter of 1775–1776 passed the hope of reconciliation grew faint; more and more the logic of events forced steps which could hardly be reconciled with the theory of civil war. The last vestiges of British authority disappeared even in the royal colonies, leaving control in the hands of the revolutionary organizations. These served as temporary or provisional governments, but their status was too indefinite to be satisfactory. Under the advice of Congress province after province adopted governments of a more formal kind, based on the authority of the people, and disarmed those who refused to join in the effort against England. In March, 1776, Congress decided to appeal to France for aid. The cessation of commercial intercourse with England necessitated new trade relations, and in April, in disregard of the navigation acts, colonial ports were opened to vessels of all nations.

In spite of the widening breach the tide of opinion set but doubtfully towards independence. In this crisis of indecision Thomas Paine, a recent immigrant from England, wrote *Common Sense*. "Reconciliation is . . . a fallacious dream. . . . Everything that is right or natural pleads for separation. The blood of the slain, the weeping voice of nature cries, ''Tis time to part.' Even the distance at which the Almighty hath placed England and America is a strong and natural proof that the authority of the one over the other was never the design of Heaven." . . .

"Freedom hath been hunted round the globe. Asia and Africa have long expelled her. Europe regards her like a stranger, and England hath given her warning to depart. O! receive the fugitive and prepare in time an asylum for mankind." Published in pamphlet form and scattered broadcast — a copy for every three families within three months — this bold and incisive argument for independence was the seed of "a new method of thinking" in the minds of hesitating men.

In the early months of 1776 there was evidence that the southern colonies were ripe for the change. By May Congress had gone so far as to recommend that each colony form a government based on the assumption that all authority under the Crown was at an end. The provincial convention of Virginia had already in this same month drawn up a state constitution, at the same time instructing the Virginia delegates in Congress to propose a resolution of independence. Such a resolution was offered on June 7 by Richard Henry Lee. Still the moderates hung back and the vote on the resolution was postponed, but the radicals were able to secure the appointment of a committee to draft a declaration.[1] While the committee worked the friends of independence strove to secure a favorable vote on Lee's resolution, and on July 1 it received the support of nine state delegations. On a later vote assent was unanimous.

The formal declaration reported by the committee was adopted on July 4. This justly famous document, prepared by Jefferson, falls logically into three parts: The first sets forth principles which are regarded as self-evident — that men are by nature endowed with certain inalienable rights; that governments are instituted to preserve these rights; that governments derive their just powers from the consent of the governed; that the governed may alter or abolish their government if it proves destructive of the ends for which it was established.

These ideas did not originate with Jefferson. They had been developed by John Locke nearly a century before (see page 86). No doctrines were more familiar to Americans in the revolutionary era, and Jefferson merely gave them a new application. They were not the principles to which appeal had been made

---

[1] The committee consisted of Jefferson, Franklin, John Adams, Roger Sherman, all radicals, and Robert R. Livingston, a moderate.

during the controversy with Parliament. For a dozen years the British constitution had been invoked in vain in defense of American rights. Now resort was had to natural rights, which were conceived of as above all constitutions.

The second part of the Declaration enumerated the acts of the King which were destructive of the purposes for which governmental relations existed between the Crown and the colonies. The Declaration differed from earlier statements of grievances in laying the blame for infractions of American rights upon the King; he, it asserted, has done the wrongful acts, although in some of them he "has conspired with others," *i.e.*, Parliament.

The third part, or conclusion, is that "these united colonies are, and of right ought to be, free and independent states." Reduced to a single statement, the Declaration meant that the King, having repeatedly violated his "compact" with his American subjects, had forfeited his claim to their allegiance.

The Declaration was received with wild rejoicings, "as though," said Samuel Adams, "it was a decree promulgated from heaven." America had turned a sharp corner. Hesitation was no longer possible. From this moment every man was either a Patriot or a Loyalist. And from this moment the Loyalists suffered much at the hands of the Patriots. Many were driven into exile in Canada, the West Indies, or England, losing their immovable property through acts of confiscation. Others joined the hostile armies or took refuge within the British lines upon the occupation of New York and other coast towns. In modern warfare peaceable resident subjects of an enemy country are usually protected in their personal and property rights. In a revolution which divides a people against itself, such treatment is not likely to be accorded to the members of the losing party, even when noncombatants.

But it cannot be said that the conduct of the Loyalists was inoffensive. Even in Boston, which was the very hotbed of the Revolution, they boldly promised some "fine hangings" when the King's men came back. Their aristocratic instincts provoked many a sneering comment on the humble origin of continental officers. Throughout the country many of them gave all the aid they dared to give to the King's cause. In the later years of the war bands of Indians and Tories from Canada returned to burn, plunder, and scalp on the frontiers of New York and Pennsylvania. Other Loyalists took part with British sailors in raids upon the coast. The fairest-minded Americans, such as Franklin and Washington, were inflamed against the Tories, and it is hardly surprising that they were generally regarded as traitors. "A Loyalist," said the Patriots, "is a thing whose head is in England, whose body is in America, and its neck ought to be stretched."

Besides forcing a sharp cleavage between Patriots and Loyalists, the Declaration made it much easier to obtain foreign aid. France, especially, was now glad to help since success promised the break-up of the empire of her great rival. Although not ready yet to lend aid openly lest it involve her in war, she did not hesitate to do so secretly, while protesting to Great Britain that she was both neutral and friendly. Large quantities of munitions were "sold" to a company formed for the express purpose of turning them over on credit to the agents of Congress. Under this disguise the French government supplied the "rebels." [1]

The Declaration also altered the military problem. Now that America aimed at independence England was certain to put forth much more vigorous effort. Could the United States withstand the might of a power three times as populous, and ranking first among European states in wealth and naval strength? To their advantage was the fact that the foe must be the aggressor; if they could hold out until she tired of the struggle, they would win. Their people would fight on their own soil, protected by a broad ocean across which all hostile forces must be transported.

A modern well-knit nation with a population equal to that of the states in 1776 (approximately two and a half million whites) could command an army of nearly two hundred and fifty thousand men. The Whig population alone must have included about one hundred and seventy-five thousand men of military age. But the states were only in the first stages of union, and there existed neither the strong central authority nor the public sentiment necessary to make the best use of the very considerable potential resources. The only centers of real authority were the new state governments. Congress had neither the power to draft men nor to lay taxes. For filling the ranks it relied upon the uncertain

[1] International law permits the sale of munitions to belligerents by the *citizens* of neutral countries, but not by neutral *governments*.

process of volunteering and upon quotas of state militia, assigned to service for short periods; for funds, upon contributions by the states, loans, and issues of paper money. Even the state governments, being in the experimental stage, dared not risk the odium which heavy taxation might bring upon them. Under such conditions we need not wonder that Washington's army never rose above one sixth of its potential strength and was often less than one twentieth of it.

The personnel of the armies shifted so rapidly that, with the inexperience of the officers, it was difficult to create a fighting machine which could meet European regulars and professional soldiers on equal terms. A great debt of gratitude is due the Europeans — Lafayette, Steuben, Kalb, Kosciusko, and others — who gave their skill to the work of organizing the army, and to the governments which made loans. Without aid from abroad, especially that which France gave, and the diversion of British strength which came when war was renewed in Europe, it is quite possible that the resistance of the Americans would gradually have been crushed.

## CAMPAIGNS AFTER INDEPENDENCE

One of the darkest periods of the war came in the campaign which followed the Declaration of Independence. At the moment of its passage General Howe was preparing, with an army larger than the American commander ever had under him, to drive Washington from the vicinity of New York, whither he had transferred his troops after the evacuation of Boston. Howe easily succeeded, for his men outnumbered the Americans four to one. But he let slip several opportunities to crush his opponents. For example, after defeating them on Long Island in August, he neglected to cut off their retreat to the mainland. One by one the American positions on the lower Hudson were taken, however, as the British carried out their plan of securing control of the Hudson Valley in the hope of cutting off New England from the other colonies.

Autumn found Washington slowly retreating across New Jersey towards Philadelphia with the foe in pursuit. The patriot army was dwindling, because the men were discouraged, and it was impossible to get recruits to replace the soldiers whose terms of enlistment were expiring. Howe did not press Washington to battle, for he did not wish to shed blood to hasten the end of what appeared to be a dying cause. He was, in fact, a critic of his country's conduct towards America, and his object now was to save the colonies for England without the loss of their loyalty and affection. He preferred the olive branch to the sword for the work in hand, and proclaimed the royal pardon for all who would take an oath of allegiance. By December thousands of the inhabitants of the middle states had made their peace, and Washington wrote on the twentieth that "ten days more will put an end to the existence of our army."

When winter came Howe placed most of his army in quarters at New York, scattering a few thousand men, mostly German mercenaries, in garrisons across New Jersey. He planned to place a garrison in Philadelphia. Meantime the end of his line rested on the Delaware at Trenton in an exposed position, but safe enough, in his judgment, from the insignificant force with which Washington had crossed to the Pennsylvania side of the river.

Something was desperately needed to reanimate the hope and courage of the Americans and refill the thinning ranks. That something was a military success. Washington "in very truth snatched victory out of the jaws of defeat" when he recrossed the Delaware on Christmas night, while he still had a force of four or five thousand, and surprised the Hessians at Trenton. By this movement he took a thousand prisoners. When Lord Cornwallis, Howe's lieutenant, took the field, Washington avoided battle and then bewildered him by striking another unexpected blow against the garrison at Princeton (January 3, 1777). Something like panic came upon the foe at this, and Howe drew in his lines to New York City, leaving Washington in possession of the State of New Jersey.

The Trenton-Princeton campaign "forever established Washington's reputation as a soldier." Yet even after this success the Americans might have been crushed at almost any time during the winter. Washington wrote in March: "If the enemy do not move, it will be a miracle. Nothing but ignorance of our numbers and situation can protect us." But Howe kept his soldiers in their comfortable winter quarters and by his negligence allowed the Patriots to weather the crisis.

Paine again brought his trenchant pen into action in the evil days before Trenton. His new pamphlet, *The Crisis*, beginning with the words "These are the times that try men's souls," along with Washington's victories, revived the spirits of the Patriots and swelled the number of recruits. When the army left its quarters in the spring of 1777, it counted about eleven thousand men.

Howe's great ambition now was to occupy Philadelphia. The capture of the city where Congress held its sessions he hoped would demoralize the government and discourage the insurgents. In September he defeated Washington at the approaches to the city and entered in triumph. By dividing his forces, however, he so weakened the army at New York that it was unable to aid in what the British War Office regarded as the main campaign of 1777. This was an invasion from Canada by way of Lake Champlain, to gain control of the Lake Champlain-Hudson River line, isolate New England, and crush the divided enemy piecemeal.

An attempt had been made along this line in 1776 when Howe was on the lower Hudson; but the forces employed were inadequate for the purpose and had been beaten back to Canada by Arnold's men. For 1777 the War Office planned that General John Burgoyne should enter New York by the Lake Champlain route, while Colonel Barry St. Leger led a secondary movement of Loyalist refugees and Indians down the Mohawk to unite with Burgoyne near Albany. Additional troops were to be detached from Howe's New York army to support Burgoyne.

Fort Stanwix on the upper Mohawk barred St. Leger's passage, and the German Whigs of the Mohawk Valley defeated him at the Battle of Oriskany. Deserted by his Indians and baffled before Fort Stanwix, he returned to Canada. When Burgoyne reached the rendezvous, St. Leger, of course, failed to appear. A detachment sent into Vermont for supplies was roughly handled by Scotch-Irish militiamen under Colonel John Stark at Bennington, and Howe, preoccupied with his Philadelphia campaign, sent no supporting forces. Pushing slowly into hostile territory, farther and farther from his Canadian base, while the enemy gathered in increasing numbers, Burgoyne at length found himself almost surrounded. He tried to fight his way out, but several engagements failed to relieve his situation, and on October 17 the British cause sustained its severest blow thus far in the surrender of his entire army to General Horatio Gates, at Saratoga.

Burgoyne's surrender is rightly regarded as the turning point in the war. Creasy includes it in his list of fifteen decisive battles of the world's history. The frustration of the carefully laid plan of campaign gave the Americans for the first time grounds for enthusiastic confidence in the outcome of the struggle. Most important of all, it led directly to the French alliance.

## THE FRENCH ALLIANCE

The secret aid which France had been giving the Americans has already been described. Many of the French people felt deep sympathy for the English colonists in their struggle with the British monarchy. Already French thought was permeated with the political philosophy of Rousseau, who carried the doctrines of natural rights even further than Locke. These ideas were undermining the French monarchy and preparing the way for the great revolutionary outburst of 1789. The kinship between the ideals of the Americans and those of the French liberals was too close to be overlooked.

The French government also "tingled with joy at American victories," but not from sympathy with American ideals. The Count de Vergennes, minister of foreign affairs in the government of Louis XVI, was a statesman of the old school of crafty diplomacy. He saw in the American revolt an opportunity to weaken the imperial power which had recently vanquished France in the contest for domination in India and North America. Britain would be a less formidable rival in the future if shorn of her American possessions. Especially would this be true if, to reward those who aided them in winning independence, the new states diverted their valuable commerce from British to French channels and looked to France for guidance in international politics.

After the passage of the Declaration of Independence Congress appealed to both France and Spain for alliances. In France Franklin joined Silas Deane, the original envoy. The new

American agent instantly won the heart of all classes; social Paris lost its head over him, finding something almost hypnotic in the character of the simple, unaffected man who kept his serenity and balance amid the artificialities of the world's gayest capital. Official Paris was less easily moved. Before committing his government openly Vergennes wished the revolutionists to show by some important success in the field that they possessed sufficient military strength to promise victory in case of an alliance; and to give additional assurance he besought Spain to join in the war. But Spain feared the effect of the example of revolt in the English colonies upon the loyalty of her own. Hatred of England induced her to give Congress some secret aid, like France, in the way of loans, but she would not make a treaty of alliance.

Spain's designs were, in fact, contrary to the interests of the United States. If she went to war with England, she hoped to regain the Floridas. Congress did not object to this, provided Americans were allowed to use the Mississippi River. Navigation of the river was a vital matter for the settlements which were just beginning west of the Alleghanies, since they had no other outlet for their marketable produce. But Spain in possession of Florida would hold both banks and enforce her policy of excluding foreigners from her lands and waters. In this matter she made it plain that no concession need be expected. Moreover, although the United States desired the Mississippi as a western boundary, Spain interpreted the Proclamation of 1763 and the Quebec Act as having definitely extinguished all claims of the English colonies to lands beyond the mountains. In her opinion these regions were crown lands subject to conquest by any enemy of England.

Vergennes' desire for Spain's aid delayed the success of Franklin's efforts until news came of Burgoyne's surrender. Predicting that England would offer liberal concessions which America must accept unless France came to her help, that clever diplomat now urged Vergennes to espouse the cause of independence at once. Vergennes, regarding the reconciliation of England and the colonies as one of the worst evils that could befall France, decided to wait on Spain no longer, and early in February, 1778, he concluded two treaties with the United States.

One of these treaties dealt with commerce, and provided that each country should open its ports freely to the vessels of the other. The second was a treaty of alliance. By it France agreed to make common cause against England until the independence of the United States was recognized, and renounced all pretensions to territory on the mainland of North America. In return the United States promised to defend the French possessions in the West Indies "forever." Neither country was to conclude peace or truce with the enemy without the consent of the other.

Something more than a year after this Spain also declared war on England, but not as the ally of the United States. The conflict in the interests of the two countries still kept them apart. Vergennes confined his pledges to Spain to matters relating to Europe. His most important engagement was to aid her in recovering Gibraltar, which England had held since 1714. Despite this precaution Vergennes soon found himself in a delicate situation because of the rivalry of his two allies. He could not support the ambitions of either beyond the letter of his treaty obligations without incurring the charge of partiality. The embarrassment due to this three-cornered arrangement reached its climax during the peace negotiations.

## CAMPAIGNS OF 1778

While the treaties with France were being arranged Washington's soldiers were enduring a terrible winter at Valley Forge near Philadelphia. "As the soldiers marched . . . to their winter quarters," says John Fiske, "their route could be traced on the snow by the blood that oozed from bare, frost-bitten feet." In the midst of plenty the men starved and froze because Congress could not command supplies with its depreciated paper money, nor wagons and teams to bring in clothing, shoes, and stockings. Howe, in Philadelphia, paid gold and silver for the farmers' crops, and even "Patriots" sometimes yielded to the temptation to sell in the better market. Although the common soldier has been deservedly praised for bearing his misfortunes with heroic fortitude, and laboring "barefoot . . . through mud and cold with a song in his mouth," the strain on the morale of the men was terrific, and nearly a fifth of them deserted. An efficient government would have prevented most of the suffering at Valley Forge, but Americans had yet to learn that lesson. The spirit of disaffection penetrated even to Congress and led to an intrigue which threatened to displace Washington as commander-in-chief.

The news of the French treaties came as an offset to the depression of this winter of horrors. As Franklin had predicted, the English government was ready at last to pardon the rebellion, forego taxation, restore the Massachusetts charter, consider colonial representation in Parliament — to concede any and all of the demands which the colonists had made previous to declaring independence. Even George III exclaimed that he who held the taxing of America to be justifiable was "more fit for Bedlam than a seat" in Parliament. Rockingham, Burke, and many other Whigs were ready to grant independence rather than continue the war, but recognition of independence at this juncture savored too much of a retreat in the face of the Gallic peril to be generally acceptable. On the other hand, the time had passed for holding the Americans within the empire by promises of reform. The prospect of independence was too alluring. Besides, the treaty with France amounted to an engagement that the United States would never restore the King's sovereignty as the price of peace. When therefore the royal commissioners came to Philadelphia to offer peace on terms which would have been welcomed two years earlier, Congress curtly refused to enter into negotiations.

The entry of France into the war drew the attention of England for the time being from her lesser antagonist. Troops were withdrawn from the mainland for the defense of the British West Indies, and the approach of a French fleet under Count d'Estaing threatened to cut off supplies by sea for the army in Philadelphia, necessitating the evacuation of that place and the concentration of forces at New York and Newport.

The withdrawal of the enemy from Philadelphia gave Washington one of his rare opportunities to seize the offensive. Following Sir Henry Clinton, who had succeeded Howe, as he led his army across New Jersey, he chose a favorable moment for attack at Monmouth (June 28). The cowardly insubordination of General Charles Lee — the "damned poltroon" Washington called him — who retreated when ordered to attack, cost the American leader what should have been an easy and telling victory.

Still Washington hoped with the coöperation of the French fleet to drive the British from the port cities during the summer. D'Estaing, however, was a soldier, not a sailor, and notwithstanding the superiority of his fleet, respect for the seamanship of Admiral Howe, his adversary, made him timid. Failure of coördination between the land and naval forces brought Washington's great expectations to nought. Eventually the Newport garrison was withdrawn, but the British hold on New York remained unshaken to the end of the war.

These operations of 1778 were the last major movements in the northern states. Thereafter the British contented themselves with raids which harried the countryside and plundered the towns within reach of New York. Such actions had little if any effect upon the outcome of the war, but aroused great bitterness. Connecticut especially was the scene of such raids, and those who suffered were afterwards given lands in the "Western Reserve," south of Lake Erie (see page 188).

This same season of 1778 witnessed a notable campaign in the Northwest. The settlement of Kentucky had begun in 1774. Checked by Indian hostilities efforts were renewed in 1775, when Daniel Boone, as agent for a group of speculators under the name of the Transylvania Company, cut a wagon path through the timber from Cumberland Gap to Boonesboro. The same year saw the planting of several neighboring "stations." The Transylvania Company collapsed because it could not win the approval of the government, but the scanty population of Kentucky succeeded in weathering the storm of Indian attacks which came with the Revolution, and became the first detached nucleus of population west of the mountains.

The Kentucky settlements were organized as a county of Virginia, for when independence was declared, that state reasserted her claim to western lands under the Charter of 1609. Left nevertheless to their own devices, the pioneers clung to their homes with dogged tenacity and struck blow for blow against their red foes. The pioneer period in Kentucky was a heroic age, and the story of the struggle of its people with the savages is a true epic. At last one of the leaders, George Rogers Clark, perceived that there could be no end to this kind of warfare so long as the British held the forts of the Northwest. From them the Indians were supplied with arms and incited to go against the border, not only in Kentucky, but in Pennsylvania and the West Virginia region. Clark therefore formed the bold project of carrying the war into the enemy's country.

As Virginia claimed the Northwest, Clark applied to the government of that state instead of to Congress. Receiving a commission to raise volunteers in the western counties, he gathered about two hundred men, descended the Ohio, and marched overland from a point near its mouth to the group of old French towns near Kaskaskia on the Illinois side of the Mississippi. Here, as at most of the posts, only "the flicker of a red flag" showed that the land was British. No garrison held the fort, for as a measure of economy the French villagers had been formed into a local militia. It appears that they were secretly prepared to give the Virginians a friendly reception; at any rate they were easily won to the American side by the news that France and the United States were allies. Through their connivance with their kinsmen at Vincennes on the Wabash, that post was also surrendered to Clark's men.

When the news of these happenings, which occurred in midsummer, reached Colonel Henry Hamilton, lieutenant-governor of Canada in command at Detroit, he led in person a counter expedition for the recovery of the posts. He retook Vincennes without difficulty, and there waited for the end of winter before moving on Kaskaskia. But Clark, like a good soldier, struck first. Crossing the flooded prairies in February, 1779, he caught Hamilton off his guard and compelled him to surrender, sending him and his men to Virginia as prisoners of war. Hamilton was particularly hated by the frontiersmen, who called him the "Haar buyer," because they believed that he paid the savages for bringing in scalps. It is probable that he and other British officers enjoined their red allies to kill only in actual fighting, to spare noncombatants, and to scalp none but dead men. But the use of Indians by either combatant was certain to entail barbarities. The futility of humane exhortations to such warriors was exposed by Burke in the House of Commons

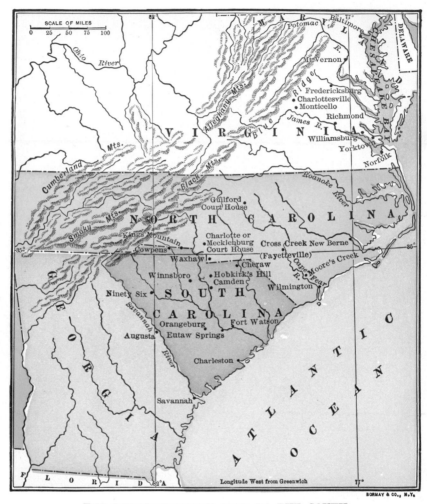

THE REVOLUTIONARY WAR IN THE SOUTH

with fine satire : "My gentle lions, my humane bears, my tender-hearted hyenas, go forth! But I exhort you, as you are Christians and members of civilized society, to take care not to hurt any man, woman, or child!"

Clark was never able to muster sufficient strength to attack Detroit. On the other hand, the British failed to recover their lost posts. Congress caused some demonstrations to be made against Detroit from Fort Pitt, and while never able to send out an effective expedition, checked the equally feeble British operations. Possession by the Americans was not mentioned in the peace negotiations, but may have been a silent factor in the decision of England to concede the demand for the Mississippi boundary. Of greater influence, probably, was the desire of the ministry to regain America's friendship.

## THE WAR IN THE SOUTH

By the close of 1778 the British were preparing a new offensive, this time in the South. With the aid of the Loyalists they hoped to overrun the southern states and recover at least a part of the revolted territory. Savannah was taken before the year ended. Little headway was made in 1779, but with the coming of fresh troops under Clinton in 1780 the march of events became swift and dramatic. Clinton laid siege to Charleston, while Banastre Tarleton, colonel of dragoons, by dashing cavalry attacks kept all American forces at a distance. Charleston surrendered in May. The British were elated, and Clinton called confidently on "every good man" to join the King's forces in the effort to "reëstablish peace and good government." In August the chief American force in South Carolina, under Gates, to whom Burgoyne had surrendered, was badly defeated at Camden by inferior numbers. Gates, whose incapacity was by this time patent, with the remnant of his army dared not stay his flight until he had put the safe distance of two hundred miles between himself and the foe. Then regaining a degree of courage he reported that he had "proceeded with all possible dispatch" to a point where he could reorganize his forces.

Events in the North added to the gloom. Clinton moved by sea from Charleston to New York, and Washington dared not detach troops to aid the southern states lest he seize the Hudson Valley. Then came Arnold's treason. Arnold, the victim of factional malignancy, had suffered rebuke for certain trivial offenses. He nevertheless retained Washington's confidence; but in the bitterness of his sense of injustice he abused this confidence by asking and receiving the command at West Point with the purpose of betraying this key to the valley to Clinton. When the plot was discovered, he fled to the enemy, returning in 1781 with British troops to share in the fighting in Virginia.

Southern Patriots were almost in despair after Camden; they fled to the mountains and swamps; but they kept up an irregular warfare under leaders like Thomas Sumter, Francis Marion, and Andrew Pickens. The British, moving with artillery and trains of baggage wagons, were hampered by unbridged streams, trackless forests, and bewildering mountains, while a few hundred farmers, accustomed to fighting from behind trees and rocks, could assemble hastily, without uniforms, baggage, or cannon, strike a blow, and as quickly disperse.

Such was the stroke delivered at King's Mountain, in October. Cornwallis, the victor of Camden, now preparing to conquer North Carolina, sent Major Patrick Ferguson to recruit Loyalists in the back counties. Not far away were the Whig pioneers of the upper Tennessee country. These, joining with their friends east of the mountains, suddenly beset Ferguson's force and almost destroyed it.

The struggle between Patriots and Loyalists in the South in 1779 and 1780 was the most ruthless phase of the war. Loyalists taken with arms in their hands were treated, not as prisoners of war, but as traitors. The Loyalists retaliated whenever possible. The passionate hatred of former neighbors knew no bounds. Regular officers on both sides sought in vain to restrain their followers. After King's Mountain the victors executed several prisoners and spared not even the dead body of the opposing leader.

The check at King's Mountain delayed Cornwallis and gave the Whigs time to collect men and leaders for more vigorous resistance when he resumed his advance towards North Carolina in 1781. Nathanael Greene, by Washington's choice the successor of the incompetent Gates, was now in command in the

South, with Daniel Morgan as his chief subordinate. In January Morgan, attacked at Cowpens, showed himself more than a match for Tarleton. Then he joined Greene, and their combined forces fell back across North Carolina as Cornwallis advanced farther and farther from his base. When Greene thought Cornwallis sufficiently weakened, he turned upon him at Guilford Courthouse (March 15), and although beaten, inflicted such losses that Cornwallis retired to Wilmington on the coast.

This campaign showed the fundamental weakness of the British plans. Operating from the coast towns, each step forward necessitated the detachment of men to hold the country and cover communications. The forces available were never adequate for war on the scale attempted, and each advance sooner or later reached a point where the Americans were able to check it if not to inflict defeat. By the end of the summer of 1781 the enemy held only Charleston and Wilmington in the South.

The feebleness of England's efforts may not be understood unless one bears in mind her growing absorption in the European situation. In 1780 Russia, Denmark, and Sweden joined in an "Armed Neutrality League," menacing her with a general war unless she modified her practices towards neutral commerce. International law was still in a nebulous state, and the rights of neutrals were in dispute. England with her great navy made her own rules, much to the injury of other nations. The Dutch suffered from seizures of French goods on their carrying vessels, and contended that "free ships make free goods." On their part they harbored American war vessels and allowed their West Indian colonies to become the base for supplying the United States with munitions. These mutual injuries led to war between England and the Dutch Republic in 1781.

Thus by 1781 the formidable array of maritime states either actually at war or threatening war with Great Britain almost counterbalanced the sea power which was her chief reliance, and sea power was about to decide the war in America. "Nothing without naval supremacy," declared the Count de Rochambeau, as he embarked for the United States with new land forces. Washington recognized the same fact independently at about the same time. While he planned to attack Clinton in New York with the aid of Rochambeau's fresh army, his watchful eye, following the campaign in the South, perceived the opportunity for the master stroke.

Greene was in South Carolina, and Cornwallis, now in Virginia, had been chasing the "boy," as he contemptuously called the Marquis de Lafayette, commanding the Americans there.   It was the old game of futile pursuit, and ended with Cornwallis's retirement to Yorktown on the narrow strip of land between the James and York rivers.   If Count de Grasse, the French Admiral in the West Indies, would bring his fleet to the Chesapeake, while Washington and Rochambeau came down from New York, Cornwallis would be caught in a trap.

De Grasse reached the Bay on August 30, in time to drive off the British fleet which sought to keep open egress for Cornwallis by water.   The land forces closed in during September, and on October 19, six years and six months after the Battle of Lexington, Cornwallis surrendered his entire army.   British dominion ended almost on the spot where it had begun in 1607.

### THE PEACE NEGOTIATIONS

So far as the United States were concerned the failure of Cornwallis ended the war.   English opinion would not support further efforts to subdue America, although its loss was greeted with lamentations as marking the extinction of the glory and greatness of the empire and the establishment of the "uncontrolled superiority" of France in Europe.   George III declared that he would forsake England rather than acknowledge the independence of the colonies, but Lord North was forced to resign and the shaping of the American settlement passed from the hands of the stubborn monarch.   A new ministry composed of men who had consistently advocated liberality towards America — the Marquis of Rockingham, who proposed the repeal of the Stamp Act in 1766; Burke, the advocate of conciliation; Charles James Fox, an outspoken sympathizer with the Americans; Shelburne, Franklin's friend of prerevolutionary days — faced the inevitability of a separation.

Since the French alliance of 1778 England had made several informal peace overtures, all based on the hope of restoring the status of America as a part of the empire.   However favorable the terms offered, the United States could not entertain them, under the provisions of the alliance. Even after Yorktown peace could not be made, for France was still fighting. But as early as 1779 Congress appointed John Adams as peace commissioner and defined the terms of an acceptable treaty. These, in addition to independence, were: full rights in the fisheries off the Canadian coast, and the Mississippi River for the western boundary.

These demands were more than France was pledged to uphold, and to Vergennes seemed by their excess to threaten a prolongation of the war. Through his influence a modification was made in 1781. Franklin, John Jay, Jefferson, and Henry Laurens were joined with Adams in the peace commission, and the terms of peace were redefined so that independence was made the only indispensable condition. In regard to all other matters the commissioners were instructed to consult with the French minister, and ultimately to guide themselves by his advice.

Jefferson, then governor of Virginia, declined the appointment as commissioner, and Laurens, a South Carolinian, who had been the presiding officer of Congress and was at the time of his appointment a prisoner in England, was not released in time to take much part in the negotiations. Jay had been since 1779 the envoy of Congress in Spain, where he had not only failed to make progress towards an alliance, but had even been denied official recognition. Of the three men who acted Franklin alone, by temperament and experience, had a sympathetic understanding of France's position.

Vergennes's problem was to satisfy, so far as possible, the conflicting pretensions of his two allies, especially with regard to the Mississippi Valley, and at the same time to avoid making such heavy demands upon England as the price of peace that she would prefer to continue the costly and uncertain war. To give reasonable satisfaction to each belligerent and bring the war to a close would require some concessions by each nation. A compromise was necessarily Vergennes's aim.

Negotiations between the American and British commissioners were begun in September, 1782. Because Jay insisted that Great Britain must recognize the independence of the United States before discussing terms of peace, the commission given

Richard Oswald, who began the negotiations for the British, authorized him to treat with the "Thirteen United States of North America."

The first step was to define the territory of the United States. It was the desire of the British to win the friendship of the former colonies by a liberal treaty. So act, Oswald was instructed, as to "regain the affections of America." Such a course might defeat the hope of France that the new nation, brought into being through her aid, would become her commercial and political satellite. If England could retain the good will of America and the lion's share of her trade, the ill results of independence would be substantially lessened.

Vergennes (or Rayneval, his secretary, who spoke for him), having to consider the interests of others besides the United States, had already suggested to Jay that the territory south of the Ohio River, from the Alleghanies to the Mississippi, be reserved as Indian country, with the Cumberland River as the dividing line between the Spanish and American "spheres of influence," and that the Northwest remain under British control. Jay, remembering his humiliating experience in Spain and noting the Spanish slant of this suggestion, construed it as evidence of an unfriendly disposition on the part of Vergennes. In this opinion he was confirmed when Rayneval was sent in haste to London, presumably to present the French view to the British cabinet.

It is now known that Rayneval's errand had to do with another matter. But Jay, convinced of Vergennes's duplicity, formed the opinion that the commissioners could obtain a better treaty if they dealt with the British without French assistance. "Let us," he wrote to Congress, "be honest and grateful to France, but let us think for ourselves." Adams shared Jay's view, and Franklin finally consented to go on with the negotiations without consulting the French court.

The good faith of this course is open to question. England's policy of conciliation detached the United States, in effect, from her alliance. Many Americans then and since have believed with James Madison that "instead of coöperating with Great Britain" to take advantage of "the embarrassment in which France was placed by the interfering claims of Spain and the

United States," the envoys "ought to have made every allowance and given every facility to it consistent with a regard to the rights" of America.

Nevertheless it is quite likely that the terms obtained were better than they would otherwise have been.  The British not only conceded the Mississippi boundary, but recognized the rights in the fisheries as unimpaired by the war and the new status of independence.

The treaty definition of the boundary was made in partial ignorance of the geography of the country through which the line ran.  Beginning on the northeast at the mouth of the St. Croix River, the line followed that stream to its source.  Thence it ran north to the "highlands," separating the streams flowing into the Atlantic from those falling into the St. Lawrence. Following the "highlands" to the upper waters of Connecticut River, and that stream to the forty-fifth parallel of latitude, it ran due west to the St. Lawrence, thence up that river and through the Great Lakes and the chain of small lakes beyond Superior, to the northwest corner of the Lake of the Woods. From this point it ran "due west to the Mississippi," thence south with the course of the river to the thirty-first parallel, thence east along that parallel to the Chattahoochee, down this stream to its junction with the Flint, thence straight to the source of the St. Mary's, and along its course to the sea.

At several points this line had subsequently to be adjusted. A dispute arose as to which stream was the St. Croix of the treaty; there proved to be no highlands forming a watershed as described;  the line through the small lakes in the Northwest had to run by actual survey; and it developed that the Mississippi would not be reached by a line running west from the Lake of the Woods.  Sixty years elapsed before these boundary questions were finally disposed of.

Besides these disputes with England over the interpretation and application of the treaty, another serious one arose with Spain over the southern boundary.  The generalship of Bernardo de Galvez, governor of Louisiana, had placed the Spanish in the British posts at Mobile and Pensacola, and in control of the east bank of the Mississippi as far north as the present Natchez. As peace terms had not been agreed on between England and

Spain when the negotiations with the United States were under way, the fate of the Floridas was undetermined. While fixing the southern boundary of the United States at the thirty-first parallel, therefore, a secret clause of the treaty provided that in case the British retained West Florida when they made peace with Spain, it should have its old northern boundary, fixed in 1767 at 32° 28'. When peace was made with Spain, England found it necessary to yield the Floridas, which she did without definition of boundaries. Spain then not unnaturally claimed

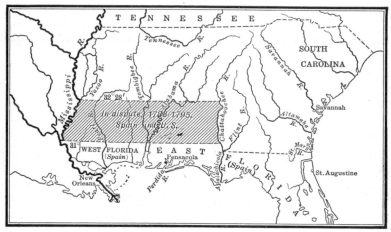

BOUNDARY DISPUTE WITH SPAIN UNDER TREATIES OF 1783.

that the provinces ceded to her were the Floridas as bounded by the British while in their possession. The United States claimed the thirty-first parallel, Spain clung to the line of 32° 28', and the quarrel dragged on until 1795.

Provisions of the treaty as to two other matters were also the cause of later disagreements. These were the stipulations that creditors in either country should encounter no legal impediments in attempting to collect debts due them in the other; and that Congress would recommend to the states restoration of the confiscated estates of Loyalists, or compensation of the losers. The purpose of the first clause was to enable English merchants to sue their American customers for pre-war debts; but as many states had passed laws requiring such debtors to pay the sums due into the state treasuries, the treaty right was nullified.

The states moreover ignored the recommendations of Congress concerning the Loyalists. The British complained of the non-performance of the treaty, and made it the ground for retaining a number of posts along the Canadian border which the treaty provided should be relinquished.

The preliminary treaty made in the autumn of 1782 became a definitive treaty when France and England made peace the next year (September, 1783). Americans had every reason to rejoice over the terms secured. Not so the French and British. "The English," wrote Vergennes to Rayneval, "buy peace rather than make it." Although the treaty was ratified, the ministry went down under the storm of criticism, and the new government was distinctly less friendly towards America.

One result of the change of ministry was the refusal to make a commercial treaty. The American commissioners hoped to conclude such an agreement in connection with the peace, but negotiations were postponed to a more convenient season. This proved unfortunate for the United States, for on account of the changed attitude of the King's government many years passed before it was possible to obtain a treaty of commerce.

When Vergennes learned of the signing of the preliminary agreement, he complained to Franklin of the violation of the instructions of Congress. "I pray you to consider," he wrote, "how you are to fulfill those [obligations] which are due to the king." Franklin could only reply that nothing had been done contrary to the interests of France, and Vergennes, although he might well have disputed the statement, did not press the matter further. To the French minister in Philadelphia he wrote, however, "If we may judge of the future from what has passed here under our eyes, we shall be poorly paid for all that we have done for the United States."

Thus was the United States ushered into the company of the nations of the earth. Many Europeans regarded its future cynically. Few believed that the feeble bonds of union would long hold the states together, much less stretch to the lands beyond the mountains without breaking. Nature herself, they said, had decreed that the Alleghanies should be the western limit of the new republic. Count de Aranda, the Spanish ambassador in France, wrote in quite another strain: "This federal republic is born a pigmy : A day will come when it will be a giant ; even a Colossus, formidable to these countries." For a decade or more the predictions of the cynics seemed likely of fulfillment ; but time has vindicated the foresight of the Spaniard.

## SELECT BIBLIOGRAPHY FOR CHAPTER VIII

The military side of the war can be followed in the histories of the Revolution cited in Chapter VII, in Van Tyne, *The American Revolution,* and in Wrong, *Washington and His Comrades in Arms.* Roosevelt, *Winning of the West,* and Henderson, *Conquest of the Old Southwest,* tell the story of the western phases of the war.

Special studies of the Declaration of Independence are : Friedenwald, *The Declaration of Independence, an Interpretation and Analysis;* Hazelton, *The Declaration of Independence;* and Becker, *The Declaration of Independence.* The last is quite recent.

On our relations with France, see the excellent work by Corwin, *French Policy and the American Alliance,* and Tower, *Lafayette in the American Revolution.* A valuable monograph on French and Spanish relations is Phillips, *The West in the Diplomacy of the American Revolution.*

The peace negotiations are narrated at length in Winsor, *America,* VII, chap. 2. A more popular account is given by Foster, *A Century of American Diplomacy.* Brief but excellent on questions of foreign relations is Fish, *American Diplomacy.*

Good biographies are : Fisher, *The True Benjamin Franklin,* Morse, *Benjamin Franklin,* and Pellew, *John Jay.*

# CHAPTER IX

## GOVERNMENT IN TRANSITION

### The State Governments

The story of the setting up of new governments in the states runs parallel in time to the story of the war. In response to the recommendation of Congress in the spring of 1776 (see page 144), Virginia was the first state to frame a constitution. This was in May, several weeks before Congress passed the Declaration of Independence. One by one the other states followed the example of Virginia, and by 1783 nearly all had adopted constitutions in place of the temporary devices of the early period of the war.

The Virginia instrument, drafted by George Mason as a member of the provincial convention, was put in force by that body without a vote of the people. This process was not quite satisfactory in a country where so much was being said about the popular origin of government, and as the other states took action a more consistent procedure was evolved. Delaware's course in August, 1776, marked a step in advance of that of Virginia, in that a convention of delegates chosen for the purpose drew up the new frame of government; but the Massachusetts convention of 1780 went still further and submitted its work to the voters for their approval or rejection.

Each of the new constitutions had a double purpose. The one aim was to provide a frame of government, the other to set forth the philosophy on which the constitution rested and to list the rights of man which the government was forbidden to violate.

It is a remarkable fact that as to its frame of government every state followed closely the model of its government before the Revolution. Connecticut and Rhode Island deemed it unnecessary to make any change at all; their charters being essentially constitutions of self-governing republics, they now merely pro-

claimed in a formal way that the charters were to be the constitutions of free and independent states.  Americans were not dissatisfied with the forms of government under which they had been
living.  All the evidence goes to show that they were deeply
imbued with the spirit of English institutions, and desired to
follow beaten paths rather than to attempt experiments and
innovations.  The Revolution was directed against external
control; it was a fight for home rule.  The states therefore made
only such changes as were required by the new status of independence.  Governors, councilors, and judges could no longer receive
their appointments from the English Crown; the authority which
the Crown had exercised passed to the people, and the new
constitutions vested the choice of all officials directly or in-
directly in the voters.

The most considerable changes were in the governor's status.
In some of the states that officer became elective by the voters;
in others the choice was made by the assembly.  In general the
office was shorn of part of its powers.  Choice by the assembly
tended to subordinate the executive to the legislature.  In some
states the governor was surrounded by an executive council,
which shared and restricted his responsibility.  Quite generally
he was deprived of the veto, which had been a vexatious power
when used by the royal governors.

The whole series of limitations placed upon the governor
reveals a suspicion of that office born of the continual friction
between the colonial assemblies representing popular interests
and the governor representing crown interests.  This suspicion
was illogical when the governor's authority was no longer derived
from the Crown.  During the early days of independence the
people reposed confidence chiefly in the elected members of the
law-making body, because in the old days they had been the
champions of colonial rights.  It took them a generation to learn
that this bias was without valid foundation.

In carrying over the features of the colonial governments the
restrictions on the right to vote and hold office were also retained.
This fact is surprising at first thought, since the Revolution was
in part a popular movement which aimed to destroy the privileged position of the merchant and planting classes.  Indeed,
the philosophy avowed by the new constitutions was demo-

cratic. For example, the Massachusetts instrument declared that "the body politic is formed by a voluntary Association of individuals; it is a social compact, by which the whole covenants with each citizen, and each with the whole people, that all shall be governed by certain laws for the common good." "The people alone have an incontestible, unalienable, and indefeasible right to institute government, and to reform, alter, or totally change the same, when their protection, safety, prosperity, and happiness require it."

The other constitutions contained equivalent, if less explicit, expressions. If one looked no further, one might easily conclude that the cause of extreme democracy had triumphed through the Revolution. But the clause of the Massachusetts constitution dealing with the suffrage restricted the right to vote to owners of a freehold of the annual value of three pounds, or other estate worth sixty pounds, and in this respect the Massachusetts constitution is again typical. In other words, there is a decided inconsistency between the theory of the constitutions and the practice which they provided for. They embody the philosophy which underlay the revolt against England; it so permeated thought that it was certain to find expression in the plans of government; but its full implications were probably not grasped at the time. At any rate, the working provisions of the constitutions left the old ruling classes in control. As a forward movement towards democracy the Revolution miscarried for the time being. Another half-century was required for the leaven of these doctrines to bring about equality of political privileges even for all white men.[1]

Another notable characteristic of the constitutions is that they took the form of written documents. How did it happen that they were put in writing? In the first place, the charters which nearly all of the colonies had possessed at some time had served virtually as constitutions, and had familiarized the inhabitants with written schemes of government. Then many Americans had come to hold the view set forth in the Massachusetts Circular Letter, that "in every free state the constitution is fixed," and to apply it even to the unwritten British con-

---

[1] Vestiges of the religious discriminations of earlier days survived in some of the constitutions in clauses restricting officeholding to Protestants.

stitution.   The idea of fixity was much more readily associated with a written instrument.   Finally, the belief that the body politic results from a social compact, as declared by the Massachusetts constitution, led naturally to the view that the articles of compact, like business contracts, should be put in writing to avoid misunderstandings and disputes.

The written constitutions of the revolutionary era, emanating theoretically from the people, fixed the powers and duties of each branch and officer of government.   No branch was made the sole judge of the extent of its own powers, but in accordance with Montesquieu's doctrine of checks and balances each was checked by the others.   Abuses of power by executive and judicial officers could be checked by impeachment and removal by the legislature. The executive veto, where it existed, was a check upon the legislative power, and the two houses checked each other.   There was no explicit provision empowering courts to declare legislative acts void, but they promptly began to do so if such acts were in conflict with the fundamental law.

### THE CONTINENTAL CONGRESS

We have had occasion to note from time to time various plans of union from the New England Confederation of 1643 to Galloway's plan of 1774.   The Stamp Act Congress is significant because it marked the first attempt to unite against the mother country, but it aimed only at a union of opinion in a temporary crisis.   The rejection of Galloway's plan gave a similar character to the First Continental Congress.

Early in the sessions of the Second Continental Congress (summer of 1775) Franklin submitted a new plan of union, much like the Albany Plan, but more detailed.   No action was taken upon it at the time.   The following June, when Richard Henry Lee moved the resolution in favor of a declaration of independence, he offered a second looking toward a permanent confederation.   Various delays prevented the adoption of anything of the sort until the war was almost over.   Meantime the task of conducting the common business fell upon the Continental Congress, which met in session after session from May, 1775, to March, 1781.

The legal status of this body has been a matter of much discussion by statesmen, historians, and students of government. Down to the Civil War the tendency in the North was to overrate its powers, in order to combat the arguments of southerners who held that the states were sovereign even under the Constitution. The present tendency is to regard the Second Continental Congress as the successor of the Stamp Act and First Continental congresses in the work of uniting public sentiment. War made its task both more important and more difficult than that of the earlier bodies, since from necessity it became the organ of common action or coöperation.

Since Congress raised and directed armies, procured the means of maintaining them, sent and received diplomatic agents, and entered into treaties with foreign countries, it performed the functions of a provisional or *de facto* government. Whether it was legally a government with authority to do what it did is a very difficult question, and one of theoretical rather than practical interest. The delegates to the first session were chosen by revolutionary conventions. After the organization of state governments the delegates were appointed by the state assemblies and acted under their instructions. No state government felt itself bound by the determinations of Congress if they ran counter to its judgment. The effectiveness of congressional measures depended upon the voluntary, not obligatory, support of the states.

The Congress has been likened to an assemblage of diplomats who as a body agree upon action to be taken by their respective governments. The indispensable necessity of union to meet the common danger gave its measures such force as they possessed. As has been said, the lack of a real government goes far to account for the small size of the continental armies, the sufferings of the soldiers, and the infrequency of aggressive movements. Full command over the country's resources would have meant a different story.

## THE ARTICLES OF CONFEDERATION

The need of defining the powers of Congress was one of the reasons for proposing the Articles of Confederation. More potent was the growing sense of permanent interests in common which required some sort of general government.   Not only the issues of war but many of the problems of peace could be handled for the common good and safety only by a common government. Lee's motion of June, 1776, led to the appointment of a committee to draft articles at the same time that the committee on the Declaration of Independence was chosen.

The chairman of the committee on articles of union was John Dickinson, who had removed from Pennsylvania and was now a delegate from Delaware.   Dickinson's committee had before it the draft which Franklin had offered the preceding summer, and used it as the basis of its own work.   The series of documents which ended with the Articles of Confederation runs back, therefore, with unbroken continuity to the Albany Plan.

The object of Franklin, and of Dickinson in his turn, was to decide what matters were of common interest, and therefore suitable to be intrusted to the care of the general government. Franklin's draft had added some items to the list in the Albany Plan, and Dickinson's committee added a few more.   As to the frame of government, nothing more was thought of than to give responsibility for these common concerns to such a body as the existing Congress.   As a result of the circumstances under which the Continental Congress had first assembled, the states enjoyed equal status, each delegation casting one vote.   Franklin had proposed to change this so that the votes of the states would be in proportion to their populations, but Dickinson, representing one of the small states, struck out this provision and inserted one continuing equality of suffrage.

A week after the adoption of the Declaration of Independence Dickinson's committee made its report.   Important as the business was, the debate proceeded slowly, for matters relating to the conduct of the war had right of way.   It was not until the autumn of 1777 (November 7), some sixteen months after the presentation of the report, that a final vote was reached, under the impulse of the enthusiasm awakened by Burgoyne's surrender.

In the debate some disputes had arisen and some changes had been made in the plan.   The equal representation of states had been confirmed, in spite of the protest of Franklin, who declared that the small states should not have as large a vote in Congress as the others unless they were willing to pay as much into the treasury.   As to money contributions, the draft had proposed that they be made by the states in proportion to population, but a dispute had arisen over the question of counting slaves, and it had been decided that each state should contribute in proportion to the value of improved lands within its borders.   Upon the insistence of the states which claimed western lands under their charter grants, control over these lands was denied to Congress.

After Congress had voted its approval of the Articles, they were sent to the states with the understanding that each legislature, when it approved, should instruct its delegates in Congress to sign on its behalf, and ratification by every one of the states was required before they were to be binding.   Now arose a difficulty over the provision concerning western lands.   Maryland, objecting to Virginia's claim, declared that the lands must be treated as a common possession of the states.

This domestic quarrel over the future of the West began long before it was certain that the lands could be held when peace was made.   The "landless" states joined Maryland in demanding cessions by the "claimant" states, and the ratification of the Articles was long delayed.   One by one, however, all of the states except Maryland gave their assent.   She stubbornly refused to ratify without the cessions, and as her assent was indispensable the claimant states finally yielded (see page 187).   The Articles went into effect March 1, 1781.

When we compare the frame of government contained in this instrument with those which the states had adopted, we find striking differences.   Not only was there no second branch of the legislature, but the familiar separation of executive and judicial functions from that of legislation was lacking.   The powers which the Articles granted were vested in Congress, to be exercised by it or its agents.   It was authorized to appoint such committees and "civil officers" as its executive business might require, and these were to perform their duties under its direction.   There was the germ, but only the germ, of a judicial system in the power to provide courts "for the trial of piracies and felonies committed on the high seas," for "determining finally appeals in all cases of captures," and for the settlement of disputes between states.

This concentration of functions in one unicameral body places the Articles in a different category from the constitutions of the states.  Moreover, the latter rested on the authority of the people in each state, and created governments acting upon and responsible to them.   The Articles declared that the Union was a confederacy, or league of friendship, in which each state retained its "sovereignty, freedom and independence, and every power . . . not . . . expressly delegated to the United States in Congress assembled."  The Articles rested upon the authority of the state governments (legislatures).   Congress was responsible to them and not to the people, and did not act upon the people. It was the organ of common action of a league.

In this body each member state was entitled to the same number of delegates, two to seven.   Each state legislature chose and paid its own delegates, or neglected to do so as it preferred. On all measures the delegation of each state cast one vote, provided at least two delegates were present.   If the delegation was equally divided, its vote was lost.   No important measure could be adopted without the concurrence of two thirds of the delegations, that is, the vote of nine states.   Amendments to the Articles, after passing Congress, required the approval of every state, by vote of the legislature.

The member states were pledged by the Articles to observe certain rules of comity in their relations with one another, and to refrain from certain actions which were inconsistent with the purposes of the league.   Thus citizens of each state were to enjoy freedom to come and go and carry on business in all of the other states, while fugitives from justice were to be given up on demand of the governor of the state from which they fled.   The public records of each state were to be given full faith and credit by the others.

As has been said, both Franklin and Dickinson had tried to make a list of the matters of common interest to the members of the league, and by the time Congress sent the Articles to the states in 1777 the list had grown to a very respectable length. First and foremost, naturally, among the powers of Congress, was that of "determining on peace and war."   Next was the responsibility for foreign relations in general — sending and receiving ambassadors and making treaties.   Then, to promote uniformity for the benefit of trade, Congress was given exclusive power to fix the standards of coinage and of weights and measures. Relations with Indians "not members of any of the states" were committed to its care, likewise the postal service. The responsibility for paying the debt incurred in the War of Independence was laid upon it. Other powers were incidental to these main ones.

Some of these powers had been included in the Albany Plan, and every one of them had been wielded in colonial days by the imperial government rather than by individual colonies. Now that independence had come, Americans were turning to the task of creating for themselves some substitute for the British government in the performance of these functions.

Unfortunately, the former relations with the British had made Americans tenacious of certain views which they should now have given up. The long struggle against parliamentary taxation had grounded them in the belief that they should be taxed only by their own assemblies. It was still quite beyond the thought of most of them to give a power to Congress which had been denied to Parliament. Instead, the Articles allowed that body to estimate its monetary needs and then to make a "requisition" upon each state for its share. The laying of the taxes to raise this and all other revenues was reserved to the states.

There was a similar defect of power in relation to the regulation of commerce. The regulation of commerce was one of the functions of Parliament which most colonists admitted as a necessity although they greatly disliked the workings of the navigation acts. The Articles consequently gave Congress only a partial and inadequate control over commerce. It was allowed to make commercial treaties, but the right to retaliate against any foreign country which discriminated against American trade was reserved to the states, and no control was given over interstate commerce.

In many ways the American league went beyond all precedents. Even such a union might have worked successfully for many years if the states had gone a little further in giving power to Congress. The lack of power to regulate commerce, the lack of power to tax, and the lack of power to act directly upon the people were fatal defects. Without these powers all of the others were mere shadows, and the Union itself a "rope of sand."

176 HISTORY OF THE UNITED STATES

## SELECT BIBLIOGRAPHY FOR CHAPTER IX

**State Governments.** Nevins, *American States during and after the Revolution*, is the first comprehensive history of this topic. Brief accounts are given in Channing, *United States*, III, chap. 14, Van Tyne, *The American Revolution*, chap. 9, and Morey, "The First State Constitutions," in *Annals of the American Academy of Political and Social Science*. See also McMaster, *Acquisition of Rights of Man in America;* Hockett, *Western Influences*, 22–27. There are a few good monographs which deal with particular states. One of the best of these is on Massachusetts: Cushing, *Transition from Provincial to Commonwealth Government*. The evolution of state constitutions from colonial charters is discussed by Morey, "The Genesis of a Written Constitution," in *Annals*.

**The Continental Congress.** Small, *Beginnings of American Nationality;* Van Tyne, *The American Revolution*, chap. 11, and "Sovereignty in the American Revolution," in *The American Historical Review*.

**The Articles of Confederation.** McLaughlin, *The Confederation and the Constitution*.

# CHAPTER X

## THE CONFEDERATION PERIOD

### COMMERCIAL READJUSTMENT

The troubles of the United States were not ended by the treaty of peace. It was no slight undertaking to set up an independent political household. The years of the war had seriously dislocated the industrial as well as political organization, and the confusion and uncertainty of the next half-dozen years have fastened upon them the name of the "critical period of American history." The interruption of intercourse with Europe had forced the United States to attempt to supply their own needs, but their manufactures, still in the handicrafts stage, were far too weak to withstand the competition of the rising factory system of England. For many years still America was to depend upon England for most manufactured goods, and agriculture and commerce were to be her chief industries. Both of them had been badly deranged by the war.

The irksome restrictions imposed upon colonial trade by the navigation system had been contributory causes of the Revolution. Independence freed the Americans from these restrictions on their trade, but with the loss of their status as British subjects the navigation acts automatically excluded them, as foreigners, from the British West Indies. They hoped that England could be persuaded to make a treaty allowing their intercourse with all parts of the empire to continue with the same freedom as in the old days. If there ever was a moment when such an agreement could have been obtained, it was when the Shelburne ministry, intent upon regaining the affections of America, signed the preliminary peace treaty in 1782. The change in ministry which came in consequence of the liberality of that treaty indicated that the hope of commercial favors was vain. With the exception of products like fish, which competed with the industry of

British North America, exportation from the United States to the British West Indies was allowed, but the goods had to be carried in English ships. As for exports to England, they might be carried in American vessels, but in that case some articles were subject to higher duties than when brought in English bottoms.

Calculations of national interest swayed the British government, and its ancient policy was not modified at the plea of the infant republic of the West. England had nothing to gain by concessions and nothing to lose by refusing to make them. The war was hardly over before it became apparent that the French hope of supplanting England in the American market was illusory. The habits of generations were too firmly fixed. While they sought some articles of luxury from France, Americans preferred the staple manufactures of the English to the French goods of the same class. English firms solicited new orders from their former customers in the states, and it proved easy to reëstablish the old credit system. In spite of restrictions, commerce soon flowed back into its old channels.

Freedom brought other losses besides that of the right to enter British colonial ports. The bounties which England had paid on the production of certain articles ceased, and were sadly missed, for instance, by the rice-growers. American tobacco lost its special privileges in the English market, and a time of depression followed in that industry.

The recovery of the privilege of trading with the West Indies became a prime object of diplomacy. John Adams, sent to England as minister in 1785, was courteously received by the King, but could not make headway with the ministry. Despite the recommendations of Congress, the states had not restored the property of the Loyalists, and had passed laws sequestering debts due Englishmen (see page 164). The British government therefore refused to make an agreement on commerce, and charged the Americans with breaches of the treaty of peace. The ministers intimated that they doubted whether the Articles gave Congress power to make a treaty which the states would be bound to observe.

The inadequacy of the powers of Congress was, indeed, a chief root of the difficulty in negotiating treaties. If Congress could have imposed the same restrictions on British ships as American vessels were subjected to in England, it might have brought England to terms.    That, at least, was Adams's conclusion from his humiliating experience.    An amendment to the Articles had been proposed in 1784, called the "commerce amendment," to give Congress this very power, but only two states consented to part with their control.

Meantime Jefferson in France was faring hardly better than Adams.    "We are the lowest and most obscure of the whole diplomatic tribe," he wrote.    France, like England, was little disposed to treat the new republic with distinguished consideration.    During the war she had given American vessels considerable liberty in her ports, both in the West Indies and in Europe, but concessions were made rather as a means of embarrassing the British than because of friendship for the United States, and with peace she like England resumed her navigation system. Spain pursued a similar course for like reasons.

Nevertheless within a year or two conditions began to improve slowly.    In 1784 and 1785 France and Spain made concessions for their own convenience by which the vessels of the states were allowed restricted trade privileges in the West Indian ports. Treaties were concluded with some of the countries of central Europe, notably Prussia, embodying the most advanced contemporary views of international law.    Unfortunately the amount of trade with these countries was small, so that the treaties were for many years hardly more than formal statements    ideals.

But the demand for American agricultural products grew, and the open ports of the Danish and Dutch West Indies proved to be back doors to the neighboring British islands.    A beginning was made, besides, in the Pacific.    The first American vessel returned from China in 1785, and within a few years Yankee skippers were second only to the English in the trade with Canton. In conjunction with the Asiatic commerce came the development of the fur trade on the northwest coast.    Ships from Boston and other New England ports rounded Cape Horn, carrying goods for the coast Indians, thence proceeding with furs to the Sandwich Islands (Hawaii), where conditions were favorable for wintering and curing the peltries.    China was the great fur market, and silks, tea, and spices composed the return cargoes.    Although

Spain claimed the Pacific shores of North America, the "Bostons," as the natives called the American traders, outnumbered both Spaniards and English during the last years of the eighteenth century. The acquisition of Oregon and Hawaii by the United States long afterwards was in part the outgrowth of these early activities.

By the end of the Confederation period (1789) foreign commerce had regained its prewar prosperity, with added promise due to the new ventures. Boston, Salem, Newport, New York, Philadelphia, Baltimore, Norfolk, and Charleston shared in the profits. Through New York passed the trade not only of the Hudson Valley but of considerable portions of Connecticut and New Jersey. Its volume was sufficient to enable the great landowners who controlled state politics to shift the burdens of taxation largely from their own shoulders by means of customs duties. Evidence of the increasing prosperity due to commerce is found in the rise of real estate values. According to Franklin they had trebled in Philadelphia within a few years after the treaty of peace.

For this prosperity little credit is due the government of the Confederation. Greater powers would undoubtedly have enabled Congress to promote the growth of commerce, but as it was, it grew from natural causes quite independently of the action of the government. Trade was so completely under the control of the states that their rivalries led to tariff wars which caused confusion and loss where prosperity should have been general.

## The Currency Question

The French and English armies and foreign loans had brought unusual quantities of coin into the country. It was largely used in buying supplies for the forces of both belligerents. The abnormal demand had sent prices to a high level and producers had prospered. Much of the money found its way eventually into the pockets of war profiteers and speculators, who spent their gains so freely that for a time after the war the value of imports far exceeded that of exports. This took coin out of the country again to pay for luxuries, and as it became scarce many a poor man found increased difficulty in paying taxes or other obligations which required hard money.

Men who were in debt therefore began to clamor for relief legislation — for stay laws deferring payment of interest or principal of debts, and especially for legal-tender paper.

The paper money issue has been so perennial in the history of the United States that it is well at the outset to notice certain fundamental principles. Paper put out in large quantities to circulate as money, without an adequate specie reserve for its redemption (known as "irredeemable" or "inconvertible" paper), is likely to depreciate and cause changes in the general level of prices. Changes in the price scale are constantly occurring, through the operation of complex forces affecting the production and marketing of goods, and are usually slow and little felt. Even when slow, they may cause hardship, as in the case of obligations running through many years before maturing.

Ideally, the principal of a debt should be repaid in dollars of the same purchasing power as those borrowed, but as yet no way has been found of stabilizing the value of the dollar. If its purchasing power increases (that is, if prices fall), the creditor receives a greater value than he loaned; if the change is in the other direction, he gets back a smaller value than he parted with. The debtor loses or gains inversely.

Legislation which affects the monetary system in either direction is very questionable, because it promotes the interest of one class or the other. Issues of irredeemable paper are dangerous for this reason. Depreciation, moreover, leads to a double scale of prices, one measured in specie, the other in paper, and the double scale aggravates the evils incident to changes in the price level.

The Second Continental Congress did its full part in demoralizing the currency, corrupting sound thinking, and teaching the people to demand paper money. When hard pressed for funds, it resorted to the issue of paper which it used in paying for whatever it needed. The receivers in turn passed on these "continental notes" to others in the course of their own business. These notes were mere promises that Congress would pay the bearer the amount printed on the face, not on demand, but at some unstated time in the future. To promote their circulation the states were asked to give them legal-tender character, and as Congress had no power of taxation, each state was requested to provide a tax for raising a fund which in time would pay off and retire its share.

This policy was adopted cautiously, and the quantity of notes authorized for the first issue in 1776 was only $2,000,000. But the temptation to make new issues proved too great, and in proportion as the volume increased public confidence in the ability of Congress to carry out its promises of payment declined and depreciation proceeded. By 1779 one dollar of silver would buy twenty in continental notes. The next year the notes had dropped to half of this value.

Congress then adopted a policy of partial repudiation; the old notes were called in at forty dollars to one, in payment of taxes due the states. There were thus paid in and destroyed $120,000,000 of the $200,000,000 which had been issued. Then Congress put out notes of a "new tenor," one dollar of which was rated as equivalent to forty of the former issues.

This attempt to float new notes at par with specie did not stay the downward course of either series, and the currency of Congress finally became so nearly worthless as to give rise to the saying still in use — "not worth a continental." After the adoption of the Constitution, Alexander Hamilton, as Secretary of the Treasury, recommended the redemption of a limited amount at the ratio of a hundred to one, which was much more than the market value.[1]

Little could be done to improve the currency situation during the Confederation. Robert Morris, the able Superintendent of Finance appointed by Congress in 1781, understood the importance of a specie circulation, and had the advice of Gouverneur Morris, and of both Hamilton and Jefferson, in his efforts. It was Jefferson and the two Morrises who worked out our decimal system of coinage based on the Spanish dollar as the unit. But it could not be put into effect at once. The United States produced no appreciable quantity of the money metals, and foreign trade was the sole source of supply. In view of the adverse balance of trade and the scarcity of specie, recoining of foreign gold and silver was put off, and the coins of France, Spain,

---

[1] A small percentage of the amount of a subscription for stock in the United States Bank might be paid in notes at this rate. The continental currency should be carefully distinguished from the certificates of indebtedness issued by the same authority. These were redeemed at par.

and England formed a large portion of the hard-money circulation of the United States for many years.

With so scanty a supply of specie, the best use which could be made of it was to form a reserve for the redemption of a paper currency.[1] A few of the states had already made a slight beginning in the direction of sound money by chartering specie-paying banks, when the Superintendent of Finance, in consultation with Hamilton, recommended in 1781 that Congress charter a Bank of North America. This institution, patterned after the Bank of England, began business in Philadelphia with a capital of $400,000 in specie.[2] Its notes, circulating at par, enabled business men to carry on their buying and selling without fear of losses due to fluctuations in the value of the currency.

These constructive measures did not meet the desires of the debtor class. With the fall of prices and the collapse of the continental currency, men who had incurred debts while their corn and wheat were bringing high prices found it harder to meet their payments than they had expected. The products of their labors brought fewer dollars, but their debts were not scaled down. The burden of their debts, if paid in specie or the notes of the new Bank, was actually increased.

This was a real hardship. Not unnaturally they wished to avoid payment in the scarce specie, and demanded new issues of paper by the states under laws making it legal tender for debts. They did not desire the redemption of the issues, but wished the paper to depreciate gradually, operating as a tax, shifting the burden of debt from the poor and diffusing the loss throughout the community. In all of the states the advocates of paper money tried to gain control of the legislatures in order to enact their program.

The paper-money advocates of the Confederation period were almost identical with the rural classes which had before and during the Revolution sought democratic reforms. They had some moral support from the wage-earners of the towns who

---

[1] Such a currency is very different from the irredeemable issues of the war period, being exchangeable for coin on demand. Such use of specie supports a sound circulation of two or three times as many dollars as are held in reserve.

[2] Doubts of the power of Congress to grant the charter led the Bank to reincorporate under a Pennsylvania charter. During the Civil War it became a National Bank, and has continued in business to this day.

could not vote.  The success of the old aristocracy in shaping the state constitutions along conservative lines disappointed and angered the masses, who felt that the new governments did not rest upon their consent.

The Revolution had weakened the old respect for established authority and institutions.  The casting off of British control had brought all government into question, and the philosophy by which rejection of the King had been justified was susceptible of dangerous interpretations.  If governments derived their just powers from the consent of the governed, what obedience did individuals owe to a government which failed to secure economic justice?  The limits of the revolutionary philosophy had not been defined, and the country reaped a harvest of social and economic disorders.

Some extremists demanded the abolition of private property, contending that the property of all the people had been protected from confiscation by the joint exertions and common victory in the war, and should therefore become the common possession.  In their eyes the state governments, with their machinery of courts for the collection of debts, took on more or less of the appearance of a mechanism for the exploitation of the masses by the few.  The wealthy merchants and money lenders who made up the creditor class were the same men who dominated the legislatures, and the lawyers and judges seemed to be their allies in enforcing laws passed to protect property interests.  Such thoughts tended to violence where no other means existed of redressing grievances, whether real or fancied.

In most of the states, on account of the restrictions on voting and the rules of apportionment in the legislatures, the conservatives were able to defeat the paper-money party at the polls and retain the upper hand in the assemblies.  In some they won by narrow majorities only, and in Rhode Island the radicals gained control of the legislature and passed a legal-tender law.  When creditors and merchants avoided debtors and customers, unwilling to accept cheap money as required by the act, another bill was passed, permitting debtors to post notices declaring that they had vainly sought their creditors.  Thereupon they were absolved from further obligation.  As these notices began with the words "Know ye," the acts on which they rested were nicknamed the "Know ye laws." They gave rise to a famous case (Trevett *vs.* Weeden) — one of several during the Confederation which raised the question of the right of the courts to pass upon the validity of acts of the legislature.

In Massachusetts the paper-money party, defeated at the polls and rendered desperate by their debts, rose in insurrection. Farmers in the barren hill country of the western counties found a leader in Daniel Shays, a veteran of Bunker Hill, and broke up the sittings of the courts at Northampton and Worcester engaged in the trial of debt cases in which many of them were defendants. From the United States arsenal at Springfield they tried to get arms, and for a while laid the town under siege. This was in 1786. So general was the sympathy with the "rebels" that conservatives feared the state authorities would not succeed in restoring order. Governor James Bowdoin, however, sent out an army of militia which drove Shays in flight from Springfield and finally dispersed his followers. Popular sympathy saved all of the insurgents from punishment, and was supposed to account for the defeat of Bowdoin by John Hancock at the next election.

The conservatives found in these commotions additional reason for distrusting popular majorities. It seemed to them that new safeguards of law and order were needed rather than more democracy. They thought that Congress should be enabled to protect the states against domestic violence. They were humiliated by its inability even to defend its own property when Shays attacked the arsenal at Springfield. Being of the creditor class, they were much concerned about the sanctity of contracts, and began to feel that some check should be placed on the power of the states to pass legal-tender laws. While, of course, the weakness of Congress was not the cause of the turbulence of the times, the propertied class became more and more convinced that a general government was necessary which could deal with discontent and preserve order.

## GROWTH OF THE WEST

Notwithstanding all discontent and tumult, America was stirring with vigorous life, as is shown by the increase of population and its expansion into new areas. The inhabitants were estimated at about three millions at the close of the war. By 1790 they numbered four millions — probably twice as many as the colonies contained in the days of the Stamp Act. Activity of speculation in western lands and the broadening current of migration westward showed confidence in the future.

At the close of the Revolution, settlements in Kentucky and Tennessee were the only ones in the Ohio Valley. North of the river the native tribes enjoyed almost undisturbed possession. From the missions established, on the eve of the Revolution, by the Moravians at Gnadenhütten and Schoenbrunn in eastern Ohio to the French villages on the Wabash and the Kaskaskia, only an occasional trading post foreshadowed the coming of the white man. A sprinkling of Americans was to be found among the French at the old posts, followers of Clark who had remained and friends who had joined them. On the north bank of the Ohio as far as the mouth of the Muskingum, and along the east bank of that stream, squatters were making "tomahawk claims" in defiance both of the natives and the government of the United States.

South of the Ohio the first stages of pioneer life were already past. Cultivated farms and well-built houses were replacing the cabins in the clearings, and a steady tide of immigration was pouring in. Many of the newcomers hailed from Virginia and the Carolinas, coming by way of the headwaters of the Tennessee, Cumberland Gap, and Boone's "Wilderness Road." An easier route, save for the danger of Indian attacks, was the river. Virginians sometimes followed the Kanawha through the mountains to its mouth, but many of them preferred the longer but easier way down the Monongahela to the "forks of the Ohio." This was the favorite path also for the Marylanders who ascended the Potomac and then crossed to "Redstone" where Brownsville now stands, most of the way following the old trail of Washington and Braddock.

Across Pennsylvania from Philadelphia the trails of the fur-traders became the paths of the pioneers. The one chiefly used ran through Lancaster and Bedford to the village of Pittsburgh at the "forks." Upon this point all routes converged as all roads led to Rome in ancient days. Here or at Redstone the pioneer embarked on a flatboat and floated with the current to Limestone (Maysville) or the Falls of the Ohio (Louisville).

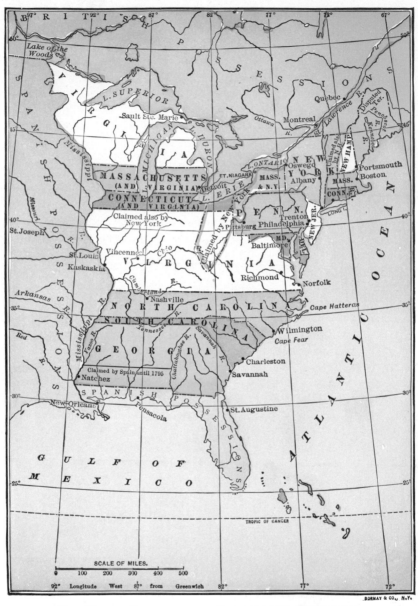

THE UNITED STATES AT THE CLOSE OF THE REVOLUTION,
Showing Western Land Claims of States.

Settlers bound for the Nashville district in Tennessee crossed overland from the North Carolina settlements, or by boat followed the circuitous course of the Tennessee River to its mouth and thence ascended the Cumberland.

The Kentucky settlements contained from thirty to forty thousand people by the close of the eighties. Kentucky and Tennessee, being parts of Virginia and North Carolina respectively, were already open to settlement under the laws of those states when the Revolution ended. Very different was the situation in the Northwest. Interest in this region was growing, but authorized settlement had to await the completion of the cessions to Congress and the action of that body.

Maryland's refusal to ratify the Articles of Confederation started the movement for cession of the western lands to Congress. Seven of the thirteen states were numbered among the claimants of these lands. Connecticut, Massachusetts, Virginia, North Carolina, South Carolina, and Georgia based their claims on charter grants made by the Crown. New York, the seventh, rested its pretensions on its suzerainty over the Iroquois, who had maintained a shadowy superiority over the western tribes as far as the Mississippi and Ohio.

The validity of all these claims was open to question. The British government had repudiated them, in effect, by consenting to the Vandalia grant and by the Quebec Act. During the Revolution France as well as Spain had considered them extinguished by these acts of the British, and even Congress would have been less tenacious of the Mississippi boundary if it had meant only the territorial satisfaction of the claimant states. Clark's campaign under the authority of Virginia strengthened the contention of that state, but Maryland insisted that Clark's conquest was made possible only by the common military efforts in the East, and that therefore the winning of the region resulted from the common sacrifice.

In solicitude for the adoption of the Articles, Congress finally appealed to the claimant states to yield. New York, whose title was least defensible, responded first, and the others slowly followed. Maryland accepted the Articles in 1781, as soon as it became evident that she had won her fight, but the cessions were not completed until 1802. Georgia was the last to act.

The Carolinas also made their transfers tardily, South Carolina in 1787 and North Carolina in 1790.

The cessions of the land north of the Ohio River were completed by 1786, through the action of New York, Virginia, Massachusetts, and Connecticut.   Kentucky remained a part of Virginia, but that state yielded all claims to the Northwest with the exception of certain tracts to be distributed as bounty lands to her veterans of the Revolution.   The largest of these lay between the Scioto and Little Miami rivers in the present State of Ohio. Connecticut also reserved an extensive tract lying south of Lake Erie, retaining for a time not only the title to the lands but jurisdiction.   In this way she hoped to provide an outlet for her surplus population, and to compensate her citizens who had suffered from British raids during the war.

In appealing to the states for cessions Congress made promises which formed the basis of important legislation a few years later. One of these was that the lands ceded should be disposed of for the common benefit.   At the time this pledge was understood to mean that the lands should be sold and the proceeds applied to the payment of the war debt.   The other promise was that the West when settled should be formed into distinct republican states, which should become members of the Federal Union, with the same rights as the original states.   In these pledges are found the germs both of the federal land system and of the principle on which the union of thirteen states has expanded into a sisterhood of forty-eight members.

After Virginia had made her cession and the movement seemed to be fairly under way, Congress took up the problem of providing a suitable government for the West.   Thomas Jefferson was chairman of the committee appointed to draft an ordinance for this purpose.   His report was adopted, after some changes, as the "Ordinance of 1784."

It divided the whole region between the mountains and the Mississippi into tracts each of which was to enter the Union when its population equaled that of the smallest of the original states. There were eighteen of these divisions.   Previous to statehood the inhabitants were to have restricted rights of self-government under the supervision of Congress.   Jefferson's draft provided for the exclusion of slavery from the entire West after the year

1800, but this clause failed to pass Congress. If it could have been adopted and enforced, the westward march of slavery would have been stopped at the bounds of the original states, and the sectional controversy over its expansion which ended in Civil War could not have occurred.

The Ordinance of 1784 was prospective in its operation and never went into effect. At the time of its enactment the cessions had not yet been completed, and only two or three of the proposed states had any inhabitants. Before the conditions contemplated by the Ordinance of 1784 came about, the Ordinance of 1787 superseded it.

In the meantime, however, Congress enacted the Land Ordinance of 1785, which dealt with the other phase of the task undertaken by its pledge to the states. It set out the plan by which the lands were to be disposed of, providing first of all for a system of surveys which has become known as the "rectangular," or "rectilinear" system.

By this method a "base line" is first laid out running due east and west. North and south across the base line, at intervals of six miles, meridians are marked off. Then lines parallel to the base line, six miles apart, mark off the surveyed area into blocks containing thirty-six square miles. Each of these blocks is called a "township," and each tier of townships between meridians is called a "range." The subdivisions of the township, each containing one square mile, are called "sections." Each section can be subdivided into halves and quarters, each quarter into quarters, and so on indefinitely.

The plan provided an admirably accurate system, in contrast with the "indiscriminate locations" which had been permitted by Virginia and some other colonies, and which had resulted in endless litigation. In part it was based on New England precedents, although the origin of some of its features is obscure. The system worked so well that it was applied to new areas from time to time as the settlement of the West advanced, until it covered the whole of the public lands. The ordinance provided for a first survey to contain seven ranges, along a base line running due west from the point where the Ohio River crosses the boundary of Pennsylvania.

Besides the survey system, the Ordinance laid down the terms

|   |   |   |   |   |   |
|---|---|---|---|---|---|
| 6 | 5 | 4 | 3 | 2 | 1 |
| 7 | 8 | 9 | 10 | 11 | 12 |
| 18 | 17 | 16 | 15 | 14 | 13 |
| 19 | 20 | 21 | 22 | 23 | 24 |
| 30 | 29 | 28 | 27 | 26 / 25 | |
| 31 | 32 | 33 | 34 | 35 / 36 | |

SYSTEM OF LAND SURVEY

Township on enlarged scale
showing sections and subdivisions

$a$ = Section, 640 Acres;    $b$ = Half-Section, 320 Acres;
$c$ = Quarter-Section, 160 Acres;    $d$ = Half Quarter-Section, 80 Acres;
$e$ = Quarter Quarter-Section, 40 Acres.

and conditions on which lands were to be sold.  Following an old practice of the New England colonies when laying out new towns, section sixteen in each township was reserved for the support of schools.  The remaining lands of the seven ranges were to be sold at auction to the highest bidder, for cash, in plots of not less than one section.  The minimum price was fixed at one dollar per acre, but with competitive bidding the actual selling price was expected to average considerably more.  It was provided at first that an auction should be held in each state, and to each was assigned for this purpose a proportionate share of the tract to be sold.

This plan of sales was a departure from the land systems of colonial days.  In many of the provinces it became customary to grant lands on such easy terms as to make them practically free.  This was due especially to the desire to promote settlement on the frontiers as a means of defense against the Indians.  Such service was worth more than the money which might be obtained by selling lands.  Lands were also sold, and speculators had become active in nearly every colony, buying great tracts on special terms for resale.  Often, however, they received the grants on condition that they colonize them within a specified time with a certain number of settlers.

After the Revolution the straitened circumstances of the public treasury and the burden of the war debt compelled Congress to deal with the public lands as a source of revenue, and for a time easy methods of acquisition found no regular place in its system.  The terms prescribed by the Ordinance of 1785 shut out the poor men who would naturally become the actual settlers, for in those days the minimum sum required to purchase a section, $640, was a considerable fortune.  It was expected by some congressmen that groups of settlers would buy whole townships, like the New England groups which formed new towns.  This did not occur, and speculators were the chief buyers at the land auctions.

Land sold slowly under the Ordinance, and Congress showed a willingness to make better terms than the Ordinance offered in special contracts with companies which wished to buy large tracts.  As early as 1783 some officers of the continental army, whose arrears of pay Congress was unable to meet, had formed a plan to accept lands in the Ohio Valley in lieu of money, and to make a settlement there.   The project led to the formation of The Ohio Company of Associates, consisting of New England veterans.   In 1787 this company sent an agent, Manasseh Cutler,

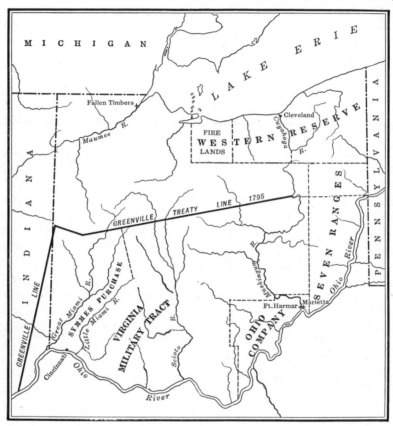

LAND PURCHASES, RESERVATIONS, AND SURVEYS IN OHIO.

to make a contract with Congress.   He proposed to purchase a tract of a million and a half acres on the Muskingum for a million dollars, to be paid in the certificates of indebtedness held by the members, then worth about twelve cents on the dollar.

Cutler procured his contract in the face of considerable opposition, by coupling with it a speculative scheme in which some members of Congress were interested.   This latter was the Scioto

Company, which asked an option on several million acres. The Scioto Company had a brief and disreputable career, but it aided the sounder Ohio Company to get fairly started.

In 1788 another organization, known from its promoter as the Symmes Company, and composed of New Jersey and Pennsylvania soldiers and speculators, obtained a contract for the purchase on similar terms of the lands between the Big and Little Miami rivers. Thus by 1788 three groups were ready to begin settlements in the Ohio country, on the Muskingum, Scioto, and Miami rivers.

A part of the plan of Congress in dealing with the Northwest was not to permit settlement before surveys were finished, and not to make surveys until the Indian title had been extinguished. To prepare the way for settlement, Congress sent out agents immediately after the peace with England to make treaties with the tribes.

The Indians showed the greatest reluctance to negotiate. The British fur-trading interest, much discontented over the terms of the peace which assigned the fur-bearing Northwest to the United States, had persuaded the government to find excuses for delaying the surrender of the border posts situated on the American side of the boundary.[1] Holding these posts, officials advised the Indians to refuse to cede lands north of the Ohio, and to make that river the permanent boundary between their lands and the American settlements. In short, notwithstanding the treaty, Britain sought to perpetuate her old plan of closing the Northwest to settlement, in the interest of the Indian trade.

With great difficulty the agents of Congress obtained several treaties, the last of which, signed in 1788 at Fort Harmar, at the mouth of the Muskingum, opened a large part of southern and eastern Ohio for white settlement. The Indians, however, refused to abide by the treaties, claiming that the chiefs had signed without authority, and Congress found the situation little changed for all its efforts. When the survey of the seven ranges was begun, the Indians prepared to take the war path, and the survey had to be abandoned for awhile.

This was the situation when the first contingent of the Ohio Company came from the East. Crossing the mountains of

[1] *Cf.* the complaints about non-payment of debts and treatment of Loyalists.

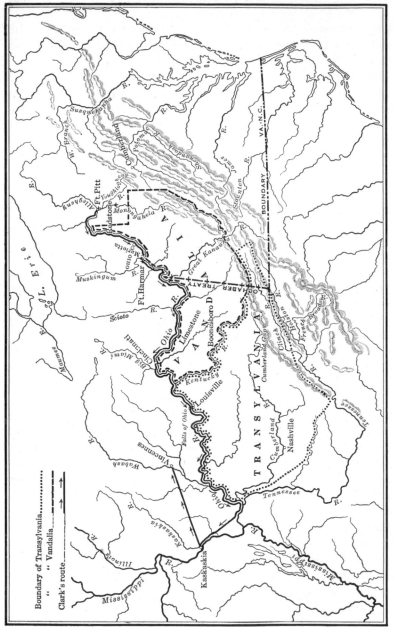

Boundary of Transylvania..............
   "     " Vandalia.............
Clark's route................

THE WEST, 1768-1788.

Pennsylvania, the party built a boat on the Youghiogheny, appropriately named the "Mayflower," in which these later Pilgrims floated down to the mouth of the Muskingum. There, opposite Fort Harmar and under its protection, they began the first authorized settlement of Americans north of the Ohio, naming it "Marietta" (1788). Almost simultaneously the Symmes Company began a settlement, while a third class of immigrants, crossing from Kentucky, contributed to the beginnings of a cluster of hamlets on the site of Cincinnati.

## THE ORDINANCE OF 1787

Before this Congress had passed the Ordinance of 1787. By 1786, when the cessions by the states had placed the Northwest under its authority, it had become evident that the provisions of the Ordinance of 1784 were unsatisfactory. It was now believed that the first ordinance provided for too many states of too small a size.

The new law applied only to the Northwest, leaving the region south of the Ohio to be organized whenever the cessions should be completed. The Northwest was to be divided eventually into not more than five nor less than three states. While the process of occupation was in its early stages, government was to be in the hands of officials chosen by Congress, but as soon as five thousand white men had removed to the territory, there was to be a government much like that of colonial Massachusetts. The qualified voters were to elect a house of representatives, while Congress (like the King) appointed the governor. Congress was also to appoint the members of an upper house, or council, from a list of persons nominated by the representatives. A delegate to sit in Congress without a vote reminds one of the colonial agent.[1]

Experience as subjects of Britain influenced the members of Congress in shaping their territorial — or as it might appropriately be called, "colonial" — system. Under the general plan first laid down in 1787, the whole wide space of the continent was to be occupied, as additional areas were brought under the

---

[1] The Ordinance shows the temper of the times by property qualifications for voting and officeholding during the territorial régime.

flag by purchase or conquest and the westward movement called for provision for government in the new regions.

The American colonial system differed from that of England in one vital respect. She held her colonies in permanent subordination. It was this inferiority of status, at bottom, that caused the severance of the bonds between her and the thirteen colonies. The Ordinance of 1787 promised that whenever any one of the divisions of the Northwest attained a population of sixty thousand, it should be admitted to the Union forthwith, on terms of full equality with the original states. Thus the American system held before the colonists of the western frontiers the prospect of early admission to all of the privileges of partnership. This equality of new and old states is one of the unique features of American federalism, and goes far to explain the strength of the bonds of union.

The pledge of statehood was one of a number of articles of compact in the ordinance which were declared to be unalterable except by common consent of Congress and the people of the territory. Other articles contained provisions similar to the bills of rights in the state constitutions, intended to safeguard freedom of worship, trial by jury, and property rights. One memorable paragraph read: "There shall be neither slavery nor involuntary servitude in the said territory, otherwise than in the punishment of crimes, whereof the party shall have been duly convicted."

This antislavery clause was the progenitor of a series of provisions which Congress applied to new territories in later years. During the controversy over slavery which preceded the Civil War, the program of the northern radicals was to extend this provision to all new territory. Hence this article of the Ordinance of 1787 was of epoch-making importance. Yet it is easy to overrate its effect. At an early date it was construed not to apply to the few slaves already in the territory, and later court decisions limited the prohibition to the territorial period. If new states entered the Union with all the rights and powers of the original members, the one class could no more be denied the right of choice in the matter of slavery than the other. The restriction undoubtedly operated in favor of settlement of the Northwest by opponents to slavery, so that when statehood came, free constitutions were preferred by the majority of the inhabitants.  There was, nevertheless, a vigorous proslavery minority, especially in Illinois, which did not give up the hope of a proslave constitution until some time after the state had been admitted.

Oddly enough, these ordinances for the West, the constructive work of the Confederation period, were not warranted by any clause of the Articles.  Congress had no better authority for what it did than the consent of the states implied in the acts ceding their claims to the western lands, and their subsequent acquiescence in the ordinances.  To make them strictly legal an amendment should have been added to the Articles.  The first Congress under the Constitution, with its fuller power, reënacted the Ordinance of 1787, and the appointment of the governor and other officials became, like other appointments, a power of the President acting with the advice and consent of the Senate.

In 1788 General Arthur St. Clair, a veteran of the Revolution, was appointed as first governor of the Northwest Territory, and the government was instituted at Marietta.  A little later it was removed to Cincinnati and then to Chillicothe.

### THE SOUTHWEST

South of the Ohio River the years of the Confederation brought discontent as well as growth.  Under the jurisdiction of Virginia and North Carolina the people west of the mountains were too distant from the seat of government.  The seaboard legislatures lacked the knowledge of conditions which they needed for the passage of suitable laws.  Speculators held great tracts of land and kept out would-be settlers, and there was no local authority which could regulate their conduct.  Adequate provision for defense, even, was not made.  The organization of county governments failed to satisfy the pioneers.  They desired to manage their own affairs and repeatedly demanded statehood.

Even in the days of the Transylvania Company the people of Kentucky had asked Congress to recognize them as a separate state.  The desire grew with time and the increase of population, and the Confederation period brought almost continuous agitation for statehood.  In western Virginia a parallel movement took place, and the settlements in the upper Tennessee Valley were equally eager for separation from North Carolina.

The passage of the Ordinance of 1784 encouraged these aspirations. The settlements on the upper Tennessee coincided almost exactly with one of the states projected in the ordinance. Moreover, in 1784, North Carolina ceded this territory to Congress on condition that certain terms be accepted within a stated time. Congress did not accept the terms, but meantime the inhabitants, assuming that statehood was at hand, set up a government, took the name of the State of Franklin, elected John Sevier as governor, and appealed to Congress for recognition. It was with great difficulty that North Carolina reasserted its authority.

A similar situation existed on the northern frontier. On the eve of the Revolution pioneers from Connecticut, Massachusetts, and New Hampshire had entered the Green Mountains, which both New Hampshire and New York claimed. When independence was declared, the question of jurisdiction was still in dispute, and the "Green Mountain boys" proclaimed their independence both of England and of the claimant states, and named their state "Vermont."

All of the regions which desired statehood looked to Congress for support of their pretensions, but Congress dared not encourage them lest it offend the states interested. At most it could indicate a willingness to act when these states assented. Such a negative position did nothing to allay discontent. Nor was Congress able to care for other interests which to the western people were of vital importance. Because of the mountain barrier the only feasible outlet for the increasing produce of these new communities was the Mississippi. Spain now held both banks of that river in its lower course, and would not concede the right of navigation by Americans. Her policy tended to make the Gulf of Mexico, almost surrounded as it was by her possessions, a "Spanish lake."

Her position gave her a strangle hold upon the American settlements, and she made the most of it. Secretly she promised the use of the river on condition that the westerners throw off their connection with the United States and enter into close association with her. Apparently she aimed either at the annexation of the territory in the southern half of the Mississippi Valley, or at an agreement which would reduce the settlements to the condition of dependent allies. To further her designs she permitted

certain persons to carry goods to New Orleans in return for their
influence in behalf of secession from the Union.   The chief of
these agents was James Wilkinson, a former officer in the Revolution, but a shrewd and unprincipled adventurer who finally
won for himself immortality in that trinity of infamy to which
Benedict Arnold and Aaron Burr also belong.

The settlers of Tennessee had an additional reason for dissatisfaction in the Indian situation.   Between them and the Spanish
on the Gulf dwelt several powerful tribes — Cherokees, Creeks,
Choctaws, and Chickasaws — occupying lands lying largely
within the bounds of the United States by the treaty of 1783 with
England, although partly within the tract the ownership of which
Spain disputed.   Fearing the Americans as neighbors and desiring, like the English in the Northwest, to prevent settlement
within the Indian lands in order to protect her trade with the
natives, Spain encouraged the tribes to resist all encroachments of
the Americans and even to exclude traders from the states.

Unfortunately Congress was less competent to deal with the
Indians in the Southwest than on the north side of the Ohio, for
the claims of the states had not been relinquished and its full
powers over Indian relations were confined to those tribes "not
members of any state."   Negotiations were undertaken with the
natives of the Gulf region, but they encountered the opposition of
the states claiming jurisdiction and came to little or nothing.

In 1786 Congress made an attempt to come to an understanding with Spain.   Three concessions were asked : the recognition
of the right of Americans to navigate the Mississippi ; the recognition of the thirty-first parallel as the boundary ; and a treaty
of commerce.   But it could offer nothing in return.   As the
Articles stood it could not close the ports to Spanish vessels nor
lay retaliatory duties.   At best it could only withdraw the
request for one or more of the concessions in the hope of per-
suading Spain to yield the others.

John Jay, Secretary of Foreign Affairs, opened negotiations
when Spain sent Don Diego de Gardoqui as minister to the
United States, only to find himself driven to pursue these tactics.
At last he decided that the least essential of the three demands
was the first.   He therefore requested Congress to authorize a
treaty by which the United States would abate her claim to the

use of the river for a term of twenty-five or thirty years in return for commercial concessions. A majority of the delegations favored the proposal, but not the necessary two thirds.

This failure is a capital illustration of the insufficiency of the power of Congress over commerce. At every point touching the welfare of the Kentuckians and Tennesseeans Congress seemed powerless. Aggrieved as they felt themselves to be, they did not hesitate to weigh the advantages and disadvantages of union with the eastern states. The matter did not present itself to their minds as a question of treason or disloyalty. Such was one of the fruits of the revolutionary philosophy. The rumor that Jay's proposal had passed Congress caused great excitement. It showed an apparent willingness to sacrifice the West for the advantage of the old states, and brought the secession movement in Kentucky to a climax. The loss of the country south of the Ohio seemed imminent. Washington, referring to the uncertain sentiment of union there, declared that the West was "on a pivot," and that the touch of a feather would turn it either way.[1] The test showed that the majority in Kentucky preferred the prospect of early statehood to a precarious independence, but the questions at issue with Spain remained unsettled as an inheritance for the government of Washington.

## FINANCIAL FAILURE

While almost every phase of the history of the Confederation shows the inadequacy of the Articles, the financial history of these years is particularly dismal. The Articles laid upon Congress the duty of paying the war debt. Apart from the continental notes, the debt amounted to about $43,000,000. Of this about $8,000,000 had been loaned by France, Holland, and Spain, the first named having supplied more than three fourths of the total obtained abroad.

Much of the domestic debt was represented by certificates issued in payment of soldiers' wages or for army supplies. Many of them had been given to the actual producers of food. Sometimes necessity had led to seizure rather than purchase of grain,

[1] Washington advocated a canal joining the Ohio and Potomac rivers, to afford an artificial outlet for the West, believing it would counteract the influence of the masters of the Mississippi.

wagons, horses, and cattle. The original receivers were fortunate
if they were able to hold these evidences of debt. In most cases
their own needs had compelled them to transfer the certificates
to others who had ready cash and could afford to speculate on the
chance of payment. Of course it was the depreciation of these
securities which caused loss to those who parted with them.

Under the circumstances the domestic debt was the last matter
of finance to which Congress could turn its attention. First of
all it must obtain funds to meet its own current expenses or cease
to function. Next was the interest on the debt, especially the
portion owned abroad. After that, if funds had been available,
would have come the principal of the foreign debt, and finally
the principal of the debt owed to Americans.

To provide for these needs the only resources made available
by the Articles were requisitions on the states and new loans.
No special provision was made for a revenue to be used in paying
the debt. The land cessions, indeed, opened an additional source
of income which, by implication, would be applied to this purpose; but so far as the Articles indicated, requisitions were to
cover the needs of Congress for all purposes.

The insufficiency of this provision was realized by Congress
almost before the Articles went into effect. To remedy it an
amendment was submitted to the states, allowing Congress to
collect a duty of five per cent on the value of all imports, to be
devoted solely to the payment of the principal and interest of
the debt. Rhode Island alone refused assent, thus defeating a
proposal of the utmost consequence.

Experience soon showed the impossibility of providing for
the debt through the use of requisitions. Congress asked for
$10,000,000 during the first two years of the Confederation, and
the states responded with less than $1,500,000. Requisitions
yielded altogether, during the entire period of the Confederation,
barely enough to meet current expenses, without paying even
interest on the debt.

Congress tried again, in 1783, to secure additional financial
powers by a "general revenue amendment," but with even less
success than before. The necessity of making some payments
on interest led to the borrowing of an additional $2,000,000 from
Holland. But most of the interest went unpaid, the arrearage

amounting in 1790 to many millions. Thus the public debt of a rich people increased continuously in time of peace because of the impotence of the government.

## SELECT BIBLIOGRAPHY FOR CHAPTER X

Fiske, *The Critical Period*, tells the story of the years of the Confederation and of the formation and adoption of the Constitution. It is one of the best of Fiske's books. McLaughlin, *Confederation and Constitution*, covers the same period; it was the first book to present the view now held of the nature of the problem of political organization which the United States faced after the Revolution. McMaster, *History of the People of the United States*, begins with the Confederation. It stresses the life of the people rather than political history, and while oddly organized is a mine of information. Its eight volumes come down to the Civil War. Schouler, *History of the United States under the Constitution*, also begins with 1783 and comes through the era of reconstruction after the Civil War. It is primarily a political history.

**Commercial Readjustment.** Channing, *United States*, chap. 13, is an excellent summary. Weeden, *Social and Economic History of New England*, is very valuable. For the efforts to negotiate commercial treaties, see Foster, *A Century of American Diplomacy*, and Fish, *American Diplomacy*.

**The Currency Question.** A good monograph is needed. Warren, "The Confederation and Shays's Rebellion," in *American Historical Review* deals with the central episode.

**The Growth of the West; The Southwest.** The general history of the West during the period is given by Roosevelt, *Winning of the West*, and Winsor, *Westward Movement*. Henderson, *Conquest of the Old Southwest*, and Hinsdale, *Old Northwest*, are most useful for the two areas dealt with. Briefer accounts are, Skinner, *Pioneers of the Old Southwest*, and Ogg, *Old Northwest*.

The story of the cessions of the western lands and congressional measures for surveying and selling them is well set forth by Treat, *National Land System*. The British policy in the Northwest is illuminated by McLaughlin, "The Western Posts and the British Debts," in American Historical Association *Reports*. Spanish policy in the Southwest is the theme of Green, *The Spanish Conspiracy*. The movements for statehood are described by Turner, "Western State-Making in the Revolutionary Era," in *American Historical Review*.

**The Ordinance of 1787.** Barrett, *Evolution of the Ordinance of 1787*.

**Financial Failure.** Dewey, *Financial History of the United States*, is a useful volume for the student of general American history. Chapter 2 deals with Confederation finance. Bullock, *Finances of the United States, 1775–1789*, is a special study of value.

# CHAPTER XI

## THE FORMATION OF THE CONSTITUTION

### STEPS LEADING TO THE CONVENTION

There was no lack of critics of the Articles of Confederation. To mention only well-known names, Washington, Hamilton, and Madison strove unceasingly to create sentiment in behalf of a more perfect government. Experience was also a faithful teacher. Each failure of Congress, each outbreak of disorder, added its quota of converts to the cause of a stronger general government.

The failure of all attempts at amendment of the Articles, however, was discouraging. It seemed impossible to secure the unanimous consent of the states to any change. Several proposals were made, now by state legislatures, now by members of Congress, again by public writers, for a convention of delegates from all of the states to consider the revision of the Articles, but Congress did not take kindly to the plan, and without its sanction a convention would be extra-legal. Besides, there was little hope that the recommendations of a convention would be accepted by the states.

In the midst of these perplexities Virginia and Maryland were seeking an agreement concerning commerce on Chesapeake Bay and the Potomac River. In general, interstate trade relations were in confusion, but these two neighbors had partially learned that coöperation is better than competition. In spite of conflicts over boundaries and other disputes they had from time to time in the past entered into agreements of various sorts, now for limiting the tobacco crop, again for joint campaigns against the Indians. Washington and Madison were eager to see the two states adopt a uniform commercial code, and at Washington's invitation, commissioners representing the two met at Mt.

Vernon in 1785. This conference revealed the need of a wider agreement, and accordingly Virginia invited all of the states to send delegates to a convention at Annapolis the next year.

The announced purpose of the Annapolis meeting was, if possible, to bring about nation-wide uniformity in legislation relating to internal and foreign trade. It was an attempt to take care of one of the great common interests by general agreement to pursue a uniform course. Delegates came, however, only from five near-by states. These were too few for effective action. Moreover, the leaders desired to broaden the aims of the movement. They had been advocating a general convention, and the moment seemed propitious for bringing about such a meeting. Before the Annapolis convention adjourned, they carried through resolutions proposing a convention to meet at Philadelphia in May, 1787, to recommend such changes in the Articles as would "render the constitution of the federal government adequate to the exigencies of the Union."

This resolution ignored Congress, which in its turn took no action for some time in support of the project. But the states responded so heartily to the invitation that Congress, outflanked as it were, was forced to issue a call for the meeting. Thus the convention obtained official standing. According to the terms of the congressional call, its recommendations were to be binding when approved by Congress and by the legislatures of every one of the states, in accordance with the amending clause of the Articles.

## THE CONSTITUTIONAL CONVENTION

By the time appointed for the meeting eleven states had chosen delegates. New Hampshire delayed action until June; Rhode Island alone failed to send delegates. Most of the fifty-five members were already well known. About three fourths of them had served in Congress, and several were, or had been, governors and judges. The rest were business men, lawyers, and planters. Even the younger members were men of large experience in public or private affairs. There was a notable absence of radicals like Samuel Adams, John Hancock, and Patrick Henry, although the last named might have attended had he not refused a place in the Virginia delegation. Jefferson and John Adams, regarded as "moderate radicals," were still abroad.

Governor Edmund Randolph, tall, handsome, and dignified, headed the Virginia delegation, in which sat also Washington, Madison, and Mason. Washington, universally acclaimed as the foremost American, guaranteed the respectability of the Convention in public estimation by his mere presence. Madison, thirty-six years old, a diligent student of government, and a ready debater, was prepared for a leading part in the discussions. Mason had drafted the Virginia constitution.

Pennsylvania sent Franklin, the premier diplomat, now too old for strenuous labor, but endowed with a calm and philosophic wisdom which was more than once like oil on troubled waters when passions ran high. His colleagues noted for previous service or activity in the Convention were: Robert Morris, former Superintendent of Finance and himself active in the "big business" of the day; Gouverneur Morris, his former associate, a keen thinker and debater with aristocratic views; and James Wilson, a Scotch lawyer, who showed an unsurpassed grasp of the problems of the Convention.

From New York came Alexander Hamilton, who as aide on Washington's staff during the war had won his admiration and confidence by his brilliant and precocious genius. Delaware sent John Dickinson to improve if he could upon his former effort at constitution-making. In the Massachusetts delegation sat Elbridge Gerry and Rufus King, both destined to become prominent figures in politics, and Nathaniel Gorham, like Robert Morris a business man and land speculator.

Roger Sherman and Oliver Ellsworth, of Connecticut, were among the most active and able members of the Convention. William Paterson, of New Jersey, is best remembered as introducer of the small-state plan. Luther Martin, of Maryland, was one of the most consistent opponents of the program of the majority. John Rutledge, of South Carolina, was an ex-governor.[1] Charles Cotesworth Pinckney, a revolutionary general, became prominent later in politics and diplomacy. Charles Pinckney, cousin of the last-named, a youth not yet out of his

---

[1] Wilson, Ellsworth, Paterson, and Rutledge later became judges of the United States Supreme Court. Rutledge and Ellsworth were in turn Chief Justice.

twenties, was the only member who came with a draft constitution in his pocket.

Although the Convention was not an "assembly of demigods," as Jefferson called it, the verdict of history agrees with the comment of Mason: "America has certainly upon this occasion drawn forth her first characters." But it cannot be said that these men represented a popular demand for a new government. Years ago one of the first historians of the Constitution (George Bancroft) wrote: "From the ocean to the American outposts on the Mississippi one desire prevailed for a closer connection." But there was no such unanimity; the rank and file of the people did not demand a strong central government. Talk about the "general interests" and "common welfare" meant little to men of the kind who had followed Shays. The problems of the federal government were far removed from the realities of the daily life of the masses.

The movement for the Constitution found its supporters, in short, among the conservatives who attributed the commotions of the time to an "excess of democracy," as Gerry phrased it, and desired to check these evils and promote business interests. The Philadelphia Convention was composed of men of the class that made the majorities in the state legislatures which chose them; it contained no representatives of the wage-earning and small-farming elements, for the one had no vote and the other was in the minority in the state assemblies. The framers of the Constitution had the bias of the old governing class, and came to Philadelphia to do on the scale of the nation what they had already done in the states. Their ideal was not government by the people. The day of democracy had not yet come.[1]

---

[1] This view is developed to the extreme by Dr. Charles A. Beard, in his *Economic Interpretation of the Constitution*. This book is a brilliant analysis of the economic groups which pushed the movement for the new Constitution and controlled the Convention. It is somewhat startling to learn that a large number of the members were holders of depreciated securities and personally benefited in fortune by the adoption of the new government and the establishment of the public credit. Dr. Beard implies, although he does not say, that self-interest was an important motive of the fathers of the Constitution. In this, in the writer's judgment, he goes beyond the evidence, which indicates that they believed that the benefits of a stronger government would be diffused throughout society. See discussion by Farrand, *Fathers of the Constitution*, pages 162–163. The present writer believes that the emphasis should be placed, as in the text, upon the view that the main features of the Constitution were determined by a process of evolution which covered at least a generation and which restricted rather narrowly the limits within which the Convention exercised a power of choice.

The Convention began its sessions on May 25 with Washington as the presiding officer. Madison assumed the task of reporting the debates for the information of posterity, and his notes, published a half-century later, are our chief source of knowledge of the proceedings. Contemporaries knew little of what went on, for the sessions were held behind closed doors, lest the discussions mar the impression of unanimity which it was hoped to make by the final report. As in the Confederation Congress, the delegation of each state voted as a unit.

As soon as the work of organization was done, Governor Randolph presented a series of resolutions as a basis of discussion. These resolutions, probably drafted by Madison, were the result of conferences held by the Virginia and Pennsylvania delegates during the preceding days. Soon after the debate began some of the delegates showed dissatisfaction with the "Virginia plan," and through Paterson offered a substitute (the "New Jersey plan," or "small-state plan"). Neither was in the form of a draft constitution; each merely set forth in resolutions the chief objects sought.

The acrimony of the debate on the issue raised by the rival plans has led many students of the Convention to give undue importance to the difference between them, and to overlook the more significant fact that the members were so thoroughly agreed on their main task that it required little discussion. This main task was to see that all matters of general, not local, importance were brought within real control of the federal authority.[1] Even in drafting the Articles of Confederation the aim had been to

[1] The adoption of the Albany Plan would have provided representative machinery by which the several colonies could have acted together in general concerns, in coöperation with the British government. Franklin believed "that if the Albany plan of union had been adopted and made effective, the subsequent separation of the colonies from the Mother Country might not so soon have happened." For want of such machinery as the plan provided, the general powers had in fact been wielded by the British government, and the local by the colonies, prior to 1763. The controversy between England and the colonies arose because it seemed to the colonies that the British government by its measures, especially those relating to taxation, and by its doctrine of parliamentary supremacy, was disregarding the limits of its general powers and invading the local, or "internal police," power of the colonies. During the years following 1763 thinking Americans and a few Englishmen were groping towards a clearer conception of the principle of "distribution of powers." If it had been grasped perfectly and applied courageously, it would have satisfied the colonists' demand for home rule on the one hand and the British demand for imperial control on the other; in essence it required nothing more than agreement as to what matters were "imperial," that is, of general concern, and what concerned the "internal police."

intrust Congress with the care of the common interests, but extreme jealousy for the rights of the states had marred the perfection of the work. The years under the Articles had clarified men's vision and shown pretty definitely where the line ran between general and local concerns. The heart of the Virginia Plan was the declaration "that the National Legislature ought to be empowered . . . to legislate in all cases to which the separate states are incompetent, or in which the harmony of the United States may be interrupted by the exercise of individual [state] legislation." These words merely stated the aim, leaving until later the enumeration of the additional "cases to which the separate states are incompetent." The New Jersey Plan accepted this same principle and began the enumeration by demanding for Congress the powers of taxation and commercial regulation.

It is surprising how few other powers of a general character the Convention was able to think of, which were not already covered by the Articles. Naturalization, bankruptcy, patents, copyrights, and the power of coercion, exhaust the list. New restrictions on the states, however, aided in separating the functions of the general and state governments. For example, states were deprived of the power of coining money (held concurrently with Congress under the Articles), of laying import duties, of emitting bills of credit, of making anything but gold and silver legal tender in payment of debts, and of passing laws impairing the obligation of contracts.

Clauses relating to taxation and commerce stood at the very head of the list of the powers of Congress in the first draft Constitution evolved out of the debates. In most comprehensive terms they authorized Congress "To lay and collect taxes, duties, imposts, and excises . . . to regulate commerce with foreign nations, and among the several states, and with the Indian tribes." But other clauses laid certain restrictions upon the use of these powers. Thus all duties, imposts, and excises were to be uniform throughout the United States; and direct taxes could be laid only in proportion to the population of the respective states. No tax could be laid upon exports from any state, nor could any regulation of trade or revenue give preference to the ports of one state over those of any other.

Some of these restrictions were made in deference to the desires of southern delegates who foresaw that in time Congress would probably be controlled by a northern majority, and feared that its new powers might be used to the detriment of southern industry.[1] The prohibition of export taxes, especially, arose from the fact that the southern states, as producers of staples such as tobacco and rice, sent abroad the great bulk of the fruits of their industry, and an export tax would fall with peculiar weight upon them. Another fear of the South was that Congress would use the power over commerce to prohibit the importation of slaves. Without some guarantee against this, Georgia and South Carolina would probably have rejected the Constitution. Hence Congress was forbidden to prohibit slave importations by the states prior to 1808.

None of the new powers was so vital as that of coercion. In fact, without it even with all the others the government must have failed as inevitably as the Confederation. Hamilton had seen the necessity of this power even before the adoption of the Articles, and had declared that Congress must have "complete sovereignty in all that relates to war, peace, trade, finance, and management of foreign affairs." By the words "complete sovereignty" he can only have meant coercive or compulsive power. In 1781 a committee of Congress, of which Madison was chairman, made a report arguing that from the necessity of such power it must exist under the Articles by implication. No result followed this report, for Congress dared not act upon this theory.

Washington again put the case in a nut-shell in 1786, when the fortunes of the Confederation were at the lowest ebb, by saying: "I do not conceive that we can exist long as a nation without having lodged somewhere a power which will pervade the whole Union in as energetic a manner as the authority of the State governments extends over the several States."

In such utterances we can trace the growth of the concept of a new type of government — a dual government, in which the states should retain authority over their internal affairs, while the general government, acting for the whole country, should wield full power over all matters that concerned the whole. Soon

[1] *Cf.* the controversy over the protective tariff, 1828-1832. See pages 385-390.

after the debates began in the Convention Gouverneur Morris explained that the existing government was "a mere compact, resting on the good faith of the parties [states]," while a supreme national government would have "a complete and compulsive operation." The Virginia Plan proposed to authorize the use of force against any state which was remiss in performance of its duties as a member of the Union. But Mason pointed out that "punishment could not in the nature of things be executed on the States collectively, and therefore such a government was necessary as could directly operate on individuals." Sherman proposed that the laws of the general legislature should be binding on the people of the United States.

The New Jersey Plan empowered the federal executive to use armed force to compel obedience to federal law by individuals as well as states; it also provided that the laws of the United States should be the supreme law, and that the state courts should be bound to uphold this supremacy even as against acts of the state legislatures.

Out of these elements the final provisions concerning coercion were constructed. The use of armed force against states was rejected as equivalent to civil war and as implying a union based on states. Even against individuals such force was feasible or desirable only in cases of insurrection involving numbers. The outcome was provision for a complete judicial system for the execution of United States law with recourse to military force in case of resistance by formidable numbers.

In happy contrast with the Articles the scope of federal judicial power was made co-extensive with the legislative power, extending to "all cases, in law and equity, arising under this Constitution, the laws of the United States, and treaties made . . . under their authority."

The distribution of powers between the governments of the United States and of the states, with compulsive operation of the laws of both (where not in conflict) upon the same persons — in a word, the creation of a dual government — was the great achievement of the Convention, and in accomplishing it the friends of the Virginia and New Jersey plans united without great difficulty. The most serious controversy in the Convention came, as already indicated, over a matter of secondary importance. Having decided that the country needed a real government on a national scale, the delegates from Virginia and Pennsylvania who sponsored the Randolph resolutions desired a Congress of two houses, with separate legislative, executive, and judicial branches, following the traditional model. Moreover, coming from populous states, they recurred to Franklin's contention at an earlier date, that the states should not have equal representation in Congress, as under the Articles, and proposed that in both houses the rights of suffrage should be in proportion to population or contributions to the common treasury. The members of the lower house were to be elected by the voters in the states, those of the upper by the lower house on nomination by the legislatures of the states.

The delegates of the small states urged that the enlargement of the powers of the existing Confederation would meet every exigency of the Union. The New Jersey Plan nevertheless accepted separate executive and judicial departments as well as new powers, but retained the one-house Congress and the equal representation of states.

There was in the two plans, as it turned out, nothing to prevent agreement except the difference concerning equality of representation in the legislature. The small states held that their equal vote was the essence of "federalism," and were fearful of a "national system" dominated by the great states through proportional representation.[1] In vain Madison and Hamilton pleaded that issues were not likely to arise which would array the large states against the small. Differences were much more likely to be sectional, they maintained, arraying the states of one part of the country against those of another part.

The small-state men were willing to accept even the two-house legislature, when they saw that it offered an opportunity to compromise. From proportional representation in one house and equal representation in the other a system "partly national, partly federal" would result. When the Convention voted for the first plan in the lower house, therefore, Ellsworth moved that equality be adopted for the upper.

---

[1] The phrase "proportional representation" has come in recent years to mean the representation of political parties in proportion to the vote polled. The student should avoid being confused by the change in the meaning of terms from period to period.

This motion failed and the chief crisis of the Convention resulted.  The large-state leaders declared that they would not confederate on the basis of equal representation, and with equal emphasis the small-state men asserted that they would confederate on no other.  A deadlock seemed to be reached and members began to talk of going home.  Fortunately a majority were not willing to abandon the hope of compromise.  A committee was appointed consisting of one member from each state for the purpose of formulating one.  Franklin was the Pennsylvania member of the committee, and to him was due the suggestion which was made the basis of the report.  Since the small states were ready to concede proportional representation in the one house, the situation demanded some makeweight to induce the large states to accept equality in the other.  The report therefore recommended this arrangement with the added condition that all bills for raising or appropriating money should originate in the lower house, and that those for the first purpose should not be amended by the upper.  Thus the large states would control the public purse.  After another bitter debate the report carried.[1]

Without a settlement of this issue of representation the Convention could not have proceeded.  The agreement is therefore rightly regarded as the "Great Compromise."  From this moment the cleavage between the large and small states ceased to be dangerous.  Other disputes divided the Convention along different lines, but while some of them aroused much feeling, none threatened a break-up.  Subsequent events proved, however, that equality in the Senate had little value for the small states.  Senators, as representatives of state governments in the "federal" branch of Congress, have been neither more nor less tenacious of state rights than representatives of the people in the "national branch."  In other ways the equality in the Senate had a very important influence upon the course of history.  The Senate became a bulwark of sectional interests during the slavery contest, enabling the South with its minority population to prevent or delay the adoption of antislavery laws.

The agreement upon representation in the lower house accord-

---

[1] By subsequent action of the Convention, the Senate was allowed to amend "money bills," thus destroying in part the advantage which the compromise had given to the large states.  Senators were also allowed to vote as individuals instead of by delegations.

ing to population raised the question whether slaves should be counted for this purpose. The same question came up in considering the apportionment of direct taxes. The rule of apportionment provided in the Articles had been difficult to apply, and in general population was held to be a sufficiently accurate index of the relative wealth of the states. Southern delegates held, however, that slaves were not the equals of white men as wealth producers, and objected to a full count as an index of tax-paying ability. Since they desired the full count as a basis of representation, while northern men took the reverse position on each of these questions, another compromise was necessary, by which it was agreed that three fifths should be counted in apportioning both representation and direct taxes.

This three-fifths ratio had been proposed several times during the dozen years preceding, as a basis for the requisitions of Congress upon the states, but never before had it been discussed in connection with representation. In later years the North chafed under it because direct taxes were rarely levied and it gave the southern whites an influence in Congress out of proportion to their numbers (see pages 330, 377).

A problem of real difficulty, although it aroused no heat, concerned the choice of the executive. After some debate a single chief executive was agreed to, but the best method of choosing him was a puzzle which long resisted solution. Choice by Congress threatened the independence of the magistrate unless his tenure of office was limited to a single term. Reëligibility, which was likely to be highly desirable in some cases, called for some other method of election. A choice by popular vote seemed utterly impracticable, both because the people were regarded as incapable of making a wise selection, and because of the lack of a means of preventing a scattered vote. When the device of an electoral college was hit upon, it was acclaimed as one of the triumphs of the Convention.[1]

One of the primary motives impelling the states to union was

---

[1] Madison, Wilson, G. Morris, and others favored popular election of the President, the first two from democratic principles. Morris thought the people would never fail to prefer some man of distinguished character and national reputation, while if Congress made the choice, he feared it would be the work of intrigue, cabal, and faction. An executive chosen by Congress and impeachable by it he held would be a mere creature of the legislative branch.

the desire that the strength of all might be available for the defense of each in case of foreign attack or internal disorders. Shays's Rebellion had shown the inability of Congress to aid a state in case of insurrection. One of the Randolph resolutions looked toward a remedy for this defect, and a section was placed in the Constitution obliging the United States to protect each state against invasion, and, upon request, against domestic violence. Congress was specifically authorized to employ military force to suppress insurrections and repel invasions, as well as to execute the laws of the Union.

A great many provisions of the Constitution deal with mere matters of detail. The Convention soon discovered that its time would be fully occupied in debating and deciding major issues, and that details would have to be left to a committee. Near the end of July the results of the discussions up to that time were referred to a Committee of Detail. These results were still in the form of resolutions stating principles, and the task of the committee was to embody them into a preliminary draft of the Constitution.

Much of the committee's work was almost mechanical. That is to say, the Convention having decided upon a government for the United States, it was left to the committee to clothe that government with familiar attributes. From the state constitutions were borrowed the provisions relating to legislative procedure, privileges of members, and powers and functions of the executive. Substantially all of these can be traced back to the practice of the colonial governments, and most of them to earlier English usage. They were the time-hallowed accessories of governments of peoples of English blood.

The committee also transcribed from the Articles the powers of the old Congress, and added those new powers, notably of taxation, coercion, and commercial control, which discussion had so clearly indicated as necessary. Finally it arranged all this matter logically in the form of a Constitution, divided into articles and sections. Its report was made on August 6 and became the basis of the Convention's debates during the last weeks of its sitting.

It was during the final period after the report of the Committee of Detail that the commerce compromise was made, the method of choosing the President determined, and control of patents, copyrights, and bankruptcies added to the enumerated powers.

Despite all care the completed Constitution had some unfortunate omissions. Territorial expansion should have been provided for. Proposals to give Congress power to build roads and canals and to grant charters to corporations were voted down. An express power to regulate all industry of more than local scope would have been of the utmost importance a century later, but the framers could not foresee the vast industrial expansion of the future, and the small-scale enterprises of 1787 seemed to fall within the police power of the states. To meet unforeseen conditions the Constitution contained provisions for amendments. The chief method required the affirmative vote of two thirds of the members of both houses of Congress and the approval of the legislatures of three fourths of the states.

The duality of the new system of government implied a duality of citizenship. In the Convention men began to speak of Americans as citizens of their states and also of the United States. A definition of citizenship in the Constitution would have prevented much confusion in after years, but it was not until after the Civil War that one found its way into the organic law through the fourteenth amendment.

As would be expected from the personnel of the Convention, the system of government which was worked out for the United States was not more democratic than the contemporary state systems. The rejection of the idea of popular election of the President is but one illustration. Many utterances show that the Senate was designed to be, not only the federal element in the government, representing the states as such, but the conservative element representing the wealthy class. Choice of senators by state legislatures was fixed upon for both of these reasons. A large majority of the Convention favored property qualifications for federal office, and attempts were made to decide what they should be. They are not found in the Constitution only because it was deemed best to leave them to be determined by Congress.

Even the so-called "popular" branch of Congress was not a democratic body, for it rested on the voting class and not on the masses. The suffrage clause of the Constitution reads: "The House of Representatives shall be composed of members chosen every second year by the People of the several states, and electors [voters for members of this house] in each state shall have the qualifications requisite for electors of the most numerous Branch of the State Legislature." This provision reached no lower into the social strata than the laws of the states, but it automatically democratized the House of Representatives as the states extended the suffrage.

The debates of the Convention show the aristocratic leanings of its members in yet another way.  In each colony and state the class from which they came had had difficulty with the democratic populations of the frontier regions.  The prejudices engendered by protracted struggles to preserve their dominance were carried by some members into the work of the Convention when it began to consider the future of the western settlements.  These men disregarded the pledge of equality which Congress had made in 1780, and which it was in the very act of confirming in the Ordinance of 1787.  "Property was the main object of Society," said Gouverneur Morris.  "He thought the rule of representation ought to be so fixed as to secure to the Atlantic States a prevalence in the National Councils."  He referred to the method by which the eastern part of his state had retained political control and urged its adoption on a national scale.  Gerry moved that the representation of the new states should never exceed that of the old, and the group holding this view was strong enough to poll four votes against five.

The report of the Committee of Detail provided for the admission of new states on terms of equality, but the conservatives were able to secure the adoption as a substitute of the colorless phrase "New States may be admitted by the Congress into this Union."  The meaning of the provision was left undetermined, to become the occasion of a dangerous sectional controversy a generation later when Missouri applied for admission (see page 377).

Madison, Mason, and Wilson advocated equal rights for new states.  Wilson's penetrating mind shows to peculiar advantage in this discussion of the rights of the West.  "The majority of the people wherever found," he urged, "ought, in all questions, to govern the minority.  If the interior country should acquire this majority, it will not only have the right, but will avail itself of it, whether we will or no.  This jealousy misled the policy of

Great Britain with regard to America. . . . Like consequences will result on the part of the interior settlements, if like jealousy and policy be ours. . . . He could not agree that property was the sole or primary object of government and society. The cultivation and improvement of the human mind was the most noble object." Wilson was a prophet at once of nationalism and democracy.

In so far as the Convention was influenced by the writings of theorists Montesquieu was their guide. American practice had always conformed closely, however, to his theory that legislative, executive, and judicial functions should be vested in independent and coördinate branches of government, each balancing the others and possessing a check upon their powers for its defense against encroachments. The Constitution gave Congress power to impeach the executive officers and judges, and gave the President a veto upon the acts of Congress. The Senate checked the executive in making treaties and appointments, and the two houses acted as mutual checks. The check of the judiciary upon the other branches was less explicit, but remarks in the course of debate show that many members thought of the power to judge of the constitutionality of acts of legislation as inherent in courts under a written constitution, and as in accordance with the theory of checks and balances.

Another theory which pervaded the work of the Convention was that the government of the United States possessed only delegated powers. In distributing powers between the federal and state governments it was intended that all not delegated to the former should remain in the states or in the people. No express clause to this effect was placed in the Constitution, as the majority in the Convention deemed it superfluous; but among the first amendments was one (the tenth) supplying the omission.

On September 17, 1787, an engrossed copy of the completed Constitution was read in the Convention and signed by nearly all of the delegates who were present. A few who had become dissatisfied did not remain for this event. According to the call of Congress, the Constitution, if approved by that body, would go to the state legislatures as an "amendment" to the Articles. The Convention, however, resolved upon a course that was really revolutionary. It proposed that ratification be by conventions of delegates in each state, chosen for the purpose by the voters, and that when the conventions of nine states had acted favorably, the Constitution should be binding upon those states. The Constitution was sent to Congress with this recommendation, and after some hesitation that body submitted it to the states to be dealt with as recommended.

## THE RATIFICATION OF THE CONSTITUTION

The opponents of the Constitution were at a disadvantage in the state contests. The secrecy with which the Philadelphia Convention had done its work kept them in ignorance of the new proposals until the moment of adjournment. In several states the conventions were called so promptly that the opposition had little time to study the Constitution and organize its forces. Moreover, the strength of the opposition was in the rural and interior parts, where the inhabitants were scattered and the diffusion of information slower than in the older, more compact communities. From Philadelphia southward, too, the rules of apportionment gave these back regions inadequate representation in the conventions, which followed the rules of the legislatures in this respect.

The friends of the Constitution were led by men who had attended the Philadelphia Convention and had come home knowing just what they wanted. Desiring to avoid the prejudice against nationalism by emphasizing the "federal" features of the new plan, they appropriated the name of "Federalists," which the opposition had first used, forcing it to accept the designation of "Antifederalists."

The Constitution being the program of the old dominant class, the question of ratification produced for the first time a nationwide division along lines of cleavage which had hitherto been only local. On the Federalist side were to be found the merchants, planters, lawyers, and speculators of the seaboard, while the Antifederalists included roughly the settlers of the isolated parts of New England, the people of interior Massachusetts who had sympathized with Shays, the Scotch-Irish and German pioneers of Pennsylvania, and the inhabitants of the Piedmont of Virginia, of the Carolina back country, and of Tennessee and Kentucky.

By the middle of January, 1788, five states had ratified. Four of these were of the small-state group which had been won by the "Great Compromise." The fifth was Pennsylvania, the first of the large states to act.

The Federalist leaders of that state deliberately hastened action to forestall opposition. The motion for calling a convention was made in the assembly before official notification of the action of Congress was received. Only a month was allowed for the election of delegates, and six weeks before the date of meeting.

In the convention the Federalists, led by James Wilson, outnumbered the Antifederalists two to one, but came almost wholly from Philadelphia and the eastern counties. The delegates of the back-country farmers feared that the strengthening of the central government would cripple the states. They objected especially to the taxing power, and to the Senate as the stronghold of the moneyed interest. Perhaps because the outcome was not in doubt, Wilson met their arguments by advocating nationalism with a frankness which Federalists in more uncertain states hardly dared to emulate. The final vote was 46 to 23 for adoption.

In Massachusetts probably a majority of the delegates at first opposed ratification. As in Pennsylvania the rural classes disliked the reduction of the powers of the state which would lessen their freedom in what they considered their own affairs, such as the issue of legal-tender paper. The Federalists, led by the ex-members of the Philadelphia Convention (with the exception of Gerry, who took his stand with the Antifederalists), won their battle by clever tactics rather than argument. It was apparent that the delegates of the plain people would be greatly influenced by the course of the two popular men, John Hancock and Samuel Adams, who were undecided. The Federalists set out to win these men. In Hancock's case they succeeded by making him president of the convention and hinting at support for federal office later. Adams, not so easily flattered, was much impressed by the declaration of the Boston craftsmen in favor of ratification. He and some others were inclined to advocate ratification only on condition that amendments be made to the Constitution, but they were finally persuaded to vote for unconditional ratification with recommended amendments, which the Federalists promised to support. The Massachusetts vote stood 187 to 168.

Massachusetts ratified early in February.   Next came Maryland and South Carolina.   Maryland was one state in which an ex-member of the Philadelphia gathering led the opposition. Luther Martin left the Convention before it adjourned, exclaiming "I'll be hanged if ever the people of Maryland agree to it !" On reaching home he published an essay entitled *Genuine Information*, in which he gave his reasons for disliking the Constitution. In spite of him the Federalists in the state convention cast 63 votes to 11.   In South Carolina the seaboard, favored by the plan of apportionment and satisfied by the compromise on the slave trade, outvoted the delegates from the Piedmont districts two to one.

The ratification of New Hampshire in June was the ninth, and gave that state the honor of putting the new instrument of government into effect.   Neither New York nor Virginia had as yet acted.   In these the lapse of time had permitted the Antifederalists to perfect their organization and it was doubtful what stand they would take.

In New York the opposition did not as in other states center in a rural democracy, but in the great landowners of the Hudson Valley, who did not wish the state to lose the revenue from import duties which the Constitution would take away.   The rivalry of the landlords and mercantile classes was of long standing, and the former controlled the convention.   Any advantage which the Antifederalists had gained by the tardy meeting was offset, however, by the fact that before the vote was reached the neighboring states had adopted the Constitution.   The geographical position of New York, in the keystone of the arch formed by the Atlantic coast, made it impracticable for her to hold out against the decision of her neighbors.   Hamilton and Jay helped to bring about a favorable decision by promising to join in requesting amendments after ratification.   After all, the final vote was exceedingly close, the Federalists winning by a margin of three.

John Marshall, later chief justice, and Madison led the friends of the new plan in Virginia, ably opposed by Mason and Henry.[1] In the main the contest followed the now familiar lines.   Madi-

[1] Washington was not a member of the Virginia convention, but used his influence, especially through correspondence, to promote ratification.

son and Marshall answered the zealous defenders of state autonomy by explaining that the states would retain all powers required for local functions, while the Union would receive only those needed to protect the interests common to all the states. The promise of the Federalists, and of Madison in particular, to work for amendments, won some votes, and the final majority for the Constitution numbered ten.

It will be noted that the question of amendments played an important part in several of the states. The Antifederalists were generally disposed to withhold assent to the Constitution unless stipulated changes were made. But there was no interstate agreement among them as to what changes should be demanded. Even so they wrung from the Federalists the promises to support amendments in return for unconditional ratification. It may here be added that the first Congress redeemed these promises, although not to the entire satisfaction of the Antifederalists, by recommending to the states a number of amendments of which ten were accepted. They constituted in effect a bill of rights, guaranteeing religious liberty, trial by jury, freedom of speech and of the press, etc., against the interference of the Federal Government. The tenth is an explicit statement of the principle of delegated powers: "the powers not delegated to the United States by the Constitution, nor prohibited by it to the States, are reserved to the States respectively, or to the people." It became the corner stone of the doctrine of strict construction.

While the Constitution was before the states Jefferson, writing from Paris, wished "that the nine first conventions may accept the new Constitution . . . but . . . that the four latest . . . may refuse to accede to it till a declaration of rights be annexed." One state convention, that of North Carolina, actually did adjourn, hoping to force the adoption of amendments. When the first Congress took up the subject, the convention met again and ratified. Rhode Island, the one state which sent no delegates to Philadelphia, was also the only one which refused to act on the Constitution. Congress really forced her to yield at last (1790) by threatening a suspension of commercial intercourse.

Beginning in October, 1787, Madison, Hamilton, and Jay joined in preparing for newspaper publication a series of explanatory essays on the Constitution since known as *The Federalist.* They are still a valuable commentary, but it must be remembered that they were intended to allay the apprehensions of those who feared nationalism. One must expect exaggeration also in the arguments on the other side, such as Martin's *Genuine Information,* but we actually find in their recognition of the Constitution as the instrument of a national government the nearer approach to the view of our own day.

Looking back after more than a century and a quarter, the student is likely to conclude that the adoption of the instrument framed by the Philadelphia Convention put an end to the sovereignty of the individual states. Some of the framers talked, indeed, of "divided sovereignty," of the relinquishment by the states of a part of their sovereignty to the general government. What was done is more accurately described by the phrase already used : governmental *powers* had been "distributed."

With state sovereignty passed all real basis for the conception of the Union as a League, formed by a contract of member states, and resting merely upon the obligations of good faith. Allegiance and obedience to the government of the United States as the supreme authority became due from every person subject to its jurisdiction, enforceable by the courts, and in case of necessity by armies and navies. The withdrawal of a state from the Union became likewise impossible (if the United States enforced its authority over its citizens within the seceding state), save as the result of successful revolution.

If the Constitution meant these things, however, hosts of people in all sections failed to grasp its true character. It became the instrument of a national government in days when the people at large were not yet conscious of national unity. Two generations were required for the national concept to master the minds even of the leading men in the majority section, while the South clung to the state sovereignty tradition until Civil War and a policy of "blood and iron" destroyed it. But we must again recall that the Constitution was the work of representatives not of the masses, but of a comparatively small upper class. Nationalism was as far beyond the ken of the people in 1787 as democracy was foreign to the purpose of the dominant group.

## SELECT BIBLIOGRAPHY FOR CHAPTER XI

**Steps Leading to the Convention; The Constitutional Convention.**
Bancroft, *History of the Constitution* (included in his *History of the United States*, last revision, and also published separately), was for a long time the standard history of the Convention. It contains much matter which is still valuable, but its point of view is antiquated. Fiske, *Critical Period*, is also somewhat out of date in its treatment of the work of the Convention. McLaughlin, *Confederation and Constitution*, is excellent. Farrand, *The Framing of the Constitution*, is a recent summary by a scholarly specialist on this topic. *The Fathers of the Constitution* is by the same authority. Schuyler, *The Constitution of the United States*, is a still more recent summary. Beard, *Economic Interpretation of the Constitution*, presents in brilliant array an abundance of evidence from a single point of view, which may overinfluence the unwary reader. For an excellent summary from a similar point of view, see Schlesinger, *New Viewpoints*, chap. 8.

**Ratification of the Constitution.** Fiske and McLaughlin give good brief accounts. See also Schuyler, and the general histories of McMaster and Schouler. The detailed history of ratification is still scattered in monographs dealing with particular states.

# CHAPTER XII

## THE ESTABLISHMENT OF THE NATIONAL GOVERNMENT

### ORGANIZATION OF THE GOVERNMENT

When formal notice reached Congress that the ninth state had ratified the Constitution, it took steps to prepare for the new régime. The first Wednesday in January, 1789, was fixed as the time for choosing presidential electors, and the first Wednesday in February as the day for casting their ballots. The first Wednesday in March was set for the meeting of Congress, with New York as the place.

The Antifederalists made efforts in some states to elect members of Congress. In Virginia they controlled the legislature and chose both senators. The great majority of the members of the first Congress, however, were Federalists, so that the new government was in the hands of its friends.

It was April before a quorum of members arrived in New York and the houses organized. The Constitution empowered the House of Representatives to choose its own presiding officer, or "Speaker," but assigned the duty of presiding over the Senate to the Vice-President. To act until the result of the electoral vote should be known the Senate chose a president *pro tempore*. The rules of procedure in both houses were adapted in the first place from the practices of the state legislatures and the Confederation Congress.

As soon as the work of internal organization had been done the houses turned to the business of counting the electoral vote. The constitutional provision for the choice of the President gave each state a number of electors equal to the sum of its representatives and senators, to be chosen as its legislature might prescribe. Several methods were used in the first election: three states used the general ticket; in five the legislatures made the choice ; the rest divided the state into districts and allowed the voters in each to choose one elector. The first of these methods eventually became universal, but for many years the second was generally used.[1]

The electors met in their own states on the day appointed and each voted for two persons, one at least a non-resident of the state. The Constitution did not provide for any indication of preference for the Presidency. From each state a certified list of the votes was to be sent to the President of the Senate, who was to open them in the presence of both houses. If a majority of the electors had voted for the same man, he was to be the President. In case of a tie, or of no person having a majority, the House of Representatives was to make the choice, each delegation voting as a unit to preserve the equal influence of the small states as under the Confederation. If no person had a majority, the names of the five leading candidates were to come before the House. After the President was chosen the candidate having the next largest vote was to become Vice-President. In case of a tie vote for the second place, the choice devolved upon the Senate.

This cumbrous machinery, which gave the Convention so much satisfaction, was expected to serve as a kind of nominating device. It was not expected that electors would often coincide in their judgment sufficiently to cast a majority for one man, hence the choice was expected to come to the House rather regularly. The framers of the Constitution failed to foresee the effect which the rise of political parties would have upon this system. The provision worked so badly that it was modified by one of the early amendments (the twelfth).

In the first election, however, no difficulty was encountered, for Washington's name was found upon the ballot of every elector. Their second votes were scattered among several men, but John Adams had more than any other candidate, although less than half of the total number.

Messengers were dispatched to notify Washington and Adams of their election, and to invite them to New York to take office. Washington, enjoying the life of a country gentleman at Mt.

---

[1] New York lost its vote in 1789 through a disagreement in the legislature as to the best method of choosing electors.

Vernon, and weary of public duties, was extremely reluctant to abandon his plantation.   Nevertheless he set out for New York, greeted everywhere by the plaudits of the people, who made of his journey a veritable triumphal procession; and upon arrival took up his abode in a house so small — sad contrast with the spacious mansion on the Potomac — that three of his secretaries had to share one room.   On April 30 he was inaugurated with great ceremony.   Adams took his seat as President of the Senate, and the government was ready for work.

New York, now a bustling town of thirty thousand people, ambitious to retain the government in its midst, presented to Congress a hall designed by the Frenchman, Charles l'Enfant, which excelled in architectural beauty any public building so far erected in the United States.   In this "Federal Hall" Congress held its sessions until the government was removed to Philadelphia, in 1791.

The work of the first Congress was second in importance only to that of the Constitutional Convention.   The Constitution, after all, was but a framework or skeleton which awaited the action of Congress to give it life.   Its provisions were not self-executing, but needed legislation to put them into effect.   The decisions involved were momentous, for they set precedents of almost constitutional force.

The Constitution referred only incidentally to "Executive Departments" and "Heads of Departments."   It rested with Congress to decide what offices were needed, to create them by law, and to define the duties of the officials.   During the summer and early fall Congress passed bills creating three departments.   First came the Department of Foreign Affairs (unfortunately renamed the Department of State).   Then came the Department of War, followed by the Department of the Treasury. The head of each Department was to be a "secretary."   In addition the offices of Attorney-General and Postmaster-General were established.

Under the Articles all civil officers had been appointed by Congress and were responsible to it.   By the Constitution the power of appointment was vested in the President "by and with the advice and consent of the Senate."   Washington offered the post of Secretary of State to John Jay, the associate of Franklin and Adams in the diplomacy of the Revolution, and Secretary of Foreign Affairs during the Confederation. The choice was a fitting one, since Franklin had passed the age for active service and Adams was Vice-President. When Jay declined, Washington turned to Jefferson, our representative in France. For the War Department he chose Henry Knox, of Massachusetts. This was a virtual continuation in office, since Knox held the corresponding post under the Confederation. Hamilton became Secretary of the Treasury and Edmund Randolph, Attorney-General.

Although the Constitution authorized the President to require the written opinions of heads of departments upon subjects relating to their respective offices, it said nothing about a cabinet. In making appointments and treaties the Senate was designed to be an advisory council. Washington's attempt to consult the Senate on an Indian treaty proved embarrassing, however, both to himself and to the members of that body. "A shamefacedness, or I know not what, flowing from the presence of the President, kept everybody silent," wrote Senator William Maclay, of Pennsylvania, in his Journal. After the one effort the President adopted the practice of submitting business requiring the Senate's advice and consent in a written message, leaving it to deliberate at its convenience.

The failure of the upper house to function as an advisory body led Washington to create his own by calling upon the three secretaries and the Attorney-General for their opinions when matters of importance were to be decided. In this and other ways the first President, like the first Congress, created precedents which have become to all intents and purposes parts of our constitutional system.

While the Constitution expressly vested the appointing power in the chief executive and Senate, it was not clear on the matter of removals. Some congressmen thought that the power of removal was incidental to that of appointment, and belonged to the President with the Senate's consent. The view prevailed that administrative officers, from heads of departments down, were subordinates of the chief executive, and that the power of removal inhered in his office. Another precedent was set by this decision, but it did not escape challenge in later times when President and Congress were at odds.

The fundamental law vested the judicial power of the United States in "one supreme court" and such inferior courts as Congress might deem necessary. It also specified the cases in which the jurisdiction of the Supreme Court should be original. Here again much discretion was left to Congress, and the framing of the Judiciary Act of 1789 was an important part of its work of organizing the government. One group of congressmen disliked the idea of creating inferior federal courts, preferring to utilize the courts of the states in federal cases, with provision for appeals to the Supreme Court. They were outvoted by those who desired a complete federal system.

The Act provided for thirteen district courts, roughly one for each state, grouped in three circuits. For each district there was to be a judge. Appeals from a district court went to the circuit court. A session of this intermediate tribunal was to be held in turn in each district of the circuit, by the judge of the district and two Supreme Court justices. The Act fixed upon six justices for the Supreme Court, one to be Chief and the others associates. As few cases were expected to reach the highest tribunal, it was not thought to be unfair to require the justices to make the round of the circuits periodically, a pair going to each annually.

An important section determined that whenever a case before a state court involved federal law an appeal should lie to the federal courts unless the decision upheld the federal law. This clause gave great offense to the friends of state rights.

Washington found at the very beginning of his term that he must protect his work from interruption by visitors. "I had no leisure to read or answer the dispatches that were pouring in upon me from all quarters," he declared. Desiring "to demean himself . . . in such a manner as to maintain the dignity of his office, without subjecting himself to the imputation of superciliousness or unnecessary reserve," he sought the advice of several men, among them Madison, Hamilton, and Adams, as to the official etiquette which would be suitable. Adams advised "splendor and majesty" to support "dignity and authority." Hamilton thought there was danger of "too much ceremony for the character of our government," and favored a simple manner to avoid exciting "dissatisfaction and cabal" in a country where "notions of equality are . . . general and strong." Although Adams and a group of senators failed — much to Washington's relief — in the effort to decorate the executive with the pompous title of "His Highness, the President of the United States of America, and Protector of their Liberties," the President did adopt enough of the grand style to draw the fire of criticism. When he rode with Mrs. Washington, he was attended by outriders in livery and the carriage was drawn by four or six horses with gay trappings and hoofs blackened and polished. Every Tuesday while Congress was in session he held a formal reception known as a levee, from three to four o'clock. At these he always appeared in black velvet knee breeches, yellow gloves, and cocked hat, wearing a dress sword in a scabbard of white polished leather. On Friday evenings Mrs. Washington held her "drawing-rooms," at which Washington desired to be regarded not as the President but as a private gentleman. From time to time the President invited diplomats, government officers, and members of Congress to formal dinners, but he and "Lady Washington" did not accept hospitalities.

## Financial Legislation

Even before it created the departments Congress passed a revenue law. Indeed, next to its own organization and the counting of the electoral vote, its earliest act was an exercise of the new power of taxation. Madison, kept out of the Senate by the Antifederalists of the legislature of his state, had turned to his neighbors as a candidate for the lower house, and it was he who moved the enactment of a five per cent duty on the value of all imports.

A Pennsylvania member asked that the duties be laid, not uniformly on all imported goods, but upon such as competed with domestic industry. At the same time that the necessary revenue was obtained, American production would then enjoy an advantage over foreign. The protective principle was thus introduced into tariff legislation at the very outset, although it was incidental to the purpose of raising a revenue. It was not until domestic manufactures developed on a considerable scale that protection became the dominant motive in framing tariffs (see page 336).

The first tariff debate was typical of all that have followed in bringing out the conflict of interest of different sections of the country.  Georgia, for example, which needed slaves, objected to any tax upon imported negroes; Virginia, with slaves to sell, desired a duty.  New England opposed an impost on molasses, the raw material of the rum distilleries of Rhode Island and Massachusetts, while other sections desired the revenue which it would yield.

The act as passed laid duties averaging about eight per cent. This first financial measure was framed hastily under pressure of urgent need, with little calculation of the relation of the probable returns to government expenditures.  The more careful consideration of needs and policies was allowed to wait until the Treasury Department was instituted and Hamilton appointed Secretary.  Meantime the public creditors became clamorous for appropriations to pay interest, at least, on the debt, and soon after Hamilton took office the House resolved that the Secretary of the Treasury should prepare a plan for the support of the public credit, to be reported to the next session.  Accordingly Hamilton presented in January, 1790, the first of a series of great reports in which was set forth his financial system.

This First Report on Public Credit dealt with the debt both of Congress and the states.  The foreign debt amounted to nearly $12,000,000, the domestic debt was about $42,500,000 more, and the state obligations aggregated about $21,500,000.  Hamilton proposed that the Federal Government should assume the state debts, and that the whole should be funded.  The essence of his plan of funding was that Congress should authorize the Treasury to accept the old securities at par in payment for new bonds.  The power of taxing made possible provision for punctual payment of interest on the new bonds and for their redemption at maturity.

Most of the securities issued by the Second Continental Congress had by this time passed into the hands of speculators who had paid much less than face value for them.  A vigorous fight was made in Congress against funding because payment of the securities at par would enrich these speculators.  Madison proposed that they be paid the market value only, and that the difference be given to the original owners.  The plan was imprac-

ticable, but this disagreement marks the beginning of a breach
between Hamilton and Madison which foreshadowed the rise
of parties. Hamilton's contention that the government was
pledged to pay the debt to the legal holders, and that it could not
establish its credit by beginning its career with an act of bad
faith, was really unanswerable, and his recommendation prevailed. The funding act established the credit of the government
at one stroke. In the rhetoric of Daniel Webster, Hamilton
"smote the rock of national resources and copious streams of
wealth burst forth."

Madison was also a leader of the group which tried to defeat
the assumption of the state debts. Hamilton urged that these
debts had been incurred in the common struggle, and were a just
charge on the common treasury. He offered no adjustment in
the case of states which had paid a portion of their debts, and he
aimed by the scheme to win support for the central government.
There could be no better guarantee of its permanence, he thought,
than to have a large number of men of wealth and intelligence
looking to it as the source of income on their investments. Such
a device had steadied the throne of William and Mary after the
Revolution of 1688.

A policy which tended to build up a moneyed interest was
certain to encounter strenuous resistance. Comparatively few
southern men had capital for speculative investments in government securities, and their representatives in Congress blocked
the assumption project for a time. The contest followed sectional lines; but another issue between North and South which
was pending at the same time made a bargain possible, an early
instance of "log-rolling." Congress was discussing the permanent location of the national capital, northern men preferring
a site on the Susquehanna or Delaware, southerners insisting on
the Potomac. The arrival of the North Carolina delegation
threw a new weight into the scales, and Hamilton made clever
use of it. At his suggestion Jefferson, who had just returned from
France to take his post in the State Department, invited a few
influential politicians to a dinner party where southern votes
for assumption were pledged in return for Hamilton's promise of
northern votes to fix the capital on the Potomac. Jefferson
later repented bitterly of his share in this transaction, claiming

that he was duped by Hamilton before he got his bearings after his return from abroad.

In December, 1790, the Secretary of the Treasury submitted two more reports. One of these proposed a Bank of the United States, to be privately owned and managed subject to conditions prescribed by a charter of incorporation to be enacted by Congress. The capital stock was not to exceed $10,000,000; and the notes of the bank, backed by specie and government bonds, were to be receivable for all payments to the United States. The charter was to run for twenty years, and during that term no similar institution was to be sanctioned by Congress. The immediate interest of the government was limited to the privilege of subscribing one fifth of the capital stock, but for the protection of the public the Secretary of the Treasury was entitled on demand to statements showing the bank's condition.

Hamilton's purpose in making this recommendation was, in the first place, to provide a sound currency. The paper issues of previous years were disappearing, and the Constitution forbade further issues by the states. Owing to the scarcity of specie, however, the state governments were under strong temptation to charter banks without requiring that their paper be properly backed by reserves of gold and silver. The multiplication of unregulated banks might lead once more to floods of depreciated notes unless steps were taken to prevent. The establishment of a great central bank, pledged to the redemption of its notes on demand, would be such a step, for by supplying the channels of business with a sound circulating medium it would dominate the situation and make it useless for unsound institutions to put out their paper.

Hamilton held that such a bank "would be of the greatest utility in the operations connected with the support of the public credit," and mentioned particularly the aid which it could give the government in obtaining loans and facilitating the collection of taxes.

There were many friends of state banks who disliked the idea of a central bank with a monopoly of valuable privileges. Such an institution would give another opportunity of investment to the moneyed class and tend to create what would today be called a "money trust." Again Madison was the leader of the congressional forces of opposition, and in his speech against the bill he stressed most of all the argument that the Constitution gave Congress no power to grant a charter of incorporation.

When the bill was passed the fight was carried to the President. Washington called for the written opinions of his cabinet. Jefferson and Randolph submitted arguments against the act and Hamilton and Knox upheld it. Much to Jefferson's chagrin, Hamilton's opinion was a reply to his own, which had been submitted to the Secretary of the Treasury because the measure was financial. Thus Hamilton had the opportunity to make the final argument by way, so to speak, of rebuttal. Convinced by his reasoning Washington signed the bill.

In a final report made a year later (December, 1791), Hamilton dealt with the subject of manufactures. This document gives the best view extant of the status of American manufactures at that time, and advocates the policy of a protective tariff for the purpose of promoting those especially which would "tend to render the United States independent on foreign nations, for military and other essential supplies." In his views on this matter Hamilton anticipated the arguments of Clay and Calhoun nearly a generation later (see page 339). But the prevailing sentiment accorded with the *laissez faire* philosophy of the English economist Adam Smith, and the protectionist plea bore no fruit for many years.

In January, 1790, Hamilton had suggested an excise on distilled liquors as a source of additional revenue. When the assumption of the state debts required further taxation Hamilton recurred to the excise in a report which accompanied the one on the bank. He recommended also an increase in the duty on imported spirits, but thought the time inopportune for a general upward revision of duties. All of Hamilton's financial plans were tinged with political motives. In this proposal of an excise he seems to have had in mind the importance of making the power of the new government felt by the farmers of the western frontier. Along the border from Pennsylvania southward the making of whisky had become the rival of the New England rum industry. Separated from the coast markets by the mountains, the transportation of grain was out of the question, and the farmers would have found grain raising profitless if they could not have converted their crop into the portable and comparatively valuable form of whisky.

The same conditions that kept the crops of the western farmers out of the coast towns kept imported goods from reaching them, so that they were hardly touched by the tariff. The excise reached them only and seemed to single them out as subjects for special taxation. Their sturdy individualism was affronted; the excise was a form of tax which they had not expected. It reminded them of the internal taxes with which England had goaded the colonists to revolution, and Congress passed the bill in the face of predictions of trouble which were soon borne out by events.

The resentment which the western border felt against the excise took the form of active resistance in southwestern Pennsylvania. Meetings were held in which defiance was urged, and the collectors began to be threatened with personal violence. At length, in 1794, when warrants were issued for the arrest of some of the agitators who were destroying the property of persons who complied with the law, actual bloodshed occurred, and the malcontents began to gather under arms.

The federal authority was directly challenged by these proceedings. Jefferson, writing to Madison, denounced the law as " an infernal one," which would become " the instrument of dismembering the Union"; while Washington, spurred on by Hamilton, decided that the time had come to call out the militia to suppress the insurrection and enforce the laws of the Union. From Pennsylvania, Virginia, and Maryland he summoned fifteen thousand men who marched towards the scene of the disturbances. Meantime commissioners sent ahead were attempting to persuade the insurgents to disband. When the troops arrived no armed opponents were to be found. Some of the leaders were arrested and two were convicted of treason, but having vindicated the national authority Washington showed clemency and pardoned them.

The incident had both good and bad results. The demonstration of the government's ability to meet rebellion with overwhelming force was complete, and a new tone of respect was noted at once in men's references to the federal power. But the resort to military force did not win friends for the administration among the people, and, as with Hamilton's other policies, the political advantages of the incident accrued to the opposition.

## FEDERALISTS AND REPUBLICANS

One important consequence of the discussion of Hamilton's financial plans was the rise of political parties. Those who followed him, being the administration party, retained the Federalist name. Madison was for a short time administration leader in the House of Representatives, but finding himself not in agreement with Hamilton, he swung into the leadership of the opposing group, which presently took the name of "Republicans," although sometimes called "Democrats" by the Federalists. Jefferson, Madison's senior and the patron and mentor of his young manhood, presently superseded him as the chief of the party.

Hamilton was of West Indian birth, his father being a Scotch merchant and his mother a French woman. He had come to New York on the eve of the Revolution as a student in King's College, but the stirring events of the hour had drawn him into public life. His brilliant ability quickly attracted attention, and his marriage to Elizabeth Schuyler introduced him into influential social and political circles. His rise was meteoric, and when called to the Treasury Department at the age of thirty-two, he was already a noted figure. In spite of small stature and slight build, his erect and dignified carriage and mental force compelled respect in all with whom he came in contact. For sheer intellectuality it is doubtful if he has been excelled by any American statesman, but in practical politics he lacked tact and persuasiveness and was somewhat domineering in manner. He had set forth his political philosophy in a speech in the Constitutional Convention, in which he said: "All communities divide themselves into the few and the many. The first are the rich and well born, the other the mass of the people. . . . The people are turbulent and changing; they seldom judge or determine right. . . . The British Government was the best in the world."

As Secretary of the Treasury Hamilton was the constructive genius of the administration. He built his hope of successful government upon the active interest of financiers, merchants, and speculators. They were the rich and well born who would check the unsteadiness of the masses. Under such a guide the Federalist party naturally attracted these elements, which were nearly identical with the old ruling class, especially in the North.

Hamilton and his followers derived their creed from the Old World. Jefferson represented the spirit of the New World, begotten of frontier conditions. He himself was born near the Virginia foot-hills, his father being one of the early settlers in the Piedmont, and his philosophy of government was permanently influenced by his boyhood environment. It harmonized with the philosophy of Locke, which he himself had incorporated into the Declaration of Independence. While in France, moreover, he had come into contact with the teachings of Rousseau, which emphasized the happiness of the supposed state of nature and stressed the natural equality of mankind.

Jefferson believed that a simple agricultural life was the best basis for a free state, because it bred equality and individuality. Such was the natural life of America, with its "immensity of land courting the industry of the husbandman." Factories and wage-labor he thought tended to destroy self-reliance and produce inequalities and class conflicts. He favored commerce with other nations as the means of exchanging the agricultural surplus for the manufactures of the Old World. Such exchange would "let our workshops remain in Europe." He preferred to let the foreign nations supply the ships, since the growth of an American merchant marine would entail a navy for its defense.

Jefferson did not believe in the possibility of democracy under all conditions. He could not trust the working classes in cities. His hope for the success of democracy in the United States was bound up with the continued preponderance of agriculture, and the wide, if not universal, distribution of land ownership. As a citizen of Virginia he would have required a small freehold qualification for the exercise of the franchise, and would then have made it the equivalent of manhood suffrage by granting estates from the public lands to all males.

He did not become a propagandist for these views while a member of Washington's administration, but he condemned policies which seemed to be conceived in the interest of the capitalists. In this he was the champion of the small farmers and the plain people in general, so that the alignment of parties followed in the main the old divisions based on economic and geographical differences. Most of the great southern planters drifted into the Republican party, however, not because they held Jefferson's liberal views, but because Federalist policies were unsatisfactory. As a class they had formed one of the groups which had promoted the movement for the Constitution; but the assumption scheme laid a burden upon them where, as in Virginia, the state debt had been partially paid; and Jay's treaty (see page 252) made them fear that their prerevolutionary debts would have to be paid. All of Hamilton's proposals tending to advance the interests of the owners of capital seeking investment favored the North, for such capital was scarce in the southern states; even the wealthy there were "land poor."

As associates in Washington's cabinet Hamilton and Jefferson were antagonists on practically every important question that came up. Their disagreement over the question of chartering the United States Bank is particularly memorable because it led to rival ways of interpreting the Constitution, and these became one of the chief differences distinguishing Republicans from Federalists.

In the opinion on the bank which Jefferson submitted he began by quoting the tenth amendment, which reserves to states or people all powers not delegated to the United States. Then examining the list of enumerated powers he found no mention of the right to incorporate a bank. Coming next to the general welfare clause, he held that Congress is not empowered by it to do just "anything they please" "but only to lay taxes" to provide for the general welfare.[1] The former construction "would render all the preceding and subsequent enumerations of power completely useless. It would reduce the whole instrument to a single phrase." Hence the general welfare clause does not authorize the charter of the bank.

Finally he considered the clause allowing Congress "to make all laws necessary and proper for carrying into execution the enumerated powers." "But," he reasoned, "they can all be carried into execution without a bank. A bank therefore is not necessary, and consequently is not authorized. . . . The Constitution allows only means which are 'necessary,' not those which are merely convenient for effecting the enumerated powers.

---

[1] "The Congress shall have power to lay and collect Taxes, Duties, Imposts, and Excises, to pay the Debts and provide for the common Defence and general Welfare of the United States." Art. I, Sec. 8, ¶1.

If such a latitude of construction be allowed to this phrase as to give any non-enumerated power, it will go to every one. . . . Therefore it was that the Constitution restrained [Congress] . . . to those means without which the grant of [an enumerated] power would be nugatory."

The heart of Hamilton's answer lies in his interpretation of the "necessary and proper" clause.   "It is not denied [by Jefferson] that there are implied, as well as express powers, and that the former are as effectually delegated as the latter."   Implied powers are those which serve as "an instrument or mean of carrying into execution any of the specified powers. . . . The only question must be . . . whether the mean . . . has a natural relation to any of the acknowledged objects or lawful ends of the government. . . . If the *end* be clearly comprehended within any of the specified powers, and if the measure have an obvious relation to that *end*, and is not forbidden by any particular provision of the Constitution, it may safely be deemed to come within the compass of the national authority."   "The powers contained in a constitution of government . . . ought to be construed liberally in advancement of the public good. . . . It will not be contended . . . that the clause in question gives any new or independent power.   But it gives an explicit sanction to the doctrine of implied powers."

Some scholars regard this doctrine of implied powers as Hamilton's chief contribution to the permanence of the Constitution. In practice the difficulty of amendment proved to be very great, but Hamilton's principles of construction supplied an element of elasticity which made it possible for the Constitution, without many formal changes of wording, to be adapted to the changing needs of a rapidly developing nation.   A rigid framework, incapable of such adaptation, must soon have been destroyed by the vital forces of the growing organism.   The doctrine of implied powers has been, not the means of destroying the Constitution, as Jefferson feared, but of preserving it.   In theory, at least, the process of construction has not changed it, but only brought out what was inherent.   The Republicans themselves, when they came to administer the government, had to abandon in large part their principles of strict construction.

Jefferson, knowing Hamilton's admiration for the British

government, fell a prey to the fear that he and his "corrupt cohorts" were subtly seeking to undermine the foundations of the Republic to prepare the way for monarchy. To combat the influence of the "monocrats" he gave a clerkship in his department to Philip Freneau, really to enable him to publish an opposition newspaper. The bitterness of this sheet, which did not spare even the President, enraged Washington, who gave Jefferson a strong hint that he disapproved of the dual rôle which Freneau was enabled to play through his patronage. To his diary Jefferson confided his determination to retain Freneau, because he had checked the tendencies of the government which had been "fast galloping into monarchy."

Over his opposite-minded secretaries Washington presided with an even hand, giving added proof of his greatness. Inferior to Hamilton in intellectual power and to Jefferson in understanding of the people, he was the superior of both in judgment and solidity of character. When at the close of the Revolution the unpaid troops were on the point of mutiny, it was he who persuaded them to disband at the command of Congress, trusting to the future for justice. Hamilton was suspected at the time of being one of a group who would have welcomed an armed uprising as a means of teaching the country the necessity of establishing a government worthy of the name. There was danger of turmoil and bloodshed and of a military despotism in such a course, and Washington's essential confidence in the people appears in his insistence that they should have the opportunity to work out the country's political salvation in peace.

Next to nobility of character judgment was the outstanding quality in his statesmanship. For this reason he held a place second to none as early as the First Continental Congress. A rather silent man, he heard others patiently, but his decisions were his own, and they were seldom wrong. Few could have yoked together men so antagonistic in temper and opinion as the two great secretaries and evoked from each his best service. In matters relating to finance his convictions supported Hamilton. In the fundamentals of foreign policy he held a middle course, differing from both advisers. In the strict sense he was also above party.

As the end of his first term drew near he desired to retire to

private life.  Hamilton demurred.  The experimental stage of
the government was not past, and the strife of parties and sections would endanger its permanence under any less commanding chief.  On this point Jefferson and Madison joined their
pleas with Hamilton's.  The first wrote: "The confidence of
the whole Union is centered in you. . . . North and south will
hang together, if they have you to hang on."  Washington
yielded to this advice, and Republicans and Federalists united
in giving him a second term (1792).  Again the electoral vote was
unanimous.  But the Republicans refused to support Adams for
the Vice-Presidency.  For this post they named George Clinton,
of New York, and gave him 50 electoral votes, while Adams, with
the support only of the Federalists, received 77.

Adams ranks next to Hamilton as a leader of the Federalist
party.  Of rather humble origin, he was during the Revolution
one of the popular leaders in Massachusetts.  The equality of
mankind, the social compact, and the consent of the governed
were dogmas which he held in common with other "fathers of
the Revolution."  Except in his attitude towards English policy
in America, however, he was not a radical; and while he insisted
upon the right of the people to choose their own plan of state
government, he hoped they would be" wise enough to follow the
English constitution" so far as circumstances permitted.  He believed in the restriction of the suffrage to freeholders but wished
to promote general ownership of land.  In these particulars his
views were much like Jefferson's.

As time passed he became distinctly less liberal.  In his admiration of British institutions he resembled Hamilton.  Like Hamilton also he believed that the rich and well born compose a
natural aristocracy, the element of stability in society.  Holding
the poor to be the more turbulent element, he thought that the
control of the propertied class would diffuse the benefits of security throughout the body politic.  He would check this control
enough to prevent oppression, for he feared the unrestrained
influence of the rich more than Hamilton did.

Adams's views were quite in harmony with those of the classes
which made up the Federalist party.  He was not a skillful politician.  He was able, honest, and patriotic, but lacked tact, was
rather stubborn and pompous, and took himself too seriously.

He had considered himself a presidential candidate in 1789, and was greatly offended when Hamilton became party to an agreement to divert a few votes from him to other persons, so as to insure Washington's election. A coolness between the two men dating from this time was the beginning of a factional division which at length split the Federalist party and contributed to its downfall.

## SELECT BIBLIOGRAPHY FOR CHAPTER XII

**Organization of the Government.** The twelve years of Federalist rule are most conveniently summarized by Bassett, *The Federalist System.* Volume IV of Channing, *United States*, begins with the constitutional era.

**Financial Legislation.** Dewey, *Financial History*, is excellent from the economic standpoint; Lodge, *Alexander Hamilton*, supplies in addition the political data. See also general histories.

**Federalists and Republicans.** Gordy, *Political History of the United States*, is inclusive in subject-matter, but gives special attention to the rise of parties. Ford, *Washington and His Colleagues*, is the work of a specialist in party history. Beard, *Economic Origins of Jeffersonian Democracy*, treats party divisions as the result of divergent economic-group interests. See also Hockett, *Western Influences*, 33–40.

Lodge, *George Washington*, Morse, *Thomas Jefferson*, Morse, *John Adams*, and Gay, *James Madison*, are helpful biographies. Lodge is somewhat of a hero worshiper. *Cf.* Ford, *The True George Washington*, and Thayer, *George Washington.*

# CHAPTER XIII

## THE FEDERALISTS AND FOREIGN AFFAIRS

### WESTERN QUESTIONS

The old dispute between New York and New Hampshire over the Green Mountain district was brought to an end in 1791 and Vermont was admitted to the Union as the fourteenth state. The next year Kentucky and Virginia reached an agreement on terms of separation and the fifteenth state took its place in the sisterhood. By this time both Carolinas had ceded their claims to jurisdiction over the lands west of the Alleghenies, and Congress organized their cessions as the Territory Southwest of the Ohio River, on the model of the ordinance already adopted for the Northwest Territory, with the exception of the antislavery provision. The growth of population was so rapid that the Southwest Territory became the sixteenth state, under the name of Tennessee, in 1796. By 1800 its inhabitants exceeded one hundred thousand, while Kentucky was approaching a third of a million.

Statehood and rapid growth did much to counteract the intrigues of Spain with the pioneers, but she stood firm on the questions of the boundary and the navigation of the Mississippi. The growth of the American communities alarmed her and made her more tenacious than ever of her influence over the Indian tribes of Florida and the disputed district. Her policy was to encourage the natives to refuse to cede lands to the United States and to have no dealings with American traders. To promote it she employed a half-breed Creek chief named Alexander McGillivray, who hated the Americans because as a South Carolina Tory in the Revolution his property had been confiscated.

To offset Spain's influence, the United States invited McGillivray to the seat of government in 1790 and paid him a liberal sum said to be in compensation for his losses. Thus mollified he and the chiefs with him made a treaty, and he accepted a military commission under the United States and promised both to promote trade among his people and to keep them at peace.   This attempt at the pacification of the Creeks did not affect the Cherokees, who harassed the border until volunteers by retaliatory raids forced them to make peace in 1794.

These relations between the whites and Indians endangered the peace between the United States and Spain.   Even more dangerous was the situation within the disputed tract.   This region was claimed by Georgia, under her charter, as well as by Spain and the United States.   Instead of relinquishing her claim to Congress as all of the other states had done, she made grants to land companies which prepared to make settlements.   Settlement in defiance of Spain might bring on war.   On the other hand recognition of her jurisdiction by the settlers would jeopardize the interests of the United States.   Washington met the dilemma and avoided international complications by issuing a proclamation warning the people to keep out of the tract.

Early in Washington's term efforts were renewed to reach an agreement over the main questions in dispute, that is, the use of the river and the boundary.   The negotiations dragged along for several years and the anger of the western people gradually kindled against the power that denied them access to the sea.   It seemed likely that they would seize the first occasion to make an attack upon New Orleans and open the river by force.

Manuel Godoy, the Spanish premier, watching events carefully, decided that the time for concessions had come when news reached Madrid in 1794 of Jay's treaty with England and Thomas Pinckney, the American representative, called for his passports, announcing his intention to go to London.   Construing this as a hint that the United States was about to seek an alliance with England with the purpose of taking forcibly what she had failed to obtain by diplomacy, Godoy, a liberal and lover of peace, agreed to make a treaty.   It was completed in 1795, and conceded the demands of the United States.   It fixed the boundary at the thirty-first parallel, and gave Americans the right to navigate the Mississippi to its mouth, and to unload goods at New Orleans for transshipment to ocean-going vessels.   This privilege, known as the "right of deposit," without which the navigation of the river would have been useless, was granted for three years, with the stipulation that it would then be renewed either at New Orleans or some other convenient point.

These years of the early nineties were a time of great stress in the Northwest Territory. The beginnings of settlement around Marietta and Cincinnati aroused the natives, who had repudiated the treaties made during the Confederation. Depredations and murders became so frequent that General Josiah Harmar, in command of the garrison at the fort of the same name, was compelled to take the field. The Indians avoided battle, but cut off some detachments of Harmar's men and had rather the better of the contest. Governor St. Clair then took command in person of an expedition directed against the heart of the Indian country. Marching into the northwestern part of Ohio, remote from his base, he allowed his army to fall into an ambush and be cut to pieces.

This was in 1791. Warned at last that most careful preparations were essential to success, the government put General Anthony Wayne, — "the chief who never sleeps," the Indians called him — in command and nearly three years were spent in plans for a decisive campaign. Then, in 1794, Wayne's army invaded the Indian country, laid waste the native villages and fields of the fertile Maumee Valley, and won a signal victory at the Battle of Fallen Timbers, a few miles from the present city of Toledo.

Forced by this defeat to make peace, the tribes in 1795, by the Treaty of Greenville, renewed the cessions made in the rejected treaties. The boundary of the Indian country was pushed northward from the Ohio to the watershed separating its tributaries from the streams flowing into Lake Erie. All but the northwest quarter of Ohio was opened, and there was peace in the Northwest for sixteen years.

Its growth now rivaled that of Kentucky. Virginians came in great numbers to the Scioto Valley, and a mixed migration from New Jersey, Maryland, Virginia, Kentucky, and even New England entered the Miami country to swell the population of Cincinnati and begin new towns like Dayton and Hamilton, as well as occupy the farm lands in the Symmes Purchase. A stream from New England, especially Connecticut, flowed into the Western Reserve. By 1800 the number of inhabitants justified the partition of the Northwest Territory. The Ohio portion retained the old name, while the remainder was christened "Indiana Territory," with William Henry Harrison as governor.

Harrison was in Congress as delegate from the Northwest Territory. Before taking his new post, he, as spokesman of the pioneers, led Congress to pass a new land law (1800) which modified the

FIRST PARTITION OF THE NORTHWEST TERRITORY, 1800.

Ordinance of 1785 in behalf of actual settlers. The main features of the new law were the introduction of the credit system and the reduction in the size of the tract which could be purchased to three hundred and twenty acres. Already (1796) the price had been advanced to a minimum of $2 per acre, but under the credit system it might be paid in four equal annual installments. Any man who had $160 in cash, plus small fees for surveying and registering, could command a farm of a half-section. Such was the scarcity of wage labor in the rising towns of Pittsburgh, Cincinnati, and Louisville that any able-bodied single man could soon earn enough above the cost of living to put himself in possession of a farm.

Speculation continued rife, and large tracts were purchased for resale. Many of the settlers bought from the speculators rather than at the government auctions. Nevertheless the new law was a quickening force in the movement of population into the Northwest. The Southwest was without this stimulus, for the unoccupied lands of Kentucky and Tennessee were under state control, and Georgia did not complete her cession until 1802. Even after that the Indians were in possession of much of the ceded area.

Only three years elapsed after the division of the Northwest before the eastern portion came into the Union. Ohio was the "first fruit of the Ordinance of 1787."

### RELATIONS WITH FRANCE AND ENGLAND

Many problems arising from our relations with the countries of western Europe crowded upon the attention of the first administration, adding to the cares of a government already heavily burdened with the task of getting under way. Some of the most difficult of these problems grew out of the French Revolution. That memorable upheaval began simultaneously with the constitutional era in the United States. In 1789 the French monarchy, top-heavy "like a pyramid on its apex," confessed the failure of absolutism by summoning the first meeting of the Estates-General, or representatives of the nation, which had been called for one hundred and seventy-five years. Like the Long Parliament which marked the failure of Charles I's attempt at personal rule in England, the Estates-General demanded reforms as the price of its aid, and thus the Revolution began.

The Revolution ran through several stages. At the beginning it was in the hands of moderate men, like Count Mirabeau, who aimed at a constitutional monarchy and the abolition of the privileges of the nobility. But as many of the nobles fled to other countries and stirred them up to attack France, the course of events enabled the Republicans to overthrow the monarchists. They were in control by 1792, and when the King was found to be plotting with the *émigrés* he was deposed, and at the end of

January, 1793, brought to the guillotine. Up to this time England was not a member of the coalition against France, but disputes now came to a head which brought her into the war.

American sympathies soon divided along party lines. The Republicans saw in the events in France the efforts of a great people to free themselves from an ancient oppression. The Federalists, on the contrary, were shocked by the violence which marked the rise of the people, and saw in it proof of the turbulence of the masses when freed from restraint. In their admiration for England they became pro-British in their foreign policy, while the Republicans were equally pro-French. The rivalries of the powers involved the territories contiguous to the United States and touched our interests so closely that Hamilton was inclined to favor an alliance with England, while Jefferson looked to a "stricter connection" with France as his "polar star."

Soon after the news of the outbreak of war between England and France came word that the Republic was sending a minister to the United States to replace the representative of the over-turned monarchy. The news made it necessary for Washington to decide upon his course. Calling together his cabinet he submitted a number of questions. By the treaties of 1778 and later the United States and France were allies, France was entitled to certain privileges in American ports, and the United States was bound to defend France's possessions in the West Indies. The cabinet disagreed on the question whether the overthrow of the monarchy had abrogated the alliance, Jefferson holding the modern view that the agreement bound the two peoples and that a change of government did not destroy it. All thought that the new minister should be received, and consented that Washington should issue a proclamation of neutrality. The proclamation announced the state of war in Europe, declared that the United States was at peace with all of the belligerent powers, and warned Americans against acts of hostility towards any of them.

Jefferson, believing that the alliance was still in force, called the proclamation pusillanimous notwithstanding his consent to it. His feelings were shared by the Republicans generally. Hamilton undertook to defend the President's course through arguments in the public press. Madison, prompted by Jefferson to take up his pen "and cut him to pieces in the face of the public," replied, and a lively debate followed. It was evidently Washington's belief that the alliance was defensive only, and that the United States was under no obligations to protect the French islands except in a defensive war. In the present case his view apparently was that France was the aggressor. Thus considered, the United States was not guilty of a breach of faith, although Washington was undoubtedly moved by a strong sense of the necessity of peace for his infant country.

The conduct of the new minister Genêt (addressed as "Citizen" after the revolutionary fashion) is a curious chapter in diplomatic history. Under the rules of international etiquette his first duty upon arriving was to proceed to the seat of government and present his credentials before attempting any official act; but he was only twenty-eight years of age and his enthusiasm for the cause of the French Republic led him to act rashly.

Landing in Charleston, perhaps because his ship was driven from its course by storms, he began at once to act as if the United States were the announced ally of France. He issued a number of commissions as privateers to Charleston shipowners, and their vessels began to prey upon English commerce. He also set on foot plans for a land attack on Spanish Florida by Americans of the southern states.

Then he set out for Philadelphia, passing through a Republican region in which he was everywhere hailed with enthusiasm. The contrast between Washington's cool dignity and the popular demonstration chilled Genêt like an arctic blast and led him to conclude that the President was not representative of the public sentiment. He did not demand fulfillment of the treaty of alliance, but insisted that the President call an extra session of Congress, apparently in the belief that the legislature would overrule his decision upon neutrality. Washington refused, but Genêt was nothing daunted.

He now entered into correspondence with George Rogers Clark, hoping to organize a force of westerners to attack Louisiana. Clark, disappointed at the neglect of his claims for services during the War of Independence, and angry like others in the new settlements because Spain still denied them the use of the river, was ready for the part of leader. To pay the expenses Genêt sought advances on the debt due France, pretending that he would use the money in the purchase of supplies for the West Indies. One of the privateers commissioned at Charleston had brought in an English vessel, "The Little Sarah," as prize. This, re-christened "The Little Democrat," and fitted out as a privateer, Genêt planned to send by sea to the mouth of the Mississippi to support Clark's attack on New Orleans.

The designs against Louisiana and the Floridas were covered by Genêt's instructions, but finding the administration unresponsive he decided to carry them out secretly and in spite of neutrality. This led to a quarrel with the government over French rights in American ports. Washington held that while the treaties permitted France's prizes to be brought into our ports and denied that privilege to her enemies, they did not permit the refitting of the prizes for hostile use. Genêt would not accept so strict a construction of the treaties, but finally promised that "The Little Democrat" should not go to sea without notice.

Genêt's conduct at several points might have strained our relations with France if his government had supported him. He actually sent "The Little Democrat" to sea in violation of his promise. Washington then requested the French government to recall him. Fortunately the request was granted readily, for another turn of events had supplanted Genêt's friends. The extreme democrats were in control in France. They sent Jean Fauchet as Genêt's successor, with instructions to arrest him and send him home. Washington refused the request for extradition and Genêt remained in America, marrying a daughter of Governor Clinton, of New York. Learning after Fauchet's arrival of the plans for the Clark expedition Washington took precautions to prevent it, although without funds there was little danger of its being attempted.

Relations with Great Britain were far from satisfactory during most of Washington's presidency. The King's government was slow in sending a minister and when one did come the situation was little improved. England still refused to make a treaty of commerce, and the question of the border posts was hopelessly entangled with the British claims on behalf of creditors and Loyalists. The Indian war in the Northwest was dangerous, for it was difficult to go against the Indians without the appearance of hostility towards their British friends. An English fort stood near the site of the Battle of Fallen Timbers, fifty miles within American territory, and Wayne's army narrowly missed attacking it.

The war between England and France brought a new crop of troubles, due to the maritime code which England saw fit to adopt. The war was a boon to American ships, since as neutrals they enjoyed many immunities denied to vessels of the belligerents. As it was no longer safe for her own vessels to visit her colonies, France relaxed her navigation system and allowed neutrals to engage in this carrying trade. In fact a great part of the carrying for all of the countries of western Europe fell into American hands.

England regarded the relaxation of trade restrictions by her enemy as a mere war measure, and applied the "Rule of 1756" to stop it. This held that a trade which France did not permit in time of peace could not be allowed in war. England began to seize American vessels laden with the products of the French West Indies when bound for France. She also asserted that provisions were contraband and subject to seizure if bound for France. The United States denied the legality of seizures of both kinds, and rejected England's interpretation of the law of blockade in addition. When England declared an enemy's port blockaded she seized vessels anywhere on the high seas if bound for that port (the "paper" blockade), while the United States maintained that the port must be guarded by a stationary naval force, and that seizures might be made only when ships were caught in the act of attempting to enter a guarded port.

The practice of impressment now also became extremely vexatious. Service on the British war-ships was hard, almost unendurable. Food was miserably bad, precautions against disease almost unthought of, and discipline brutal. Men-of-war avoided port more than the plague, for sailors deserted by hundreds on every opportunity. Only force kept the crews full, and press gangs continually, in war time, ransacked prisons and merchant ships. For a long time it had been customary for the naval officers to board foreign merchant vessels on the high seas in search of deserters. The seizure of sailors on American ships began during the Confederation, and after 1793 became very frequent, for the rapid expansion of the merchant marine attracted many deserters.   American sailors encouraged desertion by procuring "protections" — certificates that the holders were Americans — from local magistrates, which they were quite willing to transfer for a few dollars.

When every sailor whose native tongue was English was a British subject impressment seldom involved mistakes.   After America became independent the case was different, and many a bona-fide citizen of the United States was seized along with deserters.   England made no objection to the correction of errors, but long delays were unavoidable, and the victims and their families suffered great hardships.   The United States government contended that seamen on board American vessels were to be treated as Americans.   While admitting the right of British cruisers to search neutrals for munitions of war, it denied the right to search for deserters.   It offered to seek them for arrest and return; but the British would not accept this as a satisfactory substitute for impressment.   Nor would she recognize the right of expatriation.

France also began to make seizures.   Her view of the Rule of 1756 and of the law of blockade was the same as that of the United States.   She had no occasion to practice impressments, and her treaties exempted provisions from seizure.   But she held that if Great Britain did not respect the rights of the United States she would be at a dangerous disadvantage if she did so herself.

The United States had cause for complaint against both countries, but Britain's superior sea power made her offenses far more numerous and grievous.   Congress began to discuss commercial restriction.   The Republicans believed that England might be brought to terms by injury to her commerce.   The Federalists opposed the resort to such measures because American as well as English commerce must suffer, and there was danger that trade restrictions would lead to war.   While the debate was in progress Washington decided upon an extraordinary effort of diplomacy. In the crisis it seemed possible that a special envoy to the British court might gain a hearing, and for such a mission he chose John Jay.

Although his instructions made no demand for the abandonment of impressments they probably required the impossible, and he accepted the appointment knowing that "no man could frame a treaty with Great Britain without making himself unpopular and odious." To secure the execution of the treaty of 1783 in such points as the surrender of the frontier posts he found less difficult than to get compensation for the recent seizures and to persuade England to make a commercial treaty which would place our trade with the British Isles on a satisfactory basis, open the ports of the West Indies, and secure immunity for our ships in carrying French goods. Finding that he could not obtain everything that the United States desired, he made the best agreement that he thought could be obtained.

The treaty, signed late in 1794, reached the United States early the next year. It provided that the border posts should be surrendered in 1796, allowed trade with the British East Indies, placed the commerce of the United States with the British Isles on a basis of "reciprocal and perfect liberty," and admitted American boats of not more than seventy tons burden to the West Indies. The last concession contained its own guarantee that the boats would not carry their cargoes to Europe, but as a further precaution to keep the carrying trade of the islands out of foreign hands, the treaty forbade the exportation from the States of the products of the West Indies (molasses, sugar, coffee, and cotton). Although intended to prevent reëxportation, it applied equally to these articles if produced in the United States. The commercial clauses were to run for twelve years.

Joint commissions were agreed upon for settling the old question of the debts and for determining the northeast boundary. The claims on behalf of the Loyalists were dropped, offset by counterclaims for slaves carried away when the British armies sailed for home. Claims on both sides arising from alleged illegal seizures of ships were referred to commissions. The disputed questions of international law were left almost as they stood before.

Washington decided to submit the treaty to the Senate rather than to attempt further negotiations or renew the risk of war. The Senate ratified after striking out the paragraph concerning West Indian trade, England consented to the change, and Washington proclaimed the treaty as part of the law of the land.

But the agreement pleased no one. Although they accepted the treaty, the Federalists were disappointed because the commercial concessions were not greater; while the Republicans in Congress attempted at the next session, although in vain, to defeat its execution by withholding the necessary appropriations.

Republicans had denounced the negotiations from the first, as well as the choice of envoy. Had not Jay once tried to barter away our right to navigate the Mississippi? An agreement with haughty England was "a degrading insult to the American people : . . . and an insidious injury to France."

Notwithstanding the general dissatisfaction, the treaty did benefit the country in many ways. It paved the way for the settlement of several of the old disputes. It aided Pinckney to secure a treaty with Spain. Equally important, England relaxed in practice the maritime code which she refused to modify in principle. This was perhaps in part because trade was outstripping her tonnage. The commercial privileges given to Americans by the rejected article of the treaty were, at any rate, granted by executive order, and products of the French, Spanish, and Dutch islands when brought to the United States were allowed to be reëxported. In 1796 American vessels carried to Europe 35,000,-000 pounds of sugar and 62,000,000 pounds of coffee.

In the case of "The Polly," decided by the British admiralty courts in 1800, it was held that the vessel had not violated the Rule of 1756 by reëxporting a cargo which had been landed in the United States and on which duty had been paid. While the direct carrying trade between the West Indies and Europe still incurred the penalties of the rule, this decision seemed to legalize the "broken voyage," and neutral shipping prospered. The burden of the duties paid in American ports and of the increased freight charges fell upon the ultimate consumer.

## PARTY POLITICS

The year 1795 was a great one in the history of diplomacy. Within the twelvemonth treaties were signed or ratified with Spain, England, and the Northwest Indians. The vexed questions inherited from Confederation days were disposed of. These successes showed the efficiency of the new government and tended to create a spirit of confidence.  The Federalists deserved the credit for these results.  They had also established the financial system and proved that the government could cope with domestic disorders.

Yet party divisions were widening.  The Republicans dropped out of the cabinet during Washington's second term, Jefferson resigning in 1793 and Randolph in 1795.  Timothy Pickering, a staunch Federalist, became Secretary of State in that year.  Hamilton also retired from office in 1795, Oliver Wolcott taking his place ; but Hamilton continued to wield the power almost of a dictator over the Federalists.  Jefferson called him a "colossus to his party."  Adams, a man of independent views, was one Federalist who refused to follow him.

Outside of the administration the Republicans were growing in strength, and as Washington's second term neared its close they prepared for a vigorous contest in the next presidential election.  Party organization was still so imperfect that no very satisfactory method had been devised for nominating candidates.  For want of a better mode the members of the two houses met in caucuses of their parties and made recommendations.  They were entirely without authority to do so, and had no power over the choice of presidential electors, but they were fairly representative of opinion in their parties and their advice carried weight.

In this way John Adams and Thomas Pinckney (negotiator of the Spanish treaty) became the Federalist candidates in 1796, while Thomas Jefferson and Aaron Burr were named by the Republicans.  Adams was the logical candidate of his party, being far more prominent than any other leader except Hamilton, who, like many a later statesman, had made too many enemies to be an "available" standard-bearer.

To prevent a tie and consequent failure of choice by the electors, it was necessary for them to scatter votes intended for the vice-presidential candidate.  According to Hamilton it was agreed that equal support should be given to Adams and Pinckney by the Federalist electors.  Within the circle of his confidential friends, however, he let it be known that in his opinion "if the chance should decide in favor of Mr. Pinckney, it probably would not be a misfortune."  Some hint of this reached the ears of Adams's friends among the electors, in the form of a rumor that there was an intrigue on foot to bring in Pinckney over him, and to defeat it a number of them withheld their votes from Pinckney.   Adams received 71 votes, and his rival Jefferson had 68, nine more than Pinckney.

Adams was rather glad than sorry that Jefferson, his friend of olden days, had defeated Pinckney.   But the electoral system was not working satisfactorily, when one party could win the Presidency and the other the second office.   Burr moreover complained because the Republican electors did not support him equally with Jefferson, and before the next election public opinion came to require that an elector should not vote at his own discretion but according to the will of his party.   The change illustrates the growth of party discipline.   Equal support of party candidates, with a resulting tie and the necessity of choice by the House of Representatives, had its drawbacks, however, as the election of 1800 was to show.   The root of the difficulty was the lack of provision for separate ballots for the two officials.

Washington was grieved by the rise of party spirit.   He had hoped to unite men of all shades of opinion in the effort to govern the country for the good of all.   Where he had failed Adams could not succeed.   By consulting Jefferson with the thought of appointing a Republican as minister to France, he affronted the Federalists without winning the good will of the Republicans. He retained Washington's cabinet, but Pickering and Wolcott regarded Hamilton as the real head of the party and did not work in harmony with the President on many important questions. In the end the factional breach was widened by the retention of Hamilton's friends, and a drastic reconstruction of the cabinet became necessary.

Washington, meantime, made the approach of the end of his service the occasion of a Farewell Address.[1]   In it he appealed to all parts of the country to uphold the Union as the source of benefits for every section and interest, citing the Spanish treaty as an illustration of service which the Union had rendered the West.

A memorable passage dealt with foreign relations.   The interests and policies of Europe, he said, differed from those of Amer-

---

[1] The first paragraph announced his resolution to decline reëlection.   Although he gives no hint of a belief that acceptance of a third term would form an objectionable precedent, his action did much to establish the doctrine that no President should serve for more than two.

ica. "Therefore, it must be unwise in us to implicate ourselves, by artificial ties, in the ordinary vicissitudes of her politics, or the ordinary combinations and collisions of her friendships or enmities. Our detached and distant situation invites and enables us to pursue a different course. . . . Why, by interweaving our destiny with that of any part of Europe, entangle our peace and prosperity in the toils of European ambition? . . . 'Tis our true policy to steer clear of permanent alliances with any portion of the foreign world. . . . Let [existing] engagements be observed in their genuine sense.    But, in my opinion, it is unnecessary and would be unwise to extend them."

The Republicans took exception to the Address. Where "Union" was mentioned they read "Federalist party," for the deeds praised were the achievements of that party. They therefore appraised the utterance as a covert plea for their opponents.    Later generations, venerating Washington as the "Father of his country," have taken the Address as his political will and testament and have treasured his advice.    They have, in fact, probably read into the passage concerning alliances with European powers a meaning which the author did not intend. Washington himself had leaned towards an understanding with France in 1792 as an offset to the weight of England and Spain upon our flanks.    Though Europe was far away the powers of its western shores were our neighbors, as holders of colonies touching our borders on three sides.    With Spain in Louisiana, on the Gulf coast, and at the mouth of the Mississippi, and with Britain in Canada, the transalleghany areas were fruitful soil for intrigues which threatened the allegiance of citizens and the territorial integrity of the United States.

The temptation was indeed great for the government to seek support through alliances, like the nations of Europe, but Washington had finally decided upon a neutral policy as a surer means of guarding national interests at the time, since an alliance would have linked the destiny of the young Republic with the fortunes of the ally.    The advice in the Farewell Address was the outgrowth of the neutrality proclamation of 1793.    In after years the warning against "permanent alliances" was transmuted into a doctrine of "isolation" — that all participation in the wars and politics of Europe should be avoided.

### ADAMS AND THE BREACH WITH FRANCE

Although Jay's treaty relieved the tension in British relations it involved the United States in a misunderstanding with France. Our representative in that country at the time of Genêt's mission was Gouverneur Morris. His services were of great value, but his temper was aristocratic, and he became *persona non grata* after the fall of the monarchy. The Republic requested his recall at the same time that it acceded to the demand for Genêt's removal. Washington complied as a matter of international courtesy, appointing James Monroe in his stead.

Monroe was a Republican of the Virginia school, somewhat younger than Jefferson, and his devoted disciple. He had already won important rank in political life in state offices and as a member of Congress. Washington selected him partly because of his desire to preserve the bipartisan character of the government, partly because it was not likely that any Federalist would be acceptable to the French. The choice proved to be a bad one, for Monroe had not yet attained that judicial balance which characterized his later years, and conducted himself more as the representative of the Republican party than of the administration.

At the time of his arrival in Paris the only government France had was a Convention, elected by the radical Democrats to draft a constitution. Delayed in this work by the prolonged crisis of war, the Convention was still acting as a provisional government, and to it Monroe presented his credentials. His reception was so cordial that he was carried away by his emotions and made an address pledging the coöperation of the two republics in the cause of liberty. The speech voiced sentiments appropriate to nations in alliance, and misrepresented the neutral views of the administration. The British government protested, and Washington admonished him to be more circumspect.

Jay's negotiations were now in progress in England, but Monroe, insufficiently informed if not somewhat misled by his dispatches, repeatedly assured the French that the English treaty would contain nothing prejudicial to them. When the terms became known this was found not to be true. It was the desire and purpose of the American administration to adjust French relations on an entirely equitable basis, but France took the Jay treaty as evidence that the United States preferred the friendship of her chief enemy to her own.

Monroe like the French saw in the treaty evidence of a pro-British policy, and feeling that he had been duped, had no heart to defend it as he was instructed to do. On the contrary, his conduct became more than ever that of a partisan. When France proposed to send an envoy to the United States to seek a new treaty, he advised delay. The election of 1796 was at hand, with the possibility of a Republican victory, in which event he intimated the chances of success would be greatly enhanced. Monroe was doubtless moved by fear that failure of negotiations would mean war, but his conduct was indiscreet. When it was found that he was supplying friends at home with information to be used against the Federalists during the campaign, he was recalled.

The minister of France in the United States also violated the rules governing diplomats by working quietly in behalf of Jefferson's election. The defeat of the Republicans was followed by his recall, and for some time France was without a resident minister. During Adams's term the situation between the two countries developed from bad to worse until actual hostilities occurred.

Resentment against the pro-British policy of the Federalists seems to be the clew to the strange conduct of France during these years. Upon Monroe's recall in 1796 Washington sent Charles C. Pinckney to Paris. The Convention had at last framed a constitution which vested executive functions in a Directory of five members. Charles Maurice de Talleyrand was in charge of foreign affairs as a member of this Directory. Pinckney arrived before Monroe left, but was informed that France would not receive another minister from the United States until her grievances were redressed. Wishing the full responsibility for what followed to rest upon the French government, Pinckney lingered until officially notified that he was liable to arrest as a spy. At about the same time Monroe was speeded on his homeward way with many marks of esteem.

The news of Pinckney's rebuff split the Federalists into two camps. The extremists, including Pickering the Secretary of

State, were ready for war.  For once, however, Hamilton's influence was on the side of Adams, who thought that another effort should be made to reach a peaceful understanding.  For this purpose John Marshall and Elbridge Gerry, the latter a Massachusetts Republican and ex-member of the Constitutional Convention of 1787, were joined with Pinckney as special commissioners.  But they fared little better than Pinckney.  They were not received officially, but indirect intimations were given that they might be if a sum of money were provided for the pockets of the members of the Directory and a loan made to the government.  Pressing the demand for a "*douceur*," Talleyrand's agents drew from the commissioners an emphatic refusal.  Their actual words were "no, no, not a sixpence."  Transmuted by the patriotism of the orators at home, they have come down through the years in the ringing sentiment "Millions for defense, but not one cent for tribute!"

While these proposals, especially the suggestion of a bribe, reveal the corruption of the French ministers, it is doubtful whether they expected the commissioners to accept them.  It is likely that they were testing the spirit of the United States, and that they preferred not to reach an agreement.  While dallying with the commissioners the Directory was trying, as we now know, to persuade Spain to retrocede Louisiana, partly because possession of that province would provide a source of supplies for the French West Indies, and partly because it would enable France, as was believed, to control American foreign policy through the power to throttle our western settlements.

When the commissioners found negotiations blocked by these demands, they prepared to leave France.  Talleyrand thereupon invited Gerry, the Republican, to remain, and he, attributing the remonstrances of his colleagues to wounded vanity, consented in the hope of preventing a breach between the two countries.

As soon as these occurrences were reported to President Adams he ordered Gerry home and sent to Congress a message accompanied by copies of the dispatches from the commissioners.  In these, letters were substituted for the names of the Frenchmen who had acted as Talleyrand's agents, and from this fact the whole episode is known as the "X Y Z affair."  In the message

Adams declared: "I will never send another minister to France without assurances that he will be received, respected, and honored as the representative of a free, powerful, and independent nation."

The war fever now ran high. The Federalists were reunited, and in spite of Jefferson's remonstrance that the French ought not to be held responsible for "the turpitude of swindlers," many Republicans acted with them. Some time before, work had been begun on six new frigates. The building of these was hastened and supervision of the navy taken from the War Department by the creation of a new Department of the Navy. The French treaty of alliance of 1778 was abrogated, and an act was passed authorizing the raising of an army. Up to this time merchant vessels had been forbidden to arm for defense against French cruisers, lest encounters inflame the war spirit of both peoples. Now the vessels of the navy were instructed to capture French ships interfering with our merchantmen, and engagements began to take place in West Indian waters. For two years and a half the "Naval War of 1798" went on without a declaration of war on either side, with eighty-five captures of armed vessels to the credit of the new navy.[1]

No fighting occurred on land, but extensive preparations were made. Adams named Washington commander of the army. Since he was not expected to take the field in person, he, as titular chief, was in position to name the actual commander. Although Adams preferred Knox, whose claim was superior by right of seniority, he yielded at last, with very ill grace, to Washington's insistence, and appointed Hamilton to be major-general in command.

Hamilton now recurred to the idea of an English alliance and planned to conduct a land campaign for the liberation of the possessions of Spain, the ally of France, while England coöperated by sea. To these far-reaching schemes Adams gave no countenance. He adhered to Washington's safer policy of avoiding foreign alliances, and resolved to restore peace if possible. That France wished for peace seemed to be shown by the fact that she had not replied to the attacks of the American navy by declaring war. Moreover, towards the end of 1798 the assurance reached

[1] The Supreme Court ruled that a state of "limited war" existed.

our minister at The Hague, William Vans Murray, that a minister would be received by France with the respect demanded by the President's message. The cabinet, in bad humor over the "affair of the major-generals," was committed to Hamilton's war policy, and Adams, also in bad humor, without even consulting it nominated Murray as minister to France. At the suggestion of senators he consented to join Oliver Ellsworth and W. R. Davie with him as special commissioners.

In the negotiations the United States sought the consent of France to the abrogation of the treaty of alliance and asked damages for the seizure of ships contrary to the terms of that treaty. France was willing to concede one demand but not both, and an agreement was finally made on that basis. The United States was released from the guarantee of the West Indies, and in return renounced all claims on account of injuries inflicted upon her commerce. The new treaty was signed September 30, 1800.

## THE ALIEN AND SEDITION ACTS

Among the measures of the Federalists in 1798 were four which were directed against trouble-makers at home. At a time when Jefferson could seriously believe that Hamilton was plotting the overthrow of the Republic and the establishment of monarchy, it is little wonder that small men carried their attacks on officials to extraordinary lengths. Freneau's *National Gazette* made Washington regret that he had ever accepted office.[1] On the other hand, even federal judges denounced political agitators from the bench. Chief Justice Ellsworth, in a charge to a Massachusetts grand jury, thundered against "the French system-mongers, from the quintumvirate at Paris to the Vice-President and minority in Congress, as apostles of Atheism and anarchy, bloodshed and plunder."

The English war with France which began in 1793 had encountered a good deal of opposition at first from liberal Englishmen who sympathized with the aspirations of the French people, but their criticisms had been hushed by harsh treatment. In

[1] At one meeting of the cabinet Knox thoughtlessly displayed a cartoon called the "Funeral of George W-n," in which the President was placed on a guillotine. On seeing it Washington exclaimed in a rage that "that *rascal Freneau* sent him three of his papers every day, as if he thought he would become the distributor."

consequence many of these liberals came to the United States. French citizens, too, were numerous in the States, and at a time when domestic and international politics were closely inter-woven these immigrants took an active part in political discus-sions. Most of them having sought our shores in quest of ampler liberty leaned strongly towards the Republican party, support-ing it with their pens, voices, and votes.

The naturalization law permitted foreigners to become citizens after five years' residence. This seemed to the Federalists too short a period for thorough Americanization. They felt, as Harrison Gray Otis expressed it, that something must be done "to prevent the indiscriminate admission of wild Irishmen and others to the right of suffrage." Although the granting of the ballot was a power reserved to the states, Congress had control over naturalization, and doubtless with the design of robbing the Republican party of an important source of votes in future, the Federalists passed a new naturalization act extending the re-quired term of residence to fourteen years.

The second law, known as the "Alien Act," empowered the President to deal with undesirable resident subjects of a foreign government. "It was commonly supposed that the United States contained over thirty thousand Frenchmen, constantly engaged in intrigues against the government, and ready in case of invasion to rise as one man and murder their hosts." Any alien whom the President deemed dangerous to the peace and safety of the country might be ordered to depart. If he did not obey, he was liable to imprisonment. The act was limited to two years.

The third law, or "Alien Enemies Act," was not limited in duration except that from its nature it could be in effect only during war. It gave the President extraordinary power to deport resident subjects of any country with which the United States might be at war, and to prescribe the restraints to which they should be subjected if allowed to remain in America.

The second alien act may be justified as a measure of national self-defense, but the Sedition Act, fourth of the series, was an un-American law, much like the British measures of 1793 — a bold attempt to treat political opposition as crime. It was aimed less at foreigners than factious citizens. It not only provided for the punishment of persons who conspired together to impede the operation of United States laws, but forbade any person to write, print, or utter any "false, scandalous, and malicious" statement "against the government of the United States, or either house of the Congress of the United States, or the President of the United States, with intent to defame . . . or to bring them . . . into contempt or disrepute." The Republicans and moderate Federalists secured with difficulty the inclusion of a clause permitting any person charged with such an offense to present evidence that his statements were true. Hamilton, who was not in Congress, wrote urging the change. "Let us not," he advised, "establish a tyranny." This act was to expire with the term of the administration.

The alien acts were never enforced, the second one because war was not officially declared, the first because it appeared unnecessary. President Adams found it sufficient to give warning to a few agitators, and a number of Frenchmen left the country of their own accord when the Alien Enemies Act was pending. But indictments under the Sedition Act were numerous, and there were ten convictions. A Jerseyman, who had expressed a wish that the wad of a cannon fired as a salute to the President had hit him on the rear bulge of his breeches, was fined $100. Matthew Lyon of Vermont, while canvassing for reëlection to Congress, charged the President with "unbounded thirst for ridiculous pomp, foolish adulation, and a selfish avarice." He was punished with a jail sentence of four months and a fine of a thousand dollars.

The most famous of the sedition cases was that of Dr. Thomas Cooper, an English liberal and a good type of the class of men driven from that country by the repressive legislation of 1793. Cooper was a man of education and ability. He later became president of the College of South Carolina and a leader of that state during the days of the nullification controversy. He was tried in 1800 for calling President Adams incompetent, and saying that he had interfered with the course of justice. He offered to prove the truth of his statements by the testimony of Adams himself and certain members of Congress. They refused to appear as witnesses, however, and Cooper was fined $400 and imprisoned for six months.

## THE REPUBLICAN TRIUMPH

In the judgment of Republicans, the whole course of the Federalists savored of centralization and militarism. They denounced the Alien and Sedition laws with particular wrath as iniquitous and unconstitutional. Congress by the first amendment was expressly forbidden to pass any law abridging the freedom of speech or of the press. That, with control over personal rights in general, was reserved to the states. But they could not bring these laws before the federal courts in test cases with any hope that their views would be upheld. Nor would they have favored such a procedure in any event. The sedition trials were in effect test cases, which showed that the judicial branch of the government would support the legislative department.

Some Republicans despaired of checking the career of the dominant party, and suggested secession by the states of the South and West, and the organization of a new federal republic. Jefferson, without denying the right of secession, pointed out the needlessness of such an extreme remedy. His penetrating political instinct taught him that the errors of the Federalists would bring their own punishment. To treat political utterances as crime is a fatal policy for any party which depends upon the votes of the people.

Jefferson's plan was to press the mistakes of the Federalists upon the attention of the voters. As the best means of doing this, it was decided to have resolutions passed by some of the state legislatures where the Republicans were in the majority, to be sent then to all of the states in the hope of arousing opinion against the obnoxious laws. Under Jefferson's inspiration Madison drew up one set of resolutions, which the Virginia assembly passed. Concealing his authorship on account of his position as Vice-President, Jefferson drafted another set, which was introduced in the Kentucky legislature by a member named John Breckinridge, and passed with slight changes by a large vote.

The Virginia and Kentucky Resolutions were the best criticisms made of the Alien and Sedition Acts, and ably presented the Republican view. They called on the other states to concur in denouncing the acts, and to unite in maintaining their rights. It was probably the expectation of the authors that these appeals would draw out similar resolutions in many states and create such pressure upon Congress that it would promptly repeal the laws.   Beyond that it was doubtless believed that the aroused voters would visit their disapprobation upon the party which had passed the laws, at the next election.   The resolutions, in short, served the purpose of a party platform for the campaign of 1800.

The legislatures of the other Republican states failed to reply to the resolutions.   Replies came, however, from Federalist states, and the whole discussion became plainly a party controversy.   As might be expected, the replies expressed approval of the laws and maintained that the state legislatures had no right to pass judgment upon acts of Congress.   That, they held, was the function of the federal courts.

The most important part of the Virginia and Kentucky Resolutions in the long run was the part which attracted least attention at the time.   The opening paragraphs of each document advanced the compact theory of the Constitution.   Of the two the Kentucky set was the more explicit.   According to them the states as separate entities formed the Union by entering into a compact, the Constitution, delegating certain powers to a general government as a sort of agent of the states.   Whenever, therefore, this agent exceeds its powers its acts are void.   Nor is the agent the final judge of its powers — not even the federal courts, which are parts of the agency — but the states have the right to judge for themselves of infractions of the Constitution and of the mode and measure of redress.

The Virginia Resolutions held "that, in case of a deliberate, palpable, and dangerous exercise of . . . powers not granted by the said compact, the States, who are parties thereto, have the right and are in duty bound to interpose for arresting the progress of the evil, and for maintaining within their respective limits the authorities, rights, and liberties appertaining to them."

These premises warranted the legislatures in passing upon the Alien and Sedition Acts and declaring them unconstitutional and void.   Just what more the authors had in mind has been a great puzzle for students ever since.   No contemporary explanation was given, and only one state noticed the compact theory in its reply. Many years later Jefferson and Madison attempted explanations which arouse the suspicion that even they hardly realized the import of their words when first used. It is difficult to avoid the conclusion that the resolutions mean that a single state may nullify the force of a federal act within its own borders, if such act is deemed contrary to the Constitution.[1]

Such a view, and the compact theory on which it rests, was for Madison at least a lapse from the opinions held in 1787. In the Federal Convention he had been a leader of the national party, and had shown exceptionally clear understanding of the character of the Union created by the Constitution. The party controversies of a decade and the influence of Jefferson had warped him from his path.

Jefferson and Madison can hardly be called the inventors of the compact theory, but in the Resolutions they gave definite form to vague popular notions about the government which should not have survived the adoption of the Constitution. The definite formulation of the theory gave the belief in state sovereignty new life; in fact, from this time on it showed great vitality, falling in as it did with popular prejudices and local interests. Federalist New England appropriated these teachings during the War of 1812, and South Carolina justified nullification in 1832 upon the same grounds. Even the resort to secession in 1861 was a logical consequence of the doctrines promulgated in 1798.

The feeling against France in 1798 aided the Federalists in the congressional election of that year. But the reaction against the Alien and Sedition Acts more than offset this gain, and the party approached the presidential election with discouraging prospects. The factional division came to an open rupture when Adams decided to send the peace commission to France. Pickering was disgusted at the President's failure to consult his cabinet, and was not in sympathy with his pacific policy. Supported by McHenry and Wolcott, Secretaries of the War and Treasury Departments, he neglected to draft instructions for

---

[1] The word "nullification" is used in a second set of resolutions passed by the Kentucky legislature in 1799, in reply to the resolutions of some of the other states: "A nullification by those sovereignties [the states] of all unauthorized acts done under color of that instrument is the rightful remedy." This phraseology leaves it uncertain, however, whether Jefferson thought the "sovereignties" could act separately and individually.

the commissioners until the President called for his resignation. Then he refused to resign, compelling Adams to dismiss him. Intending to purge the cabinet of Hamilton's supporters, Adams also forced out McHenry, but Wolcott, whose equal culpability was unknown, escaped.   John Marshall was called to the State Department, in recognition of the steady support Adams had received from a group of Federalists in the South.

The caucus nominated Adams and C. C. Pinckney, and claimed for them the united support of the party.   Hamilton's faction refused to be bound by the caucus.   They had hoped to induce Washington to stand for election once more, but his death in 1799 put an end to their plans.   Hamilton could not bring himself to uphold Adams, nor even to maintain a discreet silence. Offended by an uncomplimentary reference to his faction, he circulated among his friends a pamphlet criticizing the President's course in severe terms.   When through Burr's agency the pamphlet came to light, it appeared to the public that Adams was without honor in his own political household.

By contrast the Republicans were harmonious and disciplined. Washington had observed with bitter humor that they had but to set up a broomstick and call it a Democrat to command every vote in the party.   Jefferson and Burr were named again by the caucus, with assurances to Burr that this time he should have equal support with Jefferson.

Burr's nomination in 1796 and 1800 showed the wish of the party to create an intersectional organization.   Indeed, both parties adopted these tactics.   A presidential candidate representing one section and a second candidate from the other promised the maximum support for the ticket.   By accepting the subordinate rôle Burr advanced his fortunes at the expense of his New York rival, George Clinton, who was less ready to acquiesce in the leadership of Virginia.   The Virginia-New York alliance thus begun lasted, with occasional interruptions, as long as the original Republican party.

The Republicans found many points at which to attack the Federalist administration.   In spite of rising taxes the public debt had increased, giving color to the charge of extravagance. The *Aurora*, a notorious paper, constantly insisted that the Federalists had "picked a quarrel" with France in order to raise

a standing army, form a British alliance, and establish a monarchy.  All their measures, from Hamilton's financial schemes
to the Alien and Sedition Acts, showed them, the Republicans
declared, to be the party of the moneyed class and aristocrats.

The Republicans carried the electoral college by a vote of
73 to 65.  As Burr, according to promise, received the same number of votes as Jefferson, an embarrassing situation resulted,
since the tie threw the decision into the House of Representatives.
The House assembled for the purpose of balloting in February,
1801.  The intention of the Republicans to make Jefferson
President was well understood, yet as the Constitution read the
House was unrestricted in making its choice.  If the Republicans
had commanded a majority of members in a majority of the state
delegations, the election of Jefferson would have resulted from
the first ballot as a matter of course; but they controlled only
eight states out of sixteen.  The Federalists had six, and in two
the parties were equally divided.

This situation made it possible for the Federalists to prevent
an election until they were ready for it to take place, but hardly
to decide it in Burr's favor as many of them would gladly have
done, believing that Burr as a northerner would be more amena-
ble to Federalist influence than Jefferson.  In a party caucus it
was decided to give him the preference.  There is no proof that
Burr made any promises to win their favor; on the contrary, he
protested openly against a plan which was contrary to the will
of his party.

After many ballots the vote still stood eight states for Jefferson
and six for Burr, with two divided, and it was Hamilton's advice
which finally broke the deadlock.  In reply to the inquiries of
friends he gave his frank opinion of both candidates.  He
denounced Burr, whose character he knew well, as "the Cataline
of America."  Jefferson, he thought, was not over scrupulous
about telling the truth, and a "contemptible hypocrit," but he
believed that he would pursue a "temporizing rather than a
violent policy."  In other words, he judged that Jefferson as
President would be too astute to disturb in any serious way the
structure which the Federalists had reared.

Following Hamilton's advice, on the thirty-sixth ballot some
of the Federalists refrained from voting or cast blank ballots,

allowing their Republican colleagues to throw the votes of the divided delegations to Jefferson and thus elect him.

Several important consequences followed the House election of 1801. Taken together with the experience of 1796 it proved the necessity of changing the method of casting the electoral votes and led to the passage of the twelfth amendment. This amendment required separate ballots for President and Vice-President, and has been called the constitutional recognition of the party system. It also reduced the number of names to go before the House, in case there was not a majority of the electoral ballots for any candidate, from five to three. The amendment was ratified in 1804, in time for the election of that year.

Hamilton's part in defeating Burr was the beginning of an enmity between the two men which, nourished by later events, led in 1804 to a duel which cost Hamilton's life (see page 287).

With their defeat in 1800 the Federalists made their exit from the administration of national affairs. They had supplied the constructive ability needed to prove the experiment in constitutional government a success. They had organized the government, put its credit on a firm basis, vindicated the national authority, and greatly improved international relations through treaties with Spain, England, and France. Their work had been done so well that, as Hamilton predicted, the Republicans did not venture to make fundamental changes.

It may seem surprising that a party which had rendered such services never succeeded in recovering from its first defeat. But for this there were several reasons. In the first place, as just stated, the Republicans built upon the foundations laid by the Federalists. In the second place the Federalists had continually offended by their aristocratic temper and acts. In so far as the masses enjoyed the right to vote they were effectually alienated and driven into the Republican ranks.

A very important part of the increasing strength of Republicanism was due to the rise of the West. The Kentucky and Tennessee frontiersmen came chiefly from that discontented stock of the Virginia and Carolina Piedmont which had in vain claimed political equality with the aristocrats of the tidewater. Even Federalists, when they migrated to the West, changed parties. It seemed that their principles could not withstand the strong solvents of the frontier. It was the younger and less prosperous men who felt most strongly the lure of the new regions, and whatever profession of Federalism they made was soon abandoned in their new homes. Their outlook on life was not that of the prosperous stay-at-homes. Pioneer conditions bred the ideas of equality and popular government for which Jefferson stood.

Southern Federalists also, for the most part, soon found Jefferson's party acceptable, and after 1800 Federalism had little vitality outside of New England.

## SELECT BIBLIOGRAPHY FOR CHAPTER XIII

**Western Questions.** See books cited for Chapter X. Ogg, *The Opening of the Mississippi,* is useful for the earlier West as well as for the topics treated in the present chapter.

**Foreign Relations.** Much of the best material for the topic is in periodical literature, but Bassett has utilized most of this literature in *The Federalist System.* See also Channing, *United States,* IV. Foster, *Century of American Diplomacy,* is sketchy and popular; Fish, *American Diplomacy,* accurate and brief. Trescot, *Diplomatic History of the Administrations of Washington and Adams,* is fuller, and while an old work is still valuable; Adams, *History of the Foreign Policy of the United States,* is just off the press.

**Party Politics and Republican Triumph.** Bassett, Schouler, and McMaster are all valuable. Gordy, *Political History,* is more particularly devoted to party politics than any of these. Stanwood, *History of the Presidency,* gives compact and accurate summaries of each presidential campaign.

The best studies of the Republican resolutions of 1798 are: Warfield, *The Kentucky Resolutions of 1798,* and Anderson, "Contemporary Opinion of the Virginia and Kentucky Resolutions," in *The American Historical Review.*

# CHAPTER XIV

## JEFFERSONIAN DEMOCRACY

### The Republican System

The advent of Jefferson marked the first change in party administration, and the political atmosphere was charged with portents of impending events. There were New Englanders who believed that the Republican party was the American counterpart of French democracy, and that its triumph would be followed by excesses like those of the Reign of Terror in Paris. Jefferson's religious beliefs were misunderstood in the strongholds of orthodox Puritanism. His faith was close to that of the Deists, but many thought him to be an atheist of the French type, and dire calamities were predicted in consequence of his elevation to office.[1] The brother of the president of Yale College declared in a public oration (July 7, 1801) that "Jacobinism" would destroy civilization. "We have a country," said he, "governed by blockheads and knaves."[2]

Jefferson himself spoke of his election as a "revolution." In putting the ship of state "on her Republican tack," however, he took pains to reassure his countrymen. His first public utterance, the inaugural address, was an appeal to men of all political faiths. "We have called by different names brethren of the same principle," he said. "We are all republicans, we are all federalists."

Then, in the hope of winning general approbation, he set forth what he deemed to be the essential principles of government: "Equal and exact justice to all men . . . peace, commerce, and honest friendship with all nations, entangling alliances with none . . . a well-disciplined militia, our best reliance

---

[1] Deism may be concisely defined as belief in God but not in revelation except through God's works. The Deists rejected all miracles.
[2] *Cf.* Ellsworth's utterance, quoted on page 261.

in peace, and for the first moments of war, till regulars may relieve them : — the supremacy of the civil over the military authority — economy in the public expense that labor may be lightly burdened : — the honest payment of our debts and sacred preservation of the public faith : — encouragement of agriculture, and of commerce as its handmaid : — the diffusion of information, and arraignment of all abuses at the bar of the public reason : — freedom of religion ; freedom of the press ; and freedom of person, under the protection of the Habeas Corpus : — and trial by juries impartially selected."

The effort to find the common ground on which all Americans could stand reduced some of these remarks to platitudes.  Others indicated views of the Republicans which genuine Federalists did not share.  Such were the references to the militia, economy, the public debt, and the mutual relations of agriculture and commerce.  The main purpose of the address came out in a private letter in which Jefferson indicated his belief that many persons who were Republicans at heart were in the Federalist ranks because of the late troubles with France.  These he hoped to lead into the Republican fold by cautious and conciliatory words and deeds.

Elsewhere in the address Jefferson stated his ideal : "A wise and frugal government, which shall restrain men from injuring one another, shall leave them otherwise free to regulate their own pursuits of industry and improvement, and shall not take from the mouth of labor the bread it has earned.  This is the sum of good government."  Such an ideal is in marked contrast with Hamilton's conception.  It reduced the functions of government to the minimum, hardly more than the preservation of order and defense against foreign attacks, and reserved the largest possible sphere for individual action.  It was entirely in harmony with Jefferson's faith in a simple agricultural state as the best basis for democracy (see page 236).  A government with so few functions would not need to "take from the mouth of labour the bread it has earned" in the form of taxes.

Hamilton's ideal of government was much more comprehensive.  For him government was an agency for the promotion of the general welfare in manifold ways.  Through its fostering care resources might be developed and industry stimulated.  Economic strength would result, permitting the levy of heavy taxes for meeting the cost of performing many functions. The prosperity of commerce would justify the expense of a protecting navy, and national power would give the country a respectable position among the nations. Hamilton's theory was akin to that of the mercantilists and much closer than Jefferson's to the tenets of European statesmen.

In choosing his cabinet Jefferson again showed his desire to conciliate New England. He appointed General Henry Dearborn, of Massachusetts, Secretary of War, and Levi Lincoln, of the same state, Attorney-General. For Postmaster-General he selected Gideon Granger, of Connecticut. The last office, though not a cabinet position, was important because the holder controlled the appointment of numerous local postmasters and clerks.

The chief cabinet posts went to Madison, as Secretary of State, and Albert Gallatin, as Secretary of the Treasury. Madison, like Hamilton, was a small man, only five feet six in stature. Beside him Jefferson towered like a giant with his six feet two and one-half inches. The two men held each other in warm affection, and although the difference in their ages was but eight years, the contrast in physical appearance made their relations resemble those of father and son. Gallatin was by birth a Swiss, but he had come to America in 1780 while still a mere lad. For a time his home was in western Pennsylvania, the part affected by the Whisky Insurrection. He attended the meetings which preceded that outbreak, counseling moderation and opposing violence, but found his influence outweighed by that of the hotheads. He entered Congress during Washington's Presidency, and at once showed a mastery of finance that made him a godsend to his party. He alone among its members was able to cope with Hamilton's genius in that sphere on terms of approximate equality. In spite of his ability and loyalty his enemies in both parties would not forget his foreign birth and embittered his life by petty persecutions.

The first departure from Federalist ways appeared in the simplicity of the conduct of the new President. The inauguration took place in the new capital city on the Potomac. Its wild surroundings, in a district still only sparsely peopled, and its uncompleted buildings and streets, were more suggestive of the frontier than of the gayety and ceremonial of European capitals, and would have made elaborate display seem out of place. Jefferson, moreover, made a virtue of "republican simplicity." He walked up Capitol Hill to take the oath of office. He gave up the state carriage with six horses which his predecessors had used, and rode horseback unattended when he went out. Being a widower whose daughters were married and in homes of their own, his household lacked feminine management. The formalities at the executive mansion which had kept plain citizens at a distance gave way to the open house, and at times informality was allowed to slip over into slouchiness, as when on one occasion the President received a foreign diplomat in dressing-gown and slippers. Even worse, because of mild international complications which resulted, was the rule of "pêle mêle" in official etiquette — gravely adopted "to maintain the principles of equality" — "of gentlemen in mass giving precedence to the ladies in mass in passing from one apartment . . . into another." After one or two experiences with the working of the rule, the British minister declined the President's invitation to dinner "awaiting instructions from his Government."

In dealing with Congress Jefferson replaced the annual address, an imitation of the English King's speech from the throne, by the written message. In making the change he explained that he "had principal regard to the convenience of the Legislature," concealing his own preference for a method of communication which would not display his lack of readiness as a speaker. Indirection was one of Jefferson's traits. He never, like Hamilton, announced aims boldly and fought his way to them against all opposition. He preferred the arts of management. Suggestion, advice, intimation, were better means of attaining objectives than dictation. Within the glove, however, was an iron hand, and few presidents have dominated their parties so completely.

The Republicans had denounced the extravagance of the Federalists and promised an economical administration. They suspected Hamilton of desiring to perpetuate the public debt for political reasons, and resolved to get rid of it as speedily as possible. The excise tax they had always disliked because of its inquisitorial character, and they promptly repealed it. Notwithstanding the loss of this revenue, Gallatin's careful calculations showed that by curtailing expenditures the debt could be paid in sixteen years. The economies for this purpose were made at the expense of the army and navy. Although a military academy at West Point was authorized in 1802, adequate support was withheld and the army was sharply reduced. Naval construction ceased and the few ships already built were tied up at the docks.

Jefferson's devotion to peace and his confidence in the reasonableness of mankind led him to believe that the nation was safe without armaments. Trusting the militia — the citizen soldiery — as a sufficient first line of defense in case of invasion, he planned a "naval militia" for protecting the coast. A number of small gunboats were built and distributed among the bays and inlets along the Atlantic, to be manned by the farmers of the vicinity in case of attack. The boats proved to be unmanageable in rough water, and, indeed, almost useless.

Unexpected events — the Tripolitan war and the Louisiana Purchase — swelled expenditures far beyond Gallatin's calculations. Nevertheless his policy of debt reduction went forward, for the receipts from customs rose rapidly, largely in consequence of importations due to the practice of the "broken voyage" (see page 253). The European war era was the golden age of the American carrying trade, and the treasury reaped a harvest from duties on goods brought in and reëxported.

The President found the appointive offices occupied by Federalists. Few men of his party had been appointed by Washington and Adams. Monroe and Gerry, selected for diplomatic missions, were notable exceptions. Republicans were eager for the spoils of victory and pressed Jefferson to remove the adherents of the defeated party to make room for his friends. Jefferson would not do so; he wished to prove the sincerity of the appeal which he had made to the Federalists in the inaugural address. The tests of a man's fitness, he said, should be, Is he honest? Is he capable? Is he faithful to the Constitution? But some room had to be made for Republicans, and as the President remarked in rather grim jest, none of the Federalist office-holders resigned and few died. So he removed the men whom Adams had appointed since the election, and in filling offices decided to choose

Republicans until a parity of parties existed in the civil service. Once started on this course the time never arrived when he found it possible to make appointments without regard to party, and few indeed were the Federalists who received office at his hands.

His treatment of one group of appointments led to a notable court decision. In February, 1801, in the last moments of Federalist majority in Congress, a law was passed authorizing the appointment of a number of justices of the peace for the District of Columbia. Adams made the nominations so late in his term that — so the story went out — he was busy until midnight on March 3 signing commissions. Commissions were, in fact, found by the new administration upon the desk of the Secretary of State, signed and ready for delivery.

Jefferson thought it indecent for Adams to make such haste to put men into office who would serve under his successor, and instructed Madison not to deliver the commissions. Marbury, one of the "midnight appointees," applied to the Supreme Court for an order (writ of mandamus) directing Madison to deliver his commission. John Marshall, now Chief Justice, gave the opinion of the Court. Marbury, he held, was entitled to the commission, but the Supreme Court could not issue the writ because, according to the Constitution, Marbury's case was one which could come before the Court only on appeal. Although the Judiciary Act of 1789 had provided for an original hearing in such cases by the Supreme Court, that part of the Act was void because it conflicted with the Constitution, which clearly specified the classes of cases in which the Supreme Court was the court of first resort. This case of Marbury vs. Madison (1803) is memorable because it was the first important one in which the Court passed upon the constitutionality of an act of Congress.

The Marbury decision greatly annoyed the Republicans. It seemed to them that the Court was placing itself above both the legislative and executive branches of government. If it could give orders to executive officials and set aside acts of legislation, was not the doctrine of equal, coördinate branches of government destroyed? However plausible their contention that the Court was bound by the opinion of the law-making body as expressed in statutes, it exalted the legislature to the position of superiority denied to the Court.

The Republicans, in fact, disliked the judicial system and thought that the legislature was much the safer guardian of the interests of the people. This was especially true now that they had the majority in Congress. They regarded the judges with all the more suspicion because they were Federalists. It seemed as if their antagonists, defeated at the polls, had fortified themselves in the judiciary, as judges were appointed instead of elected, and held office during good behavior instead of for fixed terms, like members of Congress and executive officials.

It was in their treatment of the judiciary that the new rulers showed the greatest tendency to interfere with the work of the Federalists. Even before the Marbury decision they had begun their attack. Besides the act under which that case arose, the Federalists had passed at about the same time a judiciary act making certain modifications in the court system as organized in 1789. The chief change was a provision for a distinct set of judges for the circuit courts, with a due complement of attorneys and marshals. From the outset the Supreme Court justices had demurred to the circuit-court duty required of them, not only because travel from district to district was an arduous labor, but also because they thought it bad practice for a judge to sit as supreme justice on the same causes which he had heard in the lower court. The Federalists welcomed the opportunity, moreover, when passing the new law, to place men of their own faith in the new positions. Adams had promptly nominated the judges and they had been confirmed by the Senate and were in office when the change of administration took place.

Jefferson referred to the new judges as "excrescences on the judiciary," and recommended that Congress repeal the act. The Republicans, exaggerating the cost, held that the law entailed needless expense, that the judges were not overburdened under the old plan, and that the purpose of the act was partisan. Repealing the law, they restored the original status of the circuit courts but added one judge to the supreme bench. Separate judges for the intermediate courts were not permanently provided until 1867.

In one other way the Republicans showed that their control of Congress gave them the advantage over the Federalists ensconced in the judiciary. The power in impeachment cases is lodged by the Constitution in the two houses, the right to present charges belonging to the lower house, while the Senate hears the arguments and renders judgment. The grounds of impeachment are "treason, bribery, or other high crimes and misdemeanors." At Jefferson's suggestion Congress turned the machinery of impeachment against John Pickering, judge of the New Hampshire federal district court. Pickering had appeared upon the bench in an intoxicated condition, and was clearly unfit for his position. In the course of the proceedings, however, it appeared that he was of unsound mind, and the question arose whether an insane man could be guilty of a misdemeanor in the ordinary legal sense. The Senate finally voted that he was "guilty as charged," thus evading the difficulty.

Encouraged by this success the Republicans next impeached Samuel Chase, an associate justice of the Supreme Court. Chase's real offense was partisan conduct. He had presided at some of the trials under the Sedition Act, and had shown prejudice against the accused. On another occasion, in a harangue to a jury, he had attacked the Republicans as a "mobocracy." In this case the Senate was unwilling to take ground which might lead to impeachments for mere differences of political opinion, and Chase was acquitted. The words of the Constitution imposed no check upon the discretion of the Senate when sitting as a court of impeachment, but public opinion and common sense tended to limit impeachments to cases of unethical conduct. The outcome of the Chase trial possibly prevented the Republicans from proceeding against Chief Justice Marshall for his decision in the Marbury case.

### The Louisiana Purchase

The pacific course of Jefferson's first administration was interrupted by trouble with Tripoli. The Barbary States of the African coast of the Mediterranean had enriched themselves for many years at the expense of European commerce. Strangely the powers, instead of chastising the pirates, had as the result of their own rivalries, fallen into the habit of purchasing immunity by the payment of annual tribute. As part of the British empire the American colonies had shared in the immunity from attack which this policy secured for British vessels. An unpleasant reminder of the price of independence was the seizure of some American vessels soon after the Revolution ended.

Against Jefferson's protest Washington's government adopted the European plan in dealing with the pirate states. Unhampered by the jealousies which tied the hands of the European governments, the United States, he believed, was strong enough to teach the corsairs a lesson. Therefore, when the ruler of Tripoli declared war in 1801, because of dissatisfaction with the present which the United States had sent him, Jefferson declined to humor him. The pasha meant by his declaration that seizures of American vessels would be resumed, and was little prepared for the action of the President in sending ships to blockade his coast.

Although marked by deeds of heroism, the war ran on for four years without decisive action, and in the end peace was obtained only by paying a ransom for captured American sailors and renewing the annual tribute. The only advantages derived from the war were the development of a fine morale in the little navy, and the training of a group of young officers who were to encounter British fighting ships a few years later.[1]

The most important event by far of Jefferson's first term was the purchase in 1803 of the Province of Louisiana, which spread its broad plains westward from the Mississippi River to the Rocky Mountains. First explored by Frenchmen before the middle of the eighteenth century, it received its name in honor of the King of France. At the close of the French and Indian War it had become the property of Spain. At that time a few traders of French blood had reached the site of the modern St. Louis, but thence southward to Red River wilderness prevailed, except for a lonely post or two on the Arkansas. Most of the inhabitants dwelt in New Orleans or near by. Apart from a few Spanish officials the St. Louis settlements remained French during the Spanish period, with numbers augmented about 1763 by newcomers from the eastern banks of the Mississippi, who found English rule distasteful.

[1] During the War of 1812 the pirate states took advantage of the embarrassment of the United States and renewed their captures. In 1815 a strong squadron was again sent to the Mediterranean and the corsairs were forced to sign treaties which ended their depredations forever.

Among the inhabitants of Spanish Louisiana the occasional American was conspicuous because of his rarity. The interest which the people of the United States felt in the transmississippi region was hardly that of possible settlers. Rather it was the interest of rivals who were jealous of the power which through possession of the mouth of the Mississippi held the economic life, and perhaps the political destiny, of the entire interior valley in its hand. The Spanish closure of the river and intrigues with the early settlers of the West had jeopardized the hold of the United States upon the transmontane country and taught statesmen the danger that would be involved in having a strong power in Spain's place.

No one was more aware of this danger than Jefferson. While Secretary of State, in 1790, a threat of war between England and Spain drew attention to the probable effects on the United States. If war came, England would, in all probability, attack and seize Louisiana and the Floridas. Then, as Jefferson said, she would embrace us on one side by her possessions and on the other by her fleet. Such a situation would be perilous in the extreme, for it would destroy the American balance of power, as Jefferson called it. It was to the interest of the United States to have Spain remain in possession of Louisiana and the Floridas rather than that they should pass into the hands of a more powerful nation.

But the war cloud of 1790 blew over, and the real danger came not from England but from France. Although by the alliance of 1778 that country renounced all pretensions to territory in North America, the Revolution had hardly closed before she began efforts to regain Louisiana. Genêt's plans for expeditions organized on American soil were a fruit of this ambition. After 1795 when Spain and France made peace, French influence grew apace. Appeals were made to Spain's fears of American encroachments, and she was urged to retrocede a province which only the strong arm of France could defend. French representatives in the United States significantly pointed out to their home government that the Mississippi Valley was a natural unit, that a river did not form a good international barrier, and that one nation was destined to rule the whole interior of the continent from the Appalachians to the Cordilleras.

Spain resisted the pressure of her neighbor until Bonaparte

became First Consul. He eagerly embraced the plan of a revived colonial empire, and in characteristic manner obtained the coveted cession by means which left the weaker party little choice. Almost at the same instant that the treaty of 1800 with the United States was signed, Spain retroceded Louisiana by the Treaty of San Ildefonso. Bonaparte promised never to dispose of the territory to any other power than Spain, and also to create a kingdom in Italy for the Spanish King's son-in-law. He afterwards violated both pledges without compunction.

This Treaty of San Ildefonso was made secretly. France and England were still at war, and Bonaparte dared not allow the mistress of the seas to learn of his acquisition until he had an army on the ground to defend it. He prepared an expedition, therefore, for the double purpose of reconquering Santo Domingo and occupying New Orleans.

The eastern portion of the island of Santo Domingo was the most valued possession of France in the West Indies, and after 1763, in the western hemisphere. It was a rich source of sugar and other tropical products, and formed the nucleus of the plan of a revived colonial empire. It was valued for the same reason that the English mercantilists prized colonies the resources of which supplemented those of the British Isles. But it was not self-supporting; it did not produce its own food supplies, nor could France provision it, especially in war time. In this fact lay the value for France of peace with the United States, for from America came the means of subsistence for the island population. The possession of Louisiana would free France from this dependence upon the United States and complete the economic structure of her colonial empire.[1]

During the gloomy days of the Revolution in France, when she was hard beset by her foes, the slaves of the island had risen in revolt and drenched the soil with the blood of their masters. Under the lead of the remarkable negro Toussaint Louverture a black republic had been set up and independence proclaimed. The career of the "gilded African," as Bonaparte called him, on a small scale paralleled his own and won for the negro the name of the "Black Napoleon."

[1] Recall also the political influence which France would have over the United States through the possession of Louisiana.

The preliminaries of the Peace of Amiens, made with England in October, 1801, gave Bonaparte a breathing space for putting his designs into execution. His army reached Santo Domingo early in 1802, and before summer had treacherously captured Toussaint and sent him to perish in a French dungeon. The blacks submitted, only to be roused again to frenzied resistance when the restoration of slavery was attempted. The war was thus prolonged until the heats of summer brought yellow fever to fight the battles of the islanders. The white army melted away and the reconquest of the island was given up. Without it Louisiana was less desirable, and the army of occupation had left its bones in San Domingan graves.

With the Treaty of San Ildefonso "the shadow of the Corsican fell across the seas." Rumors of the treaty revived Jefferson's fear of a strong power at the mouth of the Mississippi, and his pro-French sympathies did not for a moment blur his vision of the danger to America if France supplanted Spain. The French minister in the United States had warned his government, just after the election of 1796, that "Jefferson is an American and by that title cannot be sincerely our friend."

The President took pains to acquaint Napoleon with his views on the transfer of Louisiana in no uncertain terms. He wrote a letter to Robert R. Livingston, the American minister in Paris, declaring: "There is on the globe one single spot the possessor of which is our natural and habitual enemy. It is New Orleans, through which the produce of three eighths of our territory must pass to market. . . . [Spain's] pacific dispositions, her feeble state, would induce her to increase our facilities there, so that her possession of the place would be hardly felt by us. . . . Not so can it ever be in the hands of France. . . . The day that France takes possession of New Orleans, fixes the sentence which is to restrain her forever within her low-water mark. It seals the union of two nations, who, in conjunction, can maintain exclusive possession of the ocean. From that moment, we must marry ourselves to the British fleet and nation . . . and . . . make the first cannon which shall be fired in Europe the signal for tearing up any settlement [France] may have made. . . ."

The intensity of Jefferson's feeling was due to his conviction that France would seek and find means to unite under her control all of the territory watered by the ramifications of the Mississippi. He felt that the destiny of the country was at stake, and that, if he would not see the Alleghanies become its western limit, the designs of France must be frustrated even at the cost of a foreign alliance, such as he deprecated in his inaugural address, and an alliance at that with the England which he hated!

Some time after this letter was written news came that a Spanish official at New Orleans had withdrawn the right of deposit granted by the treaty of 1795. In this action was erroneously seen the hand of the First Consul. It turned out that the measure was due to the failure of the United States to claim the renewal of the right, in 1798, according to the letter of the treaty. The action of the official was unauthorized, and an adjustment was reached without much difficulty. But before the tangle could be smoothed out the West, expecting the French legions and aroused almost to madness by the closure of the river, was on the point of striking the weak Spanish garrison at New Orleans and seizing the city.

To prevent the recurrence of such a crisis Jefferson instructed Livingston to open negotiations for the purchase of a tract at the mouth of the river. He was given a good deal of latitude as to the extent of the territory to be acquired, provided it was sufficient to insure unmolested enjoyment of navigation and transshipment of cargoes. To reassure the West by visible efforts Monroe, who was popular there, was dispatched as special envoy to aid Livingston in the negotiations.

These steps did not indicate that the threat in Jefferson's letter would be carried into effect. They seemed to mean that the Government would not forcibly oppose the occupation of New Orleans, provided the tract asked for could be purchased. It is not likely, in any event, that Jefferson's threatening language had much to do with Napoleon's decision to part with the whole of Louisiana. The failure in Santo Domingo, and even more, conditions in Europe, were turning his thoughts from colonial empire. In March, 1803, it became certain that the Peace of Amiens would soon be ruptured, and he probably decided that the good will of the United States would be cheaply bought if obtained at the price of what, for want of an army of occupation, he could not hold against either the sea power of the British

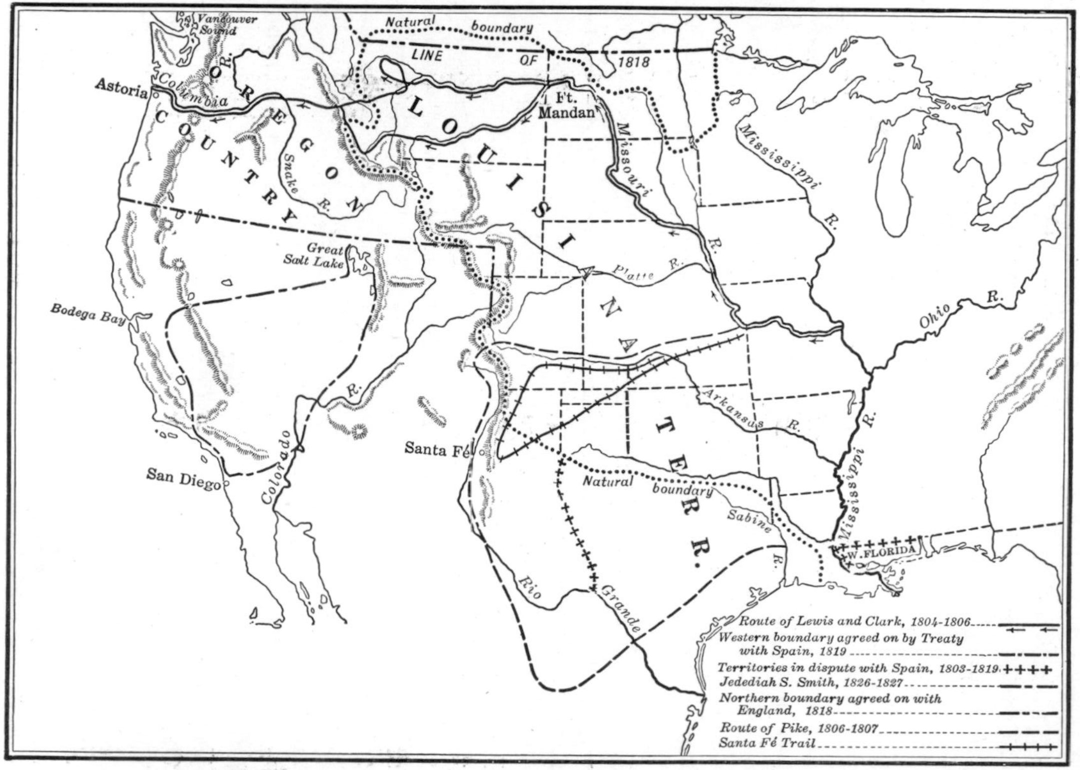
Vancouver Sound
Astoria
Columbia
R.
OREGON COUNTRY
Snake R.
Natural boundary
LINE OF 1818
LOUISIANA TERR.
Ft. Mandan
Missouri R.
Platte R.
Mississippi R.
Ohio R.
Great Salt Lake
Bodega Bay
R.
Colorado
San Diego
Santa Fé
Arkansas R.
Natural boundary
Sabine R.
Rio Grande
W. FLORIDA
Route of Lewis and Clark, 1804-1806
Western boundary agreed on by Treaty with Spain, 1819
Territories in dispute with Spain, 1803-1819
Jedediah S. Smith, 1826-1827
Northern boundary agreed on with England, 1818
Route of Pike, 1806-1807
Santa Fé Trail

The Louisiana Purchase and Explorations of the West

or the rifles of the frontiersmen.   Regardless of his promises to
Spain and of the French constitution, which did not permit the
executive to alienate territory, he resolved to sell Louisiana to
the United States.

On April 11, 1803, Talleyrand, discussing with Livingston
the sale of the Isle of Orleans, suddenly asked, "What would
you give for the whole of Louisiana?"  Livingston, surprised
beyond measure and somewhat deaf, could hardly trust his ears.
Once convinced that the First Consul was in earnest the only
question to be decided was the price.  Although Livingston
conducted the negotiations, he would not conclude them until
Monroe arrived, and both signed the treaty dated April 30
which for 80,000,000 francs more than doubled the area of the
United States.  Livingston may be pardoned for exclaiming
"This is the noblest work of our lives!"

When Jefferson learned what Livingston had done he was
perplexed.  It was not from any doubt of the immense benefits
of the cession that he hesitated.  All of his fears for the future of
the West were dispelled by the treaty.  Relieved of the menace
involved in the devious policies of European states, the great
valley gave ample room for the peaceful expansion and development of the Republic.  Possession of the lands beyond the Mississippi also suggested the possibility of removing the Indian
tribes from the eastern states.  But provision for the acquisition of territory was, as he said, a "*casus omissus*" of the Constitution.  The treaty provided, moreover, that Louisiana
should be "incorporated into the Union," and that the inhabitants should be admitted to all of the privileges of citizens.

Consistency required the President either to abandon the
treaty or to seek the powers needed to authorize it.  He decided
upon the latter course, and drafted an amendment to give constitutional sanction for what had been done, without authority,
on behalf of the nation.  "Let us not," he urged, "make blank
paper of the constitution by construction."  But he found the
Republicans whose advice he sought were not willing to risk the
uncertain outcome of an effort at amendment.  They adopted
Hamilton's doctrine of implied powers, and in the power of
making war and treaties held that there was ample warrant for
acquiring territory.

Jefferson at length yielded his scruples, for delay was dangerous, as Livingston and Monroe were warning him that Napoleon might change his mind.   In the face of vigorous protests by the Federalists, the Senate ratified the treaty and the houses joined in authorizing the President to receive the territory and to provide for its government.   On the last day of November, 1803, the Spanish governor at New Orleans transferred Louisiana to the representative of France, and twenty days later the tricolor on the *Place d'Armes* was hauled down and replaced by the Stars and Stripes.

## Plots and Conspiracies

These events filled the hearts of the Federalists with forebodings.   In the promise of incorporation and citizenship they saw a pledge of future statehood for Louisiana, and it was against this provision that they directed their main attack while the treaty was before the Senate.   They did not object to holding the territory as a permanent dependency, but denied the right of the President and Senate, as the treaty-making organ of government, to promise statehood.   They maintained that new states could be admitted into the Union only by Congress, and that such states must be formed within the original territory of the Union.

The attitude of the Federalists was due to their belief that the increase of western states would mean the relative decline of the influence of New England.   Gouverneur Morris wrote to Livingston: "Our party though with numerous exceptions opposed" the treaty; "for one reason, that it cost money the greater part of which we to the northward must pay, and it gains territory which will, in their apprehension, by giving strength to the Southern representation, diminish the Eastern influence in our councils."   Senator Uriah Tracy, of Connecticut, complained that the relative strength which "admission gives to a Southern and Western interest is contradictory to the principal of our original union."   Rufus King and John Quincy Adams were among the Federalists who saw in the acquisition the prospect of a politico-economic alliance between the South and the West, and of the perpetuation of the rule of Jefferson's party.

Some of the ultra Federalists even began to feel that the Union had failed to secure their dearest interests, and to consider secession and the formation of a northern confederation. "The people of the East," wrote Pickering to George Cabot, "cannot reconcile their habits, views, and interests with those of the South and West. The latter are beginning to rule with a rod of iron. . . . I do not believe in the practicability of a long-continued union. A northern confederacy would unite congenial characters."

The plans of the secessionists embraced New England and New York. In order to carry the latter with them they approached Burr. Jefferson distrusted the Vice-President, and deliberately cultivated the Clinton faction in New York, favoring it in federal appointments. Burr, indeed, in whose veins flowed America's best blood, whose ability was beyond question, and who was one of the most skillful political manipulators of his day, lacked the confidence even of his intimate political associates because of his predilection for unscrupulous intrigue. Angered by Jefferson's treatment, he now seemed ready to act with the New England plotters. If New York Federalists united with Burr's faction of the Republicans to make him governor of the state, he would be in position to promote the program of secession there.

It is quite unlikely that this scheme would have found much support among the people either of New England or New York. Jefferson's policy of conciliation had won wide approval in the northeastern states, as the election of 1804 was to show. When Hamilton's advice was sought by the malcontents he wrote: "Dismemberment of our empire will be a clear sacrifice of great positive advantages, without any counterbalancing good." He advised the New York Federalists to have nothing to do with Burr, thus for the second time contributing to his defeat for office. Burr in anger challenged him to a duel.

The encounter cost Hamilton his life and Burr the remnants of his reputation. Realizing that his career was blasted so far as the East was concerned, he turned to the West where the wilderness excited his adventurous genius. With the United States hesitating whether to seize West Florida in defiance of Spain's claim (see page 290) — or mayhap Texas, to which the Louisiana Purchase treaty gave even a better claim — the Spanish borderlands were in a continual state of restless apprehension.

Many were the Americans who trespassed on Spain's rights in Texas during the opening decades of the nineteenth century, with purposes ranging from the capture of wild horses to the founding of independent states. Burr's prominence made it certain that if he joined this crowd of adventurers, his name would go down to posterity as the most notorious of them all. His plans are obscure, but they aimed at the formation of an independent state from the territory either of the United States or Spain. His own words cannot be reconciled, for he spoke sometimes of Louisiana and sometimes of Mexico as his objective. That his real design was against the Spanish is the more plausible conjecture, as it fits in with conditions and the temper of the people of the West in these years.

In 1805 he began to collect supplies and men at Blennerhassett Island, in the Ohio River, near Parkersburg, West Virginia. Before any action indicating his true purpose was taken, suspicions arose which led his chief supporters to abandon him. When finally arrested, he was charged with treason against the United States. Treason is defined by the Constitution as levying war against the United States, or giving aid and comfort to the enemy in time of war, and it could not be shown that the preparations at Blennerhassett came within this definition. He was therefore acquitted and disappeared from view, punished with such a load of obloquy as the American people have never visited upon any other man, not excepting Benedict Arnold.

General Wilkinson, who was Burr's accomplice, treacherously contributed to his downfall. It was he who had led the secession movement in Kentucky. Now, while commander of the United States forces in the West he was a pensioner of Spain and faithless to both masters. Although false to every trust he successfully covered his villainy during his lifetime, and bore a supposedly honorable (although incompetent) part in the War of 1812.

## EXPLORATIONS IN THE WEST

Jefferson was a man of wide intellectual interests. A philosopher and lover of books, he had an insatiable curiosity about the physical universe and found the cultivation of his garden one of the most delightful of occupations. "Nature intended me," he wrote, "for the tranquil pursuits of science . . . but the enormities of the times . . . have forced me . . . to commit myself on the boisterous ocean of political passions." His correspondence ranged all the way from letters discussing botany with the Italian Philip Mazzei, to inquiries addressed to Kentucky pioneers about the "big bones" found at the salt licks. His curiosity was aroused concerning the unknown West long before Louisiana was acquired. In 1783 he wrote to George Rogers Clark suggesting an exploration into the transmississippi country. He recurred to the project while Secretary of State, but the Presidency gave him for the first time means to carry out the scheme. At his instance Congress provided funds for an expedition led by Meriwether Lewis, his secretary, and William Clark, younger brother of the hero of Kaskaskia. Both held commissions in the army. These steps preceded the Louisiana treaty, the President deeming the scientific character of the undertaking inoffensive even though conducted on alien soil. Before the party set out, however, the transfer of Louisiana was completed, so that the explorers were within their own country until they crossed the Rockies.

Leaving St. Louis in 1804, the party went up the Missouri to the Mandan Indian villages near the present Bismark, North Dakota, where it went into winter quarters. The next season the stream was ascended to its headwaters, where passes were found leading to the Snake River. Down this the explorers proceeded to the Columbia, and thence to the Pacific, where the second winter was passed. The mouth of the Columbia had first been entered in 1793, by Captain Robert Gray, of Boston. Alexander Mackenzie, of the Hudson Bay Company, had soon afterward crossed Canada to Vancouver Sound, but Lewis and Clark were the first white men to traverse the Columbia River basin. Their exploration gave the United States a claim to the "Oregon country" of which good use was made later.

Several other explorations of the newly-acquired territory were made at about the same time as the Lewis and Clark expedition. Some of these ascended the Red River but failed to reach its source owing to hostile Indians and even more to the jealousy with which the Spanish watched their border after the exposure of Burr.

Two notable journeys were performed by Lieutenant Zebulon

M. Pike.   In the winter of 1805 he made a search for the sources
of the Mississippi but was unable to make trustworthy observa-
tions because of the snow-covered surfaces.   In the summer
of 1806 he went up the Arkansas River, penetrating the Royal
Gorge, and gaining much geographical knowledge.   Beyond the
ridge Spanish soldiers were encountered, who took his party to
Santa Fé and later to Mexico, under the fear that its errand was
unfriendly.   When released at last Pike returned home by way
of Texas and Louisiana.   The information which he gained about
the northern provinces of Mexico through this enforced visit
aroused interest in the United States and was afterwards a factor
in opening the Santa Fé trail for trade with them.

## Dispute over West Florida

The Louisiana treaty involved the United States in a new dispute with Spain over boundaries.   The treaty said that the
United States was to receive the province "with the same extent
that it now has in the hands of Spain, and that it had when France
possessed it" before 1763.   The French had claimed the Perdido
River as the eastern boundary of Louisiana, but Spain had received nothing east of the Isle of Orleans in 1763, the part of
French Louisiana lying between the Iberville and the Perdido
going to England.   When in 1783 England transferred this
tract to Spain, Spain did not change the boundary between the
provinces of Louisiana and West Florida.   Spanish Louisiana,
therefore, included nothing east of New Orleans.   Did her
retrocession to France include the tract east of the Iberville
which had come to her through England as intermediate owner?
Livingston in perplexity asked Talleyrand what France
intended to take under the Treaty of San Ildefonso.   Talleyrand had in his possession at that moment a copy of the instructions prepared for the first French governor of Louisiana, in
which the Rio Grande and Iberville were mentioned as the boundaries; but for some reason best known to himself — perhaps a
wish to embroil the United States with Spain — he preferred to
dissimulate.   "I do not know," he replied.   "You have made a
noble bargain for yourselves, and I suppose you will make the
most of it."

Livingston, although he knew that Spain had refused to include land east of the Iberville in the retrocession to France, taking the cue from Talleyrand, worked out a theory that she had nevertheless done so inadvertently. Although the Spanish minister in the United States wrote to Madison, several weeks before the treaty was ratified, protesting that in buying Louisiana the United States had really purchased stolen goods,[1] Jefferson not only ignored the protest, but, accepting Livingston's interpretation of boundaries, claimed the territory between the Iberville and the Perdido. Without awaiting the outcome of efforts to persuade Spain to accept this interpretation of the treaty, he asked Congress to extend the revenue laws to the district, although he located the customs house on undisputed ground (1804). Then he turned to diplomacy.

Spain stood firm as to West Florida, but Talleyrand suggested that through French

WEST FLORIDA DISPUTE, 1803–1819.

mediation the United States might be able to obtain the relinquishment of Spain's claim. Having failed to gain a means of influencing American policy through the possession of Louisiana, France now found it in Jefferson's hunger for territory. The President was kept dancing for several years to the Emperor's piping. In 1806 he persuaded Congress, not without considerable difficulty, to grant an appropriation for the settlement of the dispute through the mediation of France, but by this time Napoleon had lost interest because a favorable turn of fortune had made him careless of America's good will and money.

The acquisition of Louisiana influenced America profoundly. The acceptance by the party of strict construction of interpretation in place of amendment as a means of adapting the Constitution to new needs confirmed that process. The removal of

[1] "In taking Louisiana," says Professor Channing, "we were the accomplices of the greatest highwayman of modern history."

European influence from the Mississippi Valley made real that "detached and distant" position of the United States which Washington stressed in his Farewell Address, and made possible that freedom from "entangling alliances" which Jefferson recommended in his inaugural. The undisputed control of the West gave the United States the geographical basis for becoming a great power, able to maintain among the nations a distinctive policy such as the Monroe Doctrine.

Two essential elements of that doctrine were already in evidence at the opening of the nineteenth century. Washington contributed one of them when he adhered to neutrality and in his Farewell Address advised his countrymen to avoid permanent European alliances. Jefferson was the originator of the other when he resolved that Louisiana must not pass from the hands of Spain to any other European state, because of its vital relation to the welfare of the United States. These two elements — the principle of isolation and that of paramount interest — when brought together with the third principle of non-intervention in the message of President Monroe in 1823, constituted the famous doctrine which bears his name (see page 360).

## SELECT BIBLIOGRAPHY FOR CHAPTER XIV

**Jeffersonian Democracy.** Adams, *History of the United States of America during the Administrations of Jefferson and Madison*, is a comprehensive work in nine volumes. Although somewhat unsympathetic towards Jefferson and his associates, it is one of the best pieces of historical writing yet achieved in the United States. Channing, in *United States*, IV, and *Jeffersonian System*, is juster to the Republicans. Johnson, *Jefferson and his Colleagues*, is more recent than either Adams or Channing, but lays less claim to original scholarship.

Fish, *The Civil Service and the Patronage*, is an illuminating discussion of the whole subject indicated by the title.

**The Louisiana Purchase.** In general Adams is excellent on diplomatic history. His account of the acquisition of Louisiana takes insufficient note of the influence of European factors upon Napoleon's policy. *Cf.* Ogg, *Opening of the Mississippi*, and Channing, *United States*, and *Jeffersonian System*.

For Burr's conspiracy, see, besides Adams, McCaleb, *The Aaron Burr Conspiracy*.

Roosevelt, *Winning of the West*, gives a popular account of the explorations of the transmississippi country. See also Thwaites, *Rocky Mountain Exploration*.

# CHAPTER XV

## THE STRUGGLE FOR NEUTRAL RIGHTS

### RELATIONS WITH ENGLAND

The general acceptability of Jeffersonian principles was shown by the reëlection of the President in 1804 by an overwhelming vote. Against C. C. Pinckney and Rufus King, the Federalist candidates, he carried even the New England states with the exception of Connecticut. Clinton, old-time rival of Burr, had profited by his fall, and reconciled temporarily to Virginia's leadership, received the Vice-Presidency in token that the intersectional alliance was intact.

The rupture of the Peace of Amiens in 1803 was followed by war on a scale never before equaled. Within a few years all of Europe was drawn into the struggle, and even the United States, despite its boasted isolation, was in the sequel unable to hold aloof.

The renewed conflict meant both prosperity and trouble for the United States. As in the previous decade the American carrying trade increased by leaps and bounds. In 1790 the total exports of the country were valued at about $19,000,000. Five years later $26,000,000 worth of goods were brought from the French, Spanish, and Dutch possessions and reëxported. By 1806 the value of reëxports had risen to nearly $60,000,000; tonnage was increasing at the rate of 70,000 a year, requiring 4,000 additional seamen every twelvemonth; and the relatively high wages paid were attracting sailors from all of the maritime countries of Europe. Ship-building and subsidiary industries were proportionately active and absorbed most of the capital available for investment.

The rapid growth of this neutral commerce at length alarmed the British mercantile and shipping interests, which began to fear that the position of preëminence which they had enjoyed before the wars might be lost permanently.    The decision in the case of "The Polly" encouraged a rival who was becoming a menace, and the courts were made to feel the pressure of public opinion.    In 1805 came the decision in the "Essex" case.    The "Essex" had brought a cargo from Spain to Salem.    After it had been landed and the duty paid, it was reshipped to Havana and a drawback allowed for the duty.    The highest authority in England held that the cargo was never intended for the United States market, and that, under these circumstances, the broken voyage violated the Rule of 1756 as truly as if direct and continuous.

The decision was regarded in America as a reversal of that given in the case of "The Polly," and the difference seemed to lie in the allowance of the drawback in the "Essex" case.    The profitable reëxport trade thus faced the alternative of incurring the penalties of violating the Rule of 1756 or of carrying the burden of full duties.    The British were charged with attempting to prescribe the duties which American commerce should bear in its home ports, as in the days of colonial dependence.    Under instructions from Madison, Monroe, who had gone to England as minister after the purchase of Louisiana, remonstrated with Charles James Fox, the Secretary of Foreign Affairs.    Fox, during the Revolution and since, had been friendly, and agreed that duties and drawbacks were matters of domestic regulation on which a foreign state had no right to pronounce.

The modification of the restrictions involved in the "Essex" decision was not easily arranged, however, for Fox dared not affront British opinion.    With the support of the cabinet he obtained an executive order, or "Order in Council," which had the form of a new restriction on neutrals, but was intended in fact to be a substitute for the Rule of 1756 as interpreted in the recent decision.    "Fox's Order," as it is called, dated May 16, 1806, announced a blockade of the coast of Europe from Brest to the Elbe River.    Except between Ostend and the mouth of the Seine, however, naval officers had instructions to allow passage of inbound neutrals not laden in an enemy's port and outbound neutrals not sailing for one.    Thus trade *via* American ports was tacitly permitted without inquiry as to the payment of duties.

With renewed war the question of impressments also again

became acute.  Within three years, according to a report of Madison, there were nearly twenty-three hundred cases.  Impressments and the complaints of the merchants on account of seizures under the "Essex" decision led Jefferson to decide upon an extraordinary mission, and William Pinkney, of Maryland, was sent to England as Monroe's colleague for the negotiation of a new treaty.  At the same time Congress passed a non-importation act closing the American market to certain British goods after November 15, 1806, unless meantime an equitable agreement were reached.  This was before Fox's Order had been issued.  The commissioners were instructed to make no treaty which did not provide for the abandonment of impressments. That obtained, they were to seek the repudiation of the "Essex" decision and reparation for the seizures which had followed. These objects secured, the non-importation act might be repealed.

The discussion of impressments soon led to an *impasse*.  Fox was willing to surround the exercise of the right with safeguards against abuse, but would not give it up.  To do so, he said, might result in the overthrow of British naval power on which the safety of the nation depended.  Monroe and Pinkney on their part could not recede from the position that the flag of the United States must protect the crews of American vessels.  This question was therefore dropped from the negotiations, with the assurance of the ministry that the greatest caution would be observed, in impressing British seamen found on American ships, not to violate the rights of American citizens.

At the request of the ministry the Americans, notwithstanding their instructions, took up the matter of commerce, and on the last day of the year signed a treaty which virtually accepted the "Essex" decision.  Its chief provision was that reëxports should be regarded by the British as neutral goods in case they had paid certain duties in American ports.  Jefferson did not even submit the treaty to the Senate, but under the urging of Madison instructed that negotiations be resumed.  Meantime Fox had died and a new ministry had taken office with George Canning as Foreign Secretary.  To the proposal that negotiations be continued he replied bluntly that such a course was wholly inadmissible.

Just at this moment occurred the *Leopard-Chesapeake* affair. The "Chesapeake," Captain James Barron, was an American war-ship. In June, 1807, she left Chesapeake Bay for the Mediterranean, with new armament aboard which was to be mounted during the voyage. Reports had reached the Halifax station, in command of Admiral G. C. Berkeley, that the "Chesapeake" had shipped British deserters in her crew. He therefore ordered the "Leopard" to intercept her and seize any British seamen found on board. Coming up with the "Chesapeake" the "Leopard's" commander sent an officer to demand the surrender of deserters. Captain Barron replied that he knew of none among his crew, and refused to muster the men for inspection. As a matter of fact there were three Americans aboard who had formerly been impressed and had escaped, and one British deserter who had enlisted under an assumed name and had thus escaped Barron's notice.

The commander of the "Leopard," upon receiving Barron's reply, opened fire. For fifteen minutes the defenseless "Chesapeake" sustained the attack, which killed three men and wounded eighteen. Just as the colors were struck a single gun was fired "for the honor of the flag." Then the British came aboard again and took away the four deserters.

The crippled "Chesapeake" made her way back to Norfolk to tell the tale of outrage. Never before had a government vessel been the victim of a press gang. The national honor was directly affronted. For the first time, in a surge of national emotion, Federalists and Republicans forgot their differences. "The affair of the Chesapeake put war into my hand," wrote Jefferson years afterwards. But the President did not choose war; he contented himself with ordering all British armed ships to leave American waters, while Madison prepared a demand for the punishment of Berkeley, reparation for the damages done, and the abandonment of impressments.

England was so clearly in the wrong in this affair that Jefferson and his Secretary thought she must now yield on all points at issue. When Canning heard of the insult to the flag, he voluntarily sent Monroe a letter of regret and promised reparation if British officers were shown to be culpable. But Jefferson refused reparation unless coupled with the abandonment of impressments, and this attitude made settlement impossible. As Canning said, "it showed a disposition to make a particular incident, in which Great Britain was in the wrong, instrumental to an accommodation in a case in which his Government held a different doctrine."

The climax of the impressment controversy had now been reached. The utmost endeavors to persuade England to give up the practice had been answered with refusal. With Canning's reply the alternatives left to the United States were to acquiesce or to attempt the maintenance of its rights by force, and since no warlike move was made, the decision of the administration, judged by its conduct, was acquiescence.

Monroe wrote urging that the country be put in a better state of defense. He believed the British navy was so occupied in Europe that the ministry would engage in hostilities with the United States only with great reluctance. The course pursued probably tended to confirm the opinion which he reported was prevalent in England, "that the United States are, by the nature of their Government, incapable of any great, vigorous, or persevering action." Jefferson's inaction relieved Canning of the fear of hostilities, and allowed the British to conclude that the inconvenience expected from the non-importation act was the worst they had to apprehend. Even that act never went into effect. Its passage was intended to aid our envoys in their treaty negotiations, and with the failure of the treaty the act was abandoned.

## THE WAR OF ORDERS AND DECREES

By this time (mid-year, 1807) the European war had reached a state of deadlock. England, protected by the Channel like a huge moat, and by her "wooden walls," was beyond Napoleon's reach. He had, to be sure, gathered a host with the evident intent of invading the British Isles, but that possibility vanished with Nelson's victory at Trafalgar (1805) over the combined Spanish and French fleets. Thereupon, turning quickly from the coast, Napoleon struck his continental foes, winning in succession the great battles of Austerlitz and Jena, and putting Austria and Prussia under his feet. By the end of 1806 he was the master of central Europe. The next year, by the Battle of Friedland, Russia too was forced to accept a peace (Tilsit) dictated by the Emperor.

With England in control of the seas and France invincible on

land the war became an economic contest. Unable to reach his
chief antagonist with armed forces, Napoleon devised his "Continental System." Under military pressure a combination of
European states was formed, pledged to exclude British commerce from the markets of the continent. England's trade was
the source of her economic strength, and to undermine it would
be to destroy her power in war.

Fox's blockade, ordered with the intention of doing the United
States a favor, gave Napoleon the pretext he needed for the
inception of his system. In accordance with British practice
the blockade was a "paper" one. France had hitherto agreed
with the United States that the paper blockade was illegal, but
Napoleon now decided that two could play at the game. He
saw in the device a means of enforcing the Continental System,
and of isolating England without a navy. Justifying his action
by the plea of retaliation against Fox's blockade, he issued a
decree from Berlin, in November, 1806, proclaiming a (paper)
blockade of the British Isles. This, of course, subjected to capture any neutral vessel bound to or from a British port, but for
want of ships it could be enforced only when such vessels visited
the continent.

In 1807, by the Peace of Tilsit, the Czar engaged to close
Russia's ports against Great Britain. Denmark and Portugal,
neutral hitherto, were also compelled to choose between France
and England, and saw the lesser danger in supporting the Continental System. The Italian states were likewise forced, and it
became a part of Napoleon's aim to bring the conduct of the
United States into harmony with his policy. If she conformed
to the French regulations, England might be destroyed.

Realizing her danger, England resorted to retaliatory measures
of similar nature; as Captain Mahan says, she chose war with
the United States under the forms of peace rather than acquiescence in her enemy's designs. Early in 1807 the so-called "First
Order in Council" forbade the coasting trade of neutrals between
ports under French control. In November a Second Order
blockaded the coast from Copenhagen to Trieste against neutrals
unless they first entered and cleared from a British port and
paid duties there. In other words, the United States was to
be allowed to trade with Europe only subject to regulations

intended to protect British commerce and to replenish the British treasury! Even more than the "Essex" decision the orders, if obeyed, would have degraded the United States to the level of colonies.

In December Napoleon countered with the Milan Decree under which ships were declared to lose their neutral character if they obeyed the Second Order, or even submitted to search on the high seas by British naval officers.

American commerce was thus caught as it were between upper and nether millstones.   Trade with the continent could be carried on only by evading British cruisers.   Our direct trade with England, France lacked the means of stopping, but the disastrous effects of the war of Decrees and Orders were shown by a fall of more than two thirds in the value of goods exported from the United States.

The President's remedy for all these wrongs was what he called "peaceable coercion."   Jefferson is often called a pacifist. This is an error, for he was not a non-resistant on principle.   He used force against Tripoli, threatened war with Spain over West Florida, and talked of a military and naval alliance with England during the Louisiana crisis.   Yet he believed that in most cases the appeal to reason was more likely to be availing than resort to the sword.   When the belligerent powers seemed to attach so much importance to commercial restrictions as substitutes for military measures, it is hardly surprising that the chief neutral overestimated the effect which self-imposed restrictions were likely to have upon both belligerents.   "Our commerce is so valuable to them that they will be glad to purchase it when the only price we ask is to do us justice," thought Jefferson. American tradition, moreover, favored commercial coercion, and among the Republicans widespread sentiment demanded an attempt to secure justice by such means.   They had withal but half-hearted sympathy with the carrying trade, holding that the legitimate function of commerce was to provide an outlet for our own surplus (see page 236).   During the years of expanding shipping Jefferson had declared that "this exuberant commerce brings us into collision with other Powers in every sea, and will force us into every war with European Powers."   He was, perhaps, not loth to sacrifice it in the effort to preserve peace.

Non-importation was the first of a series of efforts to defend
American rights by commercial coercion.  As it never became
operative, it amounted merely to an ineffective threat.  In
contempt for its weakness John Randolph called it "a dose of
chicken broth."  Few of the Republicans were discouraged by
its failure.  Monroe's unsuccessful negotiations, the promulga-
tion of the Orders in Council and the French Decrees, led naturally enough therefore to the chief experiment with the game
of commercial war.  Indeed, even before the full scope of the
Orders and Decrees was known, with the hearty support of his
party but in the face of determined opposition by the Federalists,
Jefferson's plan of an embargo was enacted into law in December,
1807.  This act forbade the departure of all ships for foreign
ports except foreign vessels in port at the time of the passage of
the bill, which were allowed to depart in ballast or with cargoes
already on board.  Coasting vessels were required to give bond
to land their freight at domestic ports.

Although impartial in terms the embargo did not affect France
and England equally.  It deprived the former of but little trade
not already cut off by the Orders in Council.  Federalists declared
that the bill had "France" written on its face.  "The Emperor,"
said the French minister at Washington, "applauds the embargo."  It deprived Great Britain of her intercourse with
America just when he was shutting her out of Europe, and cut
off supplies from the West Indies which were supposed to be
indispensable.  It gave him also the pretext for a characteristic
act of trickery.  To avoid being shut up in port, many American
ships had hastily put to sea while the embargo was on its passage,
while others evaded the law in every possible way.  Some of
these under British license visited French ports, and in April,
1808, by the Bayonne Decree, were seized on the ground that
they were outlawed by leaving home in violation of law.

Nor did the act produce the expected effect upon England.
There was some distress among her poor who lost employment
through the cutting down of the imports of raw cotton for
the mills, but shipowners were benefited rather than injured.
"Except with those directly interested," wrote one from London,
"the dispute with the United States seems almost forgotten, or
remembered only to draw forth ironical gratitude, that the kind

embargo leaves the golden harvest to be reaped by British enterprise alone." The sarcastic Canning replied to Pinkney's suggestion that the embargo might be repealed in return for the revocation of the Orders in Council, by expressing concern over the law as an "inconvenient restriction upon the American people." Revolts in the Spanish colonies at just this time also opened new markets and sources of supplies for the British.

The embargo fell upon American shipping with a weight which almost crushed all that had survived the European Decrees and Orders. The masts of ships thrown out of use spread out before the port towns like "huge forests of dry trees." Seamen lost their employment and reëntered foreign service. The customs fell from $16,000,000 to $8,000,000, and Gallatin reported that in its effects upon national wealth and the public revenue the embargo was not materially different from war. The paralysis of shipping affected all subsidiary industries, and the loss of the foreign market brought down the price of the produce of the farms and plantations.

Despite their losses, the planters as a class stood manfully behind the program of their party, but public opinion in the commercial regions, especially New England, was so adverse that evasion of the law was general, and the administration found it necessary to recommend several supplementary acts for enforcing it. Congress, which had refused ships to protect trade, provided armed vessels to stop it. While these watched the harbors on the Atlantic, illicit traffic throve on Lakes Champlain and Ontario and at unguarded points on the northern and southern borders. Quebec and Halifax became depots for American commodities, and from them British goods were smuggled into the United States.

The enforcement acts inflamed the opposition and were resorted to with great reluctance by the Republicans. They savored too much of the Federalists' methods of dealing with the resistance to the excise law in 1794. The administration party was not ready to uphold the embargo at the point of the bayonet. Moreover, the election of 1808 showed a distinct reaction in favor of Federalism, all of the New England states except Vermont swinging back into its ranks. In the last moments of his term Jefferson signed a repeal bill.

## The Election of 1808

In the campaign of 1808 the Republican party was somewhat divided. In Virginia Monroe, embittered by Jefferson's rejection of his treaty with England and probably desirous of a less pacific foreign policy, contested the succession with Madison. Vice-President Clinton and his New York followers felt that the time had come for a northern President. A caucus of the Virginia legislature favored Madison over Monroe, and the congressional caucus named him for President with Clinton for a second time in the second position. Clinton publicly repudiated the vice-presidential nomination, and his friends in the electoral college gave him their votes for the chief magistracy. At that he had but 6, while Madison had 122. The Federalists cast 47 electoral ballots for C. C. Pinckney and Rufus King.

Although outwardly neutral, it was an open secret that Jefferson's choice was Madison. He was, indeed, in closer accord with the outgoing administration than Monroe, and the best person for the Presidency if there were to be no change in policy. The Secretary of State was a master of argument, and his state papers dealing with the questions of neutral rights display the utmost keenness in penetrating the weak places in his adversaries' armor. This quality of mind made him an admirable member of the Federal Convention of 1787, where he probably rendered his greatest service to his country. In charge of foreign relations he became an inveterate note-writer, and unfortunately for his later reputation, he came to the Presidency at a time when a man of vigorous action was needed.

## Madison and Commercial Coercion

Some Republican members of Congress were inclined to think that war was the alternative of the embargo. Others still had faith in commercial restrictions. The outcome of considerable debate was a non-intercourse law, which went into effect a few weeks after Madison entered the presidential office (May 20). This law conciliated the domestic shipping interest by permitting commerce with all countries except France and England, and paved the way for negotiations by authorizing the President to suspend its operation against either of these upon the withdrawal of its restrictions upon American trade.  From Canning's point of view the new act was preferable to the embargo, for it held out the hope that England might draw the United States into coöperation against France.  He was willing to withdraw the Orders in Council in so far as they affected America, if the United States would allow British ships to capture vessels violating the American law by trading with France.  D. M. Erskine, the British representative at Washington, whose wife was an American, misled by his desire for cordiality between the two nations, did not inform the Secretary of State of Canning's condition; instead he announced the coming of a special envoy to make a treaty, and the immediate suspension of the Orders.

Upon this Madison issued a proclamation in June (1809) restoring intercourse with England, only to be chagrined by Canning's disavowal and recall of Erskine.  Non-intercourse was thereupon renewed, and when the special envoy, Francis J. Jackson, arrived, the chance of reaching an agreement was far from good.  Slight as it was it was thrown away.  Jackson explained the repudiation of Erskine in language which was understood to insinuate that the American government had known that he was violating instructions.  Madison, who had taken the negotiations out of the hands of the stupid Secretary of State,[1] replied, "Such insinuations are inadmissible in the intercourse of a foreign minister with a government that understands what it owes itself"; and when he received Jackson's angry answer, refused to hold any further intercourse with him.  For two critical years England was unrepresented at the American capital.

Erskine's conduct had placed England in a false light, for both France and the United States construed the supposed revocation of the Orders as evidence that she was yielding to pressure.  But while not unembarrassed she was receiving large quantities of commodities, as under the embargo, by way of Halifax or other foreign ports near our border, whence they were conveyed in British ships.  Thus in a degree the American law had the

[1] Robert Smith, Secretary of State, was an unfortunate appointment, foisted upon Madison by factions opposed to Gallatin, whom he wished to appoint.  Gallatin remained Secretary of the Treasury as under Jefferson.

same effect as the British navigation acts, one aim of which was to give British vessels the carriage of American products.

The non-intercourse law was repealed after a little more than a year, but it gave Napoleon another opportunity to seize American ships. Under the Rambouillet Decree of March, 1810, several hundred vessels were confiscated on the ground that American law forbade their entry into French ports. Napoleon's zeal for the enforcement of United States law was in proportion to his need of money.

As a means of coercion non-intercourse was weaker than the embargo, and while it had led to negotiations they had miscarried. May 1, 1810, another act passed Congress known as "Macon's Bill No. 2." It repealed all restrictions on trade with the warring powers. If either would remove its own restrictions on American trade, however, the President was directed to renew non-intercourse with the other. Thus our treatment of each belligerent was made conditional upon the conduct of the other. It was hoped that both would yield if either did.

Macon's Bill No. 2 had at least the merit of benefiting commerce, as is shown by the increase in tonnage, the rise in the value of exports, and the greater revenue from customs. And it seemed at first that it might accomplish its purpose, for the French foreign minister announced to John Armstrong, American representative in Paris, that the Napoleonic decrees were revoked and would cease to have effect after November 1 — it being understood that the English would revoke the Orders in Council, or that the United States "shall cause their rights to be respected by the English."

Madison accepted this conditional statement as a *bona-fide* revocation of the Berlin and Milan decrees, and demanded that England revoke her Orders. The notice to Armstrong was not followed by any public notice on the part of France, however, and the British refused to accept the French action as genuine. On November 2 Madison therefore proclaimed the renewal of non-intercourse with England, effective after ninety days, unless meantime the Orders in Council were withdrawn. But the French seizures of ships did not cease, and the British complained of the unfairness of non-intercourse with them alone when France was equally guilty of offenses.

Napoleon was playing a shrewd game.   He probably did not wish England to revoke the Orders in Council; and by continuing to seize American vessels he made revocation impossible. But he did not condemn the ships seized, in order that the United States might cling to the belief that the decrees were not to be enforced, and thus be led to persist in non-intercourse with England.   He doubtless aimed not only to encourage the United States to maintain non-intercourse, but to embarrass his enemy still further by inveigling the United States into war with her.

## SELECT BIBLIOGRAPHY FOR CHAPTER XV

Elections of 1804 and 1808.   For these campaigns as for others the best concise account is by Stanwood, *The Presidency*.

Relations with England.   An extraordinarily clear and readable account is that by Mahan, *Sea Power in its Relation to the War of 1812*.

The War of Orders and Decrees.   Channing, *United States*, IV, gives an excellent summary of the French Decrees and British Orders in Council.

# CHAPTER XVI

## THE WAR OF 1812

### THE RISE OF THE WAR PARTY

While difficulties in the international situation were multiplying, the peaceful temper which the Madison administration had inherited from the Jeffersonian régime had gradually vanished. The generation which had fought the Revolution was passing from the stage, giving place to a younger one, less prudent and more inclined to action. The congressional election of 1810 brought defeat to half of the old members including many of the men of pacific views; their seats were taken by new men who owed their election to a growing impatience with the policy of peace at almost any price.

Among the men who entered the arena of national politics at about this time were those who were to be the foremost leaders in Congress until the eve of the Civil War. Henry Clay of Kentucky, John C. Calhoun of western South Carolina, and Daniel Webster of Massachusetts, who took his seat in 1813, attained such preëminence as to win the title of the "great triumvirate." Less well-known and yet important names are those of Richard M. Johnson of Kentucky, Felix Grundy of Tennessee, and Peter B. Porter of western New York. It will be noted that all of these except Webster were from new states or the frontier regions of old ones. With the same exception all were Republicans. To the same group of young Republicans belonged William Lowndes and Langdon Cheves, Calhoun's colleagues from South Carolina.

The events of the year following this memorable election of 1810 added fuel to a spreading fire. As in the days before Jay's treaty, the people of the Ohio Valley believed that England was behind the Indian resistance to their efforts to obtain land cessions. The Greenville treaty line of 1795 had not long satisfied the land-hungry white man. That line left almost the whole of Indiana within the Indian country, and William Henry Harrison, as governor of Indiana Territory, was exceedingly zealous in opening new tracts for settlement. Treaty after treaty for this purpose at length stirred the tribesmen to make a concerted stand against further cessions.

The leader of this concert was the great Tecumseh, a worthy successor of Pontiac. His brother the "Prophet" introduced a supernatural element into the movement by preaching in the name of the Great Spirit a return to the aboriginal simplicity of life. Casting off the vices of the white men would be rewarded, he taught, by the aid of the Great Spirit in resisting them. Tecumseh aimed to organize the tribes of a vast territory to act as a unit in making land cessions, or, if necessary, war. Visiting Harrison, he made an eloquent plea for peace on the basis of the integrity of the territory of the Indians. Soon afterwards he visited the southern tribes (his mother was probably a Creek) hoping to win their support of his plan.

Taking advantage of his absence and believing that his activity threatened hostilities, Harrison led troops into a tract ceded in 1809 by a treaty which the natives had afterwards repudiated. His menacing approach to the Prophet's Town at Tippecanoe drew upon him an attack which was repelled only with difficulty and loss. This was in November, 1811. Because the Indians abandoned the village after the battle, Harrison became a hero in the eyes of the frontiersmen as the victor of Tippecanoe.

The fact that the natives had received guns and powder from the British traders convinced the westerners that the hostilities were incited by the Canadian officials, and that the Indians could not be permanently pacified without displacing the British power in Canada. Land speculators probably encouraged a belief which promoted their plans to dispossess the natives, and the influence of the British was doubtless exaggerated. The clash between the races inflamed the West with a desire for war with England and for the conquest of Canada.

Madison read the signs of the times as shown by the election of 1810 and his administration stiffened its tone towards England. The election almost coincided with the date set for the revocation of the Berlin and Milan decrees. With the renewal of non-intercourse with England in the early months of 1811, Pinkney, minister since the failure of the negotiations of 1806, was ordered home.   No minister had been sent to Washington in place of the dismissed Jackson, and this was made the pretext for Pinkney's withdrawal.   Taken at this time, the action was part of a studied effort to impress the British government with the gravity of the displeasure of the United States.

Although a new minister to the United States was appointed before Pinkney left London, and although the Marquis of Wellesley, Canning's successor, requested Pinkney to remain, he would not do so because the British still refused to recall the Orders in Council.   The new British minister, A. J. Foster, nevertheless proceeded to Washington, and with due formalities restored to the deck of the "Chesapeake" two survivors of the quartette of sailors who had been impressed four years before.

Notwithstanding reparation for the "Chesapeake" outrage England was still firm in her insistence upon the Orders when the new Congress assembled in November, 1811.   The Indian troubles were at their height as the new men elected the year before took their seats.   They sealed their triumph by seizing control of the House and electing Henry Clay as Speaker.   These Young Republicans, Randolph referred to as "the boys," and dubbed "War Hawks" because of their eagerness to take arms against England.   The War Hawks thought more in terms of the nation and less in terms of local interests than had the Republican "fathers" who formulated the doctrine of strict construction and the Virginia and Kentucky Resolutions; the insults to New England commerce they felt as a national affront even more than did the skippers upon whom the losses fell.   But events in the West aroused their passionate hatred of the power which, with Grundy, they believed set on "the ruthless savages to tomahawk our women and children."

The election of Clay as Speaker is said to have been prompted by the belief that he was the only man among the Young Republicans who could curb John Randolph, the free lance.[1]   Its deeper

---

[1] Randolph is the most remarkable eccentric in our history.   His membership in Congress was almost continuous for a generation, in spite of his political nonconformity.   Beginning his career as a regular Republican, he soon gave free rein to his extraordinary personality and became a thorn in the side of Jefferson.   His speeches were long and often incoherent, yet no public man has coined more telling phrases.

significance lies in the fact that the West was beginning to be felt as a power in national politics, taking its place as a third section, holding the balance between the old North and South of the seaboard.

Clay was born in Virginia in 1777. His youth was spent in poverty, but his ambition and native ability attracted the attention of prominent men and won him the patronage of George Wythe, the state chancellor. Upon attaining his majority he, like many another youth, sought the new settlements in Kentucky and "grew up with the country." His gift of oratory won him speedy recognition. Before he reached the constitutional age of a United States Senator he was appointed to fill out an uncompleted term in the upper house of Congress. Then came his election to the lower house and the beginning of a brilliant career as Speaker. He was the first to recognize the possibilities of the office, and in his hands it was carried far in the direction of the commanding importance which it has possessed in recent times. He made it a position of party leadership, and through the power to control proceedings and to appoint committees aided in carrying out the program of the War Hawks.

Against the advice of the former leaders of the party, Madison, now in harmony with the War Hawks, sent in a message recommending "putting the United States into an armor and an attitude demanded by the crisis." Cheves and Lowndes reported for a special committee in favor of building twenty frigates to be followed by a dozen battle-ships. Such a fleet, they argued, could protect our ports against any force which the enemy could spare for an attack upon them. But the Jeffersonian antipathy to a navy could not be overcome. The majority of congressmen preferred to trust to privateering in case of war. After four long months of discussion Congress refused to appropriate money for

Clay's mastery of him is illustrated by an episode which occurred in May, 1812. Randolph began to address the House in opposition to a declaration of war. No motion being before the body, a member raised a point of order and the Speaker, in spite of Randolph's protest that his remarks were introductory to a motion, ruled that the motion must come first. When Randolph moved a resolution "that it is not expedient at this time to resort to war against Great Britain," Clay again denied him the right to proceed until the motion was seconded. Randolph appealed to the House which sustained the Speaker's ruling. Finally, when Randolph had found a seconder and had again begun his speech, he was halted by a ruling that the House must vote on the question of considering the motion. By this time Randolph's ardor for his resolution had well-nigh spent itself in rage at the youthful Speaker.

naval construction, or to levy new taxes, but authorized an increase in the regular army and the enlistment of fifty thousand volunteers.

By the spring of 1812 the British government was ready to revoke the Orders in Council as soon as it could be done safely and with dignity.   England was maintaining an army of 300,000 men in Spain, to free the peninsula from the French, and to occupy Napoleon while Russia broke away from the Continental System.   This army was well-nigh dependent upon America for supplies.   Non-intercourse threatened the success of the peninsular campaign and meant scarcity of bread in England and actual distress in the manufacturing towns.

Napoleon was finally forced to show his hand by a new Order in Council, which declared that whenever the Berlin and Milan decrees should be absolutely and unconditionally revoked the British orders should automatically cease to be in force.   The United States thereupon insisted that France produce indisputable proof that the decrees were no longer operative, and the foreign minister presented a decree dated a year earlier, which declared that the Berlin and Milan decrees were to be considered as nonexistent, so far as concerned America, after November 1, 1810.   There is no doubt that this document was drawn up in 1812 and antedated; but the British ministry chose to accept it, and on June 23 announced the revocation of the Orders.

It can hardly be maintained that fear of war with the United States led England to repeal the Orders in Council.   Jonathan Russell, *chargé d'affaires* in London, wrote a short time before this action was taken, "We have indeed a reputation in Europe for saying so much and doing so little that we shall not be believed in earnest until we act in a manner not to be mistaken."   He could not see that the British apprehended a rupture with the United States.   It would therefore appear that the repeal, so far as American policy was a factor in it, was a triumph for commercial coercion.   Yet five days before this event, which was clearly foreshadowed in the utterances of the British ministry during the spring, the United States declared war.

With apparent blindness to the trend of events in Europe, the preparations for war had gone on in the United States during the early months of 1812.   Hints were given Congress before the

first of April that the President believed that war should be
declared before adjournment.   In April a ninety-day embargo
was passed, to insure that American ships would be safe in port
when war began.   Although Madison told the British minister
that the embargo was not to be considered a war measure, he
sent to Congress on June 1 a message which could only be construed as a recommendation of war.

In this message the President once more reviewed the familiar
story of British aggressions upon neutral rights.   The indictment
covered (1) impressments; (2) the "hovering" of British cruisers
near our coast to seize outbound vessels in enforcement of the
Orders in Council; (3) the paper blockade; (4) the Orders in
Council.   In addition the message alluded to the Indian war, and
adopting the view of the West, intimated that British influence
was at the bottom of it.   "It is difficult," said Madison, "to
account for the activity and combinations which have been for
some time developing themselves among tribes in constant intercourse with British traders and garrisons, without connecting
their hostility with that influence."

These aggressions, the President held, amounted to war against
the United States.   "We behold . . . on the side of Great
Britain, a state of war against the United States, and on the side
of the United States, a state of peace towards Great Britain."
"Whether the United States shall continue passive" or shall
oppose "force to force in defence of their national rights," was a
question which he recommended to the consideration of Congress.

## WAR PLANS AND RESOURCES

The debate on the President's recommendation ended in a
declaration of war on June 18.   At the moment when the policy
of peaceable coercion was nearing success, Madison's message
amounted to a public avowal that it had proved an idle dream.
Then came news of the revocation of the Orders in Council.
Indeed, most of the causes of war were removed before hostilities
began.   The paper blockade and the "hovering," of which Madison complained, were incidental to the Orders and disappeared
with their recall.   Yet it is an error to suppose that a cable,
by bringing swift news of the repeal of the Orders, would have

averted war, for the Indian question and the old grievance of impressment were not affected.

Americans should have looked to their own encroachments upon the Indian lands rather than to British influence for an explanation of the race friction in the Northwest.  As for impressments, while they varied in frequency with the fluctuating needs of the British navy and the ups and downs of American commerce, they had never been so frequent since 1807 as before, and it was extraordinary to make them a cause of war in 1812 when they had been deemed insufficient in 1807.  Since Grundy, a member of the Committee on Foreign Relations, had said in the debate on the Committee's report during the preceding winter, "I feel anxious not only to add the Floridas to the South, but the Canadas to the North of this empire"; since Clay had declared "The conquest of Canada is in your power. . . . Is it nothing to extinguish the torch that lights up savage warfare? Is it nothing to acquire the entire fur-trade connected with that country?" — the opponents of the war not without some justification charged that the real motive of the War Hawks was territorial conquest.

Yet technically the impressment grievance must stand as the *casus belli* in 1812.  The war message professed "a constant readiness to concur in an honorable reëstablishment of peace and friendship."  Immediately after the declaration, the London *chargé* was instructed to propose peace on the basis of the revocation of the orders and the abandonment of impressments.  At the same time the British government dispatched Admiral Warren to the United States to propose a suspension of hostilities in view of the recall of the orders.  The ministry would not recede on the question of impressments, however, and the war was thus professedly fought to vindicate the rights of our sailors.

On any other ground it is difficult to justify the choice of antagonist.  French seizures of vessels almost equaled those of Britain, and Napoleon's treatment of America had been marked, in addition, by the most offensive hypocrisy and deceit. Indeed, Madison consulted Jefferson as to the advisability of declaring war on both belligerents.  But he could not strike France. She presented no vulnerable point for attack, while Canada lay almost undefended, as was thought, at our door.  In effect the

war with England was for France as good as an alliance, in spite
of Madison's care to disavow all connections which might entangle
the United States "in the contests or views of other Powers."
Intent upon its own concerns and oblivious of the great issues
involved in the European war, the New World Republic, in its
provincialism, gave aid and comfort to the would-be-master of
the Old World.[1]

The country was fairly prosperous and potentially rich. At
the end of 1811 Gallatin reported that the public debt had been
reduced in ten years from $80,000,000 to $34,000,000. With a
population of nearly seven and a half millions the nominal
military strength was approximately a million men. The
prospect of success seemed excellent. England's preoccupation
with the European conflict removed the danger of an immediate
attempt at invasion. Since the United States sought to compel
her to yield to certain demands, it must succeed in an aggressive campaign in order to dictate the terms of peace. "My
plan," said Clay, "would be to call out the ample resources
of the country, give them a judicious direction, prosecute the
war with the utmost vigor, strike wherever we can reach the
enemy at sea or on land, and negotiate the terms of peace at
Quebec or Halifax."

A naval war, however, was out of the question. Thanks to
the practice afforded by the Tripolitan War, the naval officers
were experienced and skillful, but the Republic possessed less
than twenty vessels of war, only four of which were frigates
mounting more than forty guns. No ship in the entire fleet was
a match for a British seventy-four.[2] Canada was therefore the
inevitable objective of the American attack, and the War Hawks
held the defensive capacity of the enemy's provinces in slight
esteem. Clay boasted that Kentucky riflemen unaided could capture Quebec and Montreal, and even Jefferson agreed that a campaign against these places was merely a "question of marching."

The test proved that the government was not able to command
the country's actual resources in men and money. The Feder-

---

[1] It is only fair to say that the Republicans in general believed that the welfare of the
peoples of Europe would be promoted by Napoleon's success. They were suspicious of
England as a monarchy in which old abuses were still unreformed.

[2] A ship of the line was called a "seventy-four" from the number of cannon carried. It
was the most powerful type of fighting craft of that era.

alists had never become reconciled to Republican rule. Their rancor had smoldered but not died after the collapse of the secession plot of 1804. The policy of commercial restriction had revived the waning fortunes of the party, which showed large gains in the election of 1808. The war policy now showed the influence of the West, and Federalist dislike of the West had grown steadily since the purchase of Louisiana. In 1811, when the southern portion of the territory obtained from France asked admission to the Union as the State of Louisiana, Josiah Quincy, of Massachusetts, said in the House: "I am compelled to declare it as my deliberate opinion that, if this bill passes, the bonds of this union are, virtually, dissolved; that the states which compose it are free from their moral obligations, and that as it will be the right of all, so it will be the duty of some to prepare, definitely, for a separation; amicably, if they can, violently, if they must."

To the conflict into which the West had plunged the country the Federalists were bitterly antagonistic. Upon the passage of the declaration the thirty-four Federalists in Congress met in caucus and issued an address denouncing the war as "a party and not a national war," entered into by a divided people. It was suicidal, they protested, to subject the bonds of union to the strain of war under such circumstances, and they disclaimed all responsibility for the disasters which they predicted. Taking the address as their keynote, the New England wing of the party continued their factious conduct throughout the period of hostilities. They hung flags at half-mast and tolled church bells upon hearing of the declaration. They made niggardly subscriptions to the government loans, contributing less than one dollar of every thirteen that went into the treasury. They obstructed the efforts of the administration to utilize the militia as a national army, attempted to nullify federal legislation, and finally called a convention supposedly to consider secession.

The sectional character of the war, and especially the responsibility of the West for it, are well shown by the presidential election of 1812. Madison's espousal of the belligerent program won him the support of the War Hawks in the congressional caucus in June. Elbridge Gerry received the indorsement for the Vice-Presidency. George Clinton was now dead, but the jealousy of New York towards the Virginia "dynasty" found expression in the candidacy of his nephew, DeWitt Clinton. Nominated by the Republicans of the state legislature, he was later indorsed by a convention of Federalists, as a peace candidate. The returns showed that the original states were almost equally divided; they cast 90 electoral votes for Madison and war and 89 for Clinton and peace, while the five new states cast their 38 votes for Madison, tipping the scales and showing that they held the balance of political power.

Madison, "master of ideas but not of men," visited all of the offices of the War and Navy Departments in person on the day after war was declared. The effect is indicated by the words of the observer who described him as "stimulating everything in a manner worthy of a little commander-in-chief, with his little round hat and huge cockade." Incitement of clerks to perform routine tasks was not the duty of the hour for the head of the nation. The competence of department heads, however, was a matter of infinite importance. William Eustis and Paul Hamilton, the Secretaries of the War and Navy Departments, were notoriously unfit for their great responsibilities, but in spite of warnings the President lacked the courage to place strong men in their places at the outset. In 1811, after performing the duties of Secretary of State himself for some time, he had dismissed Smith (see footnote, page 303) and appointed Monroe, his late rival, to the post. By this action Monroe became "heir apparent" to the Presidency. He made a fair cabinet officer.

Quincy derided the administration as a "despotism," "composed to all efficient purposes of two Virginians and a foreigner." Gallatin, by far the ablest member of the official family, was so harassed by the continual hounding of small-minded politicians that after a year of war he welcomed the opportunity to exchange his cabinet post for a place on the peace commission. The failures of Eustis and Hamilton at length necessitated the appointment of other officials, but this was not done until great harm had been sustained.

The weakness of the executive departments was equaled by the incapacity of Congress to rise to the situation. The developed resources of the country were chiefly agricultural. The general prosperity depended in large measure upon the exportation of cotton, tobacco, corn, wheat, and flour, in exchange for imported manufactures. In spite of non-intercourse with England, foreign commerce in 1811 amounted to more than $100,000,000. Upon duties on imports the government also depended almost wholly for its revenues. Gallatin reported that the duties had fallen from $12,000,000 before commercial restriction began, to $6,000,000 in 1811, and a deficit was in sight for 1812, even with peace. War was certain to reduce commerce still further, curtailing revenues at the same time that expenditures rose.

Under such circumstances Congress performed little better than the Continental Congress of the Revolution. Although now possessed of the power of taxation, it was afraid to use it vigorously upon a people unaccustomed to heavy tax burdens. Gallatin, who for a decade had administered the treasury with scrupulous economy, seeking to wipe out the national debt and spare the people all needless taxation, saw all his work menaced by war; but when, facing the inevitable, he advocated internal taxes, the House rebuked the proposal of "unrepublican measures."[1] The tariff was indeed doubled, but the true alternative of direct taxes was loans which would saddle posterity with a burden not of its own choosing. Here too Congress was niggardly; and with most of the loanable capital of the nation in the hands of New England Federalists, Gallatin had great difficulty in securing subscriptions even for the meager sums which Congress authorized him to borrow. The securities sold at much less than par, and bore rates of interest as high as $7\frac{1}{2}$ per cent.

Gallatin also recommended the renewal of the charter of the United States Bank, which expired in 1811. A strong institution of this type could have been used to excellent advantage by the Treasury. But the Republican Congress had not yet escaped from the Jeffersonian tradition of 1791 and refused the recharter.

The declaration of war was made with the army preparations still far from complete. There were at the time less than seven thousand regulars, distributed in widely scattered posts along the coast, near the Canadian border, and in the remote interior. Eustis *guessed* the number of new enlistments up to June 8 at about five thousand. The Republicans relied upon the state

---

[1] Necessity nevertheless compelled resort to a direct tax and an excise a year later.

militia for the early campaigns, while regulars and volunteers were being recruited in adequate numbers.

The governors of the New England states refused, however, to honor the call for quotas of militia, and the United States found but a fraction of the desired number at its command.[1] Even these refused to fight on foreign soil, and proved useless for the purpose of invading Canada. The response to the call for volunteers was meager also, and for all the government's efforts, the effective forces did not at any time exceed thirty-five thousand men.

Most of the fighting had to be done along the northern frontier in a wilderness still untouched by the art of the roadmaker. The movement of large bodies of troops proved to be extremely difficult, and the proper coördination of attacks at widely separated points was almost impossible. The commissariat also was in continual confusion.

Worse than any of the physical handicaps was the inefficiency of the officers from the Secretary of War down. At the beginning of the war two major-generals and six brigadier-generals were selected. Their ages ranged from fifty-five to sixty-seven. None had served in the regular army, and only Thomas Pinckney, junior major-general, and William Hull, one of the brigadiers, had records as officers in the Revolution. "The Creator," said Jefferson, "has not thought proper to mark those on the forehead who are of the stuff to make good generals." A period of actual warfare was required to bring to the front men of real military capacity. Meantime the campaigns suffered from the incompetence of the officers chosen, as it were, by a blindfolded administration.

## THE CAMPAIGNS

Hostilities began with a triple movement for the invasion of Canada. Dearborn, the senior major-general, was to move from Lake Champlain and threaten Montreal; Stephen Van Rensselaer, a New York militia officer, and Alexander Smyth, of the regular army, were to strike the Canadian center in the neighbor-

---

[1] A decision of the Supreme Court in 1827 (Martin vs. Mott) upheld the President's right to judge of the necessity of calling out the militia. But the use of the militia as a national force, especially for warfare on foreign soil, has been beset with difficulties down to the present.

hood of Niagara ; while Hull, from Fort Detroit, was to drive the
British from upper Canada. The three strokes if properly
timed and executed would have brought the forces into united
action against Montreal. But Dearborn was conferring with
Admiral Warren when his column should have been in motion
towards the St. Lawrence, and when at last his army of militia

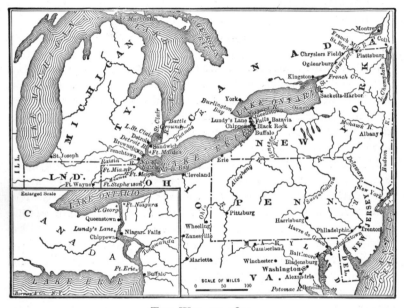

THE WAR OF 1812.

did move, it halted at the Canadian line. In the center there
was further trouble with the militia. Moreover, the two generals
there would not coöperate, and their separate attacks were easily
repulsed.

Hull's success depended upon the outcome of the movements
farther east, where due activity would have kept the enemy
occupied and prevented the sending of additional troops to upper
Canada. The sluggishness of the other commanders allowed Hull
to move first. Then, alarmed at the failure of the eastern
columns, and at the danger to his line of communications because
the British controlled Lake Erie, he fell back to Detroit. Isaac
Brock, his opponent, receiving reënforcements, took the offensive

and laid siege to the fort.  Hull then surrendered (August) without firing a shot, on the plea that capture after resistance would endanger the lives of the women and children in the fort, at the hands of the savage allies of the foe.  Although his conduct was scarcely more culpable than that of the other commanders, he was made the scapegoat.  Tried and convicted of cowardice by a court martial, he was pardoned by the President out of consideration for his honorable record in the Revolution.

The whole season's campaign utterly miscarried, and ended with the British in occupation of Detroit.  From this vantage point they threatened the entire Northwest, and actually carried the war into northern Ohio.  Harrison, who succeeded Hull, was unable to hold ground on the River Raisin, in southern Michigan, but repelled attacks directed against forts on the Maumee (Fort Meigs) and Sandusky (Fort Stephenson, the modern Fremont) in 1813.

The misfortunes of 1812 had at least revealed the incompetence of the commanding officers, and several changes were made. John Armstrong, of New York, was appointed Secretary of War to appease northern jealousy of Virginia.  Of him Dallas (later Secretary of the Treasury) said, "He was the devil from the beginning, is now, and ever will be!"  Under Armstrong the plan of campaign for the second year was substantially identical with that of 1812.  Harrison aimed at the recovery of Detroit and the invasion of Ontario from that point, while new efforts were made against Montreal and Niagara.  It had become clear that the control of Lake Erie was necessary for the success of the western phase of the campaign, and Captain Oliver H. Perry was given command of six vessels built on the lake.  With these he met and defeated a slightly inferior fleet of the enemy, in September.  Harrison was then able to force the British from Detroit and vicinity, to pursue them to the Thames River, and to win a considerable engagement on Canadian soil.  Tecumseh's death in this battle disorganized his followers and prepared the way for the pacification of the Northwest Indians some time before the peace with Britain.

In the Southwest the Creeks fell upon Fort Mims, on the Alabama River, in August, 1813, and massacred about five hundred persons.  Their pacification came, like that of the northern tribes, before the end of the war with England, in consequence of a severe defeat administered in March, 1814, by frontier militiamen in a battle which brought Andrew Jackson into prominence.

On the St. Lawrence James Wilkinson, who had replaced Dearborn, had ample opportunity to prove his incapacity. The operations near Niagara were again indecisive, preventing Harrison from following up his successes. However, events were slowly making it possible to discriminate between incapable officers and those who gave promise, and the names of Harrison, Jackson, Jacob Brown, and Winfield Scott began to inspire confidence.

A serious turn of affairs came in 1814, for the end of the war in Europe permitted England to assume the offensive in America. Napoleon, intending to chastise Russia for forsaking the Continental System which she had promised to support when she made the Peace of Tilsit, had led his armies deep into that country and occupied Moscow late in the autumn of 1812. There he found to his sorrow that possession of the Russian capital did not mean the conquest of the nation. The government and armies of the Czar forsook the vicinity, and the French found not even the means of subsistence in Moscow and the region roundabout. Napoleon was forced to forego his plan of wintering there and to attempt a mid-winter retreat to central Europe.

The season proved to be exceptionally severe, and the sufferings of the ill-fated army as it plodded westward across the vast snow-covered plains are almost without parallel. Napoleon scented the coming uprising of the peoples of middle Europe at the news of his misfortune, and hastening on to France gathered a new army with which to face the united attack of Austria, Prussia, and Russia at the Battle of the Nations (October, 1813). Suffering here his first great defeat, he fell back to France, then to Paris, vainly striving to check the columns of his adversaries as they converged upon his doomed capital. Perceiving at last the futility of the effort, he chose to abdicate the imperial dignity rather than await deposition at the hands of his triumphant foes.

These events seemed to herald the return of peace in Europe.

It only remained for the victorious powers assembled in the Congress of Vienna to redraw the map of Europe and decide the fate of the fallen autocrat. But he, banished to the Isle of Elba in the Mediterranean, escaped in the spring of 1815, and for a brief and splendid moment threatened to regain his lost glory. Then at the end of a hundred days came Waterloo, and amid its smoke and din the sun of fortune set forever upon the Corsican adventurer.

The last stage of Napoleon's career did not affect the American war, which closed six months before his final overthrow. In July, 1814, the Americans renewed the effort to invade Canada by crossing the Niagara River, no longer with the original hope of conquering a peace, but in order to make as formidable a showing as possible. Scott won a victory in a minor engagement at Chippewa, and soon after the united forces of Scott and Brown had the advantage in a hard-fought battle at Lundy's Lane. These engagements showed that capable officers were being developed and that American soldiers could fight well under good leadership. But the only use to which soldiership could now be put was to guard the territory of the United States; for, freed from the Napoleonic menace, England turned upon the little state which had been snapping at her heels while she grappled with the giant.

She planned to invade the United States at several points. A few weeks after Lundy's Lane, Sir George Prevost advanced from Canada along the well-worn route taken by Montcalm and Burgoyne in previous wars, seeking like them to isolate New England. The American land forces defending Lake Champlain were greatly outnumbered, and the fighting strength of the British boats on the lake was double that of the American vessels. But in the face of these odds, Captain Thomas Macdonough succeeded by clever strategy in turning back the invaders in the naval battle of Plattsburg.

This was in September, like Perry's victory of the previous year. The month before, a British fleet entered Chesapeake Bay to create a diversion on behalf of Prevost. An army under General Robert Ross landed on the Patuxent and marched on Washington, encountering no resistance until it reached Bladensburg, five miles from the capital. There a force which outnum-

bered the British but consisted mainly of raw militia, under
General W. H. Winder, awaited their coming.  The commander
was a politician, not a soldier, and the militia abandoned their
excellent position and fled almost at the first attack, leaving
the city at the mercy of the foe.  Directions as to the route
to be taken in the retreat were given before the battle,
which has come to be known derisively as " the Bladensburg
races."

A year before, York (Toronto) had fallen into the hands of
Americans, who had pillaged and burned the Houses of Parliament and other public build-
ings.  In retaliation the White
House, the Treasury, and the
War Office in Washington were
now burned, at the command
of Ross.  The most important
of the government records
were hastily collected and carried to a place of safety.  The
President fled from the capital
as ignominiously as the common herd, some of whom did
not hesitate to revile him as
the author of their misery.
Armstrong was now sacrificed
to appease the clamor of the
people for a victim, and the
war office was added to Monroe's responsibilities.

WASHINGTON AND VICINITY.

An attack upon Baltimore
with the support of the fleet
followed the capture of Washington.  Improvised harbor defenses
— chains stretched across the channel — kept the fleet beyond
effective cannon range, however, and forces which were landed
hesitated to press the attack.  After a brief siege the expedition reëmbarked to share in attacks on the coast of Maine
and on New Orleans.  The latter was the third point at which
the British planned to invade the United States.  Sir Edward
Pakenham replaced Ross as commander of the expedition against

New Orleans, which consisted of ten thousand veterans of the European wars.

Some months after General Wilkinson was transferred to the St. Lawrence, the command over the United States troops in the Southwest was given to Andrew Jackson. Jackson, a native of South Carolina, had "grown up" with Tennessee as Clay had with Kentucky. A smattering of legal knowledge acquired during his indigent and indolent youth, plus a great deal of native force, had made him a marked man from the early days of Tennessee statehood. He had served without distinction in the United States Senate during the Presidency of John Adams. A natural leader of men, his resourcefulness and energy had shown to much greater advantage in campaigns against the southern Indians while a major-general of the Tennessee militia, and had won him the appointment to succeed Wilkinson.

When Jackson learned of the British plan to attack New Orleans, he collected all possible forces — piratical gangs from the coast islands and marshes as well as militia of the southwestern states — and with great energy prepared to defend the city. Pakenham made his own preparations cautiously, losing the opportunity to attack before Jackson's works were ready. These consisted of a barrier across the narrow strip of land between the Mississippi and the marshes bordering Lake Borgne. Along the strip ran the only practicable approach to the city on the east side of the river. On the west bank the American position was less strong, and by carrying it Jackson's main works could have been destroyed by an attack in the rear and from the river.

From caution Pakenham passed to rashness, misled possibly by contempt for American militia. Occasional occurrences like that at Bladensburg were probably the basis of the belief of British officers, since the days of the French and Indian War, that militia could not withstand the charge of regulars. On January 8, 1815, without awaiting the success of operations on the west bank, Pakenham attempted to carry Jackson's position by assault. Many of the militia were frontiersmen whose daily companion was the rifle. Every such man was a sharpshooter, and behind their breastworks their position was almost impregnable. The British general's decision was a fatal error. Two advances were repulsed by the deadly fire, with a loss of more than two thousand killed and wounded. Pakenham fell among his men, the attack was abandoned, and the expedition reëmbarked and sailed away. According to Jackson's report his own loss was sixty-three men.

BATTLE OF NEW ORLEANS.

The Battle of New Orleans was the chief victory of the war and made Jackson a national hero. Two weeks earlier peace terms had been agreed upon at Ghent. Under other circumstances a British victory at the mouth of the Mississippi might have meant the loss of Louisiana and revived the dangers associated with the occupation of that province by a European power. Such a result was anticipated and even desired by some of the Federalists who had opposed the acquisition of the territory in the first place. The success of the West in defending the approaches to the Mississippi Valley gave it greater self-confidence and soon led it to demand more recognition from the nation.

The British plan of invasion succeeded only at one minor point. Repulsed at Plattsburg, Baltimore, and New Orleans, they succeeded in taking a few places on the coast of Maine which they held until the peace. From the military standpoint the war must be pronounced a draw. Each belligerent successfully defended its own territory but failed in the attempt to carry the war to the enemy.

## Naval Warfare

The War Hawks had desired to increase the navy but had been defeated by votes of old-line Republicans with the aid of some of the Federalists. The vessels available for service at the beginning of the war were sent out to afford what protection they could to homeward-bound merchantmen and to attack British commerce. During the first season several duels occurred between them and British ships in which the Americans were victorious, to the great elation of the people. The "Constitution" was the victor in two of these combats. In August she disabled the thirty-eight gun "Guerrière" in half an hour, and in December defeated the "Java" of her own size. In other fights the "Wasp" beat the "Frolic," the "United States" took the "Macedonian," and the "Hornet" sank the "Peacock." On the other hand the unfortunate "Chesapeake" was beaten by the "Shannon."

It had been the plan of the United States to build its frigates slightly stronger than the standard British vessels of the same class, and in nearly every battle the American boat was of greater tonnage or threw a heavier broadside than its antagonist. Yet the English were so astonished at the series of victories that they imagined the frigates to be disguised ships of the line (see note, page 313). They had felt the same contempt for American ships as for militia. Said Lord Brougham in Parliament, "The assembled navies of America could not lay siege to an English sloop of war!"

The truth is the American ships were more skillfully built than the enemy's; they were certainly well handled, and the gunnery was good. The moral effect of their success was all the greater because of the immense prestige of the British navy. Apart from their effect on the morale of the people the sea fights were without influence upon the course of the war. On the contrary the battles on the lakes were well-nigh decisive.

The early victories induced Congress to make some additions to the navy. Nevertheless one by one the ships were captured or bottled up in port. It was the privateers after all that made the great showing in the war on commerce. Such enterprises, now discountenanced by international law, attracted many ship owners and interested large numbers of citizens through popular subscriptions for the ventures. About five hundred vessels went out during the war with commissions to prey on the enemy's commerce. These boats gave additional evidence of the superiority of American shipwrights and seamen. By their swiftness they were able to avoid danger, and risked combat only where success was certain. If they fought, they were sure to win; if they fled, they were sure to escape. Although the total captures of all kinds about equaled those made by the foe, English commerce suffered far less than American. Before the end of the war the blockade of the Atlantic coast practically stopped the entry and exit of boats.

### THE PEACE NEGOTIATIONS

In the hope of freeing his ally from the embarrassment of war with the United States at the moment when Napoleon was beginning his invasion of Russia, the Czar tendered his good offices as mediator in September, 1812. Madison accepted, and appointed Gallatin and James A. Bayard, Federalist Senator from Delaware, to act with John Quincy Adams, then minister in Russia, as peace commissioners. England rejected mediation but indicated a willingness to treat directly with the representatives of the States. Clay and Russell, formerly *chargé* in England, were thereupon added to the commission, and negotiations were begun at Ghent in the summer of 1814. Britain's chief statesmen were absorbed in the discussions of the Congress at Vienna, and the conferences at Ghent were intrusted to men of little prominence, who, despite constant directions from their superiors, succeeded in making several blunders of which the American negotiators reaped the full advantage.

The instructions of the American commissioners, formulated early in the war when hopes were high, were modified as the tide of hope receded. The demand that impressments be abandoned by express stipulation in the treaty was given up, and a similar recession was made in regard to the British principles of blockade. On these points the British could not be shaken, and in the end the United States had to be content with a treaty which was silent on the matters which had been the main causes of friction before the war.

The Americans on their part resisted with equal success the demands of the British. These, framed soon after Napoleon's abdication, were in their turn excessive. The English commissioners asked : (1) for a mutual guarantee of the integrity of the territory of their Indian allies as a *sine qua non* of peace; (2) for military control of the Great Lakes, with a cession of territory in northern Maine to afford a direct route between Quebec and Halifax; and (3) for a concession in return for the renewal of the fishing rights of the United States within Canadian waters. The severity of these terms was such as to cause our commissioners to reply in effect that they could not be entertained unless America were completely conquered.

Back of the British demands was the expectation of success in the operations of Prevost and Ross. The news of the reverses at Plattsburg and Baltimore, and the threat of renewed hostilities in Europe because of disagreements at Vienna, made the British falter. Abandoning the *sine qua non* as to the Indian territory, they proffered a settlement on the basis of *status uti possidetis* — that the treaty should leave each belligerent in possession of the territory held when peace was made. The insistence of the Americans upon the *status quo ante bellum* — which would require the mutual restoration of conquered territory — was regarded by the statesmen of Downing Street as the reply of stiff-necked Yankees who could not understand the logic of the war. But the American position was sound, according to the greatest military mind in the British Empire, the Duke of Wellington. In response to the appeal of the ministry that he take command of the Canadian army, the Duke declared that he could not conquer America without first regaining control of the Lakes. Could he do this? He could not promise himself success. Evidently, in his judgment, the victories of Perry and Macdonough were decisive and the prolongation of the war unjustifiable. Nor did he regard the terms proposed by the ministry as warranted. "I confess," he said, "that I think you have no right from the state of the war to demand any concession from America. . . . You have not been able to carry it into the enemy's territory . . . and have not even cleared your own. . . . Why stipulate for the *uti possidetis?* You can get no territory."

While these consultations, unknown to the American commissioners, were disposing the ministry to acceptance of the *status quo ante*, Gallatin and his colleagues were drafting a treaty on this basis for submission to the British commissioners. Dissensions now appeared — not for the first time — within their own commission. Clay, champion of the new West which had arisen since 1783, was unwilling to purchase the renewed recognition of fishing rights by continuing the British liberty to navigate the Mississippi; Adams, true heir of his father as guardian of the fishermen, was ready to contest the point to the uttermost. With the patience which made him in a double sense a great peacemaker, Gallatin persuaded the disputants to agree to offer a renewal of both rights; but the British counter-proposal that these questions be left to be dealt with at a later time was finally accepted.[1]

Already the Americans had consented to make peace with the Indians still at war, on the basis of restoring all their prewar rights, while rejecting everything in the nature of an international guarantee under which Great Britain might claim a right to intervene in their behalf in future. Other portions of the treaty related to matters not connected with the war. They provided for joint commissions to determine the boundary at several disputed points.

On December 24, 1814, Clay who had pictured the victorious hosts of his countrymen dictating terms of peace at Quebec, signed a treaty which added not a foot of territory to the United States; Adams, who had called impressment "man stealing," accepted a peace which was silent on the subject which had caused the war. Nevertheless benignant peace smiled again upon foes of kindred blood. In token of restored harmony the British delegates entertained the Americans at dinner on Christmas Day. "The roast beef and plum pudding was from England, and everybody drank everybody else's health." So wrote young James Gallatin, who had been his father's clerk during the long negotiations. "The band played *God Save the King,*

---

[1] The fisheries question was covered by a convention or agreement made in 1818, by which the rights and privileges of the United States were curtailed somewhat as compared with the provisions of the treaty of 1783. Disputes grew out of the new agreement and the fisheries continued until the twentieth century to be a vexatious problem in Anglo-American relations. The British right to navigate the Mississippi was not renewed, since its sources were found not to be within British territory.

to the toast of the King, and *Yankee Doodle*. Congratulations
on all sides and a general atmosphere of serenity; it was a scene
to be remembered. God grant there may be always peace between the two nations."

## THE HARTFORD CONVENTION

While the peace negotiations were nearing their close New
England discontent came to its climax. Again as in the revolutionary days the town meetings became centers for the discussion of grievances, and the state legislatures, like those of
Virginia and Kentucky in 1798, passed resolutions denouncing
the acts of the federal government. The Federalists now talked
of the Constitution as a compact and spoke of the states as
sovereign. In 1814 the Massachusetts General Court used the
very words in which the President had once maintained the right
of a state to interpose its authority in cases of violation of the
"federal compact"; and a few months later Connecticut passed
an act intended to thwart the execution of a law of Congress for
the enlistment of minors.

In consequence of the refusal by the New England states of
the call for militia, the federal government had stationed no
troops in that quarter, and when the British invaded the coast
of Maine in 1814, New England was left to defend herself.
Massachusetts thereupon asked the neighboring states to join
with her in sending delegates to a convention to be held at
Hartford, in December.

The Massachusetts, Connecticut, and Rhode Island legislatures, and counties in New Hampshire and Vermont, appointed
delegates to the convention. Although the purpose stated in the
call was to devise means of security and defense "not repugnant
to their obligations as members of the Union," and to "procure
such amendments to . . . the national constitution as may secure
them equal advantages," it was generally believed that the leaders
contemplated secession unless their demands were met.

Color was given to this conjecture by the utterances of some
of the more radical Federalists. For example, one of them, writing in the Boston *Advertiser*, urged the convention to recommend
that the states declare the Constitution "suspended," and the

*Centinel,* another Boston newspaper, announced Connecticut's decision to send delegates to Hartford as the rearing of the "second pillar of a new federal edifice." "Refederator," who was quoted with approval by many papers, wanted, not the secession of New England, but the expulsion of the western states from the Union. "*Let the Western States go off,*" he argued; "then let us, who belonged to the old family [of original states], try, by the agency of such men as are to meet at *Hartford* . . . [to] revise our family compact." Gouverneur Morris, writing of the doings of Congress while the convention was sitting, declared that they were "indifferent to one whose eyes are fixed on a Star in the East, which he believes to be the day spring of freedom and glory. The traitors and madmen assembled at Hartford will, I believe, if not too tame and mild, be hailed hereafter as the patriots and sages of their day and generation."

Additional suspicion was aroused by the secrecy of the sessions, and to this day little is known of what was said.[1] When after nearly three weeks the convention adjourned to meet again at the call of the presiding officer, the parallel with the course of the First Continental Congress was too striking to be overlooked, for the Hartford Convention had formulated certain demands to be presented at Washington, and the presumption was strong that some revolutionary action would follow rejection.

The demands took the form of amendments to the Constitution : apportionment of taxes and representatives in the House on the basis of free population; a two-thirds vote of both houses for the admission of new states, the interdiction of foreign commerce, or the declaring of war; the limitation of embargoes to sixty days; the disqualification of naturalized citizens for federal office; and the limitation of the President's tenure to a single term, no two Presidents to come in succession from the same state. The first of these proposals sprang from an ancient dissatisfaction with the three-fifths compromise; the rest from sectional jealousy due to the Virginia dynasty and the growth of the West. Sober

---

[1] The Journal of the Convention was published in 1823 to show the mild temper of the meeting. Members declared that it recorded every motion and vote, and that no proposal was made to divide the Union, organize a separate government, or form any foreign alliance. The man chosen as president of the gathering was George Cabot, one of the original founders of the Federalist party, but a moderate man, now sixty-two years of age. In 1813 he had said to Pickering, "Why can't you and I let the world ruin itself in its own way?"

afterthought questions whether any of the changes except perhaps the first would have been wise.

Massachusetts and Connecticut appointed commissioners to present the proposals to the government at Washington. Yet in spite of appearances, most of the Federalists probably wished for nothing more than a redress of their supposed grievances. It is more than doubtful whether the majority of the people of any New England state would have supported secession. As an indication of their loyalty it is worthy of note that as many volunteers entered the army from Massachusetts as from Virginia.

In the columns of the *National Advocate*, a New York paper, appeared in January, 1815, the following mock advertisement: "Missing: three well-looking, responsible men, who appeared to be travelling towards Washington, disappeared suddenly from Gadsby's Hotel, in Baltimore, on Monday morning last, and have not since been heard of." The jibe was aimed at the New England commissioners. On their way to Washington they had learned of Jackson's victory at New Orleans, and news of the peace had arrived before them. Realizing that amid the universal rejoicing their errand would appear ridiculous, they had quietly turned their faces homeward.

## SELECT BIBLIOGRAPHY FOR CHAPTER XVI

Mahan, *Sea Power*, is excellent on the whole war period and the peace negotiations. This writer, himself an officer in the United States navy, was the first historian to point out the importance of sea power in the history of international relations. Adams' treatment is able and full on all the topics of the chapter. Babcock, *Rise of American Nationality*, gives a good brief account of the war but pays slight attention to diplomacy. Paine, *The Fight for a Free Sea*, is another brief account.

**Rise of the War Party.** A good life of one of the leaders of the "War Hawks" is Schurz, *Henry Clay*.

**War Plans and Resources.** Bogart, *Economic History of the United States;* Dewey, *Financial History.*

**The Campaigns.** McMaster and Schouler are briefer than Adams and more easily read.

**Naval Warfare.** Roosevelt, *Naval War of 1812*, is an older work than Mahan's, but has fuller details on naval operations.

**The Hartford Convention.** Lodge, *Life and Letters of George Cabot*, is best on the convention. The work of Powell, *Nullification and Secession in the United States*, contains a brief account (chap. 5).

# CHAPTER XVII

## THE NEW NATIONALISM

The War of 1812 was one of the most futile of conflicts, judged by the contrast between its objects and the terms of peace. The easy confidence with which the leaders had predicted a peace dictated at the Canadian capital contrasted sadly with the meager successes along the border. Neither force nor diplomacy wrested from England the recognition of neutral rights. Yet the war profoundly affected the American people. In spite of the inconclusive duel they had a sense of vindicated honor. The victories at the Thames and Lundy's Lane, the repulse of the enemy at Plattsburg and New Orleans, and most of all, the gallant performance of the seamen, appealed powerfully to the national pride; while the darker experiences — the lack of preparedness, the failure of the militia, the recalcitrancy of New England, the financial mistakes — were warnings to plan more wisely for the future.

The Republicans had been undergoing a process of nationalization since 1801. Jefferson had come to the Presidency as the apostle of localism and the foe of centralized authority, but from the moment of his inauguration the logic of circumstances had proved stronger than his theories. After the purchase of Louisiana Gouverneur Morris wrote: "By downright demonstration it is shown that the republican party were not dissatisfied because the power of the Government was too great, but because it was not in their hands." In proportion, moreover, as the Republicans had gravitated towards the standard of strong government set up by the Federalists, the latter, as the party of the "Outs," had swung around to states' rights and localism. Thus there had been an actual exchange of positions. But the opposition of New England to the war, culminating in the

Hartford Convention, brought home to the whole country the dangers in the weakening of political authority towards which states' rights sentiments tended, and peace was accompanied by an access of patriotism and nationalistic feeling. Gallatin wrote in 1816: "Under our former system we were becoming too selfish . . . too much confined in our feelings to local and state objects. The war has renewed the national feelings and character which the Revolution had given."

## After-War Readjustment

The spirit of nationalism had never before attained the vigor shown at the close of the second war with England. It pervaded all of the measures of reconstruction which followed the peace. One of its first manifestations is found in the plans for placing the army and navy on a peace basis. Madison's message of 1815 recommended adequate provision for the national defense. Clay, now returned from Ghent and reëlected Speaker, pointed to the unsatisfactory state of the relations with several European powers, and urged the retention of the direct tax as a measure of financial preparedness. New wars were not unlikely to come, and the former trust in pacific methods of preserving national rights was gone. There was no more talk of reducing the navy to the vanishing point, as in Jefferson's early plans. On the contrary, it was maintained at its full, though meager, war strength, with provision for some additions. The peace footing of the army was put at ten thousand men. Although this was but half the number recommended by Monroe, as Secretary of War, the action of Congress indicated that faith had been lost in the militia as a trustworthy first arm of defense.

Having provided for the military and naval establishments, the Republicans, still following Madison's lead, set about restoring the currency. The evils of unregulated issues of paper, which Hamilton avoided by the creation of the United States Bank, had fallen upon the country when the Republicans refused to grant a renewal of the charter in 1811. Banks chartered by the states had multiplied, and while nominally specie paying, their issues were so little regulated that a total of possibly $170,000,000 was put into circulation upon the basis of specie reserves not exceeding $15,000,000. This was about four times as much as sound methods permitted.

Any unusual demand for specie, under such conditions, was certain to result in the suspension of specie payments. The shock came with the capture of Washington. All of the banks in the South and West suspended payments in the autumn of 1814, throwing the country upon a paper basis again, as at the close of the Revolution. Almost indescribable confusion followed. The paper of each bank had its own scale of depreciation, which varied with the strength of the bank and its distance from the point where the paper was in use. Tables, frequently revised to show the current value of the different notes in circulation in each community, were necessary to enable merchants to transact business at all, and even then the constant fluctuations discouraged activity in business through fear of loss by further depreciation. The government was involved also, since most of the money received for bonds was in the form of bank-notes. Only in New England where specie payments were maintained did bank-notes remain at par.

An attachment to state banks has been one of the striking manifestations of localism in the United States. In early days, when the issue of circulating notes was regarded as the chief function of banks, the business was one of the most profitable forms of investment. The idea of a great central institution endowed with special privileges by favor of government has always been repugnant to a large portion of the people, as tending to give a monopoly of such profits, and an undue control over credit, to a privileged few.

The necessity of a uniform currency, however, was felt even in colonial days, as shown by the parliamentary enactments fixing the value at which money of various kinds should circulate in the provinces. The Constitution recognized this need by giving Congress power to regulate the value of money; and Hamilton resorted to the United States Bank as the most expedient mode of exercising this power, in so far as it applied to paper.

With some hesitation Madison turned to Hamilton's ideas and suggested in the message of 1815 that if the operation of the state banks could not restore a uniform circulation, a national bank would "merit consideration." For the Republicans, such a course was a humiliating confession of error.  But the confusion of the currency imperatively demanded remedial action, and they had no substitute to offer.

/ Calhoun was chairman of the committee which, working in touch with A. J. Dallas, the new Secretary of the Treasury, as the guiding spirit in financial reconstruction, reported a bill for the creation of a second United States Bank.  The capital now authorized was $35,000,000.  The government was to subscribe one fifth and to appoint a like proportion of the directors.  The new bank was to issue notes redeemable on demand in specie. The charter was to run for twenty years; branches might be established in the states as needed; the bank was to be the depositary of public funds unless they were removed by the Secretary of the Treasury for reasons satisfactory to Congress.  It was to be exempt from federal taxation, but was required to pay a bonus of $1,500,000 for its charter.

In presenting the bill Calhoun insisted that it was the duty of Congress to regulate the currency and restore specie payments. So far was he from the position of Jefferson in 1791 that he waived discussion of the constitutional aspects of the question as "a useless consumption of time."  Clay supported him heartily, attributing his change of mind since 1811 (when he had been among those who voted against rechartering the first bank) to "the force of circumstances and the light of experience."  In April Madison placed his signature on the bill, thus virtually adopting the doctrine of implied powers which he had combatted twenty-five years before.

The opening of the bank enabled the government to bring about a general resumption of specie payments.  With the notes of the new institution in circulation, the Secretary of the Treasury was able to announce that, in accordance with a joint resolution of Congress, on and after February 20, 1817, government dues would be received only in the notes of the United States Bank and other specie-paying institutions.  This and other measures of pressure compelled the banks to get ready for resumption, and those which were not essentially unsound were able to do so by the date set.

Along with liberal provision for national defense and a new United States Bank, Madison's message recommended a protective tariff.  The war had taught him the importance of building up such domestic manufactures "as will relieve the United States from a dependence on foreign supplies . . . for articles necessary for the public defence or connected with the primary wants of individuals."  Here again the Republicans were adopting Hamilton's policies.  Aid to manufactures for this very purpose had been advocated by him with little avail.

England, where the factory system was first established, thanks to the genius of the inventors of the steam engine and of power-driven machinery, carefully guarded the secret of the construction of the machines which gave her preëminence; but it was the greater profitableness of agriculture and commerce which long prevented serious efforts at manufacturing in the United States.  When the embargo, non-intercourse, and war cut off the accustomed supply of foreign goods and at the same time destroyed the shipping of the country, capital was diverted perforce into manufacturing to prevent actual want of necessaries.  By the end of the war very considerable sums, probably amounting to a hundred million dollars, had found investment in manufactures of various kinds, mostly textiles, which employed more than half of this total.  These new enterprises were located chiefly in New England and the Middle States.  Rhode Island was the home of most of the cotton mills.  But some factories were to be found in the towns of the Ohio Valley, where the difficulty of transportation across the mountains had much the same effect as the embargo and war had in the Atlantic states.

The English were uneasy over this effect of the war.  Having succeeded in retaining their American market after the Revolution, they were now in danger of losing it unless means could be found to destroy the infant industries in the States.  As Lord Brougham said in Parliament, "it was worth while to incur a loss upon the first exportation, in order, by a glut, to stifle in the cradle those rising manufactures in the United States which the war had forced into existence, contrary to the natural course of things."  For this purpose British goods began to be "dumped" upon the American market and sold at auction for whatever they would bring.

The privations of the war period had shown others besides Madison the importance of preserving the manufactures of America until they could stand alone in spite of foreign competition. Even Jefferson overcame his antipathy to them and wrote: "There exists both profligacy and power enough to exclude us from the field of interchange with other nations; . . . to be independent for the comforts of life we must fabricate for ourselves. We must now place the manufacturer by the side of the agriculturist. . . . He . . . who is now against domestic manufacture, must be for reducing us either to dependence . . . or to be clothed in skins, and to live like wild beasts in dens and caverns."

The investments of the owners of the new plants were also at stake, but their interests were not the basis of the demand for protective legislation by the political leaders. For example, Calhoun professed to lay the claims of the manufacturers "entirely out of view." Economic independence, it was urged, was as essential as political; indeed, political independence was hardly a reality without economic self-sufficiency. As the War of the Revolution had been fought for the one, so now it was proposed to win the other by the protection of home industry.

The import duties, doubled at the beginning of the war for revenue purposes, and averaging about twenty-five per cent, were continued by the tariff act of 1816. On some classes of goods, especially cottons, the rates were increased. Imported cottons selling in the case of India prints for as little as six cents a yard were to be valued for the levy of the impost at not less than twenty-five cents. This device is known as the "minimum principle." [1]

Another recommendation of the President's message was a national system of roads and canals. An express authorization of such works by Congress was one of the omissions from the Constitution which had soon been regretted. When in 1806 Jefferson found a treasury surplus accumulating, he recommended the adoption of an amendment to confer this power. A little later Gallatin prepared an elaborate report on canals and roads, and Congress appropriated money for a coast survey. No steps were taken looking towards the adoption of the suggested amendment, and with the passage of the embargo the surplus disappeared and along with it the possibility, for the time being, of a federal system.

[1] For discussion of the opposition to the tariff see page 341.

Nevertheless the seeds of a national system of roads were planted during Jefferson's presidency.   When Ohio was admitted in 1803, an agreement was made with the new state by which, in return for the exemption of federal public lands within the state from taxation, Congress pledged a percentage of the proceeds of the sales of the lands for use in building a road connecting the state with the eastern seaboard.   This agreement was the origin of the Old National Road, or "Cumberland Road," as it is sometimes called, from the fact that its original eastern terminus was the town of Cumberland, in western Maryland.   Its construction was begun in 1811, but at the end of the war only about twenty miles had been completed.

Madison's recommendation of internal improvements repeated that of Jefferson in 1806, including the proposal of an amendment to the Constitution.   The prosecution of the war had been hampered by the lack of military roads, and the increasing population of the West laid new stress upon the importance of means of communication and transportation as bonds of union.   Congress took no action, and the President renewed his recommendation in the message of 1816, particularly inviting attention "to the expediency of exercising . . . existing powers, and, where necessary, of resorting to the prescribed mode of enlarging them, in order to effectuate a comprehensive system of roads and canals."

Thus prompted a second time, Congress took up a bill reported by Calhoun which proposed to use for roads and canals the bonus paid by the bank for its charter, together with the dividends on the bank stock owned by the government.   The discussion of this measure soon brought out the fact that the Republicans of the Old and New Schools had drifted far apart.

## CLEAVAGE OF THE REPUBLICANS

Although the Old School Republicans had been swept into the current of the New Nationalism, they had a deep-seated respect for the letter of the Constitution and the importance of the amending process.   The doctrine of implied powers which Madison was willing to accept in the erection of the bank he rejected in the case of internal improvements.   When the "Bonus Bill" passed Congress and came to him for signature, he vetoed it, apparently in the hope of recalling his party to original principles.

Opinion within the Young Republican group was outrunning that of the old leaders. Taking up the ideal of economic self-sufficiency which Madison's message suggested in its recommendation of protection for manufactures, they outlined a complete national system of political economy. Clay and Calhoun were the chief exponents of this phase of the New Nationalism.

"Whenever we have the misfortune to be involved in a war with a nation dominant on the ocean," said Calhoun, in discussing the tariff bill, "the moneyed resources of the country to a great extent must fail. . . . Commerce and agriculture, till lately almost the only, still constitute the principal, sources of our wealth. . . . They both depend on foreign markets. . . . When our manufactures are grown to a certain perfection, as they soon will be under the fostering care of Government . . . the farmer will find a ready market for his surplus produce; and, what is almost of equal consequence, a certain and cheap supply of all his wants. . . . The arm of Government will be nerved; and taxes in the hour of danger . . . may be greatly increased. . . . To give perfection to this state of things, it is necessary to add, as soon as possible, a system of internal improvements, and at least such an extension of our navy as will prevent the cutting off of our coasting trade."

Discussing the Bonus Bill Calhoun made light of constitutional difficulties. Was not Congress authorized to lay taxes to "provide for the common defense and general walfare?" He held that this clause authorized appropriations for roads and canals which the general welfare demanded, for the very greatness of the country and the rapidity of its growth tended to weaken the bonds which held together its widely separated parts. "We are under the most imperious obligation to counteract every tendency to disunion. . . . Whatever impedes the intercourse of the extremes with this, the center of the Republic, weakens the Union."

This scheme of things had much in common with the thought of the English mercantilists. Both were based on a belief in the desirability of governmental regulations to develop national resources and industry for the sake of strength and safety in war time. The system was implied in Madison's recommendations, especially those relating to protection and internal improvements; but he did not develop the implications, and on the question of the interpretation of the Constitution the President and the Young Republicans were far apart. The latter adopted implied powers as a principle of general validity, and as sharp a difference developed between the two groups of Republicans in their views of constitutional construction as had once separated Republicans and Federalists. When Monroe came to the Presidency, he, like Madison, displayed a tenderness for the letter of the Constitution which exasperated the younger men. In his first message (1817), while expressing his belief in the desirability of internal improvements, he announced his conviction that a constitutional amendment was necessary to authorize Congress to establish them.

Monroe's message showed that the plans of Calhoun and Clay as to internal improvements were blocked by the certainty of a veto of any bill which Congress might pass. They on their part would not consent to an effort to amend the Constitution. Said Clay, "if an amendment be recommended, and should not be obtained, we should have surrendered a power which we are bound to maintain if we think we possess it." The views of the Old School he called a "water-gruel regimen," an interpretation which would construe the Constitution to a dead letter and make it a bar to the country's progress. Was the Constitution by its grant of power to establish post offices and post roads and to regulate commerce between the states (in all of which he found power implied to build roads and canals) made for the Atlantic margin of the country only? "We are not legislating for this moment only, or for the present generation, or for the present populated limits of the United States; but our acts must embrace a wider scope, — reaching northwestward to the Pacific, and southwardly to the river Del Norte. Imagine this extent of territory covered with sixty, seventy, or an hundred millions of people. The powers which exist in this government now will exist then; and those which will exist then exist now." Clay seemed to have discarded altogether the necessity of the amending process.

There were many Republicans who, like Presidents Madison and Monroe, approved of national policies in themselves but could not follow Clay and Calhoun on account of constitutional scruples. There were others who, in spite of the prevailing nationalism, were still controlled by considerations of sectional interest. This division is apparent in the votes both on the Bonus Bill and the Tariff of 1816. New England Federalists and Old School Republicans voted against the Bonus Bill, which promised more benefits for other sections than for their own; and although Lowndes was chairman of the Ways and Means Committee which reported the tariff bill, and Calhoun its most eloquent supporter, many southern members could not be moved by the nationalistic arguments. Aside from the general advantage of national self-sufficiency, the benefits of protection, they perceived, would be very unevenly distributed.

John Randolph presented the sectional point of view on the tariff in his characteristic way. Said he: "It eventuates in this: whether you, as a planter, will consent to be taxed, in order to hire another man to go to work in a shoemaker's shop, or to set up a spinning jenny. . . . No, I will buy where I can get manufactures cheapest, I will not agree to lay a duty on the cultivators of the soil to encourage exotic manufactures; because, after all, we should only get much worse things at a higher price." In the vote part of the South followed Lowndes and part Randolph; it cast twenty-three votes for protection and thirty-four against it. Twenty negative votes came from the maritime districts of the North, whose carrying trade would be injured by the lessening of America's dependence upon Europe.

## THE SUPREME COURT AND NATIONALISM

The decade following 1815 is memorable on account of a series of great decisions by the Supreme Court which were quite in the spirit of the New Nationalism. For the first few years after the adoption of the Constitution the judiciary was regarded as the weakest of the three branches of the Federal Government. In its first great decision the Court held that a state might be sued by the citizen of another state (Chisholm vs. Georgia, 1793). While this decision was a sound interpretation of the words of the Constitution as they stood,[1] it was unpopular and led to the adop-

---

[1] "The judicial Power shall extend to all Cases . . . between a state and Citizens of another State." Const., Art. III, Sec. 2.

tion of the Eleventh Amendment, which denied the jurisdiction of the federal courts in such cases.

The amendment was damaging to the prestige of the Court. Chief Justice Jay soon afterwards resigned to become a candidate for governor of New York. When a few years later President Adams offered to reappoint him, he declined. "I left the bench," he replied, "perfectly convinced that under a system so defective, it would not obtain the energy, weight, and dignity which was essential to its affording due support to the national government; nor acquire the public confidence and respect which, as the last resort of the justice of the nation, it should possess." [1]

The greatness which Jay could not foresee was achieved under John Marshall (appointed January 31, 1801), to whom Adams turned upon receiving Jay's declination. The appointee, while known as an able lawyer and diplomat, had up to this time given little evidence of peculiar fitness for the supreme bench. Adams lived to regard his "gift of John Marshall to the people of the United States as the proudest act of his life." Indeed, as Hamilton ranks as the greatest master of finance in our history, so Marshall stands preëminent among our jurists.

Marshall, although a Virginian, was one of the small group of southern men who remained steadfast in the principles of Federalism in spite of the cross currents which carried both political parties so far from their original courses. Jefferson thoroughly distrusted him, and we have already seen how the Republicans attacked the court system of which he was head. In the hope of counterbalancing the weight of his opinions, Jefferson appointed Republicans to the bench as vacancies occurred. But these fell under the spell of Marshall's powerful mind, and the ablest of them, Joseph Story, of Massachusetts, became a worthy second to his great chief as a nationalistic expounder of the supreme law.

The first of Marshall's great decisions was the opinion in the Marbury case, holding an act of Congress to be unconstitutional. In Fletcher vs. Peck (1810) the Court held void an act of the Georgia legislature; the decision applied that provision of the Constitution which forbids a state to pass any act impairing the obligation of contracts. In Martin vs. Hunter's Lessee (1816)

[1] Jay especially disliked the circuit-court duty required of members of the supreme bench.

the Court upheld the provision of the Judiciary Act of 1789 concerning appeals from the state courts in cases involving federal law. The highest court in the State of Virginia had rendered a decision in the case and denied the right of appeal, but the Supreme Court asserted its paramount authority in the face of this denial. The prohibition of state legislation impairing the obligation of contracts was again involved in the case of Dartmouth College *vs.* Woodward (1819). The State of New Hampshire had modified by act of the legislature, and against the will of the trustees of the college, the charter granted to the college in colonial days. Such a charter the Court held to be a contract which could be modified only by mutual consent of the parties. The winning of this case, as counsel for the college, his alma mater, was a step in Daniel Webster's rise to fame.

In the same year the Court gave its sanction to the doctrine of implied powers in a suit involving the United States Bank. Friends of local banks in several southern and western states brought about the enactment of laws taxing the branches of the United States Bank, really for the purpose of forcing them out of business. The cashier of the Baltimore branch refused to pay the tax on its notes as required by the Maryland law, and appealed from the decision of the highest state tribunal.

This case of McCulloch *vs.* Maryland involved two questions: 1) the constitutional right of Congress to incorporate the bank; and 2) the right of a state to tax an agency of the federal government, used in the performance of its functions. The first issue was the old one discussed by Jefferson and Hamilton while members of Washington's cabinet. Now in words really quoted from Hamilton's opinion Marshall sustained the constitutionality of the charter act and at the same time the doctrine of implied powers: "Let the end be legitimate, let it be within the scope of the Constitution, and all means which are appropriate, which are plainly adapted to that end, which are not prohibited, but consist with the letter and spirit of the constitution, are constitutional."

As to the second point, the power to tax was held to be equivalent to the power to destroy. "If the States may tax one instrument employed by the government in the execution of its powers, they may tax any and every other instrument. They may tax the mail; they may tax the mint; . . . they may tax judicial process; they may tax all the means employed by the government, to an excess which would defeat all the ends of government." The only tax which states could lay upon the branches of the bank, he concluded, was the regular property tax on their buildings and land.

By these and other decisions Marshall became one of the great builders of the American constitutional system. Unlike the jurists of later times, he was not bound by the interpretations of predecessors, for there were few of consequence. His constructive mind and his long tenure, from 1801 to 1835, enabled him to create a consistent body of constitutional law on which all of his successors have built. The decisions discussed went far towards clarifying the limits of the powers of the states and federal government respectively. Some of them set restrictions on the authority of the states while others asserted the prerogatives of the national government. The Old School Republicans took alarm at the trend of the decisions, without being able to put forward a champion who was a match for Marshall. "All wrong," groaned John Randolph, "but no man in the United States can tell why or wherein." To him and his associates the decisions seemed to be undermining the rights of the states and bringing about a "consolidated" republic.

Some of Marshall's decisions have since been modified. While they struck out the first bold outlines of our constitutional law, the finer shading was added by later hands. For example, the states learned that by means of general laws prescribing the conditions under which charters might be had, they could reserve the right to alter or repeal charters, and that, despite the Dartmouth College case, the courts would uphold such laws.

## Beginnings of a National Literature

Another evidence that national consciousness was stirring in this period is found in the appearance of the first signs of a truly American literature. The first generation after independence was an era of political writing. The controversy with England, the establishment of the Constitution, the contests of parties, furnished themes which filled men's minds, and left little energy for productive effort in the field of polite literature.

Then came, with the opening of the nineteenth century, writers of fiction and verse who were, for the most part, dull and uninspired imitators of English models. In the next decade, however, a new American school appeared in which the names of Washington Irving, James Fenimore Cooper, and William Cullen Bryant stand foremost.

Irving's *History of New York, by Diedrich Knickerbocker* (1809) drew its inspiration from local sources, and displayed a quality of humor which stamped the author as a genius. He was the first American writer of fiction to command respect abroad, and while he later allowed himself to be diverted from native to foreign themes, some of the best of his work, such as the story of *Rip Van Winkle* (1819), found its setting in the Hudson Valley or Catskill Mountains.

After an attempt at a novel of the conventional English type, Cooper published *The Spy* (1821). It was a tale of the Revolution, and won immediate popularity. Next came *The Pioneers*. James K. Paulding had already published, in 1818, a poem, *The Backwoodsman*, which won the praise of critics because the writer forsook the giants, castles, and distressed maidens of European romances and portrayed the simple life of the American frontier. *The Pioneers* gave a vivid prose picture of the same life. Cooper's own experience provided the background for the book, as his father, an early settler of central New York, had brought him as an infant into what was then the wilderness. Although the stories of this pioneer among our novelists include tales of the sea, their significance in the history of our literature lies in the fact that they were products of American influences, little affected by English traditions.

With Bryant our poetry began. A few men before him had written a poem or two each; he was our first poet who wrote both much and well. *Thanatopsis*, written when the author was but a lad of seventeen, appeared in 1819.

The beginning of good work in literature is properly associated with the founding of *The North American Review*, in 1815. Innumerable magazines had sprung up in the years preceding, only to wither away after a few issues for lack of root and nourishment. The essays on natural and moral philosophy, and the "agreeable and entertaining moral tales" with which they were filled, were substitutes for real literature which bored even the long-suffering reader of those days.   In the hands of Jared Sparks as editor, the *Review* set a new standard of excellence, drawing both contributions and subscriptions from the young intellectuals of New England in sufficient numbers to give it a place as a permanent factor in the developing culture of the nation.

## SELECT BIBLIOGRAPHY FOR CHAPTER XVII

**After-war Readjustment.** Adams, *History*, covers the attempts at reorganization during the last months of Madison's term.   McMaster is exhaustive on the currency situation.   Babcock has chapters on the Second Bank, the Tariff, Internal Improvements, and the Supreme Court.

Taussig, *Tariff History of the United States*, is a standard work by a leading economist.   The political aspects of the tariff are brought out more fully by Stanwood, *American Tariff Controversies in the Nineteenth Century*.

Von Holst, *John C. Calhoun*, has a brief account of Calhoun's congressional career.

**Cleavage of the Republicans.** This topic has been little developed by writers.   In this connection Gilman, *James Monroe*, and Adams, *John Randolph*, may be studied along with the lives of Clay and Calhoun.   See also Hockett, *Western Influences*, chap. 4.

**The Supreme Court and Nationalism.** Corwin, *John Marshall and the Constitution*, is a handy summary of the topic.   Beveridge, *Life of John Marshall*, is a monumental work both in bulk and value.

# CHAPTER XVIII

## EXPANSION

The legislation of 1816–1817 was enacted while the country was still in the shadow of the war, and all that Congress did was colored by the supposed necessity of preparing for other wars which might come. As it turned out, nearly a century was to pass before the United States again found itself embroiled in hostilities with a European nation. The year 1815 marked the beginning of a new era, in which for the first time the government found itself free from international entanglements. Peace permitted both government and people to "turn their backs on Europe" and devote their energies as never before to the settlement and development of their own vast, rich territory. Out of domestic activities were to arise most of the public questions of the "middle period" (1815–1860).

### The Westward Movement

The westward movement of population had been somewhat retarded by the war, but with the Peace of Ghent it rose to unprecedented volume. The entire Atlantic Seaboard was affected by conditions which stimulated migration to the newer regions. The thin soils of the New England hillsides were incapable of producing grain in competition with the cheap and fertile lands already opened farther west. The decline of shipping added its quota of men upon whom altered economic conditions forced a readjustment in manner of life. The opportunity to earn wages in the factories which were increasing in number under the stimulus of protective legislation did not attract these sturdy seamen and sons of the soil. They preferred a hazard of new fortunes elsewhere, leaving the indoor toil of the mills to women and children.

Equally conducive to migration were conditions in the southern states. The inhabitants of the back settlements of the Carolinas and Virginia were handicapped by the lack of roads and canals giving access to the markets of the coast, and they still suffered under the discriminations which since colonial days had maintained the political dominance of the tidewater planters. Many of them, moreover, belonged to religious sects, like the Quakers, which abhorred slavery. In the eighteenth century these interior settlements had been a region of small farms and free labor, but the cultivation of cotton by slave labor was now spreading into the South Carolina Piedmont, while tobacco planting was encroaching upon the area of small farms in Virginia and North Carolina.

The original region of cotton growing was the coast of Georgia and South Carolina. In this limited belt flourished the sea-island, or long-staple variety. Short-staple cotton throve in almost any southern soil, but was not a profitable crop before the invention of Whitney's cotton gin (1793), which reduced the cost of removing the seed to a negligible figure. Then, under the stimulus of the increasing demand of the European factories, its cultivation rapidly increased and it soon became a more important crop than any of the older staples, rice, indigo, or even tobacco.

As if to meet the demand of the restless population, the early years of peace saw the opening of new lands in the West. Even before the Treaty of Ghent was signed, the Creeks paid the price of their defeat at the hands of Jackson's men, by the cession of a large portion of their lands in Alabama, a district stretching northward from Mobile Bay almost to the Tennessee River.

In the Northwest the soldiers who followed Harrison had cast hungry glances upon the fertile fields of the Maumee Valley, reserved to the natives by the Treaty of Greenville; and the tribesmen, no longer having the moral support of the British in Canada, were soon persuaded to part with nearly all of their possessions in Ohio. Other treaties, some of them after wars, opened large tracts in Indiana, Illinois, Michigan, Wisconsin, Iowa, Georgia, Alabama, Mississippi, and Florida. As a corollary of this policy of opening up the Indian country, there was developed the plan of removing the dispossessed tribes to tracts west of the Mississippi, where, as was fondly imagined, they might forever remain untroubled by the white man's cupidity. The execution of the removal policy was accomplished in the thirties.

An additional incentive to migration was given in 1820 by new land laws. From the view-point of the federal treasury the law of 1800 had not worked well. Many purchasers under the credit system, expecting to meet deferred payments through the profits of resale or cultivation, defaulted in their obligations. Since whole communities were sometimes delinquent, eviction proved impracticable. The land code was therefore revised. The credit system was abolished, but to offset the hardship of cash payments the minimum price of lands was reduced from $2 to $1.25 per acre, and the size of the tract which might be bought to eighty acres. The auction system was retained, but it was now easier than ever before for the poor man to obtain possession of land.

For a decade or more after 1815 the chief force in pushing the frontier onward was the Piedmont stock. From the interior counties of the South Atlantic states, and from Kentucky and Tennessee to which this stock had contributed Boone and the other transalleghany pioneers of the eighteenth century, thousands of settlers poured into both Northwest and Southwest. From the same Kentucky neighborhood the families of Abraham Lincoln and of Jefferson Davis removed, the one to Indiana, the other to Mississippi. Quakers, Baptists, and other antislavery sects from Virginia and the Carolinas chose new homes in the Northwest because slavery was not allowed. The steam-boat appeared on the western waters (1812) and gave command of up-stream navigation on the important rivers. The bottom lands of southern Indiana and Illinois filled up with small farms.

After 1820 any man who possessed a hundred dollars could exchange it for eighty acres of government land and become the owner of a farm in fee simple. Want of this small sum was hardly a deterrent, however, to thousands of poor men, and squatting became extremely common; the public domain was so vast that the practice had the sanction of public opinion in the West, and even the government was lax in enforcing the law against trespassers. The advantage which the auction system of disposing of lands gave to speculators, the squatters overcame by banding together in land-claims associations. Such organizations generally succeeded, by collusion or intimidation where necessary,

in preventing any except actual occupants from bidding for occupied lands at the sales.

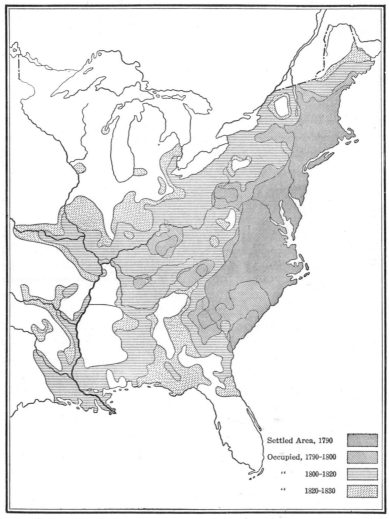

SPREAD OF POPULATION, 1790–1830.

Many of the people who came to the Northwest in these years
were extremely poor.   Some of them brought their entire worldly
possessions in wheelbarrows or packs upon their backs, and spent

their first winter in "half-faced camps." These were rude shelters of poles, backed by a huge fallen log, with the southern face open to the weather. Such a camp was the home of the Lincolns for a year after their removal to Indiana in 1816, when Abraham was a boy of seven. It was replaced by a one-room log cabin which had no floor, and no covering, even of deer-skin, for the holes which served as windows and door. The table and chairs were mere slabs with legs fitted into holes. Abraham's bed was "a heap of dry leaves in the corner of the loft, to which he mounted by means of pegs driven into the wall."

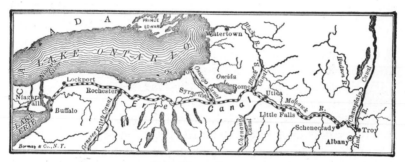

THE ERIE CANAL.

Prior to 1830 most of New England's emigrants went to central and western New York or to Ohio. After the opening of the Erie Canal they began to reach the remoter Northwest. The project of the canal to join the Lakes and Hudson River had long been discussed by New Yorkers, who cherished the hope — until Madison vetoed the Bonus Bill — that it would be adopted as part of a comprehensive national system. Disappointed by the veto the work was begun as a state enterprise. It was ready for use in 1825 and became a great route for westward-bound emigrants. Steam-boats, in use on the Lakes after 1819, connected with the canal at Buffalo and brought the pioneers to southern Wisconsin and northern Illinois. Approaching from the Northeast, they entered the prairies and became the first successful cultivators of lands which from their lack of trees had been regarded as infertile.[1]

[1] A beginning had been made in southern Illinois in cultivating the prairie lands adjoining the wooded bottoms of the streams.

The "Piedmontese" carried the small farm of the pioneer type into Alabama and Mississippi as well as into the Northwest. But here was an opportunity for the planter, and the small farmer was not able to hold his ground.   Capitalism in the form of the seeker after good cotton lands bid up the price at the auctions to $20 or $30 per acre, and occasionally much more.   Choice lands already in the hands of small farmers were secured by the offer of prices which the owners could not afford to refuse, when other good lands farther on were to be had for so much less.   Thus the planter pushed the farmer on to a new frontier, or crowded him, if thriftless, back into the hills to join company with "poor whites."   Excluded from the Northwest, the plantation spread over the Gulf states, and by the middle thirties the alluvial soils of this new South had become "black belts" in a double sense, since the slaves outnumbered the whites.

On the south, at the close of the war, settlers were already pressing upon the Florida boundary and chafing under the Spanish control of the coast, which barred them from their natural outlets by way of the small rivers flowing into the Gulf. The American advance-guard passed the boundary of the United States during the twenties and settled in Texas under Mexican jurisdiction.   Within our limits the extreme western frontier of agricultural settlement in this decade was on the Missouri River in the "Boone's Lick country," opposite the mouth of the Osage River.

Americans had begun to settle in Missouri immediately after the purchase of Louisiana.   Even before this came the aged Daniel Boone, seeking the "elbow room" no longer to be had in Kentucky or western Virginia.   When Missouri Territory was organized in 1812, however, he already had twenty thousand "neighbors" along the river below his settlement, and on the west bank of the Mississippi.   Missouri Territory gained population rapidly during the rush after 1815.   Lying beyond the Old Northwest, it was open to the planter with his slaves.   No ordinance such as barred him from Illinois operated here.   Consequently, from Virginia, North Carolina, Kentucky, Tennessee, slaveholders went thither in numbers, in preference to the Gulf region.

The tremendous shift of population in the early decades of the nineteenth century led to the division of old territories and the drawing of new boundaries with bewildering rapidity. Then as new states were admitted the political map was stabilized east of the Mississippi. Within a half-dozen years as many states were created. The appearance of Indiana (1816), Mississippi (1817), Illinois (1818), Alabama (1819), Maine (1820), and Missouri (1821), however, because statehood was granted when the population of each numbered only a few thousands, really marks only an early stage of the movement which was to convert the frontier settlements into populous commonwealths. These new states (except, of course, Maine) were the fruit chiefly of the Piedmontese migration, and were already members of the Union before the main movement of New Englanders and planters set in.

## THE FAR WEST

Save for the migration into Texas beyond the bounds of the United States, the westward march of the agricultural frontier did not pass Missouri until after 1840. The admission of the new states named was followed by a process of filling in and compacting of population east of the Missouri River. While this was in progress the Far West became a field of great activity in the fur trade. The Americans infused new life into the trade which the Spanish and French had carried on in rather desultory manner from St. Louis, and soon made that town the outlet for the whole great Rocky Mountain area.

William Clark was one of the organizers of the Missouri Fur Company (1809), the chief promoter of which, however, was the Spaniard, Manuel Lisa. A dozen years later (1821) the Rocky Mountain Fur Company was founded by General William H. Ashley. About the same time John Jacob Astor, a rich New York merchant, extended the operations of his American Fur Company from the Old Northwest to the transmississippi country. During the best days of the trade furs worth many hundreds of thousands of dollars were annually collected by the employes of these companies and brought to market through St. Louis. The industry was short-lived, and by 1840 the beaver trade was declining. For several decades more there was an immense traffic in buffalo hides, but by the middle of the century the West of the fur-trader was giving way before the advance of the farmer and miner.

The significance of the fur trade in the history of the Far West is not found in the value of the skins which were collected. As in the first days of French exploration in the Mississippi Valley — indeed, as in the first steps of the English and Dutch westward from the Atlantic coast — the trader was the pathfinder for the settler. The French *engagés* and Scotch-Irish "free trappers" of the companies in the West explored the great rivers and their tributaries and found all of the passes of the Rockies and Sierras. General Ashley penetrated to the Great Basin in 1824, and within the next few years his associate, Jedediah S. Smith, several times traversed the mountains and deserts to the shores of the Pacific. Through the knowledge they gained of the geography of the western regions the traders made possible the overland migrations of the forties and the later occupation of the interior.

While the fur industry was at its height another type of commerce was opened with the Spanish settlements of the Southwest. Pike's involuntary visit in 1807 revealed the possibility of profitable relations between Santa Fé and the Missouri River settlements except for the Spanish law, which forbade intercourse between New Mexico and the outside world save through the far-distant port of Vera Cruz. The enforcement of the law thwarted all efforts to open trade until the revolt of Mexico against Spain inaugurated a more liberal régime. In 1821 came the first successful expedition, and thereafter the "commerce of the prairies" gradually grew until it attained considerable magnitude. The outbound wagons carried cotton and woolen cloth and garments, hardware, and other manufactures, and brought back hides, mules, and silver coin or bullion.

Beyond the Rockies, which formed the boundary of the Louisiana Purchase, the United States was one of four powers which contested the possession of the basin of the Columbia River, known as the "Oregon country." Spain claimed it by right of priority of exploration of the Pacific coast; Russia by virtue of the activities of her traders who operated southward from Alaska as far as Bodega Bay, just above San Francisco. English traders had also been active in the last two decades of the eight-

eenth century, not only on the coast north and south of Vancouver
Sound, but inland. The enterprise of the Canadian fur com-
panies covered western Canada from the Arctic Ocean to the
Pacific.

To the valley of the Columbia itself the claims of the United
States seemed to its government paramount. Discovered by
Captain Gray and first explored by Lewis and Clark, its trade
likewise was first opened by Americans. In 1810 John Jacob
Astor organized the Pacific Fur Company for operations on the
northwest coast. The post of Astoria was established for this
purpose near the mouth of the Columbia. But the War of 1812
was at hand, and the men at Astoria sold out to the British
Northwest Company, which was also now ready to exploit the
Oregon country, rather than run the risk of capture by a hostile
warship.

After the Peace of Ghent the fate of Oregon was involved in
the interpretation of the clause of the treaty which required the
mutual restoration of occupied territory. Astoria was actually
reclaimed under this provision, in spite of the fact that it had
been sold, not captured. However, the respective rights of
England and the United States to the region as a whole were left
as before the War, and in 1818 a settlement was postponed by a
treaty in which it was agreed that for ten years the citizens of
both countries should enjoy equal rights of trade and occupation.

The "joint occupation" agreement, renewed in 1828, worked
in the long run to the advantage of the United States. The
trade of the Northwest Company declined with the passing years.
On the other hand the thirties saw the beginning of a migration
of permanent settlers from the United States which by the forties
gave the Americans the major interest in the country. Thus the
way was prepared for a final adjustment with England in 1846.

By the treaty of 1818 the boundary between the United States
and Canada from the Lake of the Woods to the Rocky Mountains
was fixed along the forty-ninth parallel. West of the mountains
the line remained undetermined under the joint occupation agreement, but both England and the United States were alarmed
when in 1821 a Russian ukase forbade all foreigners to trade on
the Pacific coast north of the fifty-first parallel. Three years
later, however, by separate treaties with England and the United

States, Russia agreed to claim no territory south of 54° 40'. Meantime (1819) Spain yielded to the United States her interest in everything above latitude 42°. Thus after 1824 the joint occupiers of Oregon were the remaining rivals for the region between 42° and 54° 40', with the rights of the United States strengthened by whatever of validity the Spanish contention possessed.

## THE ACQUISITION OF FLORIDA

The same treaty which dealt with the Spanish claim to Oregon transferred Florida to the United States. The situation on the Gulf coast east of the Mississippi was very unsatisfactory after the purchase of Louisiana. The possession by Spain of the strip of territory through which flowed the streams giving outlet to the southern portions of the United States was extremely inconvenient. As in the case of New Orleans before 1803, the interests of the United States forbade its transfer to any other European power, and both Jefferson and Madison were on the alert constantly for any move which seemed to tend in that direction.

In 1810 President Madison took advantage of an insurrection in West Florida to annex that province. The revolutionists had declared independence and appealed to the United States for annexation. Although the leaders were Americans and the whole proceeding savored of conspiracy, Madison by proclamation took possession of most of the province, professing "that in the hands of the United States it will not cease to be a subject of fair and friendly negotiation and adjustment" with Spain.

England, as the ally of Spain in the war against Napoleon, protested against this breach of international usage, but the protest was unheeded, for American relations with her were nearing the breaking point. Indeed, Madison went still further, for fearing British occupation of East Florida, he asked and received from Congress, in January, 1811, authority to take temporary possession of that province on the ground that "the United States could not see without serious inquietude any part of a neighboring territory in which they have . . . so just a concern, pass from the hands of Spain into those of any other foreign Power."

England made no effort to acquire the Floridas, but she used them as a base of operations against the United States during the War of 1812. The Gulf coast became in effect hostile territory, for Spain was careless of her obligations as a neutral, or unable to enforce them. British agents used the Spanish posts as

THE GULF REGION, 1812–1818.

centers from which to incite the Creeks and other southern tribes against the Americans. Creeks took refuge among the Seminoles of East Florida after their defeat in 1814 and continued hostilities. These facts help to explain the eagerness of the people of the Southwest for the conquest of the Floridas. Jackson actually occupied Mobile and Pensacola after the Creek campaign, to prevent their use by the English, and in the course of his movements drove British forces from the nominally neutral ground.

The situation along the Spanish border did not improve after the peace.   Amelia Island, at the mouth of the St. Mary's, was a nest of smugglers and freebooters; runaway slaves escaped to the Seminoles; British adventurers told the Creeks that the lands ceded by them in 1814 were restored by the treaty of peace;[1] raids against the settlements in Georgia and Alabama brought on border warfare.

By the treaty of 1795 Spain was pledged to prevent exactly such disorders as were now rife, but her impotence threatened a chronic state of confusion and uncertainty.   Late in 1817 the United States Government decided to take matters into its own hands.   Amelia Island was occupied by troops, and Jackson, as major-general of the southern department, was dispatched to the Florida border with the Georgia and Tennessee militia.   His instructions from the Secretary of War permitted him to "adopt the necessary measures to terminate" the conflict, and authorized him to pursue the Indians across the borderline into Florida, if necessary, in order to punish them severely enough to put an end to their marauding expeditions.

Jackson, moved by his old desire to conquer Florida, sent a letter to President Monroe, saying: "Let it be signified to me through any channel (say Mr. J. Rhea)[2] that the possession of the Floridas would be desirable to the United States and in sixty days it will be accomplished."   He afterwards asserted that he received the President's approval of his plan.   Monroe on his part denied that he made any reply, being ill at the time.   Supposing that he had the President's sanction, Jackson crossed the line, seized the Spanish posts, deprived the governor of his office, and even court-martialed and executed two British subjects whom he believed to be guilty of stirring up the Indians.

This vigorous conduct made Jackson more than ever a hero, especially with the people of the West.   But it stirred the wrath of England and Spain and created a delicate situation for the administration to deal with.   For several days the cabinet deliberated on the course to be pursued.   They agreed that

---

[1] The interpretation of the treaty accepted by both governments was that the United States was to make peace at once with the tribes still at war, and that these should not be deprived of lands as punishment for their share in the war.   It had no bearing upon the terms of earlier treaties with the Indians.

[2] One of the congressmen from Tennessee.

Jackson had exceeded the discretion allowed him.  Calhoun, Secretary of War, held that he should be punished for insubordination.  In the Secretary of State, however, he found a defender.  Even the extreme measure of seizing the posts, Adams held, was the logical consequence of such a punitive expedition as Spain's neglect of duty had necessitated.  She had drawn the consequences upon herself.

Upon Adams fell the task of satisfying the complaints of the foreign governments.  To England he represented that the traders whom Jackson had put to death had by their bad conduct forfeited their right to the protection of their government.  This view the British at length accepted.  Spain was not so easily appeased.  Her minister angrily declared that negotiations on all other matters would await the disavowal and punishment of Jackson and the restoration of the posts.  To his surprise, Adams, instead of adopting a conciliatory tone, in reply declared that the President would not punish Jackson, although he had acted without authority, because the Spanish commandant had made himself "a partner and accomplice of the hostile Indians."  The posts would be restored whenever a sufficient garrison was sent to control the Indians.

This was the crux of the whole matter.  In a dispatch to the minister of the United States at Madrid, the Secretary of State reviewed the conduct of Spanish officials in Florida, detailed the long series of abuses which they had condoned, and ended with an ultimatum: "The United States can as little compound with impotence as perfidy, and Spain must immediately make her election, either to place a force in Florida, adequate at once to the protection of her territory and to the fulfillment of her engagements or cede to the United States a province of which she retains nothing but the nominal possession, but which is in fact a derelict, open to the occupancy of every enemy, civilized or savage, of the United States, and serving no other earthly purpose than as a post of annoyance to them."

Of the two alternatives the maintenance of order was quite beyond the resources of the Spanish government.  Of necessity cession was chosen, and negotiations were begun with this in view.  In February, 1819, a treaty was signed which made final disposition of all phases of the vexatious question of the two

Floridas.  As compensation for the cession, the United States agreed to cancel all claims of itself or citizens against Spain for damages or injuries up to the date of the treaty, assuming the payment of private claims to an amount not to exceed five million dollars.

Besides the Florida question, the treaty of 1819 settled the boundary between the Louisiana Purchase and the territory of Spain in the Southwest.  Under the French treaty of 1803 the United States had a good claim to Texas, but having insisted upon its title to West Florida it now seemed best to concede the Spanish right to the region west of the Sabine River.  Up that river the line agreed upon ran to the thirty-second parallel; thence north to the Red River, which it followed to the hundredth meridian; thence north to the Arkansas River and along its right bank to its source; thence due north to the forty-second parallel, and along that line to the Pacific.[1]

Although signed in 1819, the Spanish treaty was not ratified by the Cortes until October, 1820, and not until July, 1821, was Florida formally transferred to the new owner.  It was thereupon organized as a territory with Andrew Jackson as governor.

## THE MONROE DOCTRINE

By the treaty of 1819 the United States tightened its hold upon the shores of the Pacific and reached out to the waters of the Gulf of Mexico.  It is rather as a phase of its expanding interests in the western hemisphere than as a matter of European relations that the Government now formulated that unique statement of policy known as the "Monroe Doctrine."

There were three elements in this policy, all of which, separately, were already well recognized American principles.  Washington had contributed the germ of the principle of isolation in his Farewell Address (see page 256); Jefferson had emphasized the same idea when he advised against "entangling alliances" (see page 271); Madison, even in his war message of 1812, had

---

[1] This boundary provision, in connection with the French treaty of 1803, has sometimes been construed to mean that the Oregon country was a part of the Louisiana Purchase. This is an error.  The Rocky Mountains were the western limit of Louisiana, and the treaty of 1819 gave us Spain's claim to a region above 42° which had never been a part of either French or Spanish Louisiana.

carefully disavowed all entanglement "in the contests or views
of other Powers." [1]

Jefferson had brought the second element, the doctrine of the
paramount interest of the United States in the fate of neighboring
territory, to the fore, when he protested against the transfer of
Louisiana by Spain to any other power than the United States
(see page 282); in 1808 he foreshadowed the extension of this
solicitude to more remote regions by writing to Gallatin that
the United States desired Cuba, and Spanish-America generally,
to remain in "its present condition of dependence upon Spain";
in 1811 Madison applied the doctrine of paramount interest
specifically to East Florida (see page 356).   Moreover, it underlay the demand which Adams made for the proper government or
the cession of Florida, and nerved him in the negotiations with
Russia relating to the northwest coast (see page 364).

The third element arose in large part from the sympathy
which the people of the United States felt for the inhabitants of
the Spanish-American colonies in their struggle for independence.
It was the principle of self-determination.

Ever since the English colonies had gained their freedom the
hope of a like liberty had stirred the breasts of the peoples of
Latin America.   For more than twenty-five years following the
American Revolution, Francisco de Miranda, a Venezuelan
patriot, sought with remarkable persistence to arouse the interest
of one European court after another in the freeing of the Spanish
colonies.   Captured at last, he died in a Spanish prison in 1816,
but not before the fires of revolution which he had kindled had
burst into flame.

Rising against the Napoleonic domination about 1810, the
Spanish-Americans resumed their allegiance upon the restoration
of the Bourbon dynasty by the Congress of Vienna, only to rise
again when reforms were refused.   King Ferdinand attempted
to coerce his rebellious subjects into submission, but under the
leadership of José de San Martin and Simon Bolivar, of Argentina
and Venezuela, the South American states won by 1822 an independence which the proud Dons refused to recognize.   The
Spanish Empire, like that of ancient Rome, declined and fell.

---

[1] *Cf.* the habitual reference to the enemies of Germany in the World War as our "associates," not "allies."

Revolution spread to Central America and Mexico, leaving only Cuba and Porto Rico in the West Indies as sad reminders of the departed glory of Castile.

To the people of the United States it seemed that their Latin neighbors were treading in their footsteps, and enthusiasm ran high for their cause. In Congress Clay led a demand for the immediate recognition of the revolutionary republics. Again and again the chamber resounded with his eloquent appeals on behalf of "eighteen millions of people struggling to burst their chains," but the administration could not be hurried into premature action. President Monroe showed his sympathy with the revolutionists by sending agents to investigate conditions, but he would not recommend recognition until he had satisfied himself that they were able to maintain their independent status. Besides, the Florida question was pending, and there was danger that precipitate acknowledgment of Spain's colonies as independent states would interfere with the success of the negotiations. In March, 1822, the President at last announced his readiness to send ministers to the new states as soon as appropriations were made for their maintenance. Thus he proclaimed that the time for recognition had come.

In the freedom of the Latin-American countries Clay saw the promise of a great New-World association of republics, united by ties of kindred institutions and of commerce, with the United States at its head. Such an American system built upon liberty would stand in sharp contrast with the despotisms of the Old World. "We look too much abroad," he said. "Let us break these commercial and political fetters; let us no longer watch the nod of any European politician; let us become real and true Americans, and place ourselves at the head of the American system."

This enticing prospect of a group of free states was threatened by the policy of the European powers. Under the lead of the Czar, the rulers of Russia, Prussia, and Austria formed an association, upon the fall of Napoleon, sometimes called the "Holy Alliance," for mutual aid in the spirit of Christian brethren. After the restoration of the Bourbon dynasty in France that country was also admitted.

The prime purpose of these powers, under this fair name, was to guard the "legitimate" rulers of Europe against revolution. To invert a famous modern watchword, the intention was "to make the world safe for autocracy." Adopting the practice of intervening in countries where popular movements threatened the thrones of monarchs, they hoped to prevent the spread of revolution into their own dominions. This policy was the very antithesis of the American principle of self-determination. In carrying it out, at one Congress of the allies Austria was commissioned to put down with arms democratic movements in the Italian states of Naples and Piedmont, while at another France was directed to send troops into Spain on a like errand. Finally, at the Congress of Verona in 1822 the French representative proposed intervention in Spanish America.

Action on the proposal was postponed, and it is doubtful whether it would ever have claimed serious consideration. But it set in motion efforts to prevent the possibility of an attempt at intervention. England had acted with the other powers in the after-war period, because of her interest in the steps taken for composing the affairs of Europe, but she consistently discountenanced intervention as a violation of the rights of the invaded states.[1] The suggestion of interference with the *status quo* in America was objectionable to her both on this ground and for economic reasons. In proportion as Spanish domination in the western hemisphere had declined British trade had increased; and the independence of the colonies was much more favorable to her commerce than the colonial status could possibly be.

It seemed quite probable also that any power which incurred the burden of intervention on behalf of Spanish authority would be compensated by the grant of territory in the New World. England feared that France, if commissioned to intervene, would seek Cuba as her reward. She was almost as fearful of the growing interest of the United States in the island. In the summer of 1823, therefore, Canning, the Foreign Secretary, proposed a joint declaration by England and the United States against any project of intervention or territorial acquisition in Spanish America by any European power. To add weight to the declara-

[1] Strictly speaking, a distinction is to be made between the Holy Alliance and the Quadruple Alliance. Of the latter, formed for the purpose of general readjustment of Europe, England was a member.

tion Canning proposed that both parties should disavow all designs on their own part of acquiring any portion of the possessions of Spain.

This proposition, three times urged by Canning, the American minister in London referred to the President. He consulted Jefferson and Madison, and the three great Virginians concurred in the judgment that the moment had come to depart from the traditional policy of isolation and form an entente with Great Britain. Said Jefferson, "Our endeavor should surely be, to make our hemisphere that of freedom. One nation, most of all, could disturb us in this pursuit; she now offers to lead, aid, and accompany us in it." At this juncture it was Adams, the Secretary of State, who held fast to isolation. In sessions of the cabinet he insisted that the United States should act alone, "rather than come in as a cock-boat in the wake of the British man-of-war," and that the government should disclaim all interference in the affairs of Europe. He insisted, moreover, that it should give no pledges concerning its own future policy towards Spanish America — Cuba, he was sure, was destined "by the laws of political as well as physical gravitation" to belong one day to the United States — and that it should make an "earnest remonstrance against the interference of European powers by force with South America." With the doctrine of isolation he thus joined those of paramount interest and self-determination (or non-intervention). The advice of the masterful Secretary triumphed over that of the ex-presidents, and shaped the famous message which Monroe sent to Congress in December, 1823.

With this background it is possible to interpret the message. Out of the negotiation with Russia over Oregon arose the declaration that "the American continents, by the free and independent condition which they have assumed and maintain, are henceforth not to be considered as subjects for future colonization by any European powers." This declaration against further colonization, a phase of the doctrine of paramount interest, has since been construed to forbid the acquisition of territory in America by any foreign power even by purchase with the free consent of the seller.

The intervention of the Holy Alliance in the Spanish peninsula

gave the opportunity for the message to reiterate the principle
of isolation: "In the wars of the European powers, in matters
relating to themselves, we have never taken any part, nor does
it comport with our policy so to do. It is only when our rights
are invaded, or seriously menaced, that we resent injuries, or
make preparations for our defence."

Then comes a passage in which the doctrines of paramount
interest and non-intervention are closely interwoven. "With
the movements in this hemisphere, we are, of necessity, more
immediately connected, and by causes which must be obvious
to all enlightened and impartial observers. The political system
of the allied powers is essentially different, in this respect, from
that of America. This difference proceeds from that which
exists in their respective governments. And to the defence of
our own, which has been achieved by the loss of so much blood
and treasure, and matured by the wisdom of their most enlightened citizens, and under which we have enjoyed unexampled
felicity, this whole nation is devoted. We owe it, therefore, to
candor, and to the amicable relations existing between the
United States and those powers, to declare, that we should consider any attempt on their part to extend their system to any
portion of this hemisphere, as dangerous to our peace and safety.
With the existing colonies or dependencies of any European
power, we have not interfered, and shall not interfere. But with
the governments who have declared their independence, and
maintained it, and whose independence we have, on great consideration, and on just principles, acknowledged, we could not
view any interposition for the purpose of oppressing them, or
controlling, in any other manner, their destiny, by any European
power, in any other light than as the manifestation of an unfriendly disposition towards the United States."

The Monroe Doctrine is not a doctrine of indifference to
Europe. On the contrary, the message of 1823 expressly affirmed
that "of events in that quarter of the globe, with which we have
so much intercourse, and from which we derive our origin, we
have always been anxious and interested spectators." The
policy of the Holy Allies in Spain and Italy was an especial cause
of anxiety to the United States, which nevertheless adhered to
its own policy of isolation, "adopted at an early stage of the wars

which have so long agitated" Europe. The autocratic system of the Old World, maintained through forcible prevention of the exercise of the right of self-determination by weak peoples, was, however, not to be allowed to extend to the western hemisphere. Left to themselves the new republics would maintain their independence and establish popular forms of government. Through the preservation of the right of self-determination the New World, at least, should be made safe for democracy.

The immediate effect of Monroe's message is somewhat problematical. There was no further talk of intervention in Latin America. England's manifest opposition was a factor of great if not decisive importance in preventing any undertaking of the sort. Canning afterwards claimed credit for Monroe's stand, and boasted, "I called the New World into existence to redress the balance of the Old." But Canning claimed too much. Our analysis of the antecedents of the message shows how deep-rooted its elements were. Through the pen of Adams the international situation in 1822–1823 combined and welded them into the form in which they were given to the world.

## THE PANAMA CONGRESS

Two years later Adams as President had further opportunity to define the policy of the United States with reference to Latin America, in a way which indicated that at the time it was not eager for the rôle of protector of weaker states. Spain had not recognized the independence of the revolted republics. Under the lead of Bolivar these planned a congress to meet at Panama with the purpose, as was supposed, of organizing a sort of League of American Nations. Such a league could offer united resistance to Spain's attempts at reconquest, or to efforts of other powers at intervention or colonization. Moreover it would make possible the conquest of the remaining Spanish possessions, Cuba and Porto Rico, the freeing of the slaves, and the independence of the islands or their annexation to Mexico or Colombia.

Clay, now Secretary of State, was disposed to accept the invitation to participate in the congress. He saw in it the possibility of promoting his visionary plan of an American system under the leadership of the United States. President Adams was less enthusiastic. He did not welcome the idea of a strong union of the other states of the western hemisphere, which might become a formidable counterweight to the influence of his own country, and the possibility of annexing Cuba to any of the Latin states was only less repugnant to him than the idea of its transfer to a European power. He tried to dissuade Colombia and Mexico from attacking Cuba and Porto Rico, and through Russia endeavored to induce Spain to avert the danger by recognizing the independence of her lost colonies.

Nevertheless he was willing to send delegates to Panama, under instructions which would safeguard our neutrality and independence of action. He saw no objection to an agreement that each American nation should "guard by its own means against the establishment of any future European colony within its borders."

The President's enemies in Congress professed to see the danger of a surrender of sovereignty or at least of an entangling alliance in participation at Panama, and southerners took alarm at the possibility of a discussion of slavery (which they regarded as a purely domestic concern) in an international gathering. The Senate at last approved the mission, but one delegate died while on the way to the isthmus and the congress adjourned before the other arrived. Disagreements among the Latin states themselves prevented further sessions.

## SELECT BIBLIOGRAPHY FOR CHAPTER XVIII

**The Westward Movement.** Babcock's story of the migration of population is continued by Turner, *Rise of the New West*. McMaster supplies many episodes and illustrative incidents, while Turner gives a masterful interpretation of the significance of the movement. The essays in his *Frontier in American History* are even more brilliant as interpretations.

The importance of mountain, forest, stream, and other physiographic features as forces in American development is discussed by Semple, *American History and its Geographic Conditions*, and Brigham, *Geographic Influences in American History*. See also Schlesinger, *New Viewpoints*, chap. 2.

**The Far West.** Very useful are Coman, *Economic Beginnings of the Far West*, and Paxson, *The Last American Frontier*.

**The Acquisition of Florida.** The standard monograph is Fuller, *The Purchase of Florida*. For the larger aspects of Spanish relations, see Chadwick, *Relations of the United States and Spain*, I.

**The Monroe Doctrine.** A good account of the revolutions in the Spanish-American states is Paxson, *Independence of the South American Republics*.

There is a considerable literature on the Monroe Doctrine, most of it dealing with interpretation and later applications. Reddaway, *The Monroe Doctrine*, is the best monograph on its origins. Turner's discussion in *Rise of the New West*, is excellent.

# CHAPTER XIX

## SLAVERY AND THE MISSOURI COMPROMISE

### SECTIONAL RIVALRY IN THE WEST

By migrating to the West the democratic frontiersmen of the back country of the old states escaped from the domination of the aristocratic class. In founding the new states which entered the Union between 1815 and 1821 they formed constitutions to suit themselves. By these judges as well as governors and legislators were made elective and manhood suffrage became the almost universal rule.

The democracy of the West and its devotion to the party of Jefferson in the early years of the nineteenth century had aroused the jealous apprehension of the Federalists, as has been shown. They regarded even the New England emigrants to the West as the refuse of society.[1] Nevertheless the New England settlers carried with them many of the ideals and institutions of the states from which they came. The same was true of the southerners, and in a sense the whole process of colonizing the West was a race between rival sections. The southerners transplanted the county as the unit of local government, while the men of the Northeast were equally tenacious of the town. As a result Illinois, for example, adopted the county system for that portion of the state where the Piedmont stock predominated, while the New Englanders succeeded in introducing many features of the township system into the region which they occupied later. The educational ideals and methods of the two classes presented another occasion for dispute.

The rival stocks showed remarkably persistent sympathy with the sections from which they sprang. Even as late as the Civil

---

[1] Timothy Flint, one of the contemporary authorities on conditions in the West, wrote about 1826: "The people in the Atlantic states have not yet recovered from the horror inspired by the term 'backwoodsman.' This prejudice is particularly strong in New England, and is more or less felt from Maine to Georgia."

War the southern element in the Northwest retained a lively
partiality for the Confederacy, as the Copperhead movement
shows.   The affinity of the people of the upper Mississippi Valley
with the South was enhanced by geographical influences, since
the river and its branches formed the natural system of communication, while the mountains were a barrier to intercourse with
the East.   To some extent artificial factors tended to modify
the original bias of the people.   The construction of the Erie
Canal turned the course of the Mississippi, as it were, and made
New York rather than New Orleans the chief entrepôt of the
great interior.   Thereafter the East gained relatively in influence
over the West.   The Ordinance of 1787 had a profound influence
upon this rivalry, for by interposing a legal barrier to the expansion of slavery into the Old Northwest it discouraged proslavery
men from becoming residents in any great numbers, and thus gave
a decisive advantage to the free states in the contest for institutional control.

Because slavery was excluded from this northwest region
where the streams of migration met, their rivalry was not too
intense to permit adjustments and compromises.   If slavery
had been tolerated, this would not have been the case.   Experience proved that slavery and free labor could not prosper
together in the same community.   The inevitable effect of the
one had been to degrade or expel the other.   Many of the
southerners in the lower counties of the states north of the Ohio
were in a real sense driven from their former homes by the irrec-
oncilable character of the two systems of labor.

### HISTORY OF SLAVERY IN AMERICA

Chattel slavery had disappeared from western Europe long
before the discovery of America.   However, when the expansion
of Europe brought Spaniards, Frenchmen, and Englishmen into
contact with primitive, non-Christian races, the institution
was revived in their colonial possessions.   There was much
labor to be performed which whites refused to do for hire, and the
scruples which had put an end to slavery in Europe were much
less felt amid New-World conditions.   There was some Indian
servitude in the possessions of all of the powers which colonized

America.   It was especially common in the Spanish dominions until prohibited by the government, which inconsistently encouraged the importation of negroes to serve in the stead of the natives.

The rise of the plantation in the English colonies was accompanied by the use of servile labor — red, white, and finally black.   But negro slavery had hardly become established before American opinion began to turn against it.   Repeatedly during the colonial era provincial legislatures tried to restrict the importation of blacks, but the trade was a source of profit to British merchants, and the colonial acts were invariably set aside. When the Revolution brought freedom of action, the Association of 1774 included negroes among the forbidden imports, and later regulations of the Continental Congress continued the non-importation until the end of the war.   Then control over the whole matter passed to the states.

Jefferson's first draft of the Declaration of Independence included in its charges against the British Crown that of vetoing the colonial acts relating to the slave trade, but this clause was dropped out of deference to South Carolina and Georgia, where alone at that time were to be found apologists for human bondage. Under the influence of the revolutionary philosophy of the rights of man the belief was quite general that slavery was iniquitous. Patrick Henry affirmed that "every thinking honest man rejects it in speculation," and Jefferson exclaimed, "I tremble for my country when I reflect that God is just; that his justice cannot sleep forever."

There were slaves in every state when independence was declared.   Above Mason and Dixon's line they were employed chiefly as coachmen, butlers, cooks, and body-servants in well-to-do families, and their numbers were relatively few.   In the years following the Revolution, consequently, the Northern states found slavery a simple matter to deal with.   In one case, that of Vermont, the state constitution abolished it outright.   In Massachusetts emancipation resulted from judicial interpretation of the constitution of 1780, which declared that all men are by nature free.   This clause, the court ruled, was incompatible with the existence of chattel slavery within the commonwealth.   Most of the Northern states adopted some plan of gradual emancipa-

tion.  Pennsylvania was the first to take such action (1780),
and its law is typical.  It left unchanged the status of persons
already held in bondage but gave their children freedom when
they attained adult years.

Southern states also discussed plans of emancipation.  The
depression of the tobacco, rice, and indigo industries after the
Revolution made the support of the laborers burdensome to the
masters, and fostered the growth of humanitarian sentiments.
It was difficult, however, to break away from established custom.
In the same letter quoted above Patrick Henry wrote, "I am
drawn along by the general inconvenience of living without
them.  I will not, I cannot, justify it.  However culpable my
conduct, I will so far pay my devoir to virtue as to own the
excellence and rectitude of her precepts, and lament my want of
conformity to them."  Moreover, the large number of blacks in
the Southern states made emancipation a much more difficult
undertaking than in the North.  In some regions they outnumbered the white inhabitants, and it was feared that freeing an
ignorant and undisciplined race would result in an idle, vicious,
uncontrollable population.  Slavery had at least the merit of
keeping the negro under management.

Emancipation in the South, therefore, waited upon some practicable plan of dealing with the free blacks.  In 1816 the American Colonization Society was formed for the purpose of transporting freedmen to Africa.  For a time its program awakened some
enthusiasm, especially in the South, where its chief support was
found.  The little republic of Liberia was the fruit of its activities,
but its means proved to be quite insufficient for an undertaking
of such magnitude, and its efforts in sum made no appreciable
impression upon the black mass of American slavery.  Then as
cotton culture spread and southern prosperity increased conditions demanded a greater labor supply and sentiment changed.

From the close of the Revolution slavery was regarded as a
question for the states.  The fathers of the Constitution have
been criticized for not incorporating in the supreme law a provision for gradual emancipation.  Such criticism rests on an
entire misconception of the task of the Convention.  It was
believed that the states separately would provide for emancipation; any such antislavery provision would have insured the

rejection of the Constitution; above all, the intent of the Convention — to intrust to the federal government only matters of general concern — excluded the relation of master and slave as naturally as it did that of employer and employee from its sphere.

Yet the Constitution touched slavery at many points — in restricting the control of Congress over commerce, in fixing the rule of apportionment of taxes and representatives, in defining the obligations which states owed to one another as members of the federation, such as the rendition of fugitives from justice and service, and otherwise. The first Congress was confronted with petitions from antislavery societies, praying it to use its powers for the furtherance of the cause of freedom. The petitions led to the appointment of a committee of inquiry into the scope of the powers of Congress in the matter. The report set forth that the legislature could not interfere in any way with slavery in the states; that it could not prohibit the importation of slaves prior to 1808 but might lay a duty of ten dollars per head upon such importation and regulate the conditions of ocean transportation in the interests of humanity; and that the slaveholders were entitled to the enactment of a law for the rendition of fugitive slaves escaping into other states.

This report led to some legislation for the mitigation of the horrors of the "middle passage," by way of securing for the miserable blacks reasonable air space and of preventing needless suffering — much like provisions of our own times regulating shipments of live stock in railway cars. Another result was the Fugitive Slave Law of 1793. Any white person who claimed a negro as his runaway property had merely, by oath, to satisfy a federal or state magistrate of the validity of his claim. The law made the recovery of fugitives easy, but it did not safeguard the rights of free persons of color, whom unprincipled white men were willing to enslave by perjuring themselves.

As the year 1808 approached, Jefferson congratulated Congress that the time was near when it might constitutionally make an end of the African slave trade. Accordingly an act was passed to take effect January 1, 1808. It laid heavy penalties in fines and imprisonment upon slave importers, but found no better disposition for the blacks illegally brought into the country than to turn them over to the state concerned to be sold. Despite the law, the smuggling in of negroes continued more or less actively. Additional acts were passed, and in 1820 the trade was made piracy, punishable by death. But it is not recorded that any execution occurred for transgression of the law before 1861.

## THE MISSOURI COMPROMISE

The discussions in Congress accompanying the passage of these early bills, while sharp, did not produce any alarming clash of sectional opinion. Northern and southern men agreed that slavery was an evil. Perhaps Jefferson voiced a general sentiment when he likened it to a wolf held by the ears, equally dangerous to hold or to let go.

Down almost to 1820 the rivalry of the North and South for the institutional control of the West did not involve slavery. In general the expansion of sections tended to follow lines of longitude, and the Ordinance of 1787 divided the territory of the Union into two spheres, the northern one open only to free labor. The new states had entered the Union in pairs, as it happened, each new slave state balancing a free state. This equality of the sections was deceptive, however, for it did not hold true in Congress. While in the Senate there was an actual balance, in the House of Representatives the preponderance had long since passed to the North. Beginning in 1790 with an equilibrium in both houses, the North, through more rapid growth, had, by 1820, 105 representatives as compared with eighty-one from the slave states.

The disparity would have been greater still but for the advantage which the South derived from the three-fifths ratio, under which sixty per cent of its slaves were counted in apportioning representation. By virtue of this clause the southern states enjoyed twenty votes in the House and in the electoral college, more than their white population would have given them. The numerical superiority of the North, moreover, had hitherto been partially offset by the division of its strength between two political parties, while the South and West had been united. The opposition of the Federalists to the admission of new states and their grumbling over the three-fifths provision had been only the ineffectual declamation of a minority.

The situation was full of danger for the slave section, in case an issue should arise to unite the people of the free states against them.   So long as the South could preserve its equality in the Senate, however, no legislation affecting its interests could be enacted without a concurrent majority of the two houses.   The preservation of equality in the Senate was therefore a vital consideration.

This was the general situation when Missouri applied for statehood in 1818.   Although beyond the river, in the territory purchased from France in 1803, Louisiana had already been admitted (1812) with slavery, largely because of its southern position and the fact that its inhabitants held slaves at the time of the purchase.   In contrast, Missouri lay almost wholly above the latitude of the mouth of the Ohio, in the zone of the free states of the Northwest, as did the major portion of the Purchase, and the decision on its admission was likely to determine the fate of slavery in the rest of the territory acquired from France.

Northern leaders therefore judged that the time had come to make a stand against the spread of an institution attended by so many moral and political evils; and when a committee of the House reported a bill for the admission of the new state, James Tallmadge, a member from New York, proposed (February 13, 1819) a restrictive amendment.   One clause forbade the further introduction of slavery into the state, and a second provided that "all children of slaves, born within the said state, after the admission . . . thereof . . . shall be free, but may be held to service until the age of twenty-five years."

The Tallmadge amendment aroused the South in panic fear. Here was a measure which promised both to unite the North and to deprive the slave section of its equality in the Senate.   If the amendment prevailed, bounds would be set to the expansion of slavery, and as new states were carved from the territory of Louisiana, the South would be more and more hopelessly outweighed in the political scale.   On the other hand the slave states might gain a permanent preponderance through unrestricted expansion.

The vote on the amendment followed sectional lines.   On the first clause the House stood 87 to 76.   All of the yeas were cast by northern members, but eleven northerners — contemptuously called "doughfaces" by John Randolph — voted with the South. The Senate rejected the amendment and the session ended in a deadlock.

The debate on the Missouri bill startled the aged Jefferson "like a fire bell in the night." It was no moral issue that awoke his fears, but the sectional alignment, which threatened the severance of the Union. "In the gloomiest hour of the Revolutionary War," he declared, "I never had any apprehensions equal to those which I feel from this source."

The whole country was greatly stirred. During the summer recess of Congress a whirlwind of anti-Missouri feeling swept the North. Everywhere mass meetings were held and resolutions passed against the perpetuation of slavery by permitting its spread to new states. Legislatures resolved, pamphlets poured from the press, and newspapers teemed with articles indicative of the public excitement. Doughfaces were burned in effigy, and great mass meetings at Boston, New York, Philadelphia, Trenton, and Baltimore appointed committees of correspondence to distribute literature and organize the people against the admission of a new slave state.

The contest in Congress was renewed in the session of 1819–1820. Tallmadge having retired, John W. Taylor of the same state led the anti-Missouri forces in the House. Maine, hitherto a part of Massachusetts, was now with the latter's consent seeking separate statehood. The Senate therefore joined bills for the admission of Maine and Missouri, hoping thus to compel northern congressmen, especially those from the Maine district, to forego the Tallmadge-Taylor program of restriction.

The situation which developed was critical in the extreme. The dissolution of the Union was openly discussed and to many seemed imminent. But the very danger was an incentive to compromise. At the end of six weeks of acrimonious debate, Senator J. B. Thomas, of Illinois, offered an amendment to the Maine-Missouri bill proposing that Missouri be admitted without restriction, but that in all the remainder of the territory ceded by France, north of 36° and 30′ north latitude, "slavery and involuntary servitude, otherwise than in punishment of crime whereof the party shall have been duly convicted, shall be and is hereby forever prohibited."

In the Senate the vote of the slave states on Thomas's motion stood 14 to 8, that of the free states 20 to 2.   The House at first rejected it; but some of the northern Republicans were becoming suspicious that the slavery issue cloaked a design of certain of the leaders of the nearly defunct Federalist party to unite the North in a new party under their leadership.   Although at first zealous supporters of the Tallmadge restriction, this suspicion led a few of them to change sides.   A conference committee recommended the acceptance of the Thomas amendment, and when the House took a trial vote on restriction, it was rejected by a small majority.   The change of the few Republican votes broke the anti-Missouri phalanx, and the Thomas amendment (generally spoken of as the "Missouri Compromise") was then accepted, 134 to 42.   On this final ballot the North was almost unanimous in the affirmative, casting only five negative votes. The South was divided, 38 to 37.   Virginia cast 18 of her 22 votes in the negative.

Throughout the debate northern speakers contended that the clause in the Constitution reading "New states may be admitted by Congress into the Union," authorized that body to prescribe the terms of admission.   The most notable speech upholding this opinion was made by Senator Rufus King, of New York. He had been one of the members of the Federal Convention who had sought to empower Congress to restrict the privileges of the new states.   The reason for the exercise of the power now he found in the injustice of extending the three-fifths ratio of representation to new states created out of territory not originally a part of the United States.   King's prominence in the Federalist party was one of the main reasons for the Republican suspicions of a new party movement.

Senator William Pinkney, of Maryland, replied to King, basing his argument upon the concept that the Union is composed of equal states.   The words of the Constitution, he held, might warrant Congress in rejecting the application of a territory for statehood, but if statehood were granted, the new state must possess all of the powers of the original ones.   Consequently Missouri must be as free as any of the older states to determine her domestic institutions.

The balance of power in the nation was the chief political

issue in the contest, and this question of the right of a new state to control its domestic institutions was the chief legal one.  The extreme states' rights men denied the power of Congress to prohibit slavery even in the territories, since they were the common property of the states both slave and free.  This accounts for the considerable southern vote against the compromise.

During the summer of 1820 a convention met at St. Louis and framed a constitution for Missouri.  One provision made it the duty of the legislature to pass laws to prevent the immigration of free negroes.  This clause irritated the North and brought on a new debate in Congress.  Many questions were raised in this discussion.  Was Missouri a state by virtue of the act passed at the previous session, or did statehood await approval of her constitution by Congress?  Did the provision for the exclusion of free negroes abridge the privileges and immunities of citizens (Constitution, Article IV, Section 2)?  The outcome of much debate was a signal demonstration of the ability of statesmen to evade difficulties.  Although no agreement was reached on the points in dispute, a second compromise was adopted, largely through Clay's efforts, which directed the President to announce by proclamation that Missouri was a state, upon receipt of a promise from the legislature that it would never pass a law abridging the privileges and immunities of citizens of the United States.  Meaningless as this pledge was, the legislature complied with the requirement, and on August 10, 1821, the admission of the state was proclaimed.

## SELECT BIBLIOGRAPHY FOR CHAPTER XIX

**History of Slavery in America.**  Phillips, *American Negro Slavery*, is the most elaborate work on the subject.  There is an excellent brief sketch in the first volume of Rhodes, *History of the United States from the Compromise of 1850*.  Hart, *Slavery and Abolition*, contains a brief sketch. Of value is Du Bois, *The Suppression of the African Slave-Trade*.

**The Missouri Compromise.**  All of the general histories give this topic considerable space.  One of the best accounts is that by Gordy, *Political History*, II.  Turner's brief chapter in *Rise of the New West* is marked by keen interpretation.

# CHAPTER XX

## SECTIONALISM AND POLITICAL PARTIES, 1816–1828

### The Conflict of Sectional Interests

The West was not merely a bone of contention between the older sections; its rapid growth soon made it a third section comparable in population and importance with the groups of states on the Atlantic. By the census of 1790 the population of the country was somewhat less than four millions, and of these only one person in fifteen dwelt west of the mountains. By 1830, however, six out of every fifteen of the inhabitants were west of the Alleghanies, and the population of the new section alone exceeded five millions. As measured by increase in population the West had grown in importance six times as fast as the rest of the country.

The great shift westward caused a radical readjustment of the nation's life. As circumstances connected with the War had impaired the shipping interest and stimulated the growth of manufactures, so now the farming, manufacturing, and planting interests had to adjust themselves to the changing geographical basis. A recent writer has said that the "improvement in the economic condition of the West which set in about the time of the second war with England, and which in a decade or two entirely changed the relation of that region to the rest of the country," is "the most important event in our economic history during the first half of the nineteenth century."

The West was predominantly agricultural. The abundance of cheap land was the lure which drew to it the great majority of its inhabitants. The first comers had found themselves cut off from the rest of the world by stretches of unpeopled forest and mountain. Their isolation was even greater than that of the back-country folk of the coast states, and the privations and perils of frontier life were intensified. Theirs was the task of building society from its very foundation stones. Thrown upon their own resources, their first productive efforts were devoted to securing the rudest necessities of existence.

But with astonishing rapidity the clearing about the pioneer's cabin widened, and the huts which clustered here and there upon the river banks grew into towns. The very isolation of the West acted like a duty on imports; the difficulty of intercourse with the remote East was a stimulus and protection to the manufactures which it was compelled to set up for itself. By the beginning of the War of 1812 a few factories were appearing at Pittsburgh, Steubenville, Cincinnati, and Louisville. These led the people to dream of a self-sufficing economic province, a western world, maintained by exchange between town and country, the farmer supplying the wants of the townsman in the way of food and receiving in return the products of the craftsman's art.

But the local market was not sufficient to absorb all of the surplus yield of the fields. The growth of manufactures did not keep pace with that of agriculture, and it became the chief problem of the farmer to find an adequate market. The quest for a market broke down the provincialism of the West and brought it into closer relations with other sections and countries. From the days of the first settlements in the Ohio Valley some of the grain and meat of Kentucky and Tennessee found an outlet down the Mississippi, in spite of Spanish policy, to the West Indies and Europe. Western grain was also converted into whisky for easy carriage over the mountains to the eastern seaboard. Cattle and hogs, too, were driven in increasing numbers across the mountains as time passed. The expansion of the plantation area in the South enlarged the market for the western farmer.

The difficulties of transportation were a great impediment to all intercourse, and the western states were for a long time too poor to shoulder the financial burden of improving the streams or building roads. They looked to the Federal Government as the only agency by which the country could be provided with the roads and canals which were essential to their progress and to the general welfare.

Unfortunately the period of rapid expansion of western agriculture coincided with years of increasing production in Europe.

The end of the wars allowed soldiers by thousands to resume their normal occupation as tillers of the soil. The supply of farm produce in the world market increased much more rapidly than the demand for it, and prices fell. European governments took pains to protect their own agriculture. For example, England revived her Corn Laws, which had been relaxed during the war period. These forbade the importation of foreign grain except when the price of the domestic crop reached an abnormal height. Under these conditions American agriculture suffered severely from overproduction and low prices during the years around 1820.

When the western farmers learned the causes of the hard times, they began to believe that a protective tariff would help them, on the theory that if a larger proportion of the people were encouraged to engage in manufacturing and a smaller part in agriculture, the farmer would find a profitable home market in supplying the needs of the manufacturing population. "Agriculture has been pursued to its acme," runs the comment of a western editor. "The number employed in it is disproportionate to that of the mechanical branch — and the true interest of the whole community will be promoted by producing an equilibrium between them."

The growth of the West was a serious matter for the eastern states. While its population rose by leaps and bounds, that of the old states, except those which, like New York and Pennsylvania, had broad unsettled spaces within their limits, came almost to a standstill. New England, which had formerly felt concern about the West for political reasons, now grew anxious on economic grounds. In 1817 Governor Wolcott, of Connecticut, recommended that the legislature investigate the causes of the "Ohio fever," as by far the most important subject that could engage its attention. Southern legislatures also made investigations, seeking means of counteracting the attractions of the newer regions. Some of them proposed to improve the facilities for marketing the produce of their own inland counties by constructing roads and other means of transportation.

Partly because it would be one way of inducing their people to remain at home several of the old states amended their constitutions or adopted new ones extending the suffrage. Maryland and South Carolina led in this democratizing movement, enfranchising all adult white male citizens by constitutional changes in 1810. Connecticut took a similar step in the constitution of 1818, which replaced her old colonial charter, and Massachusetts (1821) and New York (1826) followed. Rhode Island framed a constitution to supersede her charter, but it was rejected by the voters (1824). Virginia extended the franchise somewhat in 1830, but did not adopt full white manhood suffrage.

The depression of the commerce and agriculture of the states of the northern seaboard made them more and more dependent for their prosperity upon the new manufacturing industries. These looked hopefully to the West and South for their markets, and demanded a continuance of the protective system to give them the advantage over foreign competitors in the home market. The hard times following 1819 especially were years when the manufacturers were clamorous for additional protection. The demands of the manufacturer and farmer were kindred in the matter of the tariff, and brought the northeastern states into economic alliance with the Northwest. The Southwest, on the contrary, tended towards the plantation system too strongly to be attracted into this combination.

The interests of the eastern factory owners and the western farmers were not entirely in harmony. The westward movement made labor scarce and wages high, and the abundance of land open to settlement was looked upon as a retarding factor in the growth of manufactures. Men whose capital was invested in factories were therefore tempted to seek legislation to restrict sales of public lands, a desire with which the frontier population was not at all in sympathy.

The desire of the West for improved means of transportation was seconded by the seaboard cities of the middle states. New York, Philadelphia, and Baltimore foresaw a profitable commerce in handling the export business of the interior, and the policy of federal internal improvements received hearty support in the neighborhood of these cities. The Erie Canal enriched New York, which soon outstripped the other coast towns in population, and Pennsylvania was led, in emulation, to construct a competing route across the Alleghanies, consisting partly of canals and partly of roads. Baltimore agitated the completion of the Cumberland Road and projected a Chesapeake and Ohio Canal.

But New England was indifferent. No transportation route was likely to bring freight to her ports from beyond the Hudson.

Even Norfolk and southeastern Virginia were interested for a time in a James River Canal project, but most of the old South had nothing to gain from internal improvements except of a purely local character. The high Appalachians effectually fenced off the coast of the Carolinas from the great central valley of the continent until the era of the railroads dawned. Charleston then discovered her interest in a rail connection with the cities of the Ohio Valley. During the twenties, however, the states of the southern seaboard were the seat of opposition to federal internal improvements, which would mean the expenditure of public funds on works from which they would derive little or no profit.

The old planting states felt the full force of the competition of the fresh, cheap lands opened up as the area of cotton cultivation expanded across the Gulf plains. The lowering of the cost of producing cotton on the extremely fertile alluvial lands newly opened made the crop unprofitable on the thin soil of many a Carolina·plantation, and the owners had no such alternative as the people of the maritime states of the North. The cotton planters devoted their energies more and more to the production of their one crop. All that they produced went to market elsewhere, and all that they consumed came from without in the course of direct or indirect exchange.

Many planters neglected even to raise hay for their animals or grain for their families and slaves, deeming it better economy to supply all of the needs of the plantation from the proceeds of the sale of their staple crop. Their political economy was consequently that of "free trade" and *laissez faire*. Manufactures came most cheaply from England, where most of the cotton was sold. Any interference with this intercourse, such as a duty for the encouragement of domestic manufactures, increased the price of what the planter got, whether he bought imported or domestic goods. The steady demand for cotton abroad, moreover, left him little motive for creating a home market, such as the farmer needed.

The interests of North, South, and West, or to put it in economic instead of geographical terms, the interests of the manufacturing, planting, and farming sections, were inharmonious. For this reason the nationalism which was so pronounced just after the War of 1812 did not long survive. The votes against the tariff bill in 1816 foreshadowed a renewed conflict of sections growing out of economic divergences. Within a few years the planting region, especially, showed a marked reaction to localism, and revived the strict interpretation of the Constitution to offset the nationalizing tendencies of the Federal Government. John Taylor, of Virginia, wrote several books combating nationalism. Jefferson reverted to his former views and commended Taylor's works as a "retraction of the government to its original principles." He denounced the Supreme Court as a "subtle corps of sappers and miners constantly working under ground to undermine the foundations of our confederated fabric." The Young Republicans he stigmatized as "pseudo-republicans but real federalists."

The history of the United States from 1817 to 1828 is largely a record of the rivalry of the three sections in their attempts to deal with the great domestic questions of the day, such as the tariff and internal improvements. The political weight and aggressiveness of the West in these contests is particularly noteworthy. States carved from what had been wilderness when Washington was inaugurated sent 57 members to the House of Representatives under Jackson. During that interval of forty years the representation of New England increased only from 29 to 38; that of the South Atlantic states from 45 to 60. Only the Middle states showed an advance at all comparable with that of the West, with an increase from 29 to 75. We must trace the sectional conflict in the chief questions of the period.

Although the Young Republicans controlled the House of Representatives during Monroe's presidency, they lacked a sufficient majority to pass bills for internal improvements over his veto. But they studied the question. In 1818 at the request of the House Calhoun, then Secretary of War, submitted a report which outlined a system of internal improvements with national defense as the object. No attempt at legislation followed, but Congress and the executive clashed a few years later on a bill for the Cumberland Road.

The road had been completed as far as Wheeling, on the Ohio

River. After a period of suspended activity due to financial embarrassment following the panic of 1819, the survey was made for the extension of the road, and in 1822 a bill passed Congress for the collection of tolls to be used in the upkeep of the highway. Since violators of the regulations would have to be dealt with, the President saw in the bill an infringement on the police power of the states and vetoed it. In Congress it had received the vote of all but two members from Western states, and of nearly every member from districts along the route.

In 1824 a General Survey Bill was enacted, authorizing the President to employ the engineering corps of the army in making surveys of routes for any roads and canals which he deemed of national importance. This measure received the vote of all members who favored any of the local projects, of which there was a multitude, and Monroe signed it. Most of the opposition to this bill came from New England and the Old South, while the West was a unit in its support.

Republicans of the Old School, the southern seaboard group, saw in the Survey Bill another evidence of the trend towards nationalism. Randolph denounced it as an abuse of power, and threatened opposition by every means short of actual insurrection. Jefferson was ready in 1825 to have the Virginia legislature declare federal legislation regarding internal improvements null and void, following the precedent set by the Virginia and Kentucky Resolutions of 1798. But it was the tariff which, next to the Missouri question, caused the chief sectional conflict of the period.

The Tariff of 1816 had produced sufficient revenue for a year or two, and had made possible the repeal of internal taxes. The panic of 1819, however, called forth a demand for a new tariff with higher rates, both because treasury receipts were falling off and because the factories felt the pinch of the hard times. Friends of protection organized to procure the desired legislation, and a new bill passed the House in 1820. In the Senate it was defeated by a single vote.

Although the chairman of the committee which reported this bill tried hard to meet the criticism of those who contended that protection favored particular interests at the expense of the nation as a whole and the South in particular, it is evident from the vote that the spirit of sectionalism had already replaced the nationalism of 1816. The alignment of the agricultural West and the manufacturing areas of the East in support of the measure was almost perfect; while the union of the maritime interest with the cotton, tobacco, and cane growers in opposition was no less so.

The battle was now joined in earnest, and year after year the protectionists returned to the attack, under the prod of continued hard times. In 1824 they succeeded in carrying through a new act, with increased duties. The debate on this bill is noteworthy because of great speeches by Webster, Clay, and Robert Y. Hayne. The first, whose constituency was still maritime in interest, argued cogently against legislative interference with the natural course of trade. Clay on his part elaborated the home-market theory, and advocated protection as a means of creating a genuine "American system."

"We have shaped our industry, our navigation, and our commerce, in reference to an extraordinary war in Europe, and to foreign markets which no longer exist," said he. "The consequence of the termination of the war of Europe has been the resumption of European commerce, European navigation, and the extension of European agriculture and European industry in all its branches. Europe, therefore, has no longer occasion, to anything like the same extent as that she had during her wars, for American commerce, American navigation, the produce of American industry."

Explaining that the surplus produce of the United States was increasing much more rapidly than the consuming power of Europe, even if the foreign states received American food products, he argued that "a genuine American policy" would create a home market for the products of our agriculture "in all its varieties, of planting, farming, and grazing." The establishment of manufactures would create a home market for the planter and farmer, and a source of supply for their necessaries. "But this home market . . . can only be created and cherished by the protection of our own legislation against the inevitable prostration of our industry which must ensue from the action of foreign policy and legislation."

Clay professed to speak for all sections. "The inquiry should be in reference to the great interests of every section of the Union. . . . If they come into absolute collision . . . a reconciliation, if possible, should be attempted, by mutual concession, so as to avoid a sacrifice of the prosperity of either. . . ." But Clay's logic was the logic of the farm and factory, not the plantation. His scheme of sectional reciprocity was rejected by the planter. Senator Hayne, of South Carolina, spoke for the latter, protesting against a system which for the South meant only burdens.

In this debate the southern speakers began to invoke the Constitution against the tariff, urging that import duties were permissible only as a means of regulating commerce or raising revenue and not for the purpose of protection. In general they spoke with moderation, but Randolph, with his usual eccentricity, threw off all restraint. "A fig for the Constitution!" he cried. "When the scorpion's sting is probing to the quick, shall we stop to chop logic?" With a sarcastic fling at the West, he exclaimed: "Men in hunting-shirts, with deerskin leggings and moccasins on their feet, want protection for manufactures!"

The Tariff of 1824 proved unsatisfactory to the woolen manufacturers, who found that the duty on English woolens was evaded by deliberate undervaluation of the goods, to deceive customs officials. To prevent this, a new bill was introduced in Congress in 1827, known as the "Woolens Bill," which proposed to apply the minimum principle to woolen as well as cotton goods. Passing the House, it was defeated in the Senate by the casting vote of the Vice-President, Calhoun.

This rebuff led the friends of protection to call a convention at Harrisburg, in July, 1827, for the purpose of agreeing upon the features of a new bill to be presented at the next session of Congress. The Tariff of 1828, however, did not follow the Harrisburg plan. Its provisions were shaped for political ends, as will be seen later, and as an economic measure it was such a monstrosity that it was dubbed the "Tariff of Abominations."

The persistence of the protectionists goaded the South to desperation. Randolph flamed as usual. His declamation recalls the comment of a representative from western Virginia in the state convention of 1830: "The difference, sir, between a

*talking* and a *working* politician is immense. The Old Dominion
has long been celebrated for producing great orators. . . . But
at home, or when they return from Congress, they have negroes
to fan them asleep." The heroic age of Virginia ended with
the generation of Washington, Jefferson, Madison, and Monroe,
and hegemony in the South passed to the cotton belt. Tobacco
yielded the scepter to cotton as king of the staples, and the
premiership was seized by the ministers of the new monarch.
In the antitariff agitation South Carolina eclipsed Virginia. Dr.
Cooper, of sedition trial fame, now president of South Carolina
College, declared that the time had come to calculate the value
of the Union. Agitation spread throughout the state and the
temper of the discussions became alarming to those who loved
the Union.

The development of the issues of the years 1815 to 1828 played
havoc with the reputation for consistency of many a public
man. Jefferson changed ground twice, once when he indorsed
the tariff, and again when he reverted to states' rights. Webster
supported the Tariff of 1828 and explained his new stand by
saying that his constituents had accepted protection as the
policy of the government since 1824, and had adapted their
economic activities to it. No statesman of the time showed a
greater change of front than Calhoun. His last public utterances
before entering Monroe's cabinet were in the strain of exalted
nationalism. In 1816 and 1817 his advocacy of protection and
internal improvements was quite on a par with Clay's speech on
the Tariff of 1824. As Secretary of War his report on internal
improvements fixed his place in the public mind as a foremost
champion of such measures. Then after a long interval during
which he was silent his vote against the Woolens Bill revealed
him as the enemy of protection and the champion of sectional
interests.

This somersault was due primarily to disappointment at the
way in which protectionism had grown. Calhoun's original
idea had been that protection for a few years would establish
manufactures so firmly that they would be able to hold their
own against foreign competition without further aid. But having tasted government bounty the manufacturing interest seemed
to him to have become insatiable, and, aided by the votes of the

representatives of agriculture, to have determined to lay the planters under permanent tribute. His chief concern, therefore, became the defense of the rights of the minority section.

Loving the Union and feeling alarm at the temper of his own state, he set himself, about the time of the passage of the Tariff of 1828, to formulate a plan by which a single state might constitutionally prevent an abuse of power by the Federal Government. The outcome was the South Carolina Exposition of 1828. It was presented to the state legislature, late in the year, in the form of a committee report, since it was deemed inexpedient for the Vice-President's hand to appear. Like Jefferson when in a similar position, he made his theory public through the medium of confidential friends.

Like Jefferson, also, Calhoun built the doctrine which the Exposition advanced upon the compact theory of the Constitution. Indeed, he claimed to be reasserting the doctrines of 1798. But he was much more explicit than the authors of the Virginia and Kentucky Resolutions. Calhoun held: 1) that the Constitution is a compact or contract between sovereign states; 2) that the Federal Government in all of its branches is the common agent of the states; 3) that the Constitution is a body of instructions for the agent; 4) that the agent's acts are null and void if they are not within the powers given by the instructions.[1] Thus far Calhoun substantially restated Jefferson's views of thirty years before. But he added 5) that a *single state* might judge of the constitutionality of any act of Congress (a point which Jefferson had left uncertain), and if held unconstitutional, might declare it null and void within its bounds; 6) that the proper organ of the sovereign state in exercising this right was a convention especially summoned for the purpose; and 7) that the judgment of the state convention was final unless three fourths of the states (the amending power) upheld the nullified act of Congress.

Such was the theory of nullification. In later documents Calhoun refined and elaborated but added nothing essential. The Exposition gave much space to the statement of southern grievances, and the nullification theory was appended to serve

---

[1] The Exposition did not state these propositions categorically, but that they are a correct interpretation of its meaning is made clear by Calhoun's own later explanations.

as a warning to the northern majority, to show that each state
held in its hand a weapon with which to defend itself against
oppression.   Calhoun and his friends did not think the time
had come to use the weapon.   When the committee's report came
before the legislature, the election of Jackson, himself a cotton
planter, was already assured, and in this fact Calhoun's friends
saw the prospect of a change of policy with regard to the tariff.
They therefore contented themselves with adopting and pub-
lishing the Exposition.

## THE RESHAPING OF PARTY LINES

The dozen years following the War of 1812 witnessed the
dissolution of the old Federalist and Republican parties and the
emergence of the National Republican and Democratic parties.
The original pair had grown out of social and economic problems
which found their geographical basis in the strip of territory
between the Atlantic and the Alleghanies.   Their disintegration
and the rise of the new political groupings were the natural
consequences of the growth of the West, and the divergence of
sections over the new problems.

The Federalist organization was the first to dissolve.   The
acceptance by the Republicans of so much of its nationalism —
Josiah Quincy said that they "out-Federalized Federalism" —
left it nothing to stand for which had distinctive value.   It was
undermined by the growth of the West and discredited by its
aristocratic temper and opposition to the War.   The campaign
of 1816 was its death struggle.   "If we cannot make any impression upon the presidential election, this time, I see no hope for
the future," wrote one of the leaders to Rufus King.   King himself thought the party should not continue a hopeless struggle,
and conceded that "it has probably become the real interest and
policy of the country, that the Democracy should pursue its own
natural course."   The only possible way for the Federalists to
be of use, he thought, was as a makeweight in support of the
"least wicked section of the Republicans" in case of factional
divisions.

In somewhat this way the Federalists were factors in local and
congressional politics for another decade or more — the "Indian

summer of Federalism" — but they kept up no general organization. Even in 1816 there was no formal nomination of a party candidate. Their thirty-four electors cast their ballots for King. Monroe, the Republican candidate, received 183 votes.

Monroe had been indorsed by the Republican caucus, thanks to the support of Madison (see page 315), triumphing over William H. Crawford. Although not a man of the caliber of Washington, Jefferson, or Madison, he had learned much by experience. The impulsiveness of his youth had given way to a poise which passed with admirers for wisdom, and caused him to be likened to Washington himself. He proved capable of giving the country a safe and sane, if not brilliant, administration, thanks to a judicious selection of official advisers. To John Quincy Adams he intrusted the State Department, to Crawford the Treasury, which had been in his charge for a time under Madison, and to Calhoun the portfolio of war. Crawford was by birth a Virginian but was now a resident of Georgia. He was ranked as an able man by contemporaries, but appears to the historian to have played the rôle of politician rather than statesman. Clay, somewhat disappointed at not receiving the State Department, refused any other cabinet office, and continuing in Congress was soon at odds with the administration, especially on the questions of Latin-American relations and internal improvements.

The party antagonisms of other years faded into complete oblivion with Monroe's election. During a tour which he made soon after his inauguration, he was received even in the old strongholds of Federalism with outbursts of enthusiasm and assurances of the fraternal affection with which New Englanders regarded their countrymen. The *Boston Centinel*, which had appeared in mourning upon Jefferson's elevation to the Presidency and had hailed the Hartford Convention as the beginning of a new federal edifice, now commented on the President's visit under the headline "The Era of Good Feelings," a phrase by which Monroe's eight years of office have come to be designated. The new temper of New England was one manifestation of the widespread sentiment of nationalism. At the end of four years no opposition appeared to Monroe's reëlection; even John Adams served as a Republican elector in Massachusetts; and the President would have shared with Washington the honor of a unanimous vote but for the dislike of one elector.[1]

This appearance of calm in 1820 was an illusion.   The Republican Party was undergoing dissolution as certainly as the Federalist but more slowly.   The forces of disintegration were not of the obvious kind, although during Monroe's second term a number of factions sprang up favoring the pretensions of the several candidates for the succession.   It was the conflict of sectional interests which worked quietly and almost unseen to divide into antagonistic groups men who continued to call themselves by the same party name.   The personal rivalries of Monroe's second term must be interpreted with due regard to these more fundamental rivalries between sections.

The Republican Party of 1816 really comprised two incipient parties.   The Young Republicans, with their strength in the West, formed the national wing and inherited the Federalist conception of the powers and functions of the General Government.   Although it was more democratic in spirit than Federalism, to it gravitated, for economic reasons, the capitalists of New England and the middle states, who were becoming manufacturers.   Many of them had been Federalists.

The Old School Republicans, zealous for a conservative construction of the Constitution, formed the nucleus of the other party, which reacted decidedly towards localism as the sectional conflict developed.   This faction of the planters found its seat in the seaboard South, and in the Southwest as the plantation area spread in that direction.

The party was still outwardly intact in the campaign of 1824, but these internal differences foreshadowed an early breakup. Being without a rival, a problem arose as to how candidates were to be named.   Obviously a nomination by a congressional caucus in the usual way would be equivalent to election if the nomination were regarded as binding on all members of the party. Dissatisfied with the caucus, the sections began to nominate their favorites by resolutions of the state legislatures.   South Carolina led in 1821, naming William Lowndes.   Tennessee followed the next year with Jackson, while Kentucky indorsed Clay and Massachusetts put forward Adams.   In 1824 Crawford

[1] William Plumer, of New Hampshire, who cast his vote for John Quincy Adams.

received the nomination of a small congressional caucus which the friends of the other candidates refused to attend.

Other states later indorsed one or other of these men. Calhoun waited in vain for a nomination, but finding himself favored for the Vice-Presidency by the friends of several of the other candidates, he decided to accept the certainty of the second place in preference to a doubtful fight for the first.

In deciding which of the candidates to support, the voters were not deceived by the fact that all called themselves Republicans. They were not, as has often been said, influenced merely by the personalities of the men. Each section endeavored to determine which one best represented its interests. "It will be recollected that the promotion of domestic manufactures is the ground we assume as the criterion of our choice," wrote one western editor whose comment is typical. The candidates made the voters' task difficult, however, for in their efforts to please everyone they obscured their views more or less by ambiguous language. The voters groped in more or less uncertainty. "Is Mr. Adams really a friend to the limited interpretation of the constitution — does he stick to the doctrines of Virginia — is he opposed to the Bank of the U. S. — to a general system of internal improvement? We cannot make out from his address." So wrote the editor of the *Richmond Enquirer*.

The candidacy of Jackson was more than that of any of his rivals a matter of personality. Lacking the experience in civil affairs which the others possessed, and scorned by the aristocratic element among the voters as an ignorant, hot-headed frontiersman, he was nevertheless the most popular candidate of all. His military successes had endeared him to the people of the West and his candidacy expressed the popular confidence in the political capacity of the common man. It bespoke the growing spirit of democracy, with its antipathy to machine politics (as embodied in the caucus method of nomination, for instance) and to the control of the Federal Government by an "aristocracy" of trained office-holders. The West took it for granted that he held western views on economic questions. The South took it for granted that he held southern views because he was a cotton planter.

The division of the electoral vote among so many candidates

prevented any one of them from receiving a majority. Jackson led with 99 votes, Adams came next with 84, and Crawford third with 41. Clay had sacrificed all hope of support in the planting states by his outspoken nationalism, and Jackson divided with him the vote of the middle and western states where the alliance of manufacturing and agriculture was strongest. He received but 37 electoral votes, and his name was excluded from the balloting in the House of Representatives, upon which the choice devolved under the provisions of the Constitution.

Clay was now generally believed to be in position to play the part of "king-maker," for the congressmen of the states which had supported him (Kentucky, Ohio, and Missouri) were likely to vote as he decided. In fact the situation was not so simple. Crawford had suffered a stroke of paralysis during the campaign, and his physical disability made it likely that his friends would abandon his cause after giving him a complimentary ballot. The contest would then narrow down to Jackson and Adams, with the probability of prolonged balloting, for the Clay states did not hold an actual balance of power, and the action of the four Crawford states (Virginia, Georgia, North Carolina, and Delaware) would be equally important in the final result.

As between Jackson and Adams Clay's mind had long been made up. The former he regarded as a mere "military chieftain," unfitted for the Presidency. His election, he believed, would form a dangerous precedent. With Adams he had had sharp personal differences, but they were in agreement on current questions. Clay maintained a discreet silence while the friends of the candidates importuned him to cast his lot with them. He did not make his decision known until some of the western delegations had reached the determination to support Adams. For his own satisfaction he sought an interview with Adams, which confirmed his determination to give him his vote.

In the House election in February, 1825, contrary to general expectation, enough doubtful states supported Adams on the first ballot, in addition to the Clay states, to give him the thirteen votes needed for election. The realignment of political groups followed with great rapidity. Adams appointed Clay as his Secretary of State, a personal alliance which was the true index of a tendency of their followers to fuse into an administration party; for Adams was the second choice of the Clay states, so far as can be judged from the available evidence. The administration program as set out in the first message to Congress was all that the manufacturing-agricultural alliance could wish. The Adams party, which came to be known as the National Republicans, was a political coalition of these economic groups. In its sectional aspect it represented an alliance between the Northeast and the northern portion of the West.

The sting of defeat at once drove Jackson's friends into opposition, while the nationalism avowed in the inaugural address and first message led most members of the Crawford and Calhoun factions to join the opposition, thus creating a strong antiadministration coalition. This incipient party of Jacksonian democracy was composed of incongruous elements, for it united the planters, whose views were local, with many westerners whose economic views agreed with those of Adams and Clay.

A great many persons were ill-disposed towards the administration because of the means used, as they believed, to defeat Jackson. Some of the latter's clever political friends, foreseeing the appointment of Clay if Adams became President, had discounted that event in advance. George Kremer, a dull-witted member from Pennsylvania, used as the tool of these schemers, alleged a few days before the election in the House, that Adams had offered Clay the post of Secretary of State in return for his support, and that Jackson might have had it if he had been willing to pay the same price. "None of Jackson's friends would descend to such mean barter and sale," ran the statement.

Clay demanded an investigation by the House, which Kremer evaded. But when Adams actually did appoint Clay, uncritical people believed, as the plotters had intended, that the charge of bribery was proved. Jackson was one of these. He had taken his defeat with equanimity up to this point, but convinced that he had been defrauded, he denounced Clay as the "Judas of the West," and withdrew his decision not to stand as a candidate in the next election.

The "bargain and corruption" charge gave Jackson's managers a capital campaign issue for 1828. Reasoning on the basis of the plurality vote in the electoral college, and incomplete statistics of the popular vote, they argued that Jackson was the people's choice, and that their will had been defeated by the alleged agreement between "corrupt" politicians. With this plea they made a powerful appeal to the growing sentiment in favor of popular government, and identified the cause of Jackson with that of democracy itself. "Vindicate the people's right to govern by electing Jackson," was well-nigh the whole of their platform. By this cry they won the mass of the plain people, both of the new states and of the old ones where so many of them had recently been enfranchised.

At the same time they kept economic issues in the background. To win the election it was necessary to unite the South and West and this could not be done on economic grounds. Many of the planters doubtless believed the bargain charge. We know that Calhoun did. But the planters with their aristocratic traditions had little enthusiasm for the issue of popular government raised by the politicians. It was Adams's nationalism which made it impossible for them to support him. Jackson was their only alternative, and they were ready to try him even without assurance as to his views on public questions.

Few issues of the four years of Adams's term were dealt with on their merits. His administration was one long campaign for the election of 1828. Party malice had seldom before gone to such extremes. When the antimasonic frenzy broke out, Adams was falsely alleged to hold high rank in the Masonic order. Baseless scandals were spread of immoral conduct while he was minister of the United States in Russia. His attitude and purpose relative to the Panama Congress were grossly misrepresented in the congressional debate by partisans who thought less of the important interests at stake than of their desire to discredit the President.

The masterpiece of manipulation came in the framing of the Tariff of 1828. The House committee composed of opponents of the administration reported a bill designed to please the producers of raw materials — wool, hemp, flax, and iron — but to leave New England manufacturers without the protection they wished. Southern members, of course, would vote against the bill, as would (it was supposed) those from New England. It would be defeated, and the West, as producer of raw materials, would be sacrificed by the President's own section. Thus the seeds of discord would be sown between the protectionists of the two sections. Randolph was guilty of less exaggeration than usual when he declared that "the bill referred to manufactures of no sort or kind, but the manufacture of a President of the United States."

A kindred purpose was to discredit protectionism in the house of its friends. George McDuffie, of South Carolina, made this plain when he explained "we determined to put such ingredients in the chalice as would poison the monster, and commend it to his own lips." The plan miscarried, for enough of the New Englanders accepted the bill to secure its passage, and those who mixed the cup had to drink it.

Against Jackson, in whose behalf all of these electioneering schemes were carried on, Adams was a candidate for reëlection. Son of the second President, he had spent his life in almost continuous service of the public. At the age of fourteen he had accompanied the envoy to Russia as private secretary. Next he was a member of the secretariat of the commission which negotiated peace with England in 1782, and was still young enough after that task was done, to become a Harvard student.

During his father's presidency he was sent successively to Holland, Portugal, and Prussia as minister. Under Jefferson he represented Massachusetts in the United States Senate. On the embargo issue he broke with the Federalists and lost his seat. Thereafter he considered himself a Republican. Minister to Russia during the War of 1812, he came thence to Ghent to serve on the peace commission. Eight years more of intimate contact with public affairs as Secretary of State gave him an equipment for the chief magistracy equaled by that of few statesmen before or since.

In intellectual caliber few contemporaries approached him, and his code of private and public morality had lost little of the strictness of his Puritan ancestors. He felt keenly responsible for the administration of his high office in such a way as to promote the lasting welfare of the nation. He planned a national university, desired to promote scientific explorations, and especially wished to manage the public domain as a national trust and with expert efficiency. He would have made grants for the promotion of road- and canal-making in such wise that the ungranted land would be enhanced in value by the improvement at the same time that the country's resources were developed and brought within reach of the people.   His plans were comprehensive and statesmanlike, but far beyond the grasp of the masses upon whose will hung the fortunes of public men in this dawning day of the new democracy.   Besides, they involved stretches of power which strict constructionists could never allow.

Adams firmly believed that office should seek the man, but his coldly intellectual temperament was not calculated to win friends, and his rejection of the arts of the politician deprived him of the effectual means of winning votes.   He would not use his control over appointments to create a party machine.   He would not remove from office men who had worked for Jackson and Crawford, in 1824–1825.   He would not remove the Postmaster-General when it became an open secret that he was laboring in Jackson's behalf in the campaign of 1828.   He would not even deny the calumnies of his enemies.   Small wonder that a friend, after vainly endeavoring to persuade him to dismiss a disloyal office-holder, warned him that he would find himself "dismissed" in the election.

And so it proved.   The West and the South were solidly for Jackson, who received, besides, the votes of Pennsylvania and 20 out of 36 in New York.   The New England states were loyal to their native son ; but Adams received no votes south of Maryland and Delaware.   The figures stood 178 to 83.   Calhoun was reëlected Vice-President.

Thus did the last of the old-line statesmen depart from the capitol, making way for a crowd of politicians whose advent signalized the triumph of the people.

## SELECT BIBLIOGRAPHY FOR CHAPTER XX

**The Conflict of Sectional Interests.**   The fifth volume of Channing, *United States*, opens with a survey of social and economic conditions in the period 1815–1845, which formed the basis of sectional rivalries.   The climax of the tariff controversy is the theme of Houston, *Nullification in the United States*.   See also histories of the tariff.   Hunt, *John C. Calhoun*, follows the strife of sections from the biographical point of view.   See also Lodge, *Daniel Webster*.   The earlier phases of the economic rivalry which gradually disintegrated the Republican party are discussed by Hockett, *Western Influences*, 112–126.

**The Reshaping of Party Lines.** Hockett, *Western Influences*, chap. 5. McMaster gives a wealth of detail on such episodes as the House election of 1825. The lives of the statesmen of the period give the personal aspects of politics. See especially Morse, *John Quincy Adams*, Sumner, *Andrew Jackson*, and Bassett, *Andrew Jackson*.

# LIST OF BOOKS

For convenience of reference all of the books and articles mentioned in the Select Bibliographies at the close of each chapter are here listed in one alphabet according to the names of the authors.

Abbott, Wilbur Cortez, *Expansion of Europe, a history of the foundations of the modern world.* 2 v. Henry Holt & Company, New York, 1918.

Adams, Henry, *History of the United States of America during the Administrations of Jefferson and Madison.* 9 v. Charles Scribner's Sons, New York, 1890–1891.

Adams, Henry, *John Randolph (American Statesmen).*

Adams, James Truslow, *Founding of New England.* The Atlantic Monthly Press, Boston, [c1921].

Adams, Randolph Greenleaf, *History of the Foreign Policy of the United States.* The Macmillan Company, New York, 1924.

Alvord, Clarence Walworth, *The Illinois Country, 1673–1818 (Centenary History of Illinois*, Vol. I). Illinois Centenary Commission, Springfield, 1920.

Alvord, Clarence Walworth, *The Mississippi Valley in British Politics.* 2 v. Arthur H. Clark Company, Cleveland, 1917.

Alvord, Clarence Walworth, and Bidgood, Lee, *First Exploration of the trans-Alleghany region by the Virginians, 1659–1674.* Arthur H. Clark Company, Cleveland, 1912.

*American Nation.* See Hart, Albert Bushnell, editor.

*American Statesmen.* See Morse, John Torrey, Jr., editor.

Anderson, Frank Malloy, "Contemporary Opinion of the Virginia and Kentucky Resolutions," *American Historical Review*, Vol. V, Nos. 1 and 2 (Oct., 1899, and Jan., 1900), pp. 45–63, 225–252.

Andrews, Charles McLean, "Colonial Commerce," *American Historical Review*, Vol. XX, No. 1 (Oct., 1914), pp. 43–63.

Andrews, Charles McLean, *Colonial Folkways (Chronicles of America*, Vol. IX).

Andrews, Charles McLean, *Colonial Self-Government, 1652–1689 (American Nation*, Vol. V).

Andrews, Charles McLean, *Fathers of New England (Chronicles of America*, Vol. VI).

Ashe, Samuel A'Court, *History of North Carolina.* 2 v. (only one published). C. L. Van Noppen, Greensboro, 1908.

Babcock, Kendric Charles, *Rise of American Nationality, 1811–1819 (American Nation*, Vol. XIII).

Bancroft, George, *History of the United States.* Author's last revision. 6 v. D. Appleton & Company, New York, 1883–1885.

Barrett, J. A., *Evolution of the Ordinance of 1787; with an account of the earlier plans for the government of the Northwest Territory.* University of Nebraska, Department of History and Economics, New York, 1891.

Bassett, John Spencer, *The Federalist System, 1789–1801 (American Nation,* Vol. XI).

Bassett, John Spencer, *Life of Andrew Jackson.* New edition. The Macmillan Company, New York, 1916.

Beard, Charles Austin, *Economic Interpretation of the Constitution of the United States.* The Macmillan Company, New York, 1913.

Beard, Charles Austin, *Economic Origins of Jeffersonian Democracy.* The Macmillan Company, New York, 1915.

Becker, Carl Lotus, *The Declaration of Independence; a study in the history of political ideas.* Harcourt, Brace & Company, New York, [c1922].

Becker, Carl Lotus, *The Eve of the Revolution (Chronicles of America,* Vol. XI).

Beer, George Louis, *British Colonial Policy, 1754–1765.* The Macmillan Company, New York, 1907.

Beer, George Louis, *Commercial Policy of England towards the Colonies* (Columbia University *Studies in History, Economics, and Public Law,* Vol. III, No. 2). Columbia University, New York, 1893.

Beer, George Louis, *The Old Colonial System, 1660–1754.* The Macmillan Company, New York, 1912.

Beer, George Louis, *The Origins of the British Colonial System, 1578–1660.* The Macmillan Company, 1908.

Bell, Herbert C., "The West India Trade before the American Revolution," *American Historical Review,* Vol. XXII, No. 2 (Jan., 1917), pp. 272–287.

Beveridge, Albert Jeremiah, *Life of John Marshall.* 4 v. Houghton Mifflin Company, Boston, 1916–[c1919].

Blauvelt, Mary Taylor, *The Development of Cabinet Government in England.* The Macmillan Company, New York, 1902.

Bogart, Ernest Ludlow, *Economic History of the United States.* Third revised edition. Longmans, Green & Company, New York, [1923].

Bourne, Edward Gaylord, *Spain in America (American Nation,* Vol. III).

Brigham, Albert Perry, *Geographical Influences in American History.* Ginn & Company, Boston, 1903.

Brodhead, John Romeyn, *History of the State of New York.* 2 v. Harper and Brothers, New York, 1853–1871.

Bruce, Henry Addington, *Daniel Boone and the Wilderness Road.* The Macmillan Company, New York, 1910.

Bruce, Philip Alexander, *The Economic History of Virginia in the Seventeenth Century.* 2 v. The Macmillan Company, New York, 1896.

Bruce, Philip Alexander, *The Institutional History of Virginia in the Seventeenth Century.* 2 v. G. P. Putnam's Sons, New York, 1910.

Bruce, Philip Alexander, *Social Life of Virginia in the Seventeenth Century.* Whittet & Shepperson, Richmond, 1907.

Bullock, Charles Jesse, *The Finances of the United States from 1775 to 1789, with especial reference to the budget* (University of Wisconsin *Bulletin,* Economics, Political Science, and History Series, Vol. I, No. 2). University of Wisconsin, Madison, 1895.

Carter, Clarence Edwin, *Great Britain and the Illinois Country, 1763–1774.* American Historical Association, Washington, 1910.

Chadwick, French Ensor, *Relations of the United States and Spain.* 3 v. Charles Scribner's Sons, New York, 1909–1911.

Channing, Edward, *History of the United States.* 5 v. (In progress.) The Macmillan Company, New York, 1905–.

Channing, Edward, *The Jeffersonian System (American Nation,* Vol. XII).

Cheyney, Edward Potts, *European Background of American History (American Nation,* Vol. I).

*Chronicles of America.* See Johnson, Allen, editor.

*Chronicles of Canada.* See Wrong, George M., editor.

Colby, Charles W., *The Fighting Governor (Chronicles of Canada,* Vol. VII).

Colby, Charles W., *The Founder of New France (Chronicles of Canada,* Vol. III).

Coman, Katharine, *Economic Beginnings of the Far West.* 2 v. The Macmillan Company, 1912.

Corwin, Edward Samuel, *French Policy and the American Alliance.* Princeton University Press, Princeton, 1916.

Corwin, Edward Samuel, *John Marshall and the Constitution (Chronicles of America,* Vol. XVI).

Cushing, Harry Alonzo, *History of the Transition from Provincial to Commonwealth Government in Massachusetts* (Columbia University *Studies in History, Economics, and Public Law,* Vol. VII). Columbia University, New York, 1896.

Dewey, Davis Rich, *Financial History of the United States.* Eighth edition. Longmans, Green & Company, New York, 1922.

Dickerson, Oliver Morton, *American Colonial Government, 1696–1765, a study of the Board of Trade in its relation to the American Colonies* . . . Arthur H. Clark Company, Cleveland, 1912.

Doyle, John Andrew, *English Colonies in America.* 5 v. Henry Holt & Company, New York, 1889–1907.

Du Bois, William Edward Burghardt, *Suppression of the African Slave Trade to the United States of America (Harvard Historical Studies).* Longmans, Green & Company, New York, 1896.

Earle, Alice Morse, *Child Life in Colonial Days.* The Macmillan Company, New York, [c1899].

Earle, Alice Morse, *Colonial Dames and Goodwives.* Houghton Mifflin Company, Boston, 1895.

Earle, Alice Morse, *Colonial Days in Old New York.* Charles Scribner's Sons, New York, 1897.

Earle, Alice Morse, *Customs and Fashions in Old New England*. Charles Scribner's Sons, New York, 1896.

Earle, Alice Morse, *Home Life in Colonial Days*. The Macmillan Company, New York, 1898.

Earle, Alice Morse, *Stage Coach and Tavern Days*. The Macmillan Company, New York, 1901.

Egerton, Hugh Edward, *Short History of British Colonial Policy.* Second edition. Methuen & Company, London, 1905.

Egerton, Hugh Edward, *The Causes and Character of the American Revolution*. Clarendon Press, Oxford, 1923.

Farrand, Max, *Fathers of the Constitution (Chronicles of America*, Vol. XIII).

Farrand, Max, *Framing of the Constitution of the United States*. Yale University Press, New Haven, 1913.

Faust, Albert Bernhardt, *German Element in the United States*. 2 v. Houghton Mifflin Company, Boston, 1909.

Fish, Carl Russell, *American Diplomacy*. Second edition. Henry Holt & Company, New York, 1916.

Fish, Carl Russell, *Civil Service and the Patronage (Harvard Historical Studies)*. Longmans, Green & Company, New York, 1905.

Fisher, Sydney George, *The Quaker Colonies (Chronicles of America*, Vol. VIII).

Fisher, Sydney George, *Struggle for American Independence*. 2 v. J. B. Lippincott Company, Philadelphia, 1908.

Fisher, Sydney George, *The True Benjamin Franklin*. Fifth edition. J. B. Lippincott Company, Philadelphia, 1903.

Fisher, Sydney George, *The True William Penn*. J. B. Lippincott Company, Philadelphia, 1899.

Fiske, John, *Historical Works*. Riverside Pocket edition, 12 v. Houghton Mifflin Company, Boston, 1915.

Ford, Henry Jones, *The Scotch-Irish in America*. Princeton University Press, Princeton, 1915.

Ford, Henry Jones, *Washington and his Colleagues (Chronicles of America*, Vol. XIV).

Ford, Paul Leicester, *The True George Washington*. J. B. Lippincott Company, Philadelphia, 1904.

Foster, John Watson, *A Century of American Diplomacy*. Houghton Mifflin Company, Boston, 1901.

Friedenwald, Herbert, *Declaration of Independence, an interpretation and an analysis*. The Macmillan Company, New York, 1904.

Fuller, Hubert Bruce, *Purchase of Florida*. Burrows Brothers Company, Cleveland, 1906.

Gay, Sidney Howard, *James Madison (American Statesmen)*.

Gayarré, Charles Étienne Arthur, *History of Louisiana*. 4 v. Third edition. Hawkins, Armand & Company, New Orleans, 1885.

Gilman, Daniel Coit, *James Monroe (American Statesmen)*.

Goodwin, John Abbott, *The Pilgrim Republic; an historical review of the colony of New Plymouth . . .* Tercentenary edition. Houghton Mifflin Company, Boston, 1920.

Goodwin, Maud Wilder, *Dutch and English on the Hudson* (*Chronicles of America*, Vol. VII).

Gordy, John Pancoast, *Political History of the United States with special reference to the growth of political parties.* 2 v.  Henry Holt & Company, New York, 1902.

Green, Thomas Marshall, *Spanish Conspiracy; a review of early Spanish movements in the Southwest.*  Robert Clarke & Company, Cincinnati, 1891.

Greene, Evarts Boutell, *Provincial America* (*American Nation*, Vol. VI).

Greene, Evarts Boutell, *The Provincial Governor in the English Colonies of North America* (*Harvard Historical Studies*).  Longmans, Green & Company, New York, 1898.

Hanna, Charles Augustus, *The Scotch-Irish* . . .  G. P. Putnam's Sons, New York, 1902.

Hart, Albert Bushnell, editor, *The American Nation; A History from original sources.*  28 v.  Harper & Brothers, New York, 1904–1918.

Hazleton, John Hampden, *Declaration of Independence; its history.*  Dodd, Mead & Company, New York, 1906.

Helps, Sir Arthur, *Spanish Conquest in America and its relation to the history of slavery and to the government of the colonies.*  2 v.  Harper & Brothers, New York, 1856.

Henderson, Archibald, *Conquest of the Old Southwest* . . .  *1740–1800.*  The Century Company, New York, 1920.

Hildreth, Richard, *History of the United States.*  6 v.  Revised edition.  Harper & Brothers, New York, 1880–1882.

Hinsdale, Burke Aaron, *The Old Northwest; the beginnings of our colonial system.*  Revised edition.  Silver, Burdett & Company, New York, [c1899].

Hockett, Homer C., *Western Influences on Political Parties to 1825* (*Ohio State University Contributions in History and Political Science*, No. 4).  Ohio State University, Columbus, 1917.

Holst, Hermann Eduard von, *John C. Calhoun* (*American Statesmen*).

Hosmer, James Kendall, *Samuel Adams* (*American Statesmen*).

Houston, David Franklin, *Critical Study of Nullification in the United States* (*Harvard Historical Studies*).  Longmans, Green & Company, New York, 1896.

Howard, George Elliott, *Preliminaries of the Revolution, 1763–1775* (*American Nation*, Vol. VIII).

Hunt, Gaillard, *John C. Calhoun.*  George W. Jacobs & Company, Philadelphia, 1908.

Johnson, Allen; Lomer, G. R.; and Jeffreys, C. W., editors, *The Chronicles of America.*  50 v.  Yale University Press, New Haven, 1918–1920.

Johnson, Allen, *Jefferson and His Colleagues* (*Chronicles of America*, Vol XV).

Johnston, Mary, *Pioneers of the Old South* (*Chronicles of America*, Vol. V).

Kellogg, Louise Phelps, "The American Colonial Charter," American Historical Association *Report* for 1903, Vol. I, pp. 187–341.  The American Historical Association, Washington, 1904.

Lecky, William Edward Hartpole, *American Revolution, 1763–1783; being the chapters and passages relating to America from the author's History of England . . . edited . . . by J. A. Woodburn.* D. Appleton & Company, New York, [1898].

Lecky, William Edward Hartpole, *History of England in the Eighteenth Century.* 8 v. D. Appleton & Company, New York, 1878–1890.

Lincoln, Charles Henry, *Revolutionary Movement in Pennsylvania, 1760–1776* (University of Pennsylvania *Publications*, Series in History, No. 1). University of Pennsylvania, Philadelphia, 1901.

Lodge, Henry Cabot, *Alexander Hamilton (American Statesmen).*

Lodge, Henry Cabot, *Daniel Webster (American Statesmen).*

Lodge, Henry Cabot, *George Washington (American Statesmen).*

Lodge, Henry Cabot, *Life and Letters of George Cabot.* Little, Brown & Company, Boston, 1878.

McCaleb, Walter Flavius, *The Aaron Burr Conspiracy.* Dodd, Mead & Company, New York, 1903.

McCrady, Edward, *The History of South Carolina under the Proprietary Government, 1670–1719.* The Macmillan Company, New York, 1897.

McCrady, Edward, *The History of South Carolina under the Royal Government, 1719–1776.* The Macmillan Company, New York, 1901.

McIlwain, Charles Howard, *The American Revolution; a constitutional interpretation.* The Macmillan Company, New York, 1923.

McLaughlin, Andrew Cunningham, *Confederation and Constitution (American Nation,* Vol. X).

McLaughlin, Andrew Cunningham, "The Western Posts and the British Debts," American Historical Association *Report* for 1894, pp. 413–444. American Historical Association, Washington, 1895.

McMaster, John Bach, *The Acquisition of Political, Social, and Industrial Rights of Man in America.* The Imperial Press, Cleveland, 1903.

McMaster, John Bach, *History of the People of the United States from the Revolution to the Civil War.* 8 v. D. Appleton & Company, New York, 1883–1913.

Mahan, Alfred Thayer, *Influence of Sea Power upon History, 1660–1783.* Eighteenth edition. Little, Brown & Company, Boston, 1904.

Mahan, Alfred Thayer, *Sea Power in its Relation to the War of 1812.* 2 v. Little, Brown & Company, Boston, 1905.

Maitland, Frederic William, *Constitutional History of England.* University Press, Cambridge, 1908.

Markham, Sir Clements Robert, *Life of Christopher Columbus.* George Philip & Son, Ltd., London, 1892.

Mathews, Lois Kimball, *Expansion of New England . . . 1620–1864.* Houghton Mifflin Company, Boston, 1909.

Merriam, Charles Edward, *History of American Political Theories.* The Macmillan Company, New York, 1903.

Morey, William C., "The First State Constitutions," *Annals of the American Academy of Political and Social Science,* Vol. IV (Sept., 1893), pp. 201–232.

Morey, William C., "The Genesis of a Written Constitution," *Annals of the American Academy of Political and Social Science*, I, 529–557.

Moses, Bernard, *Establishment of Spanish Rule in America* . . . G. P. Putnam's Sons, New York, 1898.

Morse, John Torrey, Jr., editor, *American Statesmen*. 32 v. Houghton Mifflin Company, 1898–1900.

Morse, John Torrey, Jr., *Benjamin Franklin* (*American Statesmen*).

Morse, John Torrey, Jr., *John Adams* (*American Statesmen*).

Morse, John Torrey, Jr., *John Quincy Adams* (*American Statesmen*).

Morse, John Torrey, Jr., *Thomas Jefferson* (*American Statesmen*).

Munro, William Bennett, *Crusaders of New France* (*Chronicles of America*, Vol. IV).

Munro, William Bennett, *The Seigneurs of Old Canada* (*Chronicles of Canada*, Vol. V).

Nevins, Allan, *American States during and after the Revolution, 1775–1789*. The Macmillan Company, New York, 1925.

Ogg, Frederic Austin, *The Old Northwest* (*Chronicles of America*, Vol. XIX).

Ogg, Frederic Austin, *Opening of the Mississippi*. The Macmillan Company, New York, 1904.

Osgood, Herbert Levi, *The American Colonies in the Seventeenth Century*. 3 v. The Macmillan Company, New York, 1904–1907.

Osgood, Herbert Levi, *The American Colonies in the Eighteenth Century*. 4 v. Columbia University Press, New York, 1924–.

Paine, Ralph Delahaye, *The Fight for a Free Sea* (*Chronicles of America*, Vol. XVII).

Palfrey, John Gorham, *A Compendious History of New England* . . . 4 v. J. R. Osgood & Company, Boston, 1884.

Parkman, Francis, *Works*. Centenary edition, 13 v. Little, Brown & Company, Boston, 1922.

Paxson, Frederic Logan, *The Independence of the South American Republics*. Ferris and Leach, Philadelphia, 1903.

Paxson, Frederic Logan, *Last American Frontier*. The Macmillan Company, New York, 1910.

Pellew, William George, *John Jay* (*American Statesmen*).

Phillips, Paul Chrisler, *The West in the Diplomacy of the American Revolution* (University of Illinois *Studies in the Social Sciences*, Vol. II, Nos. 2 and 3). University of Illinois, 1913.

Phillips, Ulrich Bonnell, *American Negro Slavery*. D. Appleton & Company, New York, 1918.

Powell, Edward Payson, *Nullification and Secession in the United States; a history of the six attempts during the first century of the Republic*. G. P. Putnam's Sons, New York, 1897.

Reddaway, William Fiddian, *The Monroe Doctrine*. Second edition. G. E. Stechert & Company, New York, 1905.

Rhodes, James Ford, *History of the United States from the Compromise of 1850*. 9 v. Harper & Brothers, New York, 1893–1922.

Richman, I. B., *The Spanish Conquerors* (*Chronicles of America*, Vol. II).

Roosevelt, Theodore, *Naval War of 1812.* G. P. Putnam's Sons, New York, 1882.

Roosevelt, Theodore, *The Winning of the West.* Standard Library edition, 4 v. G. P. Putnam's Sons, New York, 1894–1896.

Schlesinger, Arthur Meier, *The Colonial Merchants and the American Revolution, 1763–1776* (Columbia University *Studies in History, Economics, and Public Law*, Vol. LXVIII). Columbia University, New York, 1917.

Schlesinger, Arthur Meier, *New Viewpoints in American History.* The Macmillan Company, New York, 1922.

Schouler, James, *History of the United States of America under the Constitution.* 7 v. Dodd, Mead & Company, 1880–[c1913].

Schurz, Carl, *Henry Clay (American Statesmen).*

Schuyler, Robert Livingston, *The Constitution of the United States; an historical survey of its formation.* The Macmillan Company, New York, 1923.

Seeley, Sir John Robert, *The Expansion of England.* Roberts Brothers, Boston, 1883.

Seeley, Sir John Robert, *The Growth of British Policy.* 2 v. University Press, Cambridge, 1895.

Semple, Ellen Churchill, *American History and its Geographic Conditions.* Houghton Mifflin Company, Boston, 1903.

Sharpless, Isaac, *A Quaker Experiment in Government.* A. J. Ferris, Philadelphia, 1898.

Skinner, Constance Lindsay, *Pioneers of the Old Southwest (Chronicles of America*, Vol. XVIII).

Small, Albion Woodbury, *Beginnings of American Nationality* . . . (Johns Hopkins University *Studies in Historical and Political Science*, Vol. VIII, Parts 1 and 2). Johns Hopkins University, Baltimore, 1890.

Stanwood, Edward, *American Tariff Controversies in the Nineteenth Century.* 2 v. Houghton Mifflin Company, Boston, 1903–1904.

Stanwood, Edward, *History of the Presidency.* 2 v. Houghton Mifflin Company, Boston, 1898–1912.

Stillé, Charles Janeway, *Life and Times of John Dickinson* (Pennsylvania Historical Society *Memoirs*, Vol. XIII). Historical Society of Pennsylvania, Philadelphia, 1891.

Sumner, William Graham, *Andrew Jackson (American Statesmen).*

Taussig, Frank William, *Tariff History of the United States.* Seventh edition. G. P. Putnam's Sons, New York, 1923.

Thayer, William Roscoe, *George Washington.* Houghton Mifflin Company, Boston, 1922.

Thwaites, Reuben Gold, *Brief History of Rocky Mountain Exploration.* D. Appleton & Company, New York, 1904.

Thwaites, Reuben Gold, *Daniel Boone.* D. Appleton & Company, New York, 1902.

Thwaites, Reuben Gold, *France in America (American Nation*, Vol. VII).

Tower, Charlemagne, *Marquis de La Fayette in the American Revolution.*
2 v.    J. B. Lippincott Company, Philadelphia, 1895.

Treat, Payson Jackson, *National Land System, 1785–1820.*    E. B. Treat &
Company, New York, 1910.

Trescot, William Henry, *Diplomatic History of the Administrations of Washington and Adams, 1789–1801.*    Little, Brown & Company, Boston,
1857.

Trevelyan, Sir George Otto, *The American Revolution.*    New edition.    3 v.
Longmans, Green & Company, London, 1905.

Turner, Frederick Jackson, *The Frontier in American History.*    Henry
Holt & Company, New York, 1920.

Turner, Frederick Jackson, *Rise of the New West (American Nation,* Vol.
XIV).

Turner, Frederick Jackson, "Western State-Making in the Revolutionary
Era," *American Historical Review,* Vol. I, Nos. 1 and 2 (Oct., 1895,
Jan., 1896), 70–87, 251–269.

Tyler, Lyon Gardiner, *England in America (American Nation).*

Tyler, Moses Coit, *Literary History of the American Revolution, 1763–1783.*
2 v.    G. P. Putnam's Sons, New York, 1897.

Tyler, Moses Coit, *Patrick Henry (American Statesmen).*

Van Tyne, Claude Halstead, *The American Revolution, 1776–1783 (American
Nation,* Vol. IX).

Van Tyne, Claude Halstead, *Causes of the War of Independence.*    Houghton
Mifflin Company, Boston, 1922.

Van Tyne, Claude Halstead, "Sovereignty in the American Revolution,"
*American Historical Review,* Vol. XII, No. III (April, 1907), 529–545.

Warfield, Ethelbert Dudley, *The Kentucky Resolutions of 1798.*    Second
edition.    G. P. Putnam's Sons, New York, 1894.

Warren, Joseph Parker, "The Confederation and the Shays Rebellion,"
*American Historical Review,* Vol. XI, No. 1 (Oct., 1905), pp. 42–67.

Weeden, William Babcock, *Economic and Social History of New England,
1620–1789.*    2 v.    Houghton Mifflin Company, Boston, 1890.

Wertenbaker, Thomas Jefferson, *Virginia under the Stuarts.*    Princeton
University Press, Princeton, 1914.

Winsor, Justin, *Cartier to Frontenac* . . .    Second edition.    Houghton
Mifflin Company, Boston, 1894.

Winsor, Justin, *The Narrative and Critical History of America.*    8 v.
Houghton Mifflin Company, Boston, 1884–1889.

Winsor, Justin, *The Westward Movement,* . . . *1763–1798.*    Houghton
Mifflin Company, Boston, 1897.

Wood, William, *Elizabethan Sea Dogs (Chronicles of America,* Vol. III).

Wrong, George McKinnon, and Langton, H. H., editors, *The Chronicles of
Canada.*    32 v.    Brook & Company, Toronto, 1915–1921.

Wrong, George McKinnon, *Conquest of New France (Chronicles of America,*
Vol. X).

Wrong, George McKinnon, *Washington and His Comrades in Arms (Chronicles of America,* Vol. XII).

# INDEX

Abbott, W. C., as author, 19, 97, 118.

Acadia. *See* Nova Scotia.

Act of Settlement, 85 n., 89.

Adams, Henry, as author, 292, 331, 346.

Adams, James T., as author, 37.

Adams, John, defends British soldiers, 128, 130 n.; dines with Hancock, 129; on committee to draft Declaration of Independence, 145 n.; peace commissioner, 161 f.; minister to England, 178; Vice-President, 225; advice on official etiquette, 228; reëlected Vice-President, 1792, 240; character and views, 240 f.; dislike of Hamilton, 241; presidential candidate, 1796, 254 f.; early mistakes as President, 255; sends X Y Z commission to France, 259; X Y Z message, 259 f.; "affair of the major-generals," 260 f.; peace efforts, 260 f.; breach with cabinet, 261, 266 f.; action under Alien and Sedition laws, 263; nominated for second term, 267; loses support of Hamilton faction, 267; satisfaction over appointment of Marshall, 342; as presidential elector, 1820, 391.

Adams, John Quincy, on purchase of Louisiana, 286; member of peace commission at Ghent, 326 f.; disagrees with Clay, 328; upholds Jackson, 1818, 359; negotiates Spanish treaty, 359; influence on Monroe Doctrine, 364; Latin-American policy (Panama Congress), 366 f.; appointed Secretary of State by Monroe, 391; presidential candidate, 392 f.; elected, 394; program, 395; candidate for reëlection, 396 f.; sketch, 397; electoral vote in 1828, 398.

Adams, Randolph G., as author, 270.

Adams, Samuel, drafts Massachusetts Circular Letter, 130 and n.; use made of Boston Massacre, 130; urges committees of correspondence, 130; member of Massachusetts ratifying convention, 219.

Administration of Justice Act, 133.

Admiralty courts, recommended by Randolph, 84; established, 87; number increased, 121.

*Advertiser,* Boston newspaper, comment on Hartford Convention, 329 f.

Africa, coast explored, 3.

Age of discovery, 3.

Agriculture, dominant industry of colonies, 91 n.; chief resource in War of 1812, 313; depression of, about 1820, 381.

Aix-la-Chapelle, treaty of, 107.

Alabama, state of, admitted, 353.

Albany Congress, 1754, 95.

Albany Plan of Union, 95; discussion, 207 n.

Albemarle Sound, settlements on, 43.

Algonkins. *See* Indians.

Alien and Sedition Acts, 261 f.; effect on Federalist party, 266.

Allen, Ethan, in Revolution, 143.

Alliance with France, 153; question of good faith of U. S., 162; cabinet discussion, 1793, 247; abrogated by Congress, 260; abrogation agreed to, 261.

Alvord, Clarence W., as author, 55, 119.

Amelia Island, occupied, 358.

Amendments, suggested by ratifying conventions, 219 f.; adoption of first ten, 221; eleventh, 342; twelfth, 225, 269; suggestions of Hartford Convention, 330.

America, in fifteenth century, 1; discovery by Columbus, 4.

American Colonization Society, 372.

American Fur Company, 353.

"American System," 386.

Amherst, Jeffrey, in French and Indian War, 111.

Amiens, peace of, 283; prospect of rupture, 283; rupture, 293.

chinery of crown administration of colonies, 92 f.; features of colonial policy, 93 f.; limits of British control, 94 f.; temptation to imitate France, 95; plans of union, 95; conflict of English and American views, 96; rivalry with France, 102 f.; intercolonial wars, 106 f.; Peace of Paris, 112; problems following peace, 112 f.; organization of conquered territories, 114; vacillating policies, 117; war with Dutch, 1781, 159; recognizes independence of U. S., 161; desires to regain friendship of U. S., 162; refuses to make commercial treaty with U. S., 178; at war with France, 247; questions at issue with U. S., 249 f.; maritime code, 250; Congress considers embargo against, 251; Jay's treaty, 252; relaxation of code, 253; treatment of liberals, 261; renews war with France, 293; violations of neutral commerce, 294 f.; draft treaty of 1806, 295; negotiations on "Leopard-Chesapeake" affair, 296 f.; missions of Erskine and Jackson, 303; effects of non-intercourse, 303; restores men to Chesapeake, 308; refuses to recall Orders in Council, 308; revokes, 310; War of 1812, 311 f.; surprise at naval victories of U. S., 325; treaty of Ghent, 326 f.; uneasy over American manufactures, 336; "joint occupation" agreement, 355; boundary agreement of 1818, 355; protests against occupation of West Florida, 356; uses Florida as war base, 357; proposes joint declaration against Holy Alliance, 363. *See* War of 1812.
Entail, Virginia law of, repealed, 131.
Enumerated products, 82; list extended, 91.
"Era of Good Feelings," 391.
Erie Canal, construction, 351; effects on New York City, 382.
Erie, Lake, battle of, 319.
Erskine, D. M., British minister in U. S., 303; exceeds instructions, 303; recalled, 303.
Essex decision, 294.
Established Church. *See* Anglican Church.

Europe, in fifteenth century, 1; expansion, 1 f.; relations with Asia, 2 f.
Eustis, William, Secretary of War, 315.
Excise, recommended by Hamilton, 232, 233; revolt of West, 234; repealed by Republicans, 275.
Expansion of Europe, 1 f.
Expatriation, right of, denied by England, 251.
Explorations, Spanish, 5 f.; French, 9, 100 f.; English, 9; by Virginians, 42; by Pennsylvanians, 59; of Far West, 289 f., 354.
Exposition of 1828, analysis, 389; adopted, 390.

Factory system, in England, 177.
Fallen Timbers, battle of, 244.
Falls of the Ohio (Louisville), 186.
Family Compact, 106.
Farrand, Max, cited, 206 n.; as author, 223.
Far West, exploration of, 289 f., 354.
Fauchet, Jean, French minister in U. S., 249.
Faust, A. B., as author, 81.
"Federal Hall," 226.
"Federalist," 221 f.
Federalists, origin of name, 218; tactics in ratifying conventions, 218 f.; control First Congress, 224; party led by Hamilton, 235; Federalists pro-British, 247; oppose commercial restriction, 1794, 251; dissatisfaction with Jay's treaty, 253; successes in administering government, 253 f.; factional division, 255, 266; split on French relations, 258 f.; pass Alien and Sedition laws, 261 f.; in campaign of 1800, 266 f.; favor Burr in House election, 1801, 268; summary of services, 269; reasons for decline, 269 f.; opposition to purchase of Louisiana, 286; secession plot, 286 f.; gains in 1808, 301; oppose War of 1812, 314; hope for British conquest of Louisiana, 324; comments on Hartford Convention, 329 f.; adopt states' rights, 332; vote against "Bonus Bill," 341; disappearance of, 390 f.
Ferdinand VII, of Spain, 361.

York, burned by Americans, 322.

Yorktown, Cornwallis' surrender at, 160.

Young Pretender, 89.

"Young Republicans," rise of, 306; in control of House of Representatives, 308; principles, 308; war preparations, 309; denounced by Jefferson, 384; plan internal improvements, 384; heirs of Federalism, 392.